Marketing Fundamentals
2005–2006

D0130479

The Chartered
Institute of Marketing

Marketing Fundamentals 2005–2006

Geoff Lancaster and Frank Withey

ELSEVIER
BUTTERWORTH
HEINEMANN

AMSTERDAM BOSTON HEIDELBERG LONDON NEW YORK OXFORD
PARIS SAN DIEGO SAN FRANCISCO SINGAPORE SYDNEY TOKYO

Elsevier Butterworth-Heinemann
Linacre House, Jordan Hill, Oxford OX2 8DP
30 Corporate Drive, Burlington, MA 01803

First published 2005

Copyright © 2005, Geoff Lancaster and Frank Withey. All rights reserved

The rights of Geoff Lancaster and Frank Withey to be identified as the
authors of this work has been asserted in accordance with the
Copyright, Designs and Patents Act 1988

No part of this publication may be reproduced in any material form (including
photocopying or storing in any medium by electronic means and whether
or not transiently or incidentally to some other use of this publication) without
the written permission of the copyright holder except in accordance with the
provisions of the Copyright, Designs and Patents Act 1988 or under the terms of
a licence issued by the Copyright Licensing Agency Ltd, 90 Tottenham Court Road,
London, England W1T 4LP. Applications for the copyright holder's written
permission to reproduce any part of this publication should be addressed
to the publisher

Permissions may be sought directly from Elsevier's Science and Technology Rights
Department in Oxford, UK: phone: (+44) (0) 1865 843830; fax: (+44) (0) 1865 853333;
e-mail: permissions@elsevier.com. You may also complete your request
on-line via the Elsevier homepage (http://www.elsevier.com), by selecting
'Customer Support' and then 'Obtaining Permissions'

British Library Cataloguing in Publication Data
A catalogue record for this book is available from the British Library

Library of Congress Cataloguing in Publication Data
A catalogue record for this book is available from the Library of Congress

ISBN 0 7506 6644 7

For information on all Elsevier Butterworth-Heinemann publications
visit our website at http://books.elsevier.com

Typeset by Integra Software Services Pvt. Ltd, Pondicherry, India
www.integra-india.com
Printed and bound in Italy

Working together to grow
libraries in developing countries

www.elsevier.com | www.bookaid.org | www.sabre.org

ELSEVIER   BOOK AID   Sabre Foundation
            International

Contents

Preface
welcome to the CIM coursebooks

This coursebook has been designed to cover the Marketing Fundamentals syllabus for the CIM Professional Certificate in Marketing and is one of a series of such coursebooks that have been specially commissioned. It is important to stress at the outset that this is not a textbook but rather is designed to complement the recommended reading for this subject suggested by The Chartered Institute of Marketing (CIM). The coursebook is structured around the syllabus for Marketing Fundamentals and is designed to reflect any changes in syllabus content and examination structure. Over the years, the writers of this coursebook have developed considerable experience in tutoring and in writing material for the CIM syllabuses and both authors have considerable experience in examining for the CIM.

As in many areas of study, and certainly one such as marketing where there is much to learn and often different perspectives, as much reading around the subject as possible is to be recommended. Again, we would stress therefore that this coursebook should be used in conjunction with other recommended reading as in the CIM syllabus for this subject. The full reading list is contained in Appendix 5. In addition, at the end of each unit there is a bibliography and a guide to further reading for those parts of the syllabus which each unit encompasses. You are advised to consult as much of this further reading as you can. As well as extending your reading and knowledge by consulting textbooks, it is also essential to read about current developments in marketing activities using the marketing industry literature plus up-to-date examples of developments in marketing that you can read about in the financial pages of a good quality newspaper. Finally, remember that marketing is all around us in our everyday activities. After all, we are all consumers and we all use products and services. Take note of examples from the real world of some of the ideas and practices that you will find covered in this coursebook. You will find these invaluable in bringing marketing to life and particularly useful when answering to questions in the examination.

Essentially, the coursebook, like the others in the series, presents an overview of the main concepts and techniques encompassed by the Marketing Fundamentals syllabus. These are presented in Units 1–9 of the coursebook. In addition to reviewing these main concepts and techniques, through a series of questions, activities and exam hints, you will be encouraged to apply the concepts and techniques to the 'real world' of marketing. In addition, each unit contains examples and case studies of how the key concepts and ideas apply, and are relevant to the 'real world' of marketing. The activities in each unit together with the further study and exam preparation questions are the driving forces of the learning process in the coursebook and you should make every effort to complete them. As you would expect from the professional body for marketing, candidates for any of the CIM's examinations are expected to be able to 'apply' the tools and techniques of marketing. The examples and case studies are particularly relevant with regard to these application skills. The coursebook is designed to help you in these application skills and hence prepare you better for the examination.

We wish you every success in your studies and careers in marketing.

Geoff Lancaster
Frank Withey

An introduction from the academic development advisor

In the last 2 years, we have seen some significant changes to CIM Marketing qualifications. The changes have been introduced on a year-on-year basis, with Certificate changes implemented in 2002, and the Professional Diploma in Marketing being launched in 2003. The Professional Postgraduate Diploma in Marketing was launched in 2004. The new qualifications are based on the CIM Professional Marketing Standards developed through research with employers.

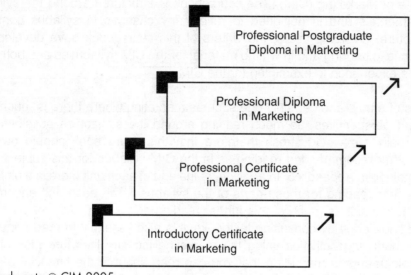

Study note © CIM 2005

As a result, the authoring team, Elsevier Butterworth-Heinemann and I have all aimed to rigorously revise and update the coursebook series to make sure that every title is the best possible study aid and accurately reflects the latest CIM syllabus. This has been further enhanced through independent reviews carried out by CIM.

We have aimed to develop the assessment support to include some additional support for the assignment route as well as the examination, so we hope you will find this helpful.

There are a number of new authors and indeed Senior Examiners in the series who have been commissioned for their CIM course teaching and examining experience, as well as their research into specific curriculum-related areas and their wide general knowledge of the latest thinking in marketing.

We are certain that you will find these coursebooks highly beneficial in terms of the content and assessment opportunities and a study tool that will prepare you for both CIM examinations and continuous/integrative assessment opportunities. They will guide you in a logical and structured way through the detail of the syllabus, providing you with the required underpinning knowledge, understanding and application of theory.

The editorial team and authors wish you every success as you embark upon your studies.

Karen Beamish
Academic Development Advisor

How to use these coursebooks

Everyone who has contributed to this series has been careful to structure the books with the exams in mind. Each unit, therefore, covers an essential part of the syllabus. You need to work through the complete coursebook systematically to ensure that you have covered everything you need to know.

This coursebook is divided into units each containing a selection of the following standard elements:

- o *Learning objectives* – Tell you what part of the syllabus you will be covering and what you will be expected to know, having completed the unit including, of course, all the activities, examination questions and so on. These objectives relate to the key areas of the syllabus, which are identified in the objectives element. The objectives also encompass the key learning outcomes and associated key skills specified in the syllabus for this subject.
- o *Study guides* – Include a brief introduction to the areas covered in the unit, tell you how long the unit is and how long its activities take to do.
- o *Questions* – Are designed to give you practice; all the questions are similar to those you get in the exam. Because of this, they are included in the further study section of the units. In this section of each unit, we have taken the opportunity to refer you to an actual exam question from a previous examination paper. As with all the questions in the units, these 'real life' exam questions are accompanied by an answer debrief in the answers and debriefings appendix. You should note, however, that for these actual exam questions you may also access a full sample answer from the relevant paper on the website www.cim.co.uk/learning zone then access past papers. Details of which paper these questions appear from are provided in each of the units.
- o *Answers* (at the end of the book) – Give you a suggested approach for answering questions. Remember there is no such thing as a model answer – you should use these examples only as guidelines.
- o *Activities* – Give you a chance to put what you have learned into practice.
- o *Debriefings* (at the end of the activities and questions) – Shed light on the methodologies involved in the activities.
- o *Exam hints* – Are tips from the Senior Examiner or examiner which are designed to help you avoid common mistakes made by previous candidates.
- o *Study tips* – Give you guidance on improving your knowledge base.
- o *Marketing in practice: examples* – These are designed to help you understand how the key marketing concepts and techniques in the syllabus are applied by actual companies in real life. These are essential in developing your application skills as a marketer.
- o *Key definitions* – Are given for key concepts and terminology, which you must know for this particular syllabus.
- o *Case studies* – As with Marketing in Practice examples, case studies are introduced to help you understand and appreciate how the key concepts and techniques discussed in each unit relate to real-life companies and marketing situations.
- o *Summaries* – Cover what you should have picked up from reading the unit.

○ *Bibliography and references* – Contain a list of all sources used in the unit and encompasses, as appropriate, not only books but journal and newspaper/magazine articles as well as website addresses.

○ *Further study* – Is intended to help you consolidate your knowledge. It includes suggestions for further reading and, as already emphasized, you are strongly recommended to read as widely as possible using this guide.

While you will find that each section of the syllabus has been covered within this text, you might find that the order of some of the topics has been changed. This is because it sometimes makes more sense to put certain topics together when you are studying, even though they might appear in different sections of the syllabus itself. If you work through each of the units in order, completing all the activities and following up with additional reading and study, together with examination preparation based around the end of unit questions, your coverage of the syllabus will be just fine.

About MarketingOnline

Elsevier Butterworth-Heinemann offers purchasers of the coursebooks free access to MarketingOnline (www.marketingonline.co.uk), our premier on-line support engine for the CIM marketing courses. On this site you can benefit from:

○ Fully customizable electronic versions of the coursebooks enabling you to annotate, cut and paste sections of text to create your own tailored learning notes.

○ The capacity to search the coursebook on-line for instant access to definitions and key concepts.

○ Useful links to e-marketing articles provided by Dave Chaffey, Director of Marketing Insights Ltd and a leading UK e-marketing consultant, trainer and author.

○ A glossary providing a comprehensive dictionary of marketing terms.

○ A frequently asked questions (FAQs) section providing guidance and advice on common problems or queries.

Using MarketingOnline

Logging on

Before you can access MarketingOnline you will first need to get a password. Please go to www.marketingonline.co.uk and click on the registration button where you will then find registration instructions for coursebook purchasers. Once you have got your password, you will need to log on using the onscreen instructions. This will give you access to the various functions of the site.

MarketingOnline provides a range of functions, as outlined in the previous section, which can easily be accessed from the site after you have logged on to the system. Please note the following guidelines detailing how to access the main features:

1. *The coursebooks* – Buttons corresponding to the three levels of the CIM marketing qualifications are situated on the home page. Select your level and you will be presented with the coursebook title for each module of that level. Click on the desired coursebook to access the full on-line text (divided up into chapters). On each page of

text, you have the option to add an electronic bookmark or annotation by following the onscreen instructions. You can also freely cut and paste text into a blank word document to create your own learning notes.

2. *e-Marketing articles* – To access the links to relevant e-marketing articles simply click on the link under the text 'E-marketing Essentials: useful links from Marketing Insights'.
3. *Glossary* – A link to the glossary is provided in the top right-hand corner of each page enabling access to this resource at any time.

If you have specific queries about using MarketingOnline, then you should consult our fully searchable FAQs section, accessible through the appropriate link in the top right-hand corner of any page of the site. Please also note that a *full user guide* can be downloaded by clicking on the link on the opening page of the website.

unit 1
the development of marketing and marketing orientation

Learning objectives

Learning outcomes

By the end of this unit you will be able to:

o Explain the development of marketing and the ways it can benefit business and organizations.

o Identify the main steps in, and barriers to, achieving a marketing orientation within the organization.

Knowledge and skills

By the end of this unit you will be able to:

o Explain the development of marketing as an exchange process, a philosophy of business and a managerial function (1.1).

o Recognize the contribution of marketing as a means of creating customer value and as a form of competition (1.2).

o Appreciate the importance of a market orientation to organizational performance and identify the factors that promote and impede the adoption of a market orientation (1.3).

o Explain the role of marketing in co-ordinating organizational resources both within and outside the marketing function (1.4).

o Describe the impacts of marketing actions on society and the need for marketers to act in an ethical and socially responsible manner (1.5).

o Examine the significance of buyer–seller relationships in marketing and the role of relationship marketing in facilitating the retention of customers (1.6).

Study Guide

This first unit is an introduction to the development, meaning and role of marketing in the contemporary organization. In short, this unit sets the scene for the remaining units in the guide. In a way, the unit reflects the process that must occur in an organization if it is to improve its performance in marketing, in as much as the first step in this improvement is an understanding of what marketing means and how it can be implemented. We shall start by looking at definitions of marketing, moving on to consider the so-called 'marketing concept' and 'marketing orientation'. We shall look at the development of marketing and the notion of marketing as an exchange process, a philosophy of business and a managerial function. We shall look at the importance of a marketing orientation to organizational performance and the issues and problems in implementing a marketing orientation through building and enhancing a marketing culture. The important contribution of marketing as a means of creating customer value and as a form of competition is considered, together with the role of marketing in co-ordinating organizational resources both within and outside the marketing function. We shall consider the changing role of marketing, and in particular the wider range of applications for marketing these days; the importance of environmental, ethical and social issues in marketing and the growth of the so-called 'relationship marketing'. Finally, we shall introduce you to the increasing importance of new technology in marketing these days, a theme that will be explored in each of the units in the coursebook.

We would expect you to take about 3 hours to work through this first unit, and suggest you allow a further 3–4 hours to undertake the various activities suggested. Other than your notebook and writing equipment you will not need anything further to complete this unit.

This first unit will also help you familiarize with the approach and style of our coursebooks. Of course if you are studying other subjects using the Butterworth-Heinemann coursebooks, you will be used to the approach. However, in case you are new to the coursebook series, you will find that the coursebooks have been developed to ensure that you acquire not only the knowledge necessary for examination success but also the skills to apply that knowledge, both in the examination and in your work as a practising marketer. Some of the elements, outlined at the start of the coursebook and especially the activities and questions and so on are designed of course to help you develop these application skills. Remember then, these activities and so on are central to the design of the coursebooks and you are therefore advised to avoid the temptation to leave them out.

Learning outcomes/unit guide

Before we start to work through this first unit, we felt it would be useful to provide you with an overview of how each of the key learning outcomes for the Fundamentals module, as set out in the CIM specification for this module, relate to this and the other units in the coursebook. The full CIM specification for the module is in fact contained in Appendix 5 of your coursebook; but the following maps out/signposts the main CIM learning objectives and in which unit(s) these are covered.

Learning outcomes	Study units/syllabus reference
o Explain the development of marketing and the ways it can benefit business and organizations (5.23.1)	Unit 1/Element 1
o Identify the main steps in, and barriers to, achieving a marketing orientation within the organization (5.23.1)	Unit 1/Element 1
o Explain the context of, and process for, marketing planning and budgeting including related models (5.23.3)	Unit 2/Element 2
o Explain the concept of segmentation and the different bases for effective segmentation (5.23.4)	Unit 2/Element 2
o Identify and describe the individual elements and tools of the marketing mix (5.23.5)	Unit 3, 4, 5, 6, 7, 8/ Elements 3, 5, 6, 7, 8
o Identify the basic differences in application of the marketing mix involved in marketing products and services within different marketing contexts (5.23.6)	Unit 9/Element 4

Having established the signposts for the major learning objectives and the coursebook units, we can now proceed to commence with your first unit.

What is marketing?

We don't expect a formal definition at this stage but do you really know what marketing is?

Study tip

Organize your study materials from the beginning of your course:

- o Use file dividers to keep broad topic areas indexed and relevant materials and articles with the relevant notes.
- o Look out for relevant articles, newspaper reports and so on that you feel provide good examples of the key concepts and techniques covered in the coursebook. You will find these useful to illustrate examination answers.

 ### Activity 1.1

In your own words describe what you think marketing is all about.

Different people will have different views of what marketing is but it would be surprising if many did not have one or more of the following in their description.

Marketing is about:

- ○ Selling
- ○ Market research
- ○ Advertising.

Or perhaps for those of you who work in marketing, it is about 'Selling products that don't come back to customers who do'.

For those of you who prefer a more formal approach, marketing may be about 'Analysis, Planning, Implementation and Control in order to develop a competitive advantage'.

The common theme that runs through this variety of viewpoints about what marketing entails is that marketing is a set of activities or, more specifically, a set of managerial activities or functions required to be performed in an organization. Certainly, marketing does encompass activities such as selling, researching markets, attracting and keeping customers, and developing and implementing plans. In short, it is true that it is a managerial function. In fact, this managerial function of marketing is enshrined in the CIM's own definition of marketing as follows.

Key definition

Marketing – Is 'The management process which identifies, anticipates and satisfies customer requirements efficiently and profitably'.

We can see, though, that the CIM definition, in addition to confirming marketing as a management process, also highlights the fact that the central focus of this process is on the 'customer' and the aim is 'satisfying' his or her requirements or 'needs'. Finally, all this must be done in the most efficient way possible with a view to achieving maximum profitability.

In fact, as you would expect, most of the formal definitions of marketing are very similar. Here, for example, are two more for you to consider.

Key definitions

Marketing – Consists of individual and organizational activities that facilitate and expedite satisfying exchange relationships in a dynamic environment through the creation, distribution, promotion and pricing of goods, services and ideas. (Dibb *et al.*, 2000)

Marketing – Means working with markets to bring about exchanges for the purpose of satisfying human needs and wants. It is a process by which individuals and groups obtain what they need and want creating and exchanging products and value with others. (Kotler *et al.*, 2000)

Extending Knowledge

The CIM website, www.cim.co.uk, provides some very useful information regarding definitions and perspectives on marketing.

So, then, if we are to understand the fundamentals of marketing, we must learn about what this management process consists of. We need to know the key tasks of marketing management and the marketing tools that are used in these tasks. Indeed, in the following units, we shall be exploring both tasks and tools more closely. However, marketing is not only or even primarily a management function or set of activities. First and foremost, marketing is a way of thinking, or, as it is often called, a 'concept' for running a business. Some have even argued that marketing is essentially a 'philosophy'. The point is that only by first understanding and accepting this way of thinking (concept or philosophy) can a company begin to develop a marketing culture or orientation and, hence, ultimately become effective at marketing.

So, what is this so-called 'marketing concept' and how does it relate to the development of a marketing culture?

The marketing concept: marketing orientation

Put simply, the marketing concept focuses on customers. A company that adopts the marketing concept puts the customer at the centre of all business decision-making and planning, and not just marketing departments decision-making and planning. A company with this approach is said to be marketing oriented. In order to understand the meaning and implications of being marketing oriented, we need to examine briefly the background to the development of the marketing concept and the distinction between a marketing- and a production-, product-, or sales-oriented company. We shall start by highlighting the distinctions between these orientations in a company.

Activity 1.2

Marketing oriented versus other possible orientations of an organization.

A company can be:

- Production oriented
- Product oriented
- Sales oriented
- Marketing oriented.

Using the following statements from the management of our hypothetical organizations, can you assess which of these four possible orientations for a company best fits the organization described by each statement. Read each of the descriptions and then place a number in the circles to indicate the following:

1. This company is marketing oriented
2. This company is sales oriented
3. This company is production oriented
4. This company is product oriented.

Company A

'We believe that our products are the most innovative on the market. Our quality is second to none and we've gone all out to develop the best design team in the business.'

No. ◯

Company B

'Our salespeople understand how to get the customer to sign on the dotted line. Most customers really want to purchase our product when they see it; they just need a little push to make up their mind.'

No. ◯

Company C

'Customers can be very fickle sometimes. We've just had to change a specification because the customer wanted something else at the last minute. This also affected our production schedules and our delivery department, and everything had to be re-costed. Still at least everyone pulled together on this one.'

No. ◯

Company D

'The customer can have any colour so long as it's black.'

No. ◯

So what conclusions did you arrive at from this activity?

Of course some of you will have recognized in Company D our old friend Henry Ford, the founder of the Ford Motor Company. Allegedly, Henry Ford was said to have uttered this much-quoted phrase about the world's first mass-produced motor car.

At the time, the 1920s, Ford's major concern was with the problems of producing cars in sufficient volume and at a price the huge latent mass market, which he rightly perceived to exist, could afford. The colour of his cars therefore mattered little to Henry Ford other than the fact that only producing one colour enabled both output to be greater and prices to be lower.

Interestingly, at the time, Ford's focus on production rather than the colour preferences of his customers was right. Customers at the time were less interested in colour than in availability and affordability. Henry Ford's approach was right for the time.

This is an important lesson to learn. The need to be marketing oriented (Company C in our example) is a function of the market and competitive conditions now faced by companies. Put another way, marketing orientation is the result of a gradual process of evolution that many, if not all, companies have passed through as societies, manufacturing economies and customers themselves have evolved.

The stages of evolution are shown in simple form below.

Era (approx.)	Orientation/emphasis
1900–1930s	Production orientation
1930s–1960s	Selling orientation
1960s–present	Marketing orientation

A good summary of the differences between the production, selling and marketing concepts is provided by Kotler as follows:

> *The production concept concentrates on production and distribution economies. This in turn is based on the notion that consumers will choose lower priced products that are readily available.*

> *The selling concept is of course based on the notion that customers need to be persuaded to buy through aggressive selling and promotion.*

> *The marketing concept is based on the notion that organizations can best meet their objectives by concentrating on customer needs and satisfying these needs better than competitors.*

> *NB Perhaps there have always been, and always will be, those inventors/companies who dangerously believe that product orientation is the secret of commercial success.*

In fact, as we shall see later, societies and therefore markets are still evolving and so too is marketing thought and practice. For example, many developed economies have now become service economies, giving rise to additional considerations in 'services marketing'. Similarly, many consumers are much more concerned about the environment and the possible effects of marketing activities, giving rise to 'social marketing'. Finally, organizations other than 'for-profit' ones are embracing the marketing concept and marketing practices. Charities, churches, political parties and personalities are only some of these wider applications of what is some-times termed 'metamarketing'.

We shall therefore be considering some of the implications of this evolving nature of the marketing culture later in this, and subsequent, units. In addition to these wider applications of marketing, however, marketing practices too are evolving and changing. In this respect, several recent developments in marketing are particularly worthy of note, namely: the growth of the so-called 'relationship marketing' and the development of 'network marketing'. Perhaps one of the most significant developments affecting all marketing managers in recent years, how-ever, is the changing nature of marketing due to an increased use, and application, of information technology (IT). As in many areas of business, IT, in all its forms, is having a significant impact on management practice. In the area of marketing, examples of this impact would include: the growth of the Internet with its implications for areas such as home shopping, marketing communications and so on; increasing sophistication in the use of databases for marketing purposes with its implications for areas such as direct mail; increasingly powerful computer-based techniques for analysing customers and markets with their implications for areas such as market segmentation and targeting, and brand positioning. Again, we shall look at the evolving and changing nature of marketing practices in more detail in this unit and the units which follow as appropriate.

Exam hint

As this is the Marketing Fundamentals paper, the examiners are unlikely to expect you to be an expert in the more specialized applications of marketing. However, the examiners will expect you to have a good basic grasp of how marketing and its applications are widening and changing in the modern world. It is vital, therefore, that you try to keep up to date as possible with what is going on in the world of marketing. The examiners will expect you to be familiar with current thinking and practices in marketing. This coursebook, of course, is designed, as far as possible, to encompass and reflect this thinking and practices, but the marketing world is very dynamic and you should try to keep up to date with current industry practices. A good general-purpose magazine on marketing designed for the marketing practitioner, such as *Marketing Today*, or even the financial pages of a good quality newspaper will help you in keeping up to date and in providing you with lots of examples that will potentially earn you higher marks in the examination.

Factors contributing to the need to be marketing oriented

Many factors have contributed to the requirement to be marketing oriented in today's business environment, but to appreciate some of the more important of these you should complete the activity below before proceeding.

Activity 1.3

Factors underpinning the need to be market oriented

Below are listed some of the key factors that have contributed to the need to be marketing oriented. In order to help you in this activity, we have described the 'state' of each factor when, as it was in the days of Henry Ford, production orientation was appropriate for organizations.

What you should do is assess the 'state' of these factors today, which in turn underpins the need to be marketing oriented.

Look carefully at each factor as it relates to the production-oriented era and then decide how you feel each factor is likely to have changed in the era of marketing orientation.

Factor	Production-oriented era	Marketing-oriented era
Demand	Latent demand high	
Average disposable income	Low	
General level of education	Low	
Mass media/access to information	Underdeveloped/low	
Supply/industry capacity	Insufficient	
Competition	Negligible/local	

You should now compare your descriptions for each of the factors with those shown in the debriefing activity.

Broad economic, political, social and technological factors have all contributed to the development of marketing orientation; however, you will not be surprised if we say that, in summarizing these factors, the overriding reason underpinning the need to be marketing oriented is customer choice. Quite simply, the organization most effectively identifying and supplying customer needs will get the business.

Again it is important to stress that both production and sales orientation were probably the right approaches to markets for their times. However, not only does it now make more sense to focus the whole of the business and hence product design, pricing policies, distribution and everything else on a careful analysis of customer needs, that is to start the planning process around those needs, but the fact is that in today's environment being market oriented is an essential – perhaps the essential – ingredient in organizational survival and success. Business planning must now start and end with the customer.

We shall be looking at marketing planning shortly, but it is important to recognize that marketing plans and business plans are different albeit totally interrelated.

The business plan, perhaps as you would expect, relates to the organization as a whole and therefore encompasses objectives and strategies for the whole company embracing all functions and activities. Marketing plans, however, again as one would expect, relate to marketing objectives and strategies and primarily involve the functions and activities of the marketing department. One could perhaps readily understand that marketing plans must start and end with customers, but under the marketing concept, and where a marketing culture exists in an organization, then business plans too, despite their wider remit, must also start and end with customers. The simple reason for this is that in the final analysis, it is the customer's needs, and the importance of identifying and satisfying these, which lie at the heart of the success or failure of business plans.

Again, it is acknowledged that business plans necessarily have a broader remit than just the marketing part of the business and must seek to co-ordinate every key function in the organization. However, the primary input into and focus for all the elements of the business plan in the company, which has a true marketing culture, must centre on the needs of the customer.

The truly marketing-oriented organization, then, is the one that places the customer and his or her needs at the centre of everything the company does. Not only marketers and the marketing function must accept this central importance of customers and hence the need to develop plans and activities to satisfy them, but every department, even every individual, in the marketing-oriented organization must be attuned to the importance of satisfying customer needs. We shall return to this aspect later.

This, then, is what is meant by being marketing oriented.

Key definition

Marketing orientation – Is a philosophy that places customer satisfaction at the centre of all organizational planning and procedures. (Withey, 2001)

Marketing as a form of competition: creating customer value

Although marketing and being marketing oriented is essentially, as we have seen, about thinking customers and focusing all the company's efforts and resources on customer needs and their satisfaction, increasingly marketers are recognizing that it is as important to be competitor as well as customer oriented. This does not detract from the importance of customer orientation but is simply a recognition that with so much competition about these days, and with so many of those competitors themselves being very customer and marketing oriented, very often the achievement of organizational and marketing objectives rests on whether or not a company can beat the competition. Beating the competition, of course, should still be viewed from a customer perspective, competitors are beaten where customers perceive a company's offerings or more specifically the value of those offerings to be superior to competitor offerings. In this sense, then, although still oriented around customers, marketing can be thought of as a form of competition. The marketer's task is to out compete other potential suppliers by creating and maintaining superior customer value through the effective application and co-ordination of the marketing mix. Obviously, there are numerous ways in which a company can attempt to create superior customer value including, for example, low prices, better service, higher quality, speedier delivery and so on. The ways in which a company creates superior value should reflect customer needs but also needs to be based on marketing assets and strengths which are superior to competitors and which can be defended and sustained in the marketplace. Marketers often refer to this process, then, as creating a sustainable competitive advantage (an SCA). The SCA, then, represents the objective and the output of successful marketing activities in the contemporary organization.

The importance of creating customer value in today's extremely competitive environment cannot be stressed enough. Customers now have substantial choice, are well informed and are prepared to shop around. This has made customers more and more demanding when they choose between competing products and services and they will, for obvious reasons, choose those suppliers and brands that offer the highest value. Increasingly, though, marketers have recognized that 'highest value' does not necessarily mean 'lowest price'. Rather customers compare price against the perceived benefits of a product or service to assess value. This seemingly simple idea, in fact, has several far-reaching implications for today's marketer. One important implication is that the marketer must look at value from the customers' perspective. In particular, the marketer first must understand what the customer values, or can be persuaded to value, in a product or service. Secondly, the marketer must then develop marketing programmes, and particularly the design of the marketing mix, based on these identified dimensions of customer value. Finally, the marketer must evaluate and surpass competitors with respect to the customers' value dimensions. Offering the best value to customers in turn leads to satisfied and hence increasingly loyal customers who as a result become valuable assets to the organization. Value-based marketing creates what is effectively a virtuous circle – the marketer delivers value, customers become increasingly loyal, the value of the company is increased which in turn enables the marketer to offer even greater value and so the process continues with competitors being increasingly shut out of the process. The future of marketing is increasingly about building and sustaining value for customers.

Building a marketing culture

We have seen that in today's environment, it is vital to become marketing oriented. But we have also seen that, although perhaps the identification of customer needs and the development of plans and programmes to meet these needs are the responsibility of the marketing function, all functions and individuals in organizations need to accept the central importance of the customer. In other words, we need to establish and encourage the right (marketing oriented) attitudes and practices throughout the company. What is required therefore is a marketing culture. Needless to say, this is easier said than done. While most managers, even non-marketing ones, would accept the importance of the customer/client to their organizations, in practice many do not 'think customers' in their day-to-day activities or even in long-term planning. So the questions are:

- How can we establish the extent to which an organization has the basics for building a marketing culture?
- How can we assess the extent to which this culture has permeated organizational thinking and planning?
- How, if necessary, can we instil and enhance a marketing culture in an organization?

These are not simple questions, and the last one, in particular, has no easy solution. Let us examine each question in turn.

Business definition and a marketing culture

The starting point for building a marketing culture in an organization is quite simply to 'think customers'. Perhaps one of the most fundamental ways in which the extent to which the management of an organization is 'thinking customers' can be assessed is in how it defines what business the organization is in.

Activity 1.4

In your own words, and as briefly as you can, summarize what business the following organizations are in:

- The Ford Motor Company
- Max Factor
- IBM
- The Catholic Church
- Your own company (or an organization you are familiar with).

Again we each might have different ideas about what business the organizations listed in the activity are in, but what really matters is our perspective or basis for defining each business. The non-marketing-oriented manager will base the definition of each of these organizations essentially on the products or services they produce. So, for example, Ford = cars and trucks; Max Factor = cosmetics/perfume; IBM = computers; the Catholic Church = religion and so on. In the marketing-oriented company, however, business definitions will be based on a customer perspective, that is the definition will stem from the benefits that the customer is seeking. So now, Ford = transport (or perhaps for some products, status); Max Factor = beauty; IBM = solutions to business problems; and the Catholic Church = hope or salvation.

Marketing in practice: example

IBM have certainly recognized the importance of business definition in building a marketing culture and in the preparation of marketing plans and budgets. IBM constantly review their business definition ensuring that it is relevant to the marketing environment and the changes taking place in constant marketing research and customer-tracking processes to ensure that their business definition is customer oriented. IBM's recent decision to finally move out of the personal computer market reflects the way in which IBM are constantly reassessing what business they are in.

Any organization that sees and hence defines its business in anything other than customer benefit terms has simply not reached first base in developing a marketing culture. An organization that defines its business in terms of what it produces is said to be suffering from what a famous marketing pundit and writer, Theodore Levitt, called 'marketing myopia'.

Key definition

Marketing myopia – Results from a company having a short-sighted and narrow view of the business it is in as a result of product- or service-based business definitions rather than customer need-based ones.

Extending knowledge

Key developments in marketing thinking/Key figures

Note: Marketing myopia/Theodore Levitt

The notions of marketing myopia and the importance of business definition are, quite rightly, much vaunted concepts in developing a marketing culture. The work of Theodore Levitt in this area therefore is considered classic.

If you can, you should read Theodore Levitt's classic article 'Marketing Myopia' (1960) *Harvard Business Review*, July–August, pp. 45–46.

Activity 1.5

Managers' definitions of their business

If you can, talk to the senior managers of an organization. This could be either the one you work for or another one you can gain access to the management of.

Ask these managers, 'What business do you feel the organization is in?' Preferably ask this question to both the marketing managers and the managers of other functional areas in the business.

From their answers, what do you conclude about the extent the organization has begun to develop a marketing culture by 'thinking customers'?

Alternative/additional activity

If it is difficult to gain access to an organization, alternatively (or better still additionally) obtain copies of the annual reports of, say, a couple of public companies. Read through the reports, noting any signs/evidence you can find of the company 'thinking customers'.

Exam hint

Given the stress placed on business definition in this unit, you will appreciate that this is an important area. Because of this you can expect marketing myopia/business definition to be a popular area with examiners. It certainly has been in past fundamental papers.

Assessing the extent of the marketing culture

'Thinking customers', then, through how we view and define the business is the first step in developing a marketing culture. But, as we have seen, 'thinking customers' must permeate all functions and levels of the organization and not just the marketing function or even senior management. Certainly, talking to managers from different functions to assess how they define the business (as you have done in the previous activity in this unit) will give us the first indication of how widespread or otherwise is the marketing culture. However, given the importance of developing this culture company-wide, not surprisingly, more formal methods of assessing the extent to which a marketing culture has permeated organizational thinking and planning are available. Many organizations now enshrine this assessment in annual marketing audits, parts of which are often the measurement of the extent to which there is a marketing or customer culture. Such measurement may entail the use of formal questionnaires in a marketing effectiveness rating review. Areas/ aspects covered by such reviews include, for example:

o   Evidence of market and customer research
o   Co-ordination between functions based on customer needs
o   Evidence of long- versus short-term planning and plans
o   Company-wide communication on customer needs.

Extending knowledge

Although space does not permit the inclusion of a full marketing effectiveness questionnaire, exposure to (and even completion of) an example of such a comprehensive and widely applied questionnaire would be very useful to understanding and knowledge in this area.

An excellent example of a questionnaire-based marketing effectiveness instrument is contained in P. Kotler (2001) *Marketing Management*, 8th edition, pp. 756–757. If you possibly can, you should read through this, and, better still, complete the questionnaire for an organization of your choice.

Instilling and enhancing a marketing culture: factors that promote and impede the adoption of a market orientation

We have seen that a marketing culture essentially means putting the customer first and 'thinking customers'. We have also seen that this must permeate the organization at all levels and all functions. Finally, we have seen that it is possible to assess the extent of such a marketing culture in an organization. But what if we find that no such culture exists and we wish therefore to instil a marketing culture? Or, as is more usual, what if we wish to enhance and extend a marketing culture throughout an organization? As mentioned earlier, this is probably the most difficult step for the majority of companies, especially when it comes to instilling such a culture into non-marketing staff. But a number of steps can be taken to grow a marketing culture.

Activity 1.6

Think about an organization you know – any organization will do. Use these questions to prompt your thoughts about the key steps in growing a marketing culture:

- ○ Is senior management in the organization totally committed to customers and improved marketing?
- ○ Has anyone the specific responsibility and authority for enhancing a marketing culture in the organization?
- ○ Do job descriptions in functions other than marketing include reference to customer satisfaction?
- ○ Are marketing staff regularly trained in developments in contemporary marketing concepts and techniques?
- ○ Are non-marketing staff trained in customer appreciation and care?
- ○ Are non-marketing and sales staff ever given a chance to meet customers/clients?
- ○ Do reward and motivation systems in all jobs encourage employees to serve customers better?

If the answer to any of the questions in the activity is no, then there are opportunities to enhance the marketing culture in the organization.

It is important to recognize that this sort of culture cannot be achieved overnight. Indeed, there is often antagonism and resistance on the part of individuals outside the marketing or sales departments. Such resistance should be anticipated and planned for. Often the persuasive (rather than authoritative) powers of a respected senior executive committed to building a marketing culture are essential here.

The development of a marketing culture and, in particular, the training and motivation of all the individuals in an organization to achieve this is now often referred to as internal marketing.

Key definition

Internal marketing – Is the creation of an internal environment which supports customer-consciousness and sales-mindedness amongst all personnel within an organization. (Christian Gröonroos)

The importance and value of internal marketing to building a marketing culture and ultimately in helping to achieve an SCA has increasingly been recognized by organizations. Only if all the employees of an organization are committed to delivering customer satisfaction can an organization be said to be truly marketing oriented. In turn, achieving this commitment, it is argued, requires the senior management through the marketing function of an organization to market the need for customer orientation and delivering customer satisfaction throughout a company's employees. Internal marketing starts then by identifying how customer orientation relates to the needs of non-marketing employees in an organization and how these needs can be met through providing customer satisfaction. At its most basic, of course, by helping meet customer needs an employee derives the benefit of helping the company stay in business and hence help keep the job. Internal marketing needs to go further than this though to convince employees that by helping generate customer satisfaction an employee's job satisfaction and motivation can be improved. Another facet of internal marketing is the use of the tools of marketing within the organization such as segmentation and targeting, that is recognizing that different employee groups or functional areas of the business will have different needs and requirements, and identifying and satisfying these. In addition, internal marketing is achieved through the application of the marketing mix elements, though in this case this would involve, for example: the use of staff training; the provision of systems and technology to help employees provide customer satisfaction through their work activities; linking reward and remuneration structures to customer satisfaction and so on. Finally, it is now suggested that marketing plans should include objectives, strategies and activities for marketing internally as well as externally.

Although internal marketing is important for all organizations, it has proved particularly popular in service organizations, for example banks, hotels and so on, where a wide range of staff are often in direct contact with customers. Not-for-profit organizations too have made extensive use of the idea of internal marketing. Some of the special and additional issues of marketing in voluntary and not-for-profit organizations are considered in more detail in Unit 9, but in the context of internal marketing, the fact that many voluntary and not-for-profit organizations also have substantial employee contact with their customers and clients, coupled with the fact that the exchange process between company and customer is often complex and multi-faceted, serve to heighten the importance of all employees being customer oriented and trying to deliver customer satisfaction and value.

Extending knowledge

A particularly useful explanation of the application of internal marketing in service and not-for-profit organizations is provided in Brassington and Pettitt (2000) *Principles of Marketing*, 2nd edition, pp. 962–969.

Marketing in practice: example

As a step towards developing a marketing culture and implementing internal marketing, the UK high street retailer Debenhams provide every employee with a card on which is printed the organization's mission statement. As part of this mission statement, Debenhams stress their objective of providing above average quality and value for money delivered through a commitment to customer dedication by all company employees. In turn, they also are committed to attracting, retaining, developing and motivating high-calibre staff who are customer centred. The start of internal marketing in this organization centres on informing employees of their role and importance in delivering customer satisfaction and company success.

Difficulties in managing the introduction of a customer-oriented culture

Needless to say, achieving a customer-oriented culture is not always easy. Some of the major difficulties and barriers in the introduction of such a culture are as follows:

o Managers fail to realize or understand the true concept.
o The structure of the organization may require change and this can lead to other managers' resistance and costs.
o People are frightened and reluctant to change.

    o The power struggle between the different departments within an organization can hinder the process, for example the production department.

    o In some organizations, the responsibility for marketing strategy and implementation are separated, and this may offer many problems.

Co-ordinating role of marketing

Effective marketing, as we shall see when we consider marketing planning and the management of the marketing mix, requires that all marketing and sales activities within the marketing function be co-ordinated. Unfortunately, the degree of co-ordination required in some organizations, particularly between sales and marketing, is not all that it should be. So, for example, in some organizations, the sales department often functions almost independently of the marketing department. In part, this is because of the traditional structure and position of the sales function in many organizations and also because some organizations even now are not truly marketing oriented. Sales and selling activities should be part of an overall co-ordinated marketing effort. As with achieving a marketing culture, this can and does give rise to problems of conflict and antagonism between sales and marketing. The senior management of a company need to ensure that the sales personnel understand their relationship to marketing and the fact that all marketing activities including selling need to be marketing department led and in the process, customer driven. This is not to suggest that selling is in any way inferior or should be subservient to marketing, but rather stresses the co-ordinating role of marketing. Other marketing activities, too, need to be co-ordinated including activities encompassing marketing research, promotion and advertising, customer service and of course the marketing mix.

In addition, and often even more problematical, marketing also has a role and responsibility in co-ordinating organizational efforts and resources outside the marketing function – hence the need for a company-wide marketing culture. In particular, marketing should help co-ordinate the efforts and activities of the other key functional areas of the business that impinge on and affect customers. This includes, then, for example, the production and quality control functions, accountancy and finance, research and development, and even personnel. Again, this is not to suggest that these other functions should be subservient to marketing, rather only that marketing should play the co-ordinating role in the efforts of these other functions, again centred on achieving customer satisfaction.

Finally, marketing also has a role to play in co-ordinating resources and activities not only outside the marketing function in the organization but also outside the organization itself. Often marketing strategies and plans encompass and involve other individuals and organizations external to an organization. A simple example would include the need to co-ordinate the activities and resources of, say, distributors. After all, distributors play a key part in achieving marketing objectives and in the levels of customer satisfaction achieved. In many ways, in fact, effective marketing requires the efforts of very many parties to be co-ordinated both internal and external to the organization. Sometimes the external parties are external marketing agencies such as market research companies, advertising agencies, or the distributors and middle persons already mentioned. But also marketers must often play a co-ordinating role with other parties in the overall value chain including, for example, suppliers. In fact, increasingly, marketers build their marketing strategies and plans taking into account and having to co-ordinate the full set of activities in the value chain.

Achieving co-ordination, both inside and outside the marketing function and including outside agencies and organizations, requires the marketer to have clear objectives and planning processes. The marketer must ensure that all parties concerned with customer satisfaction are aware of customer needs and the company's objectives and plans with respect to meeting these. Other parties must also be aware of their contribution and role in fulfilling these plans and the activities that will need to be performed. The marketer increasingly needs analysis and planning skills so as to be able to steer other parties in the right direction with regard to the use of resources to achieve customer satisfaction. In addition, the contemporary marketer must have good communication and interpersonal skills so as to be able to motivate these other parties. Co-ordinating role of marketing between customers and parties inside and outside the organization is shown in Figure 1.1. Note that the sequence shown in the diagram illustrates the process of co-ordinating beginning of course with customers.

Figure 1.1 Co-ordinating role of marketing

Technology and the marketing culture

Developments in technology are affecting every facet of marketing. Indeed, these developments are among the most pervasive of factors influencing the practice of marketing. Because of this, remember, we shall be looking at some of the more important of these developments throughout the units of the course. At this point, then, it would be perhaps useful to point to some of the ways in which technology and particularly IT is helping companies in their management of a customer-oriented culture.

Some of the ways in which technology is helping in the management of a customer-oriented culture are as follows:

- More effective and efficient internal communication via information and communication technology (ICT).
- Speedier responses to customer needs and market changes.
- Better prepared analysis of data and statistics for market and customer intelligence.
- More powerful databases which help customer profiling and therefore tailoring of products to customer needs.
- The use of intranets and extranets to keep staff and suppliers informed and to manage the value chain.
- Related to the above, the use of electronic data interchange (EDI) systems to facilitate communication through the value chain.
- Improved systems of stock control and management through use of computer applications enabling more effective customer service delivery and so on.
- Automated telephone and call-centre systems potentially improving customer response.
- Increases in the number of channels through which customers and other stakeholders can communicate with an organization.
- The Internet and website developments which enable customers, for example, to shop in alternative ways, facilitate customer choice and allow easier trading around the world.
- The use of database systems to facilitate more effective customer relationship management (CRM) through developments such as loyalty card systems and so on.

Marketing in practice: example

Most of the world's airlines are now making extensive use of IT to improve the effectiveness of their marketing, and in particular the levels of service to their customers. Singapore Airlines, Air France, Virgin Atlantic and British Airways are all examples of global airline operators who have used the Internet and databases to improve their marketing to customers. For example, customers can now save time, and often money, by using on-line booking services. Customers can check availability of flights for themselves and assess the most cost-effective times and ways to travel. Customers can even reserve certain seats on the aircraft on which they will travel. The airlines themselves can use their databases to build up detailed profiles of customers who have flown with them thereby identifying any special needs or particular preferences and requirements of individual customers, which can then be used to develop personalized service packages and offers for these customers.

Business-to-business marketers often thought to be slower to apply new marketing ideas and techniques have in fact been in the vanguard of using ICT in their marketing. Ford, for example, have been using e-marketing with their suppliers for some years now and have recently invested substantially in new databases to improve their competitiveness.

Marketing as a management function

Early in this unit, we looked at definitions of marketing, including the one proposed by CIM. We suggested that a common theme to all definitions of marketing is that it is a management function, which indeed it is. However, we also suggested that before we look at the tasks of marketing management, we need to explore marketing as a way of thinking or philosophy, the so-called 'marketing concept', and the importance of building a marketing culture in an organization. Having done this, we can now turn our attention to the tasks and tools of marketing management.

 ## Activity 1.7

Look at the advertisement below for a marketing post. Study it carefully and then write down a list of what you see as the key activities in this post.

Marketing Manager

South West circa £-

o Challenge of this new role is to develop creative approaches and long-range marketing plans while also adding immediate commercial value to the activities of operations colleagues with strong bottom-line orientation and limited application of professional marketing.

o Major retail service group which leads their market with over 100 outlets nationwide and turnover of £1 billion.

o Key accountabilities in the creation of an influential marketing function will include market analysis, building of customer database, new product/service development, corporate identity, business planning and developing cooperative relationships with suppliers.

o Operating company board member with additional line responsibility for two development businesses.

> ○ Probably 35–45, graduate calibre and possibly MBA. Successful record in senior brand marketing role in blue-chip retailing, multi-site service or FMCG company. Any general management experience would be an advantage.
> ○ Strategic visioning and business planning skills combined with ability to win credibility and make things happen with powerful line directors. Management skills to handle hybrid staff/line role and to lead change processes.
> ○ Strong but subtle influencing style. Creative but pragmatic. Common touch as well as ability to develop senior relationships. General management potential.

Clearly, the specific tasks of an individual marketing manager will vary from one organization to another but you will find that most of your list of key activities from this recruitment advertisement can be categorized under one of the following headings.

- ○ Analysis
- ○ Planning
- ○ Implementation
- ○ Control.

Turn to debriefing activity 1.7 of this unit to find out what each of these tasks entails and see examples of how the various activities referred to in the job description relate to the tasks.

Having considered debriefing activity 1.7, we can now turn our attention to each of the key activities in our list.

Analysis

Analysis includes the assessment of both internal and external factors that affect and help shape, therefore, marketing plans. Analysis encompasses the analysis of the wider marketing environment including, for example, economic, political, social/cultural and technological factors and the nearer task environment factors such as competitors, and of course customers. Effective marketing ultimately stems from effective analysis. The marketer must understand how markets operate and the trends affecting them. The analysis tasks of marketing managers require them to make use of the tools and techniques of marketing research leading increasingly to the development of marketing information systems.

Planning

Based on careful analysis, the marketing manager is responsible for developing marketing plans.

Although the marketing manager will be required to perform all four of the key activities listed above, the planning element is in some ways the central activity. It is important therefore that you understand the key steps in the planning process and how these fit together into a systematic framework.

Study tip

You should note that the marketing planning process is considered in much more detail in Unit 2. We feel, however, that it is useful to give you a basic overview of the process at this stage because this will help you to see how the various elements of marketing fit together. At this stage, therefore, you simply need to familiarize yourself with this basic overview of the planning steps.

A basic overview of the marketing planning steps is shown in Figure 1.2.

Business mission/corporate objectives
↓
Marketing audit
↓
SWOT analysis
↓
Business objectives
↓
Marketing objectives
↓
Marketing strategies
↓
Marketing tactics/marketing mix decisions
↓
Implementation
↓
Monitoring and control

Figure 1.2 Key steps in marketing planning

Extending knowledge

There are probably as many different variations on the basic marketing planning steps as there are different marketing textbooks. You should therefore consult several of the recommended texts for this subject in order to gain a feel for the different ones. Useful texts in this respect would include, for example, Brassington and Pettitt (2000) *Principles of Marketing*, 2nd edition and Lancaster *et al.* (2002) *Marketing Fundamentals*, 4th edition.

Implementation

As we can see from Figure 1.2, implementation represents the penultimate stage of the marketing planning process, though we have of course listed it separately. Implementation in fact is important enough in its own right to be considered one of the four key activities and responsibilities of the marketing manager. Implementation essentially involves getting things done. This in turn entails the marketing manager ensuring, for example, that resources and budgets are in place to implement marketing plans, plans are communicated and accepted, and that staff both within the marketing function and in other functional areas both inside and outside the business are motivated.

Control

Again, part of our marketing planning framework is shown in Figure 1.2, but is important enough to be considered in its own right. In fact, monitoring and control of marketing activities is often a neglected area, both in the literature surrounding marketing activities and also, unfortunately, in many organizations. It is the marketer's responsibility to assess the extent to which marketing strategies and plans are working, achieving the objectives set and doing this in a cost-effective manner. In addition, the control process involves making any necessary changes to marketing activities and plans to take account of, say, any changed circumstances.

These, then, are the basic activities and responsibilities of the marketing manager. Within these broad areas of activity the marketing manager has several specific marketing activities and responsibilities to perform in the organization. Among some of the most important of these activities are those of market segmentation and the development and application of the so-called 'marketing mix'. We shall now consider these two extremely important aspects of the marketing manager's job.

Market segmentation

Many feel that market segmentation lies at the heart of the contemporary marketing manager's task and it certainly represents a key facet of a marketing-oriented organization and hence a marketing culture. As with the marketing planning process, market segmentation including the related aspects of targeting and positioning are discussed in detail in Unit 2. Again, however, we feel it is useful to introduce you to the notion of market segmentation at this point as it is so central as a concept and technique to the marketing culture.

Essentially, market segmentation recognizes the fact that in most, if not all, markets, all customers are not the same with respect to their needs and wants. Market segmentation is the process of identifying and classifying customers according to these different needs and wants. By doing so, the marketer is better able to decide which groups of customers or segments to serve, and on what basis. In particular, effective market segmentation enables the marketer to develop marketing mix programmes which are much more closely tailored to the needs of different customers. As such, then, we can see how market segmentation enables the marketer to translate the marketing concept into practical marketing programmes and because of this, market segmentation represents one of those powerful tools of the modern marketer.

The tools of marketing management: the marketing mix

In performing their key tasks, marketing managers have at their disposal a number of tools or ingredients they can use to develop marketing plans, and to create customer satisfaction and, ultimately, profits for the organization. These tools or ingredients are often referred to as the 'marketing mix'.

Key definitions

The marketing mix: the 4Ps – Is the set of controllable variables the marketer uses to develop marketing plans and programmes.

First proposed by Neil Borden, the original and still basic elements of the marketing mix are the 4Ps:

- o Product
- o Price
- o Place
- o Promotion.

In the units that follow, we shall be looking at each of these in detail.

A further 3Ps – More recently, however, largely because of the growth of services marketing, the original mix has been extended to include three further Ps, namely:

- o People
- o Process
- o Physical evidence.

Again, we shall also be looking at these further elements of the mix in later units. So, at this stage, you simply need to know what they are.

Overviewing the marketing process: marketing as an exchange process

So far in this unit, we have looked at the evolution and meaning of the marketing concept and the development of a marketing orientation or culture in an organization. We have also looked at the tasks of the marketing manager and the basic tools or ingredients with which to perform these tasks. It would be helpful at this stage, however, to outline briefly how all of this translates into the marketing process.

This can perhaps most easily be done by the use of a simple diagram (Figure 1.3).

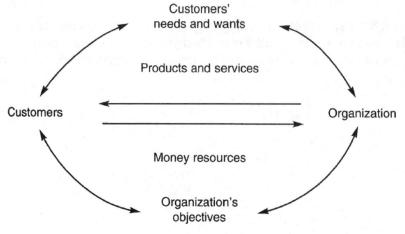

Figure 1.3 The marketing process

We can see from Figure 1.3 how the marketing process facilitates an 'exchange' process between customers and company. According to Dibb *et al.* 2000, for an exchange to take place, a number of conditions need to exist. First, two or more parties must participate. Each party must possess something of value that the other party desires, and second each party must be willing to give up its 'something of value' to receive the 'something of value' held by the other party. In our diagram, the exchange is shown as products/service (to the customer) in exchange for money/resources (to the company). The system only works if both parties (customer and supplier) receive something of value. As stated, in Figure 1.3 the exchange is based on products/services for money/resources, but those are not the only types of exchange between organizations and their customers. Clearly, the nature of the exchange process depends on the type of organization and its customers. Above all, though, we must be careful not to think of exchange processes (and hence marketing) as only being relevant to profit-making organizations. As already mentioned, it is now increasingly recognized that the need for a marketing culture, accompanied by the application of marketing principles and techniques, applies to any organization that wishes to undertake an exchange process with its customers. What differs between the profit-seeking and other types of organizations is not the need for an exchange process, but the nature of what is exchanged between the organization and its customers. A recognition of this is one reason why an increasing number and, more importantly, variety of organizations are turning to marketing. Because of this, in the final part of this unit, we shall consider in more detail this changing role of marketing. In particular, we shall look at the widening range of applications for marketing as it has spread from being initially applied to the marketing of fast moving consumer goods (FMCG), through: marketing in business-to-business marketing; the adoption of marketing in service industries; and finally to marketing in voluntary and not-for-profit organizations such as local authorities, political parties, charities and churches. Some of the key additional considerations of adopting and implementing a marketing culture in these different types of organizations are also considered and discussed, as appropriate, in later units too. Some of the key strategic implications of adopting and implementing marketing in an organization are as follows:

- o Customer orientation
- o Generic business definition
- o Information/research
- o Tailored/targeted marketing programmes
- o Integrated/co-ordinated marketing efforts
- o Long-term planning.

The changing role of marketing

Earlier in this unit we referred to the evolution of the marketing concept. In the same vein we also suggested, perhaps as one would expect, that marketing thought and practice is still evolving. In fact, marketing has changed considerably over the past 10 years. Clearly, it would be impossible and inappropriate to detail all the significant trends and changes that have occurred, but some of the more important ones are briefly introduced below. We shall introduce them here, and then consider these trends and changes in more detail in later units of the coursebook.

A wider range of applications for marketing

As already mentioned, once exclusively applied only to FMCG manufacturers, marketing has spread through business markets, service markets and finally to the 'markets' of not-for-profit organizations. We shall now briefly consider some of these markets.

Business-to-business (b2b) markets

These are markets where customers are primarily distinguished from those in FMCG markets by the fact that they are purchasing in order to further the objectives of their organizations, rather than for personal motives and use.

These days there are plenty of examples of organizations which have recognized and used the concepts and techniques of marketing in their b2b markets to good effect.

Hewlett-Packard, the multi-national computer and electronics company, for example, has long utilized many of the tools once associated only with FMCG marketers to help build a successful company. Tools such as focus group research, global media advertising and effective public relations (PR) are used together with other key marketing tools and concepts to help build a strong market position.

These markets account for a substantial amount of economic activity in most economies and they include, for example, producers (manufacturers) and distributors/intermediaries. The importance of a marketing culture and the general principles of marketing apply to just the same extent and often in the same manner in these markets as in consumer goods markets. However, there are some quite important differences for the marketer in these markets which stem, in essence, from the different nature of the buyers and the buying process encountered in these markets. There are many implications for the marketer because of this essential difference, but a major implication is in the design and use of the elements of the marketing mix. We shall therefore be considering some of these differences in b2b markets in Unit 9.

Marketing in practice: example

In the b2b marketing world, Hewlett-Packard have long been accomplished practitioners of the tools and techniques of marketing. Hewlett-Packard very quickly realized at an early stage of the company's development that the key to business and competitive success was being customer oriented. Although initially and still to a large extent they are marketing their products and services at hard headed business buyers who are concerned to drive the very hardest deals, Hewlett-Packard recognize that the tools of marketing such as strong branding and effective promotion and advertising are just as important as marketing tools as are price, service and delivery. Hewlett-Packard make extensive use of customer and market research to track their competitors' needs, and design new products and services to reflect the changing needs of their customers and the marketplace.

Extending knowledge

The website www.hp.com will help extend your knowledge of how Hewlett-Packard are using the tools of marketing to meet customer needs.

Services marketing

Already several times we have touched on the growth of service markets. The growth of service markets has, in many countries, been phenomenal in recent years. Indeed, in many developed economies such as those found in, say, the United States or the United Kingdom, service industries (as opposed to manufacturing industries) now predominate. Service industries of course include a myriad of different types of markets ranging from, for example, financial services such as banks, building societies, insurance companies and so on through to holidays, fast food, management consultancy, cleaning services and so on. It is now recognized that service products have, compared to their physical product counterparts, a number of character-istics which are different. We shall consider some of these differences and their implications in more detail in later units; but, for example, services marketing differs because service products are largely intangible compared to physical products. This, in turn, has implications, for example, for how they are promoted by the marketer. Service benefits are much more difficult for the marketer to communicate to customers. Similarly, intangibility gives rise to additional considerations with respect to, for example, branding and packaging. Having said this, like b2b markets, the essential nature of the underpinning exchange process between service organizations and their customers is as shown in Figure 1.3 with services being exchanged for money.

Asked to name an effective services marketer, many would put McDonald's, the fast-food marketer, at the top of their list. Certainly, McDonald's were one of the first service companies to fully appreciate and utilize the concepts and tools of modern marketing and they continue to do so. However, many services marketers are now just as effective as their FMCG marketer counterparts. Examples of effective service marketers include Accenture, Interbrand Newell and Sorrell, Holiday Inns, Singapore Airlines and Starbucks coffee shops.

As regards the marketing concept in a service organization, it is important to consider the characteristics of services as intangible, inseparable and perishable. We will consider these special characteristics of services in more detail later in this coursebook, together with some other important characteristics of services, such as inseparability and non-ownership. At this stage, it is sufficient to note that these characteristics will mean a need to ensure that a marketing orientation is managed well.

In the service organization in particular, regular customer audits will need to identify the consumers' expectations of the service quality and delivery. This means that the service quality must be managed well, and includes the tangibles, reliability, responsiveness, assurance and empathy of the organization. Again as we shall see in Unit 9 and as we have already mentioned earlier in this unit, marketers need to consider an extended marketing mix for services to include the additional elements of 'people', 'processes' and 'physical evidence'.

Developing a marketing-oriented service organization has implications for the management style used, the structure of the organization and its marketing strategy. Information systems, staff attitudes and skills, and shared values in the organization may all need to be considered to ensure a marketing-oriented service organization.

Not-for-profit organizations

Sometimes also referred to as 'non-business markets', these are organizations which are essentially established for reasons other than to earn profits for their shareholders. As in b2b and service markets, non-profit organizations and markets encompass a wide variety of types of organization and marketing practices. For example, they include institutions such as local authorities, hospitals, governments, universities and churches. Charities and social causes include, for example, Oxfam, Famine Relief and the Countryside Trust. With such a wide variety of types of not-for-profit organizations and markets, it is difficult and perhaps even dangerous to try to encompass the differences in the application of the marketing culture and practices in such organizations in just a few sentences. However, so long as we recognize this danger of overgeneralizing, it is possible to highlight a number of key differences in the application of the marketing concept and tools in these organizations. In particular:

- o Such organizations often operate within a much tighter regulatory framework with regard to if, and how, they apply the concepts and tools of marketing.
- o Many of the characteristics of service products, which we will introduce in later units, such as intangibility, also apply to many not-for-profit organizations.
- o The marketing mix elements and their application often differ in these organizations and markets. Again, we shall consider some of these differences in more detail in Unit 9. But, for example, it is not difficult to appreciate that the 'price' element of the marketing

25

mix is different in this setting. Indeed, often no price is set by the marketer or paid by the customer. If we take, say, a political party marketing itself for an election then as an example, customers (voters) are not asked to pay a financial price for the 'product', but rather are being asked to 'pay' with their vote. Essentially, this example illustrates differences in the nature of the 'exchange process' between not-for-profit organizations and their customers and it is to this difference that we now turn our attention.

o In overviewing the marketing process earlier in this unit, Figure 1.3 illustrated the centrality of the concept of exchange to this process. Although the essence of this process is the same for any market, and indeed underpins the very concept of a market, and although the related concept of 'value' in this process is just as relevant, as already hinted at, the notion of what is exchanged, and what constitutes value, between not-for-profit organizations and their customers differs from profit-seeking organizations. Figure 1.4 shows in simplified form some examples of exchanges which might take place between different types of not-for-profit organizations and their customers.

o The final major difference, or certainly complication, in considering marketing in not-for-profit organizations is the fact that 'the customer' can comprise several different, and often potentially conflicting groups. So, for example, if we take a university, its 'customers' could be viewed as including: students, potential employers/industry, local government, local community and national government. Because of this, often in not-for-profit organizations and marketing, a distinction is made between 'customers' and 'publics', the latter term being used to denote any party to which the organization will, from time to time, need to address its marketing efforts.

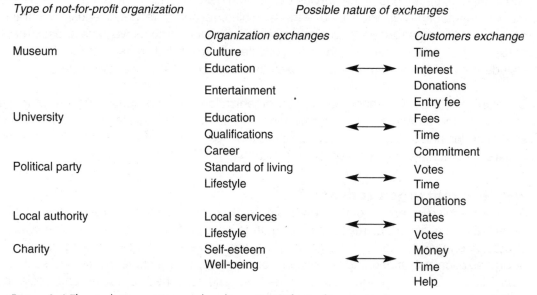

Type of not-for-profit organization		*Possible nature of exchanges*	
	Organization exchanges		*Customers exchange*
Museum	Culture		Time
	Education	←→	Interest
	Entertainment	.	Donations
			Entry fee
University	Education	←→	Fees
	Qualifications		Time
	Career		Commitment
Political party	Standard of living		Votes
	Lifestyle	←→	Time
			Donations
Local authority	Local services	←→	Rates
	Lifestyle		Votes
Charity	Self-esteem		Money
	Well-being	←→	Time
			Help

Figure 1.4 The marketing process and exchange in not-for-profit organizations

Marketing in practice: example

Notwithstanding the different nature of some of the exchanges between organization and customer in not-for-profit situations it is generally recognized that the application of the marketing concepts and tools are essentially the same as in profit-making situations. However, applying some of the marketing tools to some of the not-for-profit organizations does sometimes give rise to considerable controversy. This is particularly the case where not-for-profit marketers have made use of shock campaigns in their advertising. Although shock tactics have frequently been used in conventional marketing, particularly by companies such as Benetton, recently charity and government marketers have moved towards making extensive use of shock images in their advertising feeling that they would make more impact on their target market. However, advertisements such as the Barnados campaign showing a cockroach emerging from a baby's mouth or the recent anti-smoking campaigns in Canada and Britain warning about, for example, passive smoking and using shock tactics such as smoke emerging from a child's mouth have caused considerable controversy. However, it looks like the trend for shock tactics in advertising by the non-profit marketers is set to continue with the non-profit marketers facing the same problem as all marketers of grabbing the customer's attention.

Extending knowledge

See the following websites for issues in, and examples of, marketing in not-for-profit organizations.

www.nfpn.com.au

www.barnardos.org.uk

Activity 1.8

Select a not-for-profit organization of your choice, for example a church, a charity, a political party, and find out as much as you can about how it 'markets' its 'products'/services.

An increased recognition of environmental and social marketing: ethical and social responsibilities

Once exclusively concerned with satisfying 'wants' and profitability, marketers now increasingly are being called upon to balance these against the need to protect the environment and indeed the interest of consumers and society as a whole.

At one time, the Xerox company would not have dreamed of producing and marketing recycled paper for their office paper products. Like many companies, however, Xerox have moved with the times with specific regard to an increased concern about the environment, and in this case particularly the depletion of one of the world's scarcest resources, namely its forests. These days the Xerox company have a well-established range of paper products, which utilize recycled paper. Like Xerox many companies have become much 'greener' in their marketing activities. Green marketing is discussed shortly.

In all fairness, this recognition of the social and environmental impacts of marketing through the promotion of consumption has to some extent been forced upon the marketer by social attitudes and pressure groups. Social attitudes have changed over the past 10 years in many developed economies. Society as a whole is now much more concerned about factors such as the environment and the welfare and safety of customers, and the effect which consumption and marketing of products can have upon these. Of particular importance among these social trends have been the growth of 'consumerism' and 'green marketing'. We should look at each of these major developments a little more closely.

Exam hint

Although consumerism and green issues are relatively new for many marketers, and although in some parts of the world they are seen as being much less important, owing to factors such as the level of economic development, they are popular areas for questions on the Fundamentals paper. Because they might be less relevant issues in your own environment, do not be tempted to ignore them as topics for examination revision.

Extending knowledge

The website www.pwebs.net will help extend your knowledge on ethical and social issues in marketing.

Question 1.1

What were President Kennedy's four consumer rights, which he proposed in his now famous speech in 1962.

Activity 1.9

List as many examples as you can think of where marketers have responded to the need to protect the environment, for example the development of lead-free petrol.

Activity 1.10

Take some time to research any organizations or bodies that have been established in your own country specifically to augment the rights and power of buyers in relation to sellers. These can be formal organizations or bodies established by government, or informal ones. In addition to finding out the names/titles of any such organizations, try to establish what it is they do, that is their aims and activities.

Study tip

For many of the activities in the units you will need to look for sources of information in order to complete the activities. Obviously, the specific sources of information which may be relevant and useful will vary from activity to activity. However, many of the activities, including this one, will involve you to look for information on companies and markets other than those of your own company. There are a myriad of sources of information for markets and companies, but some of the more useful ones include, for example:

- ○ Company annual reports and accounts
- ○ Websites

- ○ Business pages of the press
- ○ Marketing trade journals and publications, for example *Marketing Week*, *Campaign* and so on.

So, for example, on this particular activity you might find the following websites useful:

www.ftc.gov
www.consumer-action.org
www.corporateinformation.com
www.euromonitor.com

Activity 1.11

Try to think of examples of products and services where their marketing has been affected by the need to cater for the consumer's increased interest in his or her own health and safety.

Green marketing

Our second and related development associated with the social-based marketing concept is an increase in environmentally friendly products and services. Not only are customers more concerned to protect their rights as consumers, but an increasing number are also concerned to protect the environment. Specifically, they are concerned about the potential effects of the marketing of products on the environment.

Activity 1.12

Try to think of examples of issues associated with marketing that are frequently raised as causing problems for the environment.

Clearly, the examples shown in the debriefing activity are indicative only. You can probably think of many other green issues for the marketer. Like the consumer movement in some countries, the Green movement, too, has increased in importance and become more powerful and influential. In several European countries this movement has become political, with representatives being elected to voice the opinions and attitudes of the members of the Green movement. The Greens are no longer a minority group, and even non-Green members of society have become more aware of the potential polluting effects associated with the production and consumption of products and services.

Like the consumer movement, the Green movement, too, has resulted in legislation designed to protect the environment from pollution. Even where there is no such legislation, we are increasingly seeing voluntary codes of practice to reduce pollution. Again, the most far-sighted marketers have responded positively to the Green movement, not only conforming to legislation but also taking proactive steps to produce and market 'greener' products. In some countries, environmental groups have combined to produce guides to products that are environmentally safe, giving them a seal of approval. This seal of approval can then be used by marketers in their advertising, packaging and promotion.

It is important to stress that the impact of green issues does differ between different parts of the world, with marketers in Europe and America perhaps seeing the largest impact. There is little doubt, however, that this importance and impact are growing and spreading and will affect most marketers in the future. It is relatively easy to find examples of how green issues have affected marketing programmes already from the materials used in some products and services, to how they are manufactured, how they are promoted and how they are designed to be used and disposed of.

Activity 1.13

Try to think of examples of products and services that have been affected by green issues and where as a consequence, the marketing mix for these products has been designed to take account of such issues.

Although consumerism and green issues are perhaps the best examples of some of the trends and changes that have given rise to a change in the underpinning concept, philosophy, and activities of marketing, there are several forces and factors that have caused the need for a more society-based marketing concept. Increasingly, the marketer of the future will have to resolve the potential for conflict between meeting profit and commercial objectives, customer needs, customer interests, and the wider interests of society as a whole.

Marketing in practice: example

A commitment to protecting and enhancing the environment, together with a recognition of the need to consider a wider variety of stakeholder interests by an organization has led many companies to include green/environmental issues and stakeholder interests in their mission statements which in turn feed into marketing objectives and strategies. The Body Shop is a company which, from its inception, has been committed to environmental protection and societal and stakeholder issues. Body Shop's ethical stance is reflected in its mission statements and its approach to corporate social responsibility. Moreover, these values translate into specific decisions regarding, for example, product development and testing, sourcing of products from low wage countries and corporate promotional and pricing practices.

An increased emphasis on quality, service and customer care

As markets have continued to become increasingly competitive, marketers have recognized that customers now demand and expect consistent quality. This applies to not only product quality but delivery, after-sales service and so on. In turn, customers also expect a high degree of service and customer care from the suppliers of the goods and services they select.

Research has shown that quality is one of the major factors accounting for differences in profitability. Companies which produce consistent quality products tend to be more profitable than their inconsistent quality counterparts. In part, the demand for high quality products reflects increasing affluence and disposable incomes in developed economies. We should not forget, however, that in some parts of the world high-quality products are not necessarily what is wanted, and in many cases are unaffordable. The marketer therefore must be careful to ensure that quality and hence price levels are not beyond the reach of the customer in a particular market.

Quality, and particularly consistency of quality, again has also become more important due to changes in manufacturing processes throughout the world. Although the Japanese were the first to use just-in-time (JIT) and kanban systems in their manufacturing, these systems are now widespread throughout the world. The JIT approach in particular means that suppliers to companies operating a JIT system must ensure and be able to guarantee zero defects. Because components and raw materials are incorporated immediately into the production process with most JIT systems without inspection, it is vital that quality can be relied on. Quality and related aspects such as customer service and care are considered in more detail in Unit 8, but related to an increased emphasis on quality and customer care is one of the most significant developments in the marketing culture, namely the growth in the concept and application of relationship marketing.

The growth of relationship marketing

Related to the growth in the importance of customer care has been the recognition on the part of many marketers that it perhaps often makes more sense to try to build long-term relationships with customers, and in particular build company and brand loyalty, than to treat each purchase a customer makes as a one-off transaction. Relationship marketing is the term that is used to describe this process of building long-term commitment and loyalty from customers. Relationship marketing itself can be defined as all of the activities which an organization can use to build, maintain and develop customer relations. The concept of relationship marketing is perhaps one of the most fundamental changes in recent years with regard to how marketers look at marketing and practise their marketing activities. However, relationship marketing is still underpinned by the concept of exchange. Remember, during the exchange process both buyer and seller exchange something of value in return for something. Relationship marketing aims to maximize such value to both buyer and seller and to ensure that both customer and company are truly satisfied. In a way, then, relationship marketing is simply a heightening of the acceptance and application of the marketing concept. But it is also much more than this. Relationship marketing requires a building of trust between the organization and its customers. It also demands long-term loyalty between both parties of the exchange. Initially, practised principally in b2b markets, relationship marketing has now grown in consumer markets too. So, for example, many of the UK's supermarket grocer retailers have developed the so-called 'loyalty schemes' designed to reward customers for continuing patronage. In the United Kingdom, examples include Tesco and Sainsbury's. In the United States, Walmart and in France, Mamouth.

Again, we cannot emphasize enough that the relationship marketing approach in marketing is based on a fundamentally different approach to customers even though it is still underpinned by the concept of exchange. Although conventional marketing, as we have seen, is based upon identifying and satisfying customer needs, it is essentially also based upon the premise that once these needs have been satisfied through an effective exchange between the two parties, then the process of marketing is complete. This concept in traditional marketing is therefore based upon the idea of effecting a transaction with the customer. So, for example, the emphasis on completing an individual sale is the measure of the success of the exchange. Not surprisingly, this approach is often now referred to as a 'transaction marketing' approach. It is increasingly recognized that this is in effect a very short term and potentially ineffective way of dealing with customers. Relationship marketing, then, is aimed at developing a long-term series of mutually beneficial exchange processes between buyer and seller.

Under a relationship marketing approach, all the activities of an organization are used to build, maintain and develop customer relations, the objective being to build customer loyalty, thereby leading to customer retention. Relationship management is concerned with getting and keeping customers by ensuring that an appropriate combination of marketing, customer service and quality is provided. In order for relationship marketing to work, however, it is important to recognize that both parties must feel that they can benefit from long-term relationships rather than one-off transactions. A key element of relationship marketing, then, is the development of such mutually beneficial long-term relationships between customers and suppliers. With relationship marketing therefore, we see a shift towards a much more interactive, two-way set of relationships between suppliers and customers. This leads, therefore, to two-way communications together with the development of much more personalized marketing strategies to ensure a unique sustained competitive advantage. Relationship marketing also widens the concept of exchange to consider all of the parties involved. So, for example, relationship marketing also considers all of the organization's partnerships – suppliers, lateral, internal – as well as the buyer/consumer.

Relationship marketing requires a fundamentally different approach to that found in transaction marketing. To ensure successful relationship marketing, there needs to be an appropriate supportive organizational culture and everyone in the company must be concerned with generating customer satisfaction. Hence, internal marketing is necessary in companies that are to successfully develop a relationship marketing approach. The growth of relationship marketing is linked to developments in information and databases by enabling the marketer to develop much more detailed understanding of customers, their expectations and needs. Customer databases help the marketer to listen to customers and interpret their problems. The use of customer databases has become so important in the contemporary marketing culture that the role and use of database marketing is considered in several of the later units. An outline of some of the most important developments in information and database marketing and developments in new technology in marketing are outlined below.

Extending knowledge

The website www.moorcroft.co.uk will help extend your knowledge of the application of relationship marketing.

An increase in information and data-based marketing

As already mentioned throughout the units in this coursebook we shall see that, increasingly, IT is being used by the marketer. There is no doubt that we shall continue to see an increase in the application of technology in marketing. Information, and particularly data-based marketing, has allowed evermore powerful and cost-effective marketing. Examples of areas where we shall see indications of this power include the growth of direct marketing and areas such as segmentation and market targeting. If we consider this last area, for example, improved information and databases are allowing marketers to identify and target smaller and smaller groups of customers but with great accuracy. This is helped by the proliferation of media channels now available to reach these smaller, more fragmented target segments. As a result, we have seen the growth of fragmented marketing approaches with a marketer being able to target more and more accurately specific groups of, or even individual, customers. Information and database marketing, then, is having a major impact on the application of marketing. More broadly, however, new technology in general is impacting marketing and marketing management.

Study tip

Because marketing is such a dynamic area of business and society, it is constantly changing and evolving. Although we have introduced some of the more important trends and developments recently in marketing, it is impossible to cover all of the changes and trends which have taken place, and obviously we cannot cover those that are yet to do so. Other developments and trends which we could have mentioned include, for example, the growth in the importance of branding, the increasing fragmentation of markets and media and the growth of network marketing. Although the examiner will not realistically expect you to be an expert in all the areas of marketing which are evolving and changing, it is important that you try and keep as up to date as possible with developments and trends. In addition to the textbooks, for the Fundamentals paper, then, you should also try to read as widely as possible the marketing press and journals. The CIM itself, of course, is a good source of information on trends and developments in marketing.

Growth of new technology in marketing

Technology, of any kind, helps to facilitate and, hopefully, improve the way we do things. Without technology many of the things we do – and often take for granted – would be at best difficult, and often impossible.

Think for a moment how different your life would be without, say, the telephone, or without access to penicillin and other modern medical treatments. What would the lives of some of us be like without the technology to, say, purify water or deliver electricity and power to our homes?

Perhaps less dramatically, but in context perhaps no less importantly, technology also affects and helps facilitate marketing and the marketing process. So much so that some areas of marketing and marketing techniques are almost totally underpinned by technology and its application. So, for example, much of advertising relies on communications technology; effective distribution and logistics relies on transport technologies; marketing research and analysis increasingly relies upon computing technology. Admittedly, this reliance on and use of technology in marketing is not new. After all, for example, trade and marketing between the Egyptians and the Phoenicians was dependent on and affected by the technology of boat-building at the time. More recently, however, business in general and certainly marketing in particular, has become more and more affected by, and reliant upon, technology. Moreover, technology itself is changing at an ever-increasing rate. We shall explore some of the more important of these changes and advances in technology as they affect the marketer in more detail shortly in this unit. Suffice it to say at this stage, that advances in technology are now beginning to fundamentally change the nature of marketing and other business and commercial activities. So much so that many believe that in as little as 10 years the process of exchange around which marketing is, of course, based would be changed beyond recognition compared to today. Certainly, at the very least, the contemporary marketer needs to be familiar with the key advances in technology which are currently affecting the marketing process. A summary of the reasons for this, which captures the importance of technological advances for marketers, are listed below:

o Competitive success increasingly is based on the application of advances in technology.
o Technology is increasingly being used by companies to both differentiate their products and reduce their costs.
o Many of the advances in technology allow the marketer to be much more customer and marketing oriented with, for example, much speedier and flexible responses to customer needs.

- ○ Technological advances have led to the emergence of new critical success factors for organizations as a result of new ways of doing business.
- ○ Advances in technology enable the marketing process to be carried out not only more effectively but more efficiently.
- ○ New technology increasingly facilitates the ease with which information, so vital to effective marketing planning and decision-making, can be collected and analysed.
- ○ Advances in technology often underpin the growth of the global company and a move towards the global market and consumer.

Another way of illustrating the importance of some of the technological advances which are now taking place in marketing is to consider some of the effects that such technology is having, or will have in the future.

Some of these effects will be considered in more detail in later units but some of the key areas of marketing thinking and practice where technological advances have had a major effect include:

- ○ Fundamental changes to retailing and shopping, for example in the future many customers will shop predominantly from home.
- ○ Much greater price competition as customers are able to 'shop around' on, say, their computers.
- ○ The potential demise of whole markets and their replacement by entirely new products and industries.
- ○ Entirely new relationships between members of the value chain and particularly between customers and suppliers.
- ○ Related to the above, the growth of new entrepreneurial companies such as the dotcom companies.

Needless to say, marketers have not been slow to grasp the advantages of the growing sophistication and application of advances in technology. The ICT in particular has assisted in the management of a customer-oriented culture in the following ways:

- ○ The sophisticated use of current databases to understand consumer behaviour.
- ○ Using the Internet as a marketing information system, for example for gathering competitor intelligence information.
- ○ Using the World Wide Web to make products more accessible for consumers, that is the use of on-line shopping, offering more information about the company or product and so on.
- ○ Building customer care systems for customers/clients using e-mail and webcasting
- ○ Considering segmentation and global niches, from the observation of the use of current, or specifically designed, Internet pages.

Together, the factors described above mean that today's marketer must not only be aware of, but understand the advances in technology which are taking place. Moreover, the marketer must also be sensitive to, and be prepared for, tomorrow's advances in technology. This in turn means that the marketer must also have the necessary skills to use the new technologies of today and tomorrow to help facilitate the marketing process. The marketer who does not possess these skills will increasingly become a dinosaur – with probably the same fate as these unfortunate creatures! Similarly, those organizations whose management and marketers are unaware of, or unable to, utilize advances in technology will become increasingly uncompetitive. The new markets and marketing of today and tomorrow are very much technology's child.

Growth of global marketing

The final element in our assessment of the changing role and nature of marketing is the trend in recent years towards global marketing. Increasingly, marketing activities encompass and are planned in the context of not just a domestic or even international setting, but from a global perspective. This growth of global marketing in turn stems from several trends and developments encompassing a broad range of cultural, economic, technological and political forces and factors. So, for example, increased travel and education coupled with developments in electronic and other forms of communication are increasingly making the world smaller in the sense of reaching and marketing to customers. The phrase 'global village' is used to capture this trend. Increasingly, customers want to buy global brands and follow lifestyle and consumption patterns of their 'neighbours' at the other side of the world. Companies too want to expand their operations from purely domestic through internal and export operations to eventually full global operations. Again there are many reasons for this but essentially the driving reason is increased profits through accessing potentially huge markets and thereby achieving economies of scale. Four of the major factors, in the context of the increasing trend towards globalization, are explained below.

Convergence of markets and global customers

A major driving force towards globalization has been the convergence of markets and related to this the emergence of the global customer. Improved communication and travel infrastructures have meant that increasingly, customers are exposed to, and aware of, products and lifestyles in other parts of the world. As a result of this, in many markets customers' needs and wants have become much more similar. A Chinese teenager wants the same Levi brand jeans and Coca-Cola soft drink products as his or her American counterpart. The Internet and the World Wide Web enable customers to shop and spend on a global basis. Hand in hand with this, companies now market their brands on a global basis with marketing, advertising and products all developed globally. There is no doubt that the convergence of markets and the emergence of the global customer has been a major factor in spurring global strategies.

Cost advantages

This driving force prompting more global approaches has a number of facets, but essentially they all relate to the potential for reducing costs by operating globally. Examples of cost advantages which accrue to the global organization include economies of scale due to, of course, sheer volume facilitated by a global approach. Similarly, a company may reap cost advantages by sourcing and/or operating from, or in, lower cost countries across the world. The often substantial costs nowadays of developing and launching new products can mean that only a global approach will enable these costs to be recouped.

Governmental and trade policies

Governmental and trade policies too are a major driving force towards global strategies. Since the Second World War, most governments have at least subscribed to the view that free trade and free markets is to the world's advantage. In some areas, this has meant that all trade barriers have been, or are being at least, removed. A good example of this is the development of the European Union which is based on free trade between member companies. Governments also sometimes prompt global strategies for reasons other than free trade such as developing closer relationships with countries which are in some ways militarily or politically strategically significant.

Global competition

This fourth factor relates to the growth of competition on a more global scale. The driving forces already mentioned have meant that more and more companies are becoming global in their strategic planning and operations. This means that even those companies who might prefer to think and plan locally can no longer afford to do so as they find themselves faced with competitors from virtually every part of the world. Furthermore, as companies become increasingly interdependent across the world, it increases the interaction between competitors on a more global scale.

Global marketing is so important these days that it touches every facet and activity of the marketer's everyday operations. Because of this, we shall be highlighting international and global aspects of the marketing activities and concepts which we shall be discussing in later units.

Activity 1.14

- Try to recall a purchase where you felt that you did not receive an adequate level of customer care.
- Describe what was inadequate/unsatisfactory about the level of care you received.
- Write down your feelings about the supplier/company you dealt with.
- What could/should the company/supplier do to improve levels of customer care?

Marketing in practice: case study

'Who needs marketing – we're bankers!'

Once notoriously product oriented, the banking industry took a long time to wake up to the need to be customer oriented and the potential for increased sales and profits by using the tools and techniques of marketing.

There are several reasons why the banks were slow to accept and implement the marketing concept and begin to utilize the full range of marketing tools and techniques, for example in many countries the banking sector comprised of a relatively small number of large banks who operated in oligopolistic market structures and hence, to some extent, were protected from intense competition.

Marketing was seen as being something that was relevant only to FMCG. Certainly, it was felt, a traditional and professional sector such as banking should not be tainting itself with marketing ideas.

Traditionally, the senior management of commercial banks came from a banking background and had few, if any, marketing skills.

Finally, it was felt that the special characteristics of what is essentially a service product meant that in any event many of the tools and techniques of marketing simply did not apply.

Over the last 10 years the situation has changed dramatically, however. Throughout the world the banking sector is now one of the most ardent users of marketing concepts and techniques. Again, there are several reasons for this but some of the most important include:

- Customers are increasingly more demanding in their needs and requirements from their banks. This stems from the fact that they are more aware of the services on offer and are better educated in their choice of financial services.
- Throughout the world the banking sector has been opened up to more and more competition. In some cases, this has been as a result of de-regulation with regard to the banking sector in many

countries leading to a much wider range of financial institutions offering banking services. But in addition, like many markets, the banking sector is now global with global competition.

o A new generation of bank employees has emerged with many senior managers in banking now coming from more commercial and often specifically marketing backgrounds as opposed to being 'pure bankers'.

Many of the banks are now as much customer oriented as their FMCG marketing counterparts. This has led to substantial and wide-ranging changes in how the banks operate; their products and services; and their marketing and organizational structures. Just some of the changes which the adoption of marketing concepts and techniques in the banking sector has given rise to include:

o Much greater use of the tools of market research and analysis. The leading banks regularly conduct marketing research exercises designed to keep abreast of customer needs and levels of customer satisfaction.

o Organizational and marketing structures which are based around customer and market requirements with, for example, product and brand manager systems being common now. Marketing has been elevated in many banks to the position of providing the overall co-ordinating role for the resources and activities of the business.

o Much more effective marketing planning and control systems with strong emphasis on techniques such as market segmentation and targeting and the application of the elements of the marketing mix extended to include the additional 3Ps of marketing services in a co-ordinated and controlled manner.

o Related to the application of the marketing mix, the banks have recognized the need for an increased emphasis on quality, service and customer care and have been particularly adept in using some of the developments in information and data-based marketing to foster the growth of relationship marketing with their customers.

o Finally, the banking sector is demonstrating an awareness of wider environmental forces and factors with its increased recognition of its ethical and social responsibilities towards customers.

Though there is always room for improvement, the global banking sector is one of the success stories in recent years of the application and implementation of the marketing concept.

'Even bankers need marketing.'

Sources: www.marketing-week.co.uk.

www.aba.com/bankmarketing/default.htm.

Summary

In this unit we have seen that:

o Marketing is first and foremost a way of thinking that puts the customer at the centre of all organizational decisions. In doing so, marketing is a form of competition which serves as the means of creating customer value.

o Marketing orientation is the result of an evolution from a production-oriented through a sales-oriented era.

o A marketing culture must be developed throughout the organization, but this takes time and resources.

Marketing is also a management function encompassing the key tasks of analysis, planning, implementation and control and involves the co-ordination of organizational resources both within and outside the marketing function. The major tools of the marketer are the elements of the marketing mix, which in turn are allied to the processes of market segmentation and targeting.

- The marketing concept is still evolving and now embraces b2b marketing, services marketing and marketing in not-for-profit organization.
- Marketing has responded to an increased awareness of environmental issues and an interest in total quality.
- Increasingly, marketers are recognizing the importance of treating customers as partners and in developing long-term customer loyalty through the development of improved relationships with customers.
- As in many areas of management, developments in IT are having, and will continue to have, a major impact on marketing practices.
- Database marketing is becoming increasingly important in the contemporary marketing culture.

Examination preparation: previous examination question

Using the previous examination questions

As this is our first previous examination question we have outlined how to use these in order to get the maximum value from them in your studies and learning.

All of the units end by asking you to complete an actual previous examination question. You will get most value from this process if you follow the steps outlined below when tackling each end of unit exam question.

First of all go to the exam paper and question as directed. These are included in Appendix 4 of the coursebook.

Read the question carefully and then preferably without using your notes or the coursebook, write an answer to the question under self-imposed 'examination conditions,' that is set yourself the same amount of time to answer the question as you would have in the examination. Prepare your answer in hand written form – which again is good practice. For obvious reasons it is up to you, but at this stage do not be tempted to read the Examiner's Comments in Appendix 4 and certainly do not consult the specimen answers to the questions which are provided.

When you have completed your own answer, you should then carefully consider the Examiner's Comments in Appendix 4 and obtain the specimen answer to the question from the website www.cim.co.uk.

At this stage, we also recommend that you read Appendix 1 of the coursebook which gives detailed guidance on examination preparation and technique.

We can now proceed with our first previous examination question.

Previous examination question

Attempt Question 3 of the examination paper for December 2003 (Appendix 4). For Specimen Answer Examination Question 3, December 2003, see www.cim.co.uk.

Bibliography

Brassington, F. and Pettitt, S. (2003) *Principles of Marketing*, 3rd edition, FT Prentice Hall, Chapters 1 and 21.

Dibb, S., Simkin, L., Pride, W. and Ferrell, O.C. (2000) *Marketing Concepts and Strategies*, 4th European edition, Houghton, Mifflin, Chapters 1 and 22.

Gröonroos, C. *Service Management and Marketing*, New York: John Wiley & Sons.

Kotler, P. (2001) *Marketing Management*, 10th edition, Prentice Hall, Chapter 1.

Lancaster, G.A., Massingham, L. and Ashford, R. (2002) *Essentials of Marketing*, 4th edition, McGraw-Hill, Chapters 1 and 13.

unit 2
marketing planning and budgeting

Learning outcomes

By the end of this unit you will:

o Explain the context of, and process for, marketing planning and budgeting including related models.

Knowledge and skills

By the end of this unit you will be able to:

o Explain the importance of the marketing planning process and where it fits into the corporate or organizational planning framework (2.1).

o Explain the models that describe the various stages of the marketing planning process (2.2).

o Explain the concept of the marketing audit as an appraisal of the external marketing environment and an organization's internal marketing operations (2.3).

o Describe the role of various analytical tools in the marketing auditing process (2.4).

o Explain the value of marketing research and information in developing marketing plans (2.5).

o Explain the importance of objectives and the influences on, and processes for, setting, objectives (2.6).

o Explain the concept of market segmentation and distinguish effective bases for segmenting consumer and b2b markets (2.7).

o Describe the structure of an outline marketing plan and identify its various components (2.8).

o Depict the various management structures available for implementing marketing plans and understand their advantages and disadvantages (2.9).

o Examine the factors that affect the setting of marketing budgets (2.10).

o Demonstrate an appreciation of the need to monitor and control marketing activities (2.11).

Study Guide

In many ways, this unit serves as an overview and framework for the rest of the units in the coursebook in as much as it encompasses the whole of the marketing process from the perspective of the steps and issues in marketing planning and budgeting. We shall be looking at the nature and the importance of the marketing planning process working through each of the various stages and introducing the relevant tools and concepts appropriate to each stage. Some fundamental areas of marketing planning and budgeting will be considered in this unit including areas such as the marketing audit and the related areas of the so-called 'SWOT and PEST analysis'. We shall also look at some of the key tools of analysis in marketing planning including the important area of portfolio analysis. In addition, we shall be looking at the concept of market segmentation, including the various bases for segmenting markets and how this relates to the elements of targeting and positioning, which are covered in more detail in Unit 3, and the creation of an integrated and coherent marketing mix. The nature of marketing objectives is considered and the various marketing strategies to achieve these. Finally, we shall look at implementation and control issues together with the role of marketing research and information in developing marketing plans. We would expect you to take about 8 hours to work through this unit and suggest you allow a further 5–8 hours to undertake the various activities suggested. Other than your notebook and writing equipment, you will not need anything further to complete this unit.

The nature and importance of marketing planning

In Unit 1, we suggested that there are four key elements of the marketing manager's task. You will recall that these are analysis, planning, implementation and control. We also suggested that of these, planning accounts for the major part of the marketing manager's responsibilities and activities. Having said this, effective plans must be built on, and reflect, careful analysis and as we shall see, implementation and control themselves can rightly be considered as part of the overall planning process. Put another way, then, the marketing manager's job is planning.

Not too many years ago, much of marketing was characterized by a lack of systematic and structured planning. Marketing managers often acted on hunch or intuition, or if you like, a feel for the market. Marketing activities were often unstructured and not set in a coherent and integrated framework. Often different marketing activities in different parts of the organization were unco-ordinated. Sometimes, for example, the sales function and the marketing function were pulling in different directions. Similarly, the important co-ordinating role of marketing with respect to other functions in the business referred to in Unit 1 was often neglected. Increasingly, however, marketing is characterized by much more systematic and structured marketing planning using a variety of powerful and sometimes sophisticated planning tools and techniques. Contemporary marketing is now imbued with a planning culture. The reasons for this move towards a planning culture are numerous, but among some of the more important reasons for this move are the following:

o A more competitive marketing environment.
o A more dynamic marketing environment.
o High levels of investment required to develop new products and markets and hence high risk.
o More sophisticated and powerful planning tools and models.
o Better trained marketing managers.
o Access to marketing data and information.
o A recognition of the need for improved co-ordination and integration of marketing and other plans.

As a result of these and other factors, then, many companies now have effective and sophisticated marketing planning systems. In addition to the move towards planning cultures in organizations, the perspective on the nature of plans has also changed in recent years. Specifically, planning, including marketing planning, has become more strategic in nature and as a result, so too has marketing itself. Strategic, as opposed to tactical, marketing planning has the following characteristics:

o Strategic marketing planning involves longer-term planning horizons.
o Strategic marketing planning involves major commitments of company resources.
o Strategic marketing planning determines the nature of what an organization is and what it is to be.
o Strategic marketing planning affects and involves all levels, functions and activities of a business.
o Strategic marketing planning reflects both internal (company) and external considerations.

There are probably as many different definitions of strategic marketing as there are different marketing textbooks. Perhaps one of the most comprehensive and yet easy to understand definitions of strategic marketing is that proposed by Cravens.

Key definition

Strategic marketing – Is a process of strategically analysing environmental, competitive and business factors affecting business units and forecasting future trends in business areas of interest to the enterprise. Participating in setting objectives and formulating corporate and business unit strategies. Selecting target market strategies for the product markets in each business unit, establishing marketing objectives, and developing, implementing and managing programme positioning strategies for meeting target market needs.

The advantages of adopting a planning culture, coupled with a more strategic approach to marketing planning are many, but among the most important are the following:

o More structured analyses of the marketing environment.
o Objectives and strategies based on exploiting company strengths and marketing assets.
o An awareness of key marketing trends and possible future developments.
o Proactive rather than reactive approaches to marketing activities.
o An increased customer focus/customer orientation.
o Integrated marketing programmes involving cross-functional activities.

Overall, these advantages have been shown to generate higher profits and more effective organizations. Let us now turn to our basic model of the marketing planning process, which you were introduced to in Unit 1 and consider the steps and stages in this process in more detail.

The marketing planning process

In Unit 1, you were introduced to a basic model of the marketing planning process. We can now examine the stages and steps in planning in more detail and see how the various stages of the marketing planning process fit together and relate to the overall corporate or organizational planning framework. Remembering again that there are many variations on the elements of the marketing planning process and their sequence, below is outlined again our basic model of the planning process showing each of the key stages and steps. This is shown in Figure 2.1.

Business mission/corporate objectives

↓

Marketing audit

↓

SWOT analysis

↓

Business objectives

↓

Marketing objectives

↓

Marketing strategies

↓

Marketing tactics/marketing mix decisions

↓

Implementation

↓

Monitoring and control

Figure 2.1 Key steps in marketing planning

We shall now take you through each of these steps again in more detail.

Business mission/corporate objectives

The first step in the marketing planning process is to determine the overall business mission and corporate objectives of the organization. It is sometimes easy to forget that marketing is only one function in an organization, albeit a central one. Marketing objectives and strategies, therefore, must be reflective and supportive of this overall business mission and corporate objectives. The business mission is the determination of what the company intends to be; if you like, its general culture and operating philosophies. An example of a business mission might be, say:

> *To be the leading provider of technological solutions in the information technology market using the greenest technologies available and with a commitment to developing community and customer relations.*

Corporate objectives may encompass several areas relating to, for example, growth, financial performance, innovation, corporate reputation, contributions to community and society and so on, and are more specific and quantified than the business mission statement. Before starting the marketing planning process, then, the marketing function must ascertain, and possibly help shape, the overall objectives of the organization. These in turn will then serve to feed into and shape marketing objectives and strategies and the individual elements of the marketing mix.

There is often confusion about the differences and/or relationships between corporate objectives and strategies, and marketing objectives and strategies. The main differences between the two are that corporate objectives and strategies relate to objectives and strategies for the organization as a whole and encompass and affect every functional area of the business. Corporate objectives relate to broad objectives concerned, as we have seen, for example, with growth, financial performance and so on as outlined above. Corporate strategies for achieving these will relate to the major routes or paths for achieving these, such as growth through mergers, acquisitions, expansion and so on. Within these broad corporate objectives and strategies each functional area of the business, including marketing, will need to develop a set of objectives and strategies which are consistent with, and supportive of, overall corporate and organizational objectives and strategies. We must stress again, however, that, of all the functional areas of business, it is the marketing function, and therefore marketing management, which will probably have most input to, and effect on, the identification and selection of overall corporate and organizational strategies.

In many organizations, and particularly the multi-product/market organization, the basic unit of marketing planning, that is the organizational element around which individual marketing strategies are planned, is increasingly the strategic business unit (SBU).

Key definition

A strategic business unit (SBU) – Is a part of a business or organization, which has its own customers/markets and its own competitors against which it is competing. It has its own management team who collectively are responsible for determining objectives, strategies and plans for this part of the business and who are responsible for the performance of the business. A strategic business unit can operate to all intents and purposes as an independent business.

While a key role of marketing management, then, is indeed to help shape overall corporate objectives and strategies, detailed marketing plans and the sequence of steps shown in Figure 2.1 are carried out at the level of the individual SBU. Obviously, where a company has multiple SBUs, then, the activities of these individual business units, including, for example, the resources they will be allocated and the related aspect of which business units are to figure most strongly in the future plans of the organization, need to be assessed and co-ordinated. In particular, although each SBU will have its own marketing objectives and strategies, the collection of business units has to be managed so as to ensure an effective balance of business units which will serve to meet the current corporate objectives and perhaps more importantly, will serve to meet future corporate objectives. A number of techniques and models for managing the collection of SBUs have been developed. Collectively, these techniques and models are often referred to as the techniques of '*portfolio analysis*'. The use of these techniques in marketing planning and budgeting has grown in recent years. A fact which is recognized by the CIM in their syllabus for this subject and because of this we shall be considering some of the key techniques of portfolio analysis shortly as they now form a central element of the marketing audit process which we shall now consider.

Study tip

It is debatable whether the techniques of portfolio analysis are tools of strategic marketing planning or more specifically tools of product management. In fact, although the different portfolio models vary, most of the portfolio analysis techniques, as we shall see, encompass and relate to both strategic marketing planning and managing the product mix. Although we have chosen to include these tools in this unit therefore reflecting the organization of the CIM's syllabus, portfolio analysis techniques are also useful and used in the context of managing the product area of the marketing mix.

The marketing audit

The second step in the marketing planning process involves the marketer in assessing the situation which faces the organization. A major tool/process here is the marketing audit.

Study tip

The marketing audit performs two key functions in the marketing planning process. The first of these relates to the next stage in the planning process, namely the identification of Opportunities and Threats, and Strengths and Weaknesses of the organisation (SWOT analysis) which you can see occurs early in the planning process. The second function of the marketing audit is as an evaluation and control mechanism at the end of the strategic marketing planning process. We shall be considering this second function of the marketing audit, that is its use in evaluation and control, in Unit 9. In this unit, then, we shall confine ourselves to look at the use of the audit in the beginning to identify and assess opportunities and threats, and strengths and weaknesses.

One half of the marketing audit will encompass the internal situation of the organization and the evaluation of its asserts, resources and competences. This is usually referred to as a 'Strengths and Weaknesses' assessment (the first half of our so-called 'SWOT analysis'). The second element of the marketing audit involves analysing the external situation facing the organization that has as its purpose the identification of 'Opportunities and Threats' (the second half of our so-called 'SWOT analysis'). It is extremely important that marketing managers are able to understand the environment in which they are operating. This means that a systematic environmental analysis will need to be undertaken on a regular basis.

PEST factors

In the context of the external environmental audit, the initials PEST are widely used and understood by marketers. These initials represent some of the major factors or elements in the wider marketing environment which the marketer must assess. The PEST initials stand for:

o *Political factors* – such as government regulations, policies and strategies, tax, education, business and industry.
o *Economic factors* – such as movements in the trade cycle, levels of disposable income, interest rates and inflation.

     o   *Social/cultural factors* – such as the ageing consumer, increases in one-parent families, changing values, attitudes and beliefs.

     o   *Technological factors* – such as the increased rate of computer capability, developments in IT and production methods.

In addition to these PEST factors, the marketing audit of the environment should also encompass factors such as competitors, suppliers and distributors, which also must be taken into account in planning marketing decisions.

With regard to the internal half of the audit, the marketer must regularly and systematically assess the resources, systems and procedures and skills of the organization so that this analysis can be fed into our SWOT analysis in the next stage. The internal marketing audit should examine these from the perspective of the extent to which they can be used to generate competitive advantage through customer satisfaction. In other words, resources, procedures and skills should be assessed from the point of view of a customer/marketing orientation. Obviously, in carrying out the internal audit, the marketing planner must decide what resources, activities and skills of the organization should be included. Many companies use standard checklists for this process encompassing, and including, the following areas or aspects of the organization:

     o   Financial
     o   Marketing
     o   Manufacturing
     o   Physical resources
     o   Personnel
     o   Research and development.

Marketing in practice: example

A good example of a company identifying a potential competitive advantage through a careful analysis and consideration of its resources through an internal analysis is that of Hewlett-Packard. Hewlett-Packard recognized that one of its key strengths is the fact that it actively encourages teamwork between the different divisions of the business. Unlike many organizations with divisional organizational structures, where each division operates as an autonomous profit centre, Hewlett-Packard have recognized that they have substantial potential synergies and therefore competitive advantage by co-ordinating marketing activities across divisions where appropriate. This may mean, for example, that customers may be offered a particular product mix which encompasses products from several divisions where it is felt such a mix would better meet an individual customer's needs.

Portfolio analysis

As already mentioned, an increasingly important area of internal analysis in conducting the marketing audit is that of portfolio analysis. Portfolio analysis comprises a collection of techniques which is aimed at assessing and analysing a company's collection or portfolio of products and/or SBUs. As we shall see, there are several techniques and approaches in this family of internal analysis techniques, but essentially they share the objective of attempting to develop more effective marketing plans in the multi-product business. The first technique of portfolio analysis we shall consider was itself one of the first to be developed and used by marketers, namely the so-called 'Boston Consulting Group (BCG) portfolio analysis method'.

The Boston Consulting Group (BCG) portfolio analysis

The technique of portfolio analysis was pioneered in the United States by the management consultants of BCG. The methods proposed identified the company's SBUs or product groups, and represented these on a matrix that considers market growth and relative market share. These are positioned in the matrix as circles with a diameter proportional to their sales revenue. Figure 2.2 explains this.

Four cells into which SBUs or product groups fall can be identified in Figure 2.2. In order to help you understand these, we have provided examples for each category.

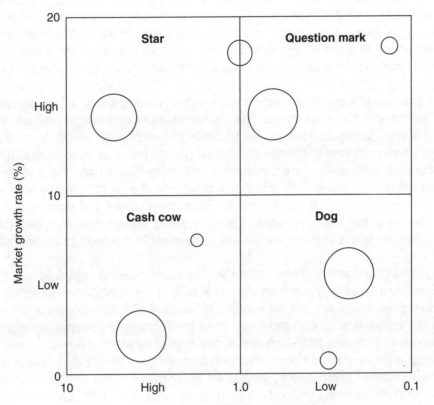

Figure 2.2 The Boston Consulting Group (BCG) matrix

- ○ 'Stars' are those SBUs that have a promising future. Significant investments of cash are necessary to develop their full potential. If managed correctly, they will develop into a valuable source of revenue as the market evolves. A good example of products, which for many companies are at this stage, is the Internet products. Most have agreed that products in this area, if properly developed and managed, will represent the 'stars' of the future for many companies.
- ○ 'Cash cows' have achieved a high market share in a mature market. They deserve the company's fullest attention, as the cash they generate can be invested in newer market areas with high growth potential. Levi jeans are a good example of a product that is probably a cash cow for the Levi Strauss company.
- ○ 'Question marks' (or problem children or wildcats, as they are sometimes called) pose a problem to management. While market growth prospects are good, question mark SBUs have a low relative market share. If they are to be moved to the left, that is

increase their relative market share, then substantial investment will be required. Based on the available marketing information, marketing management must use its skill to decide whether such investment could be better employed supporting other SBUs. Many smaller companies find themselves with the problem of too many question marks, because by definition these smaller companies have low market share. Some of the more specialist car producers at the top end of the market such as TVR, for example, have found themselves in this position. The Rover part of the BMW Rover Group had problems with products with low relative market share and with little or no growth potential in the market in which these products are positioned.

o 'Dogs' show no growth potential and their relative market share is low. Although they may not necessarily be a drain on the company's resources, they are unable to make a positive contribution to profits. Many small textile companies in the United Kingdom, for example, have brands which are in markets where there is little or no growth potential and where, due to the company size, their relative market share is low. Companies like this, therefore, tend to have an unhealthy predominance of dogs in their portfolio.

Although this model was developed for multi-industry companies, it can be used by single-industry companies; this is where the SBU is represented by a single product or product line, and it is this latter application that is now becoming more popular in use. In reality, little can be done by a single company to change the market growth rate that defines an SBU's position on the vertical axis. The options are therefore to eliminate SBUs from the portfolio, or to move them from the right to the left along the horizontal axis, that is to increase their market share. Increased sales will increase the size of the SBUs themselves and remember the size of the circles represents the value of sales. Forecast sales figures can also be plotted for each product which will help indicate the potential movement of the product in the matrix.

Similarly, although originally developed for use by profit-seeking organizations, the model can also be used by the not-for-profit marketer. The axes of the matrix, that is relative market share and market growth rate, are just as relevant in assessing the performance of products in the not-for-profit marketer's organization as in the profit-oriented commercial organization. The classifications of products into each cell of the matrix as stars, cash cows and so on would apply just as much in the not-for-profit organization as any other. Similarly, the notion of using the matrix to identify alternative strategies for different products and/or businesses together with the notion of balancing the portfolio can be used by the not-for-profit marketer. In fact, in some ways the BCG matrix, because it is based on the underlying performance factor of cash flow rather than profit, is perhaps particularly suited to the not-for-profit marketer, after all even if the not-for-profit marketer does not seek profits as a measure of performance, cash flow is always going to be important in any organization.

The accuracy of any model is only as good as the information upon which it is based. Marketing should ensure that decisions are not based on partial or misleading information. A BCG matrix-type model requires a great deal of accurate market and company information before it can be used as a meaningful management tool. In addition to presenting strategic alternatives, a well-prepared BCG matrix is valuable because it forces objective consideration of the elements of the portfolio in relation to each other.

 ## Activity 2.1

> If you have the practical resources and appropriate information at your disposal, place each of the products your company makes or the services it supplies in what you consider to be their appropriate positions within the BCG matrix. Justify your criteria in respect of each entry.

Activity 2.2

Consider and list what you feel to be the difficulties in applying, and the shortcomings of, the BCG matrix approach and compare your answer with that of the debriefing.

Essentially, only two criteria are used with respect to positioning products in the different cells of the BCG portfolio analysis matrix, namely relative market share and market growth rate. However, cash flow too can give an indication of where a product is likely to be in the matrix. Perhaps as you would expect, products in the cash cow area of the matrix have strong positive cash flows, whereas stars and dogs often have high negative cash flows. Question marks too are likely to be net users of cash rather than contributors, though perhaps to a lesser extent than star-classified products.

General Electric (GE) Business Screen matrix

General Electric (USA) and McKinsey & Co. (management consultants) developed a business screen matrix that attempted to overcome some of the criticisms of the BCG matrix. It is now known as the GE matrix and it is described in Figure 2.3.

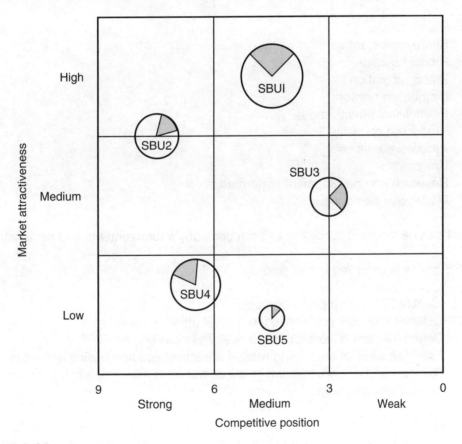

Figure 2.3 GE matrix

SBUs or product lines are considered with the two dimensions of competitive position and market attractiveness. These two criteria are good in evaluating a business or group of products in that they will be seen to be successful to the extent that they go into attractive markets and have the requisite competitive business strength to succeed in those markets. The two complement each other, for a weak company operating in an attractive market will not do well, and neither will a strong company operating in an unattractive market.

Each of the two dimensions is further analysed into a number of factors that underpin each dimension. In order to use this technique, the strategic marketing planner must first determine these various factors that contribute to market attractiveness and business position.

The following factors are used to assess product/market attractiveness:

- o Size
- o Growth rate
- o Competitive diversity and structure
- o Historical profit margin
- o Technological requirements
- o Social impact
- o Environmental impact
- o Legal impact
- o Energy requirements.

For assessing competitive position, the following factors can be used:

- o Market share
- o Share growth rate
- o Product quality
- o Brand reputation
- o Distribution network
- o Promotional effectiveness
- o Productive capacity
- o Productive efficiency
- o Unit costs
- o Research and development performance
- o Managerial personnel.

The list can be modified according to each company's requirements and circumstances.

The GE matrix is compiled in five steps:

1. Identify SBUs (or product groups).
2. Determine factors contributing to market attractiveness.
3. Determine factors contributing to business position.
4. Establish ways of measuring market attractiveness and business position.
5. Rank each SBU high, medium or low on business strength, and high, medium or low on market attractiveness.

Some kind of numerical rating should be given to the relative importance of the last two factors. Multiplying these together and totalling them for each SBU gives a composite score that enables the matrix to be compiled. In addition, the total market size for each SBU can be represented by the area of the circle with the company's SBU share of that total market represented as a segment in the circle. Thus a visual portfolio can be shown, as in Figure 2.4, and a complicated analysis can be presented in a more digestible form.

Having completed the matrix, the marketing planner can then assess the balances of SBUs or product groups within the organization, and determine future strategies for each.

According to an SBU or product group's position within the matrix, we can distinguish between three broad strategic alternatives and these are detailed in Figure 2.4.

SBUs that score high or medium on competitive position and market attractiveness are those in which a company should seek to maintain an investment and possibly grow. SBUs that score a combination of low/low or low/medium on competitive position and market attractiveness should be considered for no more investment, and as much cash as possible should be harvested from them. SBUs scoring either high/low or medium/medium combinations on competitive position/market attractiveness should be examined to see if some degree of selective investment is possible to maintain or increase earnings.

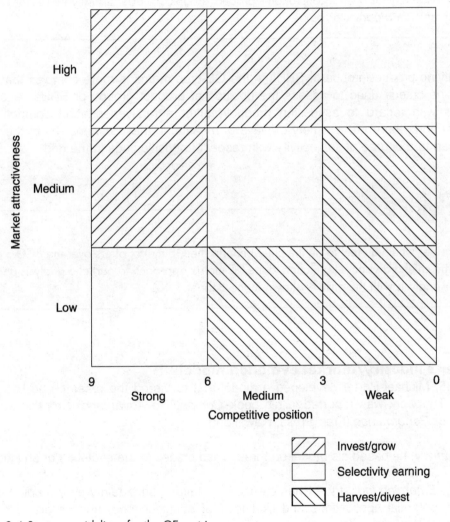

Figure 2.4 Strategy guidelines for the GE matrix

Marketing in practice: example

Mercedes identified that the 4-wheel drive products in their range represented SBUs which were ideal for investment and growth. At the same time in the larger executive saloon car end of the market, the company's relative competitive position combined with the degree of attractiveness of this market suggests that Mercedes are more likely to profit from pursuing a selectivity earning strategy.

Activity 2.3

If you have the practical resources and information at your disposal, construct a GE-type matrix in relation to your own organization's product groups or SBUs. Justify your reasons for placing each entry in a particular box.

Classifying product groups or SBUs in the GE-type matrix is more complex than in the BCG one. The criteria used to assess the position of product groups or SBUs uses many more factors with regard to assessing product/market attractiveness and competitive position. Furthermore, there are a variety of ways of measuring these dimensions of the matrix which can lead to a degree of subjectivity with respect to positionings in the grid.

Activity 2.4

Consider what you feel to be the chief benefits the GE matrix offers over the BCG matrix. Then list the chief drawbacks in relation to the GE-matrix approach to portfolio analysis and compare your analysis with the answer shown in the debrief.

Porter's industry/market evolution model

In 1985, Michael Porter developed a model that furthered the research he had published in 1980. The work was reported in his book *Competitive Advantage: Creating and Sustaining Superior Performance* (Free Press, New York).

In summary, he based his model on three broad stages in the evolution of an industry/market:

1. *Emerging industry* – Characterized by buyers' uncertainty over product performance, potential applications and likelihood of obsolescence, and sellers' uncertainty over customer needs, demand levels and technological developments.
2. *Transition to maturity* – Characterized by falling industry profits, slowdown in growth, customers knowledgeable about products and competitive offerings, less product innovation and competition upon non-product aspects of marketing.
3. *Decline* – Characterized by competition from substitutes, changing customer needs, and demographic and other macro-environmental forces and factors affecting the market.

He then used the characteristics of each stage to suggest a number of strategies as being appropriate to each, as shown in Figure 2.5.

	Growth	**Maturity**	**Decline**
Leader	Keep ahead of the field	Cost leadership; raise barriers; deter competitors	Redefine scope; divest peripherals; encourage departures
Follower	Limitation at lower costs; joint ventures	Differentation; focus	Differentiation; new opportunities

Figure 2.5 Industry life cycle and strategic position

Emerging industry strategies (growth column) should be developed to take account of industry's competitive structure characteristics:

- Threat of entry
- Rivalry among competitors
- Pressure from substitute products
- Bargaining power of buyers and suppliers.

Transition to maturity strategies (maturity column) should be developed to focus upon:

- Developing new market segments
- Focusing strategies for specific segments
- Developing a more efficient organization.

Decline strategies should:

- Seek pockets of enduring demand
- Divest the product or SBU.

 Activity 2.5

Summarize what you consider to be the similarity between Porter's model and the product life-cycle analysis and compare your answer with that suggested in the debriefing.

A.D. Little industry maturity/competitive position matrix

This was developed by the management consultant Arthur D. Little, and its approach is similar to the one developed by Porter. 'Stage of industry maturity' (similar to the stages of the product life cycle) is on the horizontal axis and 'competitive position' on the vertical axis, and it is shown in Figure 2.6.

Eight key descriptors to determine which stage a product group or SBU is in are then assessed:

1. Rate of market growth
2. Industry potential
3. Product line
4. Number of competitors
5. Market share stability
6. Purchasing patterns
7. Ease of entry
8. Technology.

Company's competitive position	Stage of industry maturity			
	Embryonic	Growth	Maturity	Ageing
Dominant				
Strong				
Favourable				
Tentative				
Weak				

Figure 2.6 A.D. Little industry maturity/competitive position matrix

Activity 2.6

Assess the shortcomings of the A.D. Little matrix and then compare your answer with that shown in the debriefing.

Shell directional policy matrix

This approach was developed by Shell Chemicals (UK) in 1975. Its approach is similar to the GE Business Screen matrix, and it has two dimensions:

1. The competitive capability of the company
2. Prospects for sector profitability.

The company's products are plotted into one of the nine cells and subsequently there is a suggested strategy for each cell, as shown in Figure 2.7.

Sector profitability includes the criteria of market growth rate, market quality, industry situation and environmental considerations. On each of these factors, a product is given from one to five stars. The same procedure is followed for each of the other three factors, so that the score on sector profitability is the total of the ratings on all four factors.

Prospects for sector profitability

	Unattractive	Average	Attractive
Weak	Disinvest	Phased withdrawal	Double or quit
		Custodial	
Average	Phased withdrawal	Custodial	Try harder
		Growth	
Strong	Cash generation	Growth	Leader
		Leader	

Company's competitive capability (vertical axis label)

Figure 2.7 Shell directional policy matrix

Competitive capability uses the same approach, except that the company's capabilities are assessed on the basis of market position, product research and development, and production capability. These are further divided into sub-factors applicable to any particular industry.

The strategy recommendations contained in each of the nine cells are shown in Figure 2.7. The chief proviso, Shell maintains, is that whatever strategy is eventually selected, the aim is that it should be 'resilient' in terms of being viable in a diverse range of potential futures. Thus, each strategy should be evaluated against all future possible scenarios and the results in all cases should be acceptable in commercial terms.

Activity 2.7

What do you consider are the limitations of the Shell directional policy matrix? Compare your answer with the debriefing.

Once the marketing audit has been completed, we can move to consider the results of the external and internal parts. The most frequently used framework for combining the internal and external audit assessment and analysis procedures is the production of a SWOT analysis.

SWOT analysis

The internal and external audit allows the marketer to produce a systematic SWOT analysis. Widely known and used in marketing planning, these initial letters stand for:

- Strengths
- Weaknesses
- Opportunities
- Threats.

The strengths and weaknesses part of the SWOT analysis come from the internal half of the marketing audit.

In conducting the internal marketing audit referred to above, the objective is to assess company resources, activities and skills with regard to establishing the extent to which the company is strong or weak. So when, for example, the marketing audits, say, the financial, managerial, marketing, production, and research and development and so on are elements of the business, it is from the perspective of assessing strengths and weaknesses.

Completing the strengths and weaknesses part of the SWOT analysis helps to point out what is possible in terms of marketing objectives and strategies. For example, it would be pointless to pursue a marketing strategy in which innovatory products feature strongly if we ourselves were not strong in this area.

The opportunities and threats of the SWOT analysis is derived, needless to say, from the analysis of the marketing environment including the PEST factors. It is relatively easy to find examples of how the marketing environment might give rise to opportunities and threats. For example:

- A downturn in disposable income may threaten the demand for, say, luxury products
- A change in government policy may give rise to opportunities for more environmentally friendly products
- A decline in the birth rate may threaten the baby food manufacturer. Developments in IT may provide opportunities for direct marketing.

 Activity 2.8

> Try to find your own real-life examples of where a trend/change in each of our PEST factors has resulted in an opportunity or threat to a company.

One of the main aims of a SWOT analysis is, having identified the company's weaknesses, to look at ways in which these can be converted into strengths; and similarly to convert the threats into opportunities. Decision-makers can then decide which are the best ways through which these conversion processes can be achieved.

A good way of representing the outcome of a SWOT analysis is to use a matrix approach as shown in Figure 2.8 which also shows the notion of conversion referred to.

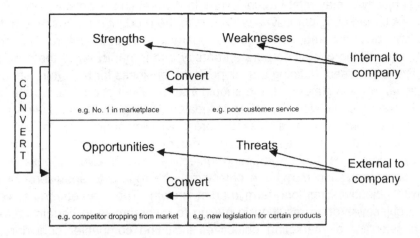

Figure 2.8 A SWOT analysis

Extending knowledge

Ideally you should extend your knowledge of the marketing environment and the PEST and SWOT analyses by consulting a good basic textbook, for example G.A. Lancaster *et al.* (2002) *Essentials of Marketing*, 4th edition, Chapters 2 and 12.

Marketing in practice: example

Because of the increasingly global nature of marketing, marketers must increasingly think of opportunities and threats in a wider context than those where in the past marketers have been concerned exclusively with the domestic marketing environment. In London, in 2004, there was a record number of restaurant closures with over 130 restaurants closing their doors for ever. One of the reasons for this record rate of closures, it was suggested, was the SARS outbreaks in China and Canada. This, it was suggested, had repercussions for many industries and markets throughout the world. Travel and tourism, of course, was particularly hard hit and hence the threat to some of London's leading restaurants. Increasingly the marketer will have to plan with global opportunities and threats in mind. Needless to say, this makes the process of assessing opportunities and threats much more difficult and uncertain.

Marketing objectives

The marketing audit and SWOT analysis enable the marketer to determine the overall marketing objectives of the organization. Marketing objectives encompass long-, medium- and short-term marketing objectives. What constitutes the timescale for these three different planning horizons will differ from company to company and industry to industry. So, for example, in the pharmaceutical industry long-term marketing objectives may encompass timescales often years or more with timescales for medium-term marketing objectives being, say, 5 years, and short-term perhaps 1 year. In the fast changing IT industry, however, long-term marketing plans may not make sense if they encompass planning horizons of, say, more than 2 or 3 years ahead, with short-term marketing plans, maybe encompassing planning horizons of no more than, say, 5–6 months.

Marketing objectives may relate to, for example, market share, sales, growth and so on. At the broadest level, marketing objectives will relate to the product market scope of the organization involving what business and markets the company is to be in the future. This area of marketing objectives links to the overall corporate strategy and in particular to the mission statement of the organization. Indeed, defining the scope of the business for the future should be part of the organizational mission statement and should in turn reflect overall corporate objectives. More specific marketing objectives will relate to goals and targets for marketing performance and might encompass areas such as sales and profits, market share, growth, and possibly areas of marketing performance such as innovation, market standing and even environmental issues. Sometimes companies have marketing objectives which can potentially conflict so, for example, an organization may have objectives with regard to short-term profit levels which conflict with objectives for long-term market growth. The marketer must carefully balance conflicting objectives often resulting in having to compromise in certain areas. Many factors affect the selection of marketing objectives including competitor considerations, customer considerations, company considerations, stakeholder considerations and environmental considerations. Objective setting is in fact often done badly in companies with objectives being set without careful consideration and analysis. In fact, objective setting is as important, if not more important, than any other element of the marketing plan as objectives provide guidance for strategy selection and facilitate the measurement of marketing effectiveness and control. In many ways, objectives provide the guiding framework with regard to how a company will compete in a marketplace, or put in another way, marketing objectives determine the competitive posture of an organization. This is illustrated in the example below.

Marketing in practice: example

There is substantial evidence that a great degree of the marketing success enjoyed by many Japanese companies in world markets stems in large measure from the aspirational and largely offensive (in competitive terms) objectives that many of these companies set for themselves during the last decade. For example, Komatsu is now one of the world's largest producers of earthmoving equipment, whereas comparatively only a few years ago it was a small player in the global market for this type of equipment. Komatsu has achieved this position, because it set itself aspirational objectives to become number one in the marketplace by encircling and beating its major competitor, namely Caterpillar. This objective has driven Komatsu to improve product quality, develop far-reaching licensing agreements and expand its product and market range. The whole of its marketing activities ranging from broad marketing strategies to detailed marketing goals stem from and reflect its aspirational objectives in the marketplace and are in no small measure a key factor in its global success.

It is important that marketing objectives, like any other area of objective setting in an organization, fulfil the so-called 'SMART criteria', namely they should be: Specific, Measurable, Actionable, Realistic and Timely. In addition, remember that marketing objectives must reflect and be integrated with the company's overall corporate objectives.

Marketing strategies

Marketing strategies represent the overall thrust of a company's marketing activities. There are a number of components to marketing strategies as follows:

Growth strategies: the Ansoff matrix

It is widely accepted that most companies want to grow. However, there are a number of strategies which a company may use to achieve growth. You may recall that earlier we suggested that one of the most useful and therefore most widely used models for identifying alternative product market growth strategies is the so-called 'Ansoff matrix'. We shall now consider this matrix. This is shown in Figure 2.9.

	Current products	New products
Current markets	Market penetration strategy	Product development strategy
New markets	Market development strategy	Diversification strategy

Figure 2.9 Ansoff's product market growth grid

This framework for delineating alternative growth strategies is based on a framework comprising 'markets' on one axis and 'products' on the other. Each of the strategies delineated in the matrix is briefly explained below.

o *Market penetration* – This strategy is based on expanding the sales of existing products in existing markets. There are a number of ways in which this can be achieved, for example the company may attempt to encourage customers to use the product more frequently or more heavily. Alternatively, market penetration can be achieved through attacking competitors' market share through, for example, heavy promotion and price discounts.

o *Market development* – This strategy for growth involves entering new markets with existing products, for example a company may achieve growth by attacking new market segments by export marketing. With this strategy, it is essential that proposed new markets are carefully assessed with respect to, say, attractiveness, and in particular the extent to which the company can match the requirements for success in the new markets.

o *Product development* – This strategy for growth involves developing and launching new products for sale in existing markets. Sometimes these may be extensions to the existing product range, such as additional features or different packaging, but also may involve entirely new products for the market. In the case of entirely new products, this can be an extremely risky, if potentially profitable, strategy. As we shall see in a later unit, it is essential to have systematic procedures for developing and launching new products where this strategy for growth is being pursued.

o *Diversification* – This strategy is probably the highest risk of all the four strategic options for growth, as it involves both new products and new markets for the organization. Diversification can take a number of forms ranging from moving into related products and markets through to entirely new products and markets. Again, this can be a very profitable route to growth but needs to be carefully planned if it is to succeed.

Overall competitive strategies

Having identified strategies for growth, a second facet of overall marketing strategy is to determine how a company will compete. We can distinguish between:

1. Cost leadership strategies
2. Differentiation strategies
3. Focus strategies.

Extending knowledge

You will perhaps recognize that this particular classification of the different types of overall competitive strategies in marketing is that proposed by Michael Porter. He referred to these strategies as 'generic strategies'. Although you will not be expected to be familiar with the work of Porter in any great depth for the Fundamentals paper, it would be useful if you could familiarize yourself with some of Porter's basic ideas. A good source is S. Dibb *et al.* (2000) *Marketing: Concepts and Strategies*, 4th edition.

The generic strategy which is selected as a basis for competing will obviously have major implications for the selection of marketing tactics, that is the design of the marketing mix.

 Activity 2.9

Try to find out what is meant by each of Porter's three alternative generic strategies. When you have done this, briefly, and in your own words, describe the possible implications of each strategy for the marketing mix.

Marketing in practice: example

In the UK grocery supermarket sector, individual key players in this market are pursuing different generic strategies. So, for example, ASDA, now owned by the American giant Walmart, are competing on the basis of a low price value-for-money strategy. They aim to offer customers the best value for money in the business, a strategy which is reflected most obviously not only in their pricing strategies but also in their product and merchandising strategies and their promotional theme of 'Its ASDA price'. In contrast, one of their major competitors, Sainsbury's, is pursuing a differentiation strategy claiming higher levels of service, with a wide range of support activities for their merchandising and an emphasis on quality. Once again, this generic strategy is reflected in their pricing and product decisions and in their promotional strapline of 'making life taste better'.

Segmentation, targeting and positioning strategies: an introduction

Many would argue that one of the most important elements of marketing plans is what is known as target marketing. This in turn comprises the sub-elements of market segmentation, targeting and positioning. Target marketing is central to contemporary marketing planning. The notion of target marketing is, in fact, an extension of the basic concept of marketing discussed in Unit 1. In essence, it is a recognition that the marketer needs to meet the specific requirements and needs of customers as closely as possible. This is especially true in today's markets, where competition for customers is intense and where customers are better informed and more demanding. Put simply, the company that comes closest to meeting the precise needs of customers through the marketing mix will get the business.

In any given market, however, different customers will have different needs. This means that rarely these days can a company succeed by mass producing a standardized product aimed at the whole market. Put another way, a modern-day Henry Ford offering customers 'any colour so long as it's black' would find difficulty marketing the product.

The fact that customers have different needs within a market means that the marketer must break down the market by identifying what these different needs are and the customer groups with which these different needs are associated. This first stage of target marketing is known as 'market segmentation'.

Having identified the different market segments, the marketer can then evaluate these various segments and decide which of them to cater for and on what basis. This second step is the 'targeting' step.

Finally, the marketer must decide the 'product positioning' strategy to be used in serving selected target markets. This final stage is where we see the impact of the process of target marketing on the marketing mix. In positioning products and services within selected target markets, the marketing mix is designed to meet the specific needs of the target market identified in the market segmentation stage so as to secure a competitive advantage.

Exam hint

The examiners may well use the terms 'target marketing' and 'market segmentation' inter-changeably. In this unit, we have seen that, in fact, segmentation is only one step in the targeting process. If the examiners nevertheless ask you to discuss market segmentation, it is likely that they are asking you to discuss all three steps in target marketing. Be careful to read any question on this area carefully in order to ascertain precisely what examiners are looking for.

In this unit, we will now concentrate on the first of the three elements or activities in target marketing, that is segmentation. The other two elements, that is targeting and the positioning process, are discussed in more detail in Unit 3 in the context of creating an integrated and coherent marketing mix.

Market segmentation

In this first element of target marketing, the marketer assesses the extent to which there are different customer groups in the market with different requirements and needs. The marketer must also determine the bases on which the market segments.

In fact virtually all markets for products and services, both consumer and b2b, usually segment into clusters of customers on some basis. You probably already have a good idea of the variety of bases on which different markets might be segmented. Some of the major categories of segmentation bases used by marketers are shown in the activity that follows.

Activity 2.10

In this activity we have listed the main categories of segmentation bases used to segment markets. We have distinguished between bases commonly used in consumer markets and those commonly used in b2b markets. To make sure you understand each of these main categories of segmentation, you should write down examples of variables used to segment markets within each major category. So in the case of the 'demographic' bases, an example of a variable would be 'age'.

o **Consumer bases**

- Demographics, for example 'age'
- Socio-economic, for example
- Geographic, for example
- Personality and lifestyle, for example
- Purchase occasion, for example
- User status, for example
- Usage rate, for example
- Benefits sought, for example

o **Business-to-business bases**

- Demographic, for example
- Geographic, for example
- Purchasing organization, for example
- User status, for example
- Usage rate, for example
- Benefits sought, for example

We can see from this activity that there are many potential bases for segmenting markets and that at least some of these are common to both 'consumer' and 'business to business'. In fact, identifying effective bases for segmentation is one of the most dynamic areas of contemporary marketing. Marketers are constantly looking for new and improved ways to segment markets. Often new approaches to segmenting markets reflect the constantly changing nature of markets and customers, so, for example, in many economies new lifestyle segments have emerged due to changes in demographic structures such as the large growth of the 55–75-year-old-age groups in many developed economies. Often referred to as the 'grey market' this represents a substantial and growing market segment. Other new approaches to segmenting markets reflect and indeed rely upon developments and improvements in the technology of marketing, and in particular something we shall explore in much more detail in Unit 9, but have already touched on in our Unit 1, namely developments in IT in general and more specifically databases in marketing. An example of the emergence of new bases for segmenting markets as a result of improved data collection and analysis has been the growth of the so-called 'geodemographic bases' for segmenting markets.

Key definition

Geodemographics – Is the identification of market segments based on where people live and their lifestyles.

This deceptively simple definition of geodemographic segmentation belies the potential complexity of many of the geodemographic segmentation techniques. This approach to segmentation often necessitates a huge amount of complex data on markets and customers in order to identify and profile geodemographic segments. Hence the fact that this approach to segmentation has emerged largely as a result of improved data collection and analysis techniques. Several commercial systems of geodemographic classifications exist whereby marketers can buy in geodemographic segmentation information and systems. In the United Kingdom and Europe, examples of commercially available geodemographic classification systems include 'Residata' provided by ABC Ltd, MicroVision from Equifax, CAMEO from EuroDirect, MOSAIC from Experian, and one of the first and best known, namely the so-called 'ACORN system' from the Caci Organization. Although all these systems differ in terms of specific data sources used in the analysis classification systems and so on, they all of course use a combination of geographical and demographic/lifestyle data.

Taking ACORN as an example, this system identifies and analyses market segments by combining information on the type of housing that consumers live in combined with lifestyle and demographic data deriving from, for example, market research and census data. Using this information, Caci's ACORN system classifies customers into 1 of 54 distinct neighbourhood types which are further classified into 11 major ACORN groups. So, for example, ACORN group D consists of low-income people living in older terraced houses of generally poor quality with few modern retail facilities. Analysis of the data in Caci's ACORN system suggests that customers in different ACORN categories have quite distinct and different lifestyles and purchasing patterns to other ACORN groups. Because of this, ACORN groupings can be used to identify and target distinct groups of customers with, for example, different propensities to buy specific products and services. As a result, and indeed the reason for the growth in popularity of geodemographic segmentation bases, marketers are able to identify distinct groups of customers together with their needs, wants and buying habits which in turn can then be used to develop targeted marketing programmes aimed at each geodemographic segment. Geodemographic segmentation bases such as ACORN have proved extremely powerful in marketing applications such as:

- Selecting new retail sites
- Targeting direct mail
- Media selection
- Sales-force organization
- The allocation of marketing resources.

Extending knowledge

Click on the website www.caci.co.uk to extend your knowledge of the ACORN geodemographic approach to market segmentation developed by CACI.

Very often the marketer will combine bases for segmentation purposes. But how do we know which bases to use in segmenting a market? The answer to this is to use bases that enable us to identify distinct and different clusters of customers with respect to the product or market in question. So, for example, we know that in segmenting the market for, say, clothing the variables of sex, income, social class and age are all related to differences in purchase requirements.

In fact, there is no one right way to segment a market. Ideally segmentation bases should allow us to reveal segments that have the following characteristics:

- *Measurable* – The segments revealed should be easy to measure.
- *Substantial* – The segments revealed should be large enough to serve.
- *Accessible* – The marketer should be able to reach the segments revealed.

63

Activity 2.11

Remembering that there is no one right way to segment a market, can you suggest what might be appropriate basis/bases for segmenting the markets shown below.

1. Holidays
2. Cars
3. Cigarettes
4. Industrial abrasives
5. Office-cleaning services.

Extending knowledge

Segmentation, targeting and positioning are complex and far-reaching areas of marketing. The coursebook therefore can only serve to introduce you to the key concepts and approaches with regard to these areas. You are therefore advised to consult one of the recommended textbooks to study this area further. An excellent source is F. Brassington and S. Pettitt (2000) *Principles of Marketing*, 2nd edition, Chapter 5. In addition, S. Dibb *et al.* (2000) *Marketing Concepts and Strategies*, 4th edition, Chapter 7 and P. Kotler *et al.* (1999) *Principles of Marketing*, 2nd European edition are also strong sources. Remember also that the stages of targeting and positioning in the process of target marketing are discussed in more detail in Unit 3.

Marketing tactics/marketing mix decisions

Having determined the key elements of marketing strategy, the next element of the marketing planning process is developing the more detailed marketing tactics. Essentially, this involves planning how the different marketing tools will be used in the marketing plan. It is therefore concerned with planning a co-ordinated marketing mix for each target market. By this stage of the planning process, the previous steps will effectively now dictate these marketing mix decisions. It is in this stage of the marketing plan that these elements are brought together to form an integrated and cohesive whole. The process of creating an integrated and coherent marketing mix in the context of targeting and positioning strategies is considered in detail in Unit 3.

Implementation, monitoring and control of the marketing mix and programmes

Plans are nothing unless they degenerate into action. Implementation is the step and activities are required to bring plans to life. Implementation involves the detailed scheduling for planning activities and involves areas such as budgets, staffing, detailed timetables and so on. In addition, organizational structures and systems must be designed in order to ensure that plans are effectively implemented. The marketer must therefore act in order to ensure that the necessary structures, people, budgets and processes are in place in order to effectively implement marketing plans.

In this section of the unit, we shall consider in particular the budgeting element of implementing marketing plans together with the alternative management structures available for implementing marketing plans. We shall then consider the key area of monitoring and control.

Marketing budgets and the marketing plan

As already mentioned, broad objectives and strategies must eventually be translated into detailed action programmes in order to bring the plan to life. These detailed action programmes will encompass the activities to be performed, by whom, when and most importantly at what cost. It is this final detail of action programmes that raises the issue of marketing budgets. Obviously, without the necessary supporting financial resources, marketing programmes and plans will never be implemented. Budgeting then is a key aspect of implementing marketing plans. But what exactly is a marketing budget?

Key definition

A marketing budget – Represents the amount of resources allocated to support marketing activities over a period of time.

Within this seemingly straightforward definition, in fact, we have several potentially complicating issues when we consider marketing budgets and budgeting further.

First of all, resources of course could include manpower, facilities, time and so on. Here, we shall discuss resource allocation in a budgeting context with specific regard to financial resources, that is monetary budgets, but we should not forget that budgets encompass more than simply financial resources.

Secondly, there are two related sub-facets when it comes to marketing budgets. The first of these concerns how decisions are made with regard to the determination of the overall marketing budget covering all marketing activities in the marketing plan. The second concerns how the overall budget will be allocated between the different elements of marketing activity within the marketing plan. So, for example, we have to determine how much of the budget will be allocated to, say, sales or selling activities, how much to branding and packaging, how much to distribution and so on. We shall be considering both overall budget determination and the issue of allocating budgets to the different elements of marketing activity in this section.

Finally, there are different time horizons with regard to all budgets, including marketing budgets. In general terms, we can distinguish between annual and longer-term budgets in marketing. Both are necessary in order to encompass, of course, different planning horizons within the marketing plans themselves. Long-term marketing strategies aimed at pursuing long-term marketing objectives require long-term budgeting procedures. Here, we shall confine ourselves principally to annual marketing budgets required to support the annual marketing plan.

With these considerations in mind, we can now consider the annual marketing financial budgeting process. We shall start by considering the alternative approaches to determine the overall annual marketing plan budget.

Alternative approaches to determine the overall annual financial budgets for marketing

There are a number of approaches to determine the overall amount to be allocated to the marketing activities in the annual marketing plan.

Affordable method

The first and perhaps the simplest way of determining the overall annual marketing budget is to base the budget on what the company can afford. You will immediately recognize, of course, that although a simple approach, there is relatively little or no real merit in adopting this approach to setting the annual marketing budget. Admittedly it does ensure that the company does not 'overspend' with regard to its financial resources but it means that, for example, in the case of a company which is making little profit, it will allocate relatively little to its annual marketing budget and hence remain at the very best stuck in its low profit situation.

Percentage of profits

In a sense, a variation on the affordable method. This approach on setting the overall marketing budget is based on setting the budget according to some percentage of the company profits. Sometimes the profits used are the previous year's profits, or in other cases can be based on forecast profits. Either way, however, the problem with this approach is that it assumes that budgets are a function of profits and not the other way around. In addition, as with our affordable method therefore, it can condemn the low profit or low profit forecast organization to remaining in the marketing wilderness. Finally, even if we accept that this method is simple and is at least related to some objective measure, it does not of itself tell us what percentage of profits is an appropriate one to allocate for the marketing budgets.

Percentage of sales

This is probably the most widely used method for setting budgets in organizations including marketing budgets. The budgeting process in this approach starts usually with a sales forecast which is then used to determine what activities will be needed to support the sales-level forecast which in turn results in not just marketing budgets but production budgets, manpower budgets and so on. Again, one can see why this is a widely used method of budgeting. It does appear to have an inherent logic and indeed many activities and costs in a company stem from and are directly related to the level of sales achieved. However, like the percentage of profits approach, this is essentially a negative way to determine the overall marketing budget. If sales are forecast to decrease, for example, then so are marketing budgets. This in turn, of course, can lead to a further drop in sales *ad infinitum.*

Objective and tasks

This approach of setting the overall annual marketing budget is in fact the most rational and defendable approach. In this approach, the budgets are determined by establishing what tasks need to be performed, in this case with regard to marketing tasks, in order to achieve the marketing objectives set out in the marketing plan. These activities can then be costed and the total of these costs represents the required total budget to support the marketing plan. The downside to this approach to setting the overall marketing budget is, of course, that it does require substantial effort, time and information. It requires, for example, detailed costings for the marketing activities in the marketing plan, or in some cases detailed estimates. The major advantage, however, is that it forces the marketing planner to think about the costs of the various marketing activities in the marketing plan, how these costs relate to the achievement of marketing objectives and therefore if they are cost effective, and how costs might be controlled.

Allocating budgets to marketing activities

Outlined, then, are the major alternative ways of determining the annual financial budget for the marketing plan. In addition, decisions must be made with regard to the allocations of this overall budget to the various marketing activities in the plan. In the multi-product company, these allocation decisions must also be made with respect to the different products or brands of the business and, where appropriate, to the different SBUs. All the four methods discussed can be used to allocate the budget between products, brands and businesses. So, for example, we can allocate the budget between different products on the basis of forecast sales for each. Often, however, these allocation decisions are made on the basis of which brand or product manager in the organization shouts loudest, is most persuasive, is friendly with the marketing director and so on. In fact, as with the overall budget allocation to support the marketing plan, the objective and task method is the only defendable way of allocating the budget between the various marketing activities. So, for example, in determining the promotional budget, the marketing manager must assess what tasks the promotional element of the marketing mix will be required to perform in the context of the overall marketing objectives in the plan. These can then be costed and the budget allocation to this element of the mix determined.

In principle, determining and allocating marketing budgets is straightforward. In practice, it can be complex. In addition to ensuring that the necessary financial and other resources have been allocated for the effective implementation of marketing plans, there must be suitable organizational and management structures in place for their effective implementation.

Management and organizational structures for implementing marketing plans

Plans are implemented by people, and particularly by managers, and in turn require suitable and appropriate organizational structures for their implementation. Companies use a myriad of different management and organizational structures to implement their marketing plans. Management structures include, for example, product manager systems where marketing plans are organized and implemented around products. A simple example of this type of structure is shown in Figure 2.10 below.

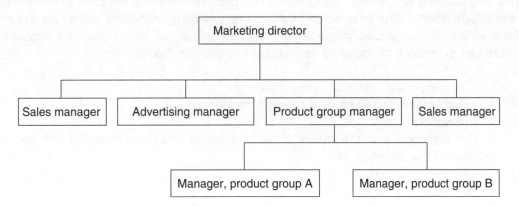

Figure 2.10 A simple product-based marketing organization

A variation on the product-based approach which is often found in b2b marketing organizations are those organizational structures which are based on brands and utilize brand managers in place of product group managers. This type of structure is very common in companies marketing-FMCG with a range of individual brands. Another structure commonly found is that which is based around customers and/or markets. An example of this type of structure is shown in Figure 2.11 below.

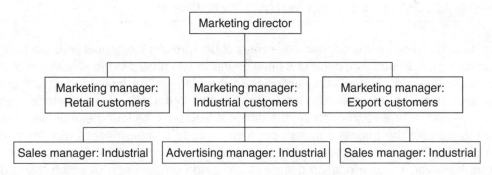

Figure 2.11 A simple customer-market-based marketing organization

These are just two of the ways of organizing marketing activities and functions. With variations on a theme, there are literally dozens of possible alternatives including, for example, category management structures, simple functional structures and matrix-type structures which are based on organization structures combining, say, product and market-based structures together. The reason for such a myriad of alternative approaches is that, in fact, there is no one method of organizing the implementation of marketing plans which is always and inevitably superior. In some circumstances, organizing around products, for example, with product managers is the most effective method. In other circumstances, organizing around markets is the most appropriate and effective method. Many factors affect what is an appropriate management and organizational structure for implementing plans including, for example:

o Organizational size and complexity
o Organizational resources
o Spread/diversity of product markets
o Speed of market and technological change
o Competition and competitive market structure
o Geographical spread of organization and markets
o Organizational culture
o Managerial skills and expertise
o Requirements for control and so on.

It is impossible and downright dangerous to be prescriptive about the form which management and organizational structures should take in implementing marketing plans. Having said this, irrespective of the precise management and organizational structures and systems, these should be selected and designed ideally so as to provide the following:

o Company-wide customer orientation
o Organizational flexibility and speed of response
o Innovation
o Co-ordination and integration between different functional areas of the business and outside the organization
o Effective communication
o Motivation and leadership.

In practice, most management and organizational systems and structures are a compromise between the above ideals, but if organizational and management structures are not appropriate and supportive of marketing plans and activities, this can be a major problem for an organization, and indeed management and organizational structural problems and weaknesses are a major contributory cause of marketing and organizational poor performance and even failure.

These, then, are the important budgeting and management/organizational issues in implementing marketing plans. Our final element of the marketing planning process involves the monitoring and control of marketing plans.

The importance of monitoring and control

> ### Study tip
>
> The evaluation and control of marketing activities, and particular the scope and use of the marketing audit in this respect is considered in some detail in Unit 9 of the coursebook.

Essentially, the process of monitoring and control comprises comparing actual performance against required or desired performance objectives and then taking any necessary action to correct differences between actual and required. Because of this, the control process in marketing stems from the marketing objectives and strategies of the company.

Without monitoring and control, it is impossible to assess the extent to which marketing objectives have been achieved and the strategies have been effective. Given the potentially large costs and use of resources in implementing the elements of the marketing mix, it would be inadvisable not to assess how well these resources have been used.

In addition, we know that markets are dynamic. The environment changes, customers change, competitors change, even the company itself can change over time. This means, therefore, that the marketing mix needs also to change to reflect and cope with these outside changes. Monitoring and control of the marketing mix facilitates the planning of such changes. Without monitoring and control, there is a danger that marketing strategies become outmoded and no longer fit the market situation.

Types of control in marketing

The major types of control used in marketing include the following:

1. Customer feedback/customer tracking, for example

    (a) Customer surveys
    (b) Customer complaints
    (c) Sales-force reports
    (d) Customer panels.

2. Sales analysis and control, for example

    (a) Sales volume/value
    (b) Sales trends
    (c) Breakdown of sales by product, customer, sales person and so on.

3. Market share analysis and control, for example

    (a) As per sales analysis above, but based on percentage of market.

4. Profitability analysis and control, for example

    (a) Analysis of costs and margins
    (b) Net profits
    (c) Return on capital.

5. Strategic control is the most wide-ranging and comprehensive of control techniques used in marketing, covering the control of the strategic planning process itself. Two main tools are used in strategic control, and both call for a wide-ranging review of the effectiveness of marketing activities, namely:

    (a) Marketing effectiveness rating reviews
    (b) The marketing audit.

Activity 2.12

If you can, try to arrange an interview with a senior marketing manager (this could be in your own company of course) and try to establish what types of controls are being used to evaluate marketing performance.

The outcome of the marketing planning process: the marketing plan

We have covered all of the major steps in the marketing planning process but remember, this is a process and not the marketing plan itself. The marketing plan represents the outcome of this process, so what does a marketing plan look like and what are the main contents of a marketing plan? Below, we have listed the structure and outline content of a 'typical' annual marketing plan. Although the structure and contents of the plan would probably not vary all that much for longer-term plans, it is important to remember that the specific layout and structure of a marketing plan can vary slightly according to the situation and the company.

Management summary

This part of the plan summarizes the main points of the plan covering key objectives, major strategies and outline marketing mix programmes.

Product market situation

This part of the plan covers the analysis of the market for the product(s)/services; included in here would be, for example, data on target market, market size, market trends and projections. This section will often include information on customer needs and buying behaviour. The product part of this section of the plan should contain information on prices, contributions and net profits for each of the major product lines encompassed by the plan. The competitive and distribution situation should also be included.

Strengths, weaknesses, opportunities and threats (SWOT) analysis

This section of the plan encompasses the external marketing audit encompassing our so-called 'PEST factors', forecast changes which will give rise to opportunities and threats. This part of the marketing plan should also contain the internal marketing audit encompassing company's strengths and weaknesses.

Marketing objectives

This element of the plan details broad sets of objectives which the plan is intended to achieve. Remember, these objectives will stem not only from the analysis encompassed in the first sections of the plan but also should reflect corporate objectives. Objectives should be stated, remember, in SMART terms and should encompass financial, marketing and any other objectives pertaining to stakeholder, social responsibilities and so on.

Marketing strategies

The marketing strategies element of the plan encompasses decisions regarding core target markets, decisions regarding product market expansion plans (the Ansoff matrix), the basis for competing, that is the competitive advantage, and the desired product/brand positioning.

Action programmes

The action programmes part of the plan involves the preparation of detailed programmes for each of the marketing mix elements encompassing as a minimum the four conventional Ps of the marketing mix, but increasingly in almost every company the additional 'People' element of the mix, and in the case of service industries and markets, the further two Ps, 'Process' and 'Physical evidence'. The action programmes should contain plans for implementing these including the allocation of tasks and responsibilities, and required marketing structures and systems.

Budgets/financial implications

This part of the plan should encompass a delineation of costs and required budgets for marketing programmes. These budgets should be allocated to the various marketing activities as appropriate. This part of the plan should also contain projected sales which will enable, in turn, projected profit and loss statements.

Controls and evaluation

This part of the plan contains information on expected standards of performance as the basis of control, it should also contain information on how results will be measured and the control mechanisms to be used.

Contingencies

The contingencies part of the plan details what actions will be taken if there be any problems. So, for example, if the marketing plan is based on a set of assumptions, say regarding levels of inflation/interest rates and so on, and should these materially alter during the period of time that the plan is in operation, requiring changes in elements of the plan, then this contingency section is aimed at encompassing any potential changes in plans of action.

Appendices

The appendices part of the plan should contain most of the detailed background analyses carried out in the production of the marketing plan. The plan itself should be as brief and focused as possible and therefore the appendices provide an opportunity to include the more detailed background analysis and information in a separate part of the plan for those who wish to examine this detail.

Further issues in marketing planning and budgeting

In this final part of the unit, we consider two further issues with respect to marketing planning and budgeting. First of all, we consider the important issue of the use of marketing research and information in marketing planning. Secondly, we look at some of the ways in which marketers are making use of technological advances and new technology in the marketing planning process.

Marketing research and information in marketing planning

At virtually every stage of the marketing process, and certainly in every stage of marketing planning, the marketer must make use of the most accurate and up-to-date information available within the time and cost constraints pertaining. A way of illustrating how marketing research and information can help in this respect is to examine the most common areas or problems given by marketers as the focus for marketing research activities. These are as follows:

- ○ Market share analysis
- ○ Market size potential analysis
- ○ Sales analysis
- ○ Business and market trends
- ○ Short- and long-range forecasting
- ○ Competitor analysis
- ○ Pricing analysis
- ○ Analysis of products
- ○ Communication analysis
- ○ Distribution and logistics analysis.

We can see that many of these areas of analysis relate to areas or aspects of the marketing plan and the marketing planning process. In addition, implicit in the areas of research listed above is the analysis of customer and market segments. A key part of marketing research activities, therefore, in marketing planning is this analysis and understanding of customers and market segments. Marketing research and information has several uses and advantages in the context of marketing planning. Among some, the main advantages and uses are the following:

- ○ It improves the marketer's ability to make decisions.
- ○ The changing values and behaviour of customers can be monitored.
- ○ Competitors' development of their strategies can be identified.
- ○ It can be used to continuously evaluate the current effectiveness of an organization's strategies and tactics, for example a television advertising campaign.
- ○ Research in the form of environmental scanning can help to identify the changes in social, legal, political and technological advancements.

Marketers therefore must, and do, make use of the tools and techniques of marketing research in preparing marketing plans. Sometimes this marketing research will be one-off *ad hoc* research aimed at addressing a specific and identified research problem and objective such as establishing the potential market size for, say, a new product. In addition, however, and increasingly, the marketing planning process is aided and abetted through marketing information systems in the organization.

Marketing information systems and marketing planning

Increasingly, often supported through improved IT (some of which we shall consider shortly in the unit) marketers have extended their concept of the scope and uses of information for marketing decisions. Marketing research is now seen in many companies as just one, though important, element of a total system of marketing information. Traditionally, marketing research is carried out to solve specific marketing problems. In this sense to a large degree it is *ad hoc*. As mentioned earlier, it is now realized that information is needed on a continuous basis. The marketing information system is designed to generate and disseminate a flow of information to marketing managers. The collection of data to solve one-off marketing problems through marketing research is, as just mentioned, one element in this system. The three other elements in a marketing information system are:

1. A marketing intelligence sub-system
2. An internal information sub-system
3. A decision support sub-system.

The marketing research and marketing intelligence sub-systems feed into the marketing information database, which in turn feeds into the analysis and decision support system part of the marketing information framework. All of these elements combine to provide information for marketing decision-making. These key elements of a marketing information system, and how they interlink, are illustrated in Figure 2.12.

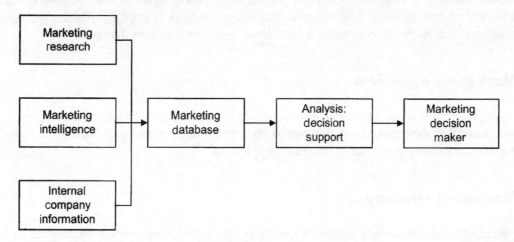

Figure 2.12 Elements of the marketing information system

Extending knowledge

For an excellent and detailed discussion of marketing information systems see, for example, F. Brassington and S. Pettitt (2003) *Principles of Marketing*, 3rd edition, pp. 221–225.

Data brought into the organization through marketing research becomes just one element in a company's marketing databank. This is a file of data collected through both the marketing information system and marketing research projects. The marketing databank allows researchers to retrieve information and this is useful for addressing problems quite different from those that prompted the original data collection. Often a research study developed for one purpose provides valuable information for developing a research method for further studies.

The marketing information system (MKIS) should be designed around the marketers' decision-making needs and should produce only the information required to take more cost-effective marketing decisions.

Activity 2.13

Try to make an assessment of the current information provided for marketing decisions internally in your organization, for example information from accounts and so on. How could such internal information provision be improved (if at all) in your organization?

Technological developments and the marketing planning process

Needless to say, the marketing planning process has not been untouched by developments in technology. You should be at least aware of some of the ways in which the marketing planning process is being affected by these developments. Below, therefore, we have given an indication of just some of the ways in which the planning process is being affected.

Marketing audit

e-Commerce and new technology is increasingly being used in the marketing audit. The Internet, on-line sources, and internal databases all help in analysing and investigating the economic environment, competitors, customer requirements and dynamics.

Marketing objectives

Again, both internal and external analysis using databases and on-line sources can be used in this area. For example, using databases to identify current rates of loyalty and retention of current customers may help to formulate objectives.

Marketing strategy

Databases are particularly useful in identifying and analysing market segments. In addition, technology can be used as a driver to underpin marketing strategy in terms of differentiation from competitors.

Marketing tactics

e-Commerce and advances in technology are affecting every element of the marketing mix, for example:

- *Product* – Computer-aided design (CAD) systems for product design and packaging.
- *Pricing* – The analysis of current database of customers and reaction to pricing variations.
- *Place* – The use of the Internet as a direct channel of distribution, for example home shopping and e-tailing.

- ○ *Promotion* – The use of DRTV, databases and direct mail and websites as a promotional driver to link with current sales promotions and advertising. The website can also be used as a communication tool for crisis management and media relations.
- ○ *Process* – Improved communications with sophisticated databases and automated customer-handling operations.
- ○ *People* – Interactive CD-ROMs, Internet-based company training for staff, use of the intranet for internal communications.
- ○ *Physical evidence* – The website as a 'window' of the organization to allow the customer to enter the organization and delve into areas which they would otherwise not have access to (e.g. a virtual tour of the factory).

Evaluation and control

Analysing the effectiveness of the marketing plan by identifying the number of Web 'hits', interrogation of the database to check the effectiveness of direct campaigns and so on. We can see, then, that e-commerce and e-technology are affecting every facet of marketing. Let us now consider some of the areas mentioned above in even more detail with regard to uses and applications of the new technologies.

Marketing in practice: example

Walmart, Tesco, Toyota, the Spanish clothing company Zara and the Italian clothing company Benetton are all examples of companies using and benefiting from the application of some of the most recent technology to their marketing planning processes. Benetton, for example, uses sophisticated IT to analyse and assess which lines of its clothing, down to the detail of which colours, are selling best in its franchised outlets. Information is fed back immediately on a daily basis and analysed at headquarters so that production, promotional, pricing and distribution plans can be amended as required to take account of purchasing patterns and demands. The information is collected and analysed so quickly that it is literally virtual information. Walmart, Tesco and Toyota are using sophisticated databases to identify and respond to customers' needs and wants. Marketing objectives and strategies are based on in-depth information again based on powerful databases to develop rapid responses in marketing strategy.

Marketing in practice: case study

'Fly me – we're good planners!'

Most have agreed that one of the business success stories in recent years has been the phenomenal rise to success of the passenger airline EasyJet. But is this success due, as some would argue, only to its low prices?

Originally started in 1995 with two aircraft and just two routes, EasyJet now operates a fleet of over 35 Boeing 737s and offers 50 routes from 21 European airports. Many factors underpin the success of EasyJet, not the least of which is the enthusiasm and expertise of the company's owner and founder, Stelios Haji-Ioannou. There is a view though that EasyJet's success is first and foremost due to its low prices. Certainly, low prices have been the thrust of its competitive strategy; however, underpinning this thrust has been probably the real key to EasyJet's success, namely its clear, co-ordinated and targeted approach to marketing planning and strategies.

One of the first indications of this was when the company swiftly recognized that changes in the regulatory environment concerning European air flight would make it possible for new and smaller companies to enter the market. At the same time, social/cultural and economic factors were also combining to increase the number of passengers who wanted to travel throughout Europe by aeroplane. The company was swift to spot a major marketing opportunity, resulting from changes in the so-called 'PEST factors'.

Looking at the market, EasyJet decided that one of the major growth segments, within what was already a growth sector, would be those passengers who wanted to fly regularly but also as cheaply as possible with little or no frills with regard to the service that was being offered. Linked to this, EasyJet realized that most of the existing companies in the market and certainly the long-established and often-global companies such as British Airways, Swissair, Air France and so on, only offered relatively high-priced flights albeit with substantial customer service. EasyJet, through careful customer and competitor analysis, recognized a gap in this growing market.

At the establishment of the company, a clear set of business and marketing objectives was formed with the objective of building market share and hence growth in the market target was identified. This involved both a market penetration and market development strategy as the company attracted more and more potential fliers with its low prices.

The core strategy pursued to achieve this growth, then, was a cost leadership strategy, the emphasis in the market mix in turn would be through competing on low price. Everything else was built around this core strategy for competing. So, for example, EasyJet determined to offer a 'no frills' product, direct booking systems and operated from out-of-city airports where landing fees and so on were much lower. This low-cost positioning strategy was also signalled through the promotional activities of the company, essentially telling the public that low-cost flights were now available and further that they were of excellent value while remaining safe. Nothing has been allowed to detract from this cost leadership strategy and the marketing mix elements, therefore, have been combined and co-ordinated so as to produce synergy through consistency.

Based on specific marketing targets and clear ideas for the future, the marketing mix in EasyJet is translated into detailed marketing plans and budgets including plans for training facilities and organizational structures. Organizational structures in the company in particular are designed to quickly effect the implementation of marketing plans and also to ensure a degree of flexibility so as to respond quickly to market and technological change. In fact, EasyJet was one of the quickest responders to the problems caused for the airline industry by the events of 11 September 2001; while its larger competitors struggled in the face of falling demand, EasyJet's quick responses produced a 27 per cent rise in its September 2001 figures compared to a near collapse of some other competitors' business.

Low prices as the key to success? Possibly. Effective marketing planning as the key to success? Certainly.

Source: www.easyjet.com.

Summary

- In this unit we have looked at the central key activity in marketing, namely marketing planning.
- We have examined, in turn, each of the steps in the planning process beginning with the identification and formulation of overall business and corporate objectives through to the evaluation and control of marketing plans.
- We have looked at the marketing planning process and introduced some of the key models that describe the various stages of this process and the various analytical tools including the

marketing audit, the tools and techniques of portfolio analysis, PEST and SWOT analysis, the Ansoff matrix and the notion of generic strategies.

o The importance of objectives and influences on these has been explored.

o We have looked at the concept of market segmentation and how this relates to the essential elements of targeting and positioning and the notion of creating an integrated and coherent marketing mix.

o Key issues in implementing marketing plans have been examined including the various management structures available and the setting of marketing budgets.

o We have described the structure of an outline marketing plan and identified its various components.

o We have seen the need for monitoring and controlling marketing activities and the way in which marketing plans make use of marketing research and information.

o Finally, we have seen that like every other area of marketing activity, marketing planning too is being influenced by developments in technology.

Examination preparation: previous examination question

A note on the mini case and questions

This is our first mini case question so obviously you will have to acquaint yourself with the approach to tackling the mini case part of the examination discussed in Appendix 1.

Previous examination question

Attempt Question 1(c) of the examination paper for December 2003 (Appendix 4). For Specimen Answer Examination Question 1(c), December 2003, see www.cim.co.uk.

Bibliography

Brassington, F. and Pettitt, S. (2003) *Principles of Marketing*, 3rd edition, FT Prentice Hall, Chapters 1, 5 and 21.

Cravens, D.W. (2002) *Strategic Marketing*, 7th edition, Irwin, Chapter 1.

Dibb, S. and Simkin, L. (1994) *The Marketing Planning Workbook*, Routledge.

Dibb, S., Simkin, L., Pride, W. and Ferrell, O.C. (2002) *Marketing Concepts and Strategies*, 4th European edition, Houghton, Mifflin, Chapters 1 and 22.

Kotler, P. (2001) *Marketing Management*, 10th edition, Prentice Hall, Chapter 1.

Lancaster, G.A., Massingham, L. and Ashford, R. (2002) *Essentials of Marketing*, 4th edition, McGraw-Hill, Chapters 1 and 13.

McDonald, M. (1999) 'How to prepare them, how to use them', *Marketing Plans*, 4th edition, Butterworth-Heinemann.

unit 3
the marketing mix and related tools: overview and issues

Learning objectives

Learning outcomes

By the end of this unit you will be able to:

○ Identify and describe the individual elements and tools of the marketing mix.

Knowledge and skills

By the end of this unit you will be able to:

○ Describe the essential elements of targeting and positioning, and the creation of an integrated and coherent marketing mix (3.1).

○ Describe the wide range of tools and techniques available to marketers to satisfy customer requirements and compete effectively (3.2).

○ Explain the development of the extended marketing mix concept to include additional components in appropriate contextual settings: product, price, place (distribution), promotion (communications), people, processes, physical evidence and customer service (3.3).

Study Guide

In this unit, we set the scene for many of the units which follow. We are going to look at an overview of the marketing mix, in particular we are going to introduce you to the wide range of tools and techniques available to marketers to satisfy customer requirements and to compete effectively. We shall also look at the importance of creating an integrated and coherent marketing mix, relating this in particular to the elements of targeting and positioning, and the significance of different marketing contexts which together serve to effectively guide the detailed marketing mix decisions. Finally, we shall take a further look at the notion of an extended marketing mix introduced in Unit 1. We would expect you to take about 3 hours to work through this unit and suggest you allow a further 3–5 hours to undertake the various activities suggested. Other than your notebook and writing equipment, you will not need anything further to complete this unit.

Introduction

You were introduced to the notion of the marketing mix and the elements which this includes in Unit 1. To remind you, the marketing mix represents those controllable factors or tools about which the marketer can make decisions with a view of developing effective marketing programmes. A key task for the marketing manager, then, is to decide which specific tools of the marketing mix to use in any given marketing campaign. In making these decisions, the marketer is seeking to develop a marketing programme that will appeal to the target market, reflect and support marketing and positioning strategies, and help build a sustainable competitive advantage. To start with, the marketer must first be aware of the range of marketing tools and techniques available to marketers to satisfy customer requirements and compete effectively.

Tools and techniques available to marketers

As we have seen, the basic building blocks of the tools available to marketers comprise of the 7Ps of the marketing mix. To remind you, these 7Ps are as follows:

- Product
- Price
- Place
- Promotion
- People
- Process
- Physical evidence.

Within each of these major tools of the marketing mix, however, there are any number of variations and ways in which the marketer may use each tool to try and satisfy customer requirements and compete effectively. For each of the mix elements, then, we can identify a number of sub-elements which reflect the myriad of decisions facing the marketer with respect to the use of the mix elements in marketing programmes. These are shown below.

Study tip

In the units that follow, we shall be looking at each of the marketing mix elements introduced here in more detail. Product decisions are the subject of Unit 4 in the coursebook, Pricing is the subject of Unit 5, Place and Promotion are covered in Units 6 and 7 respectively, and Unit 8 covers the increasingly important additional mix element of People in addition to Service and Customer Care. Finally, the way in which marketing mix decisions are affected by the so-called 'context' factors introduced in this unit are considered in detail in Unit 9 of the coursebook.

Product

Some would argue that this element of the marketing mix is the most important. Get this aspect of the mix wrong and, it is argued, it is almost impossible to sustain a competitive advantage. Certainly, product decisions often come first in the development of the mix stage of the marketing plan. Overall product decisions involve planning what products and services will be offered.

Amongst some of the key decisions about individual products and services are the following:

o Design and features
o Quality
o Materials and components
o Core product benefits
o Augmented product benefits, for example guarantees, after-sale services, installation and so on
o Branding
o Packaging.

In the multi-product firm, decisions must also be taken regarding:

o The product mix.

Finally, the product element of the marketing mix involves the management of products over time, and hence encompasses decisions regarding:

o Modifying/upgrading products
o Developing new products
o Dropping/deleting old products.

Price

Price is also a very important weapon in the marketers armoury. In particular, price is considered one of the most important tools for competing effectively. Price is the only element of the marketing mix which generates revenue and hence is directly related to profit. Price decisions encompass:

o Price levels
o Discounts/allowances
o Methods of payment
o Credit facilities
o Price negotiations
o Price changes.

In the multi-product firm, decisions must also be taken regarding:

o Price lining.

And for the international marketer:

o Transfer pricing
o Export terms/quotes.

Place

This third element of the marketing mix encompasses all those decisions and tools which relate to making products and services available to customers. Key decisions include:

o Channel length and types
o Types and numbers of intermediaries
o Market coverage
o Ordering systems
o Stocking and warehousing
o Delivery times and systems.

Promotion

This is the fourth of Borden's original four elements of the marketing mix. We can identify the following sub-elements/decisions within this marketing mix tool:

- o Advertising
- o Sales promotion
- o Personal selling
- o Publicity and PR
- o Sponsorship and exhibitions
- o Direct marketing.

Each of these promotional sub-elements can be used in a wide range of ways. So, for example, when it comes to advertising the marketer can aim advertising at, say, distributors or consumers, or both. Similarly, advertising programmes and spends may be run over an extended period of time with short bursts of advertising spend or with large advertising spends concentrated in short bursts. The content of the advertising itself can be factual, emotional or informative. Media used for advertising could be one or a combination of press, television, trade publications, magazines, newspapers and so on.

People

Remember the addition of three further elements to Borden's original 4Ps of the marketing mix was primarily prompted by the growth of the service sector in many countries. This in turn gave rise to the recognition that the marketer of service products, due primarily to the special characteristics of service products, needed to consider the use of additional marketing tools and techniques, that is a further 3Ps. The first, and some would argue the most important, element of this extended marketing mix are the marketer's employees or agents who directly or indirectly affect the process of meeting customer needs. With the often direct contact of an organization's employees with customers in services marketing and consumption, the marketers' 'people' are a potent marketing tool, in satisfying customer needs and developing a sustainable competitive advantage. Some of the key issues in managing this element of the marketing mix relate to:

- o Staff recruitment and selection
- o Training and development
- o Motivation and reward systems.

The recognition of the importance of this element of the marketing mix is that virtually all marketers now, and not just service marketers, include the people element of the marketing mix in trying to develop a competitive advantage.

Physical evidence

Particularly relevant to services marketers, this sixth element of the marketing mix includes decisions regarding those marketing tools that pertain to the physical properties of the service marketer's offer. With non-service product the customer can feel, touch, see and sometimes smell the product in evaluating whether or not the product will meet their needs. Owing to the essentially intangible nature of many service products, this physical evaluation of the product itself is simply not possible. Often then, and particularly with a new service product or with a customer who has not used the service provider before, the customer will use other physical signals or 'evidence' in evaluating the service provider's offering. So, for example, say we were new to a town and wanted to register with a dentist, we might use the 'evidence' of the appearance and facilities of the dentist's waiting room, say, to decide whether or not the services of the dentist would come up to our expectations. Banks, building societies, hairdressers, management consultants are all examples of service marketers who make use of the mix elements of physical evidence. Examples of tools in this area of the mix include:

- o   Reception and waiting areas and so on
- o   Production facilities/areas
- o   Staff appearance/uniforms
- o   Company livery/logos and so on.

Process

Again, particularly relevant to the marketing of services, this seventh element of the marketing mix pertains to the processes involved in the customer obtaining and using the service. So, for example, say in a fast-food outlet, process elements of the marketing mix might include:

- o   Ordering systems
- o   Customer queuing systems
- o   Food delivery systems
- o   Food and table clearing systems
- o   Booking and reservation systems
- o   Complaints systems.

We can see, then, that the marketer has an almost bewildering range of tools available to try and develop marketing programmes that meet customer needs. So how can the marketer begin to make sense of this range of choices and in particular how can the marketer try to ensure that the marketing mix elements eventually selected come together in a coherent way. Perhaps the marketer's greatest dilemma, and certainly at the heart of the marketing manager's key tasks is planning and managing the marketing mix.

Managing the marketing mix

With such a wide variety of marketing mix tools available to the marketer, then, the marketer is faced with two key and related problems namely:

- o   How to use the individual tools or elements of the marketing mix.
- o   How to combine these individual elements so as to achieve an integrated and co-ordinated marketing mix.

Amongst several factors that affect these two elements of managing the marketing mix, the two most important factors are:

- o   Targeting and positioning strategies
- o   The so-called 'context' of the marketing mix.

We shall now consider each of these in turn.

Creating an integrated and coherent marketing mix; targeting and positioning

A key distinguishing characteristic of effective marketing is the extent to which the individual elements of the marketing mix are co-ordinated and integrated so as to give a consistent and planned approach to the market.

As we have seen, each of the individual tools of the marketing mix calls for wide-ranging and complex decisions. Often other functions would input to these decisions. For example, in the case of pricing decisions, a key input is information on costs from the accountancy function. Similarly, new product development decisions may require the expertise and inputs from research and development, design and production. Because of this, it is vitally important that someone, or at least some function, takes responsibility for ensuring that these individual decisions come together in a co-ordinated manner. That someone, or function, is marketing.

Effective marketing planning requires that all activities that impinge on the satisfaction of customer needs must be co-ordinated by marketing. This means co-ordinating activities functions outside the marketing function in the organization, and includes the co-ordination of external organizations such as market research and advertising agencies.

If marketing does not take responsibility for this co-ordination, then it is almost inevitable that decisions about the marketing mix, such as product and price, will be taken unilaterally. If this happens, there will be little consistency between the elements of the marketing mix. We know that if the marketing mix elements are co-ordinated, we are much more likely to achieve something which has been referred to as 'synergy'.

Key definition

Synergy – Is where the outcome of combining individual elements together is greater than the simple sum total of each of the elements. It is often expressed as $2 + 2 = 5$.

An example of synergy is, say, where the marketer ensures that a high price is set to reflect a quality product sold through exclusive distribution outlets with costly and quality sales promotion. Each of the marketing mix elements acts in concert to give a marketing presence which is consistent and where each element serves to support and enhance the other elements in the marketing mix.

One could also appreciate the importance of consistency, and hence synergy, in planning the combination of the marketing mix elements by reflecting on the problems that marketers can have where this consistency is lacking. For example, one sometimes comes across examples of prestige/quality products being retailed in down-market outlets. Similarly, we see examples of marketers trying to charge premium prices for basic products. Thirdly, we sometimes see examples of where, although there is some consistency in the mix itself, the mix as a whole is inappropriate for the target market, for example top quality and premium priced products being targeted at lower income groups.

Finally, we can find examples of where the mix is consistent and was initially targeted at appropriate customer groups; but over time customers and their needs can change and competitors are always looking for new ways to compete. What this means is that planning the marketing mix is a continuous activity in what are dynamic markets.

Activity 3.1

Try to find examples yourself of marketing programmes exhibiting one or more of the problems just outlined. For each example which you find, try to assess why you think this problem occurred and what, if anything, could/should have been done to avoid/resolve the problem.

Obviously, then, the marketer has to try and ensure that the mix elements are combined and co-ordinated in an effective manner. In part, this involves no more than simple common sense, so, for example, it would not make sense to produce a luxury top end product distributed through exclusive outlets with bargain basement prices. Perhaps the most important aspect in co-ordinating the marketing mix, however, is to ensure that it is consistent with the intended target market and the positioning strategies determined earlier in the marketing planning process.

Put simply, the key to achieving an integrated and coherent marketing mix are the marketer's targeting and positioning strategies, which we now know stem from the process of market segmentation which was discussed in Unit 2.

Evaluating market segments and choosing targeting strategies

Having identified market segments, the marketer must decide which of these segments to target (i.e. market to, and on what basis). This decision will be affected by a number of factors, but the marketer will need mainly to evaluate the relative attractiveness of the different segments in the market and the company's ability to serve the different segments. Ideally we are looking for attractive segments we can serve well.

An attractive market segment is one which has the following characteristics:

- o Sufficient size/potential
- o Potential for future growth
- o Not over-competitive
- o Customers that the company could satisfy at least as well as, and preferably better than, the competitors.

Study tip

Some of the Portfolio Techniques of analysis and in particular the multi-factor GE matrix discussed in Unit 2 are useful in evaluating market segments. It might be useful to remind yourself of this particular technique at this stage.

Having evaluated the market segments, the next step towards developing an integrated marketing mix is to decide the targeting strategy to be used.

There are three broad alternative targeting strategies: 'undifferentiated targeting', 'differentiated targeting' and 'concentrated targeting'. We have defined each of these below.

Key definitions

Undifferentiated targeting – Is targeting the whole market with one marketing mix.

Differentiated targeting – Is targeting several market segments with a different marketing mix for each segment.

Concentrated targeting – Is targeting just one segment within the total market.

There are advantages and disadvantages to each targeting strategy with, again, the choice being dependent upon many factors such as company size and resources, market risks, competitors and so on. Even if you are relatively unfamiliar with these three alternative targeting strategies, you should be able to assess some of the advantages and disadvantages of each.

Activity 3.2

For each of the targeting strategies, see if you can assess what might be some of the advantages and disadvantages.

Complete the following:

- Undifferentiated targeting

    (a) Advantages, for example
    (b) Disadvantages, for example

- Differentiated targeting

    (a) Advantages, for example
    (b) Disadvantages, for example

- Concentrated targeting

    (a) Advantages, for example
    (b) Disadvantages, for example

You will no doubt already have noted in our discussion of targeting strategies that we are beginning to see the key influence of target marketing in planning an integrated and co-ordinated marketing mix. Remember, as we have seen, the marketing mix comprises the tools or ingredients at the marketer's disposal to develop effective marketing plans by creating customer satisfaction. The target marketing steps serve to begin, to influence and effectively delineate how these elements of the marketing mix will be used and in particular helps ensure a coordinated and cohesive marketing mix. Specifically, the choice of target market will serve to guide and constrain the marketing mix decisions. So, for example, if a marketer of clothing decides to target the fashion conscious 25–35 female customers with relatively high levels of income, this will begin to inform and shape the marketing mix decisions.

The final step in the process is that of determining positioning strategies.

Positioning strategies

Having segmented the market, and decided on the targeting strategy, the marketer must ensure that the targeted segment is reached and its needs served by designing the marketing mix so as to position it in the segment against the competition.

So, for example, if we are targeting the higher income segment of a market that is looking for high quality products, can pay premium prices, reads upmarket magazines and shops at exclusive outlets, to a large extent our marketing mix decisions are made for us. This is the advantage of determining positioning strategies, and this is why positioning, though only the final step in target marketing, is so important in planning a coordinated and integrated marketing mix.

Activity 3.3

Look out for examples of brands that are clearly targeting different market segments within the same product market, for example different soap powders, different cigarettes, different cars and so on. Take note of how they are positioning themselves in the marketplace against competition and in particular how the brands differ in terms of their marketing mix.

Exam hint

In collecting your examples of positioning of brands, it can be useful to use 'positioning maps' to illustrate the relative position of brands in a market. The use of such 'maps' to illustrate the relative position of brands in a market can also be very useful in the examination to make your points quickly and visually. An example of a simple positioning map with two brands is shown in Figure 3.1. You will note that it is only possible, of course, to show two dimensions or elements of the marketing mix.

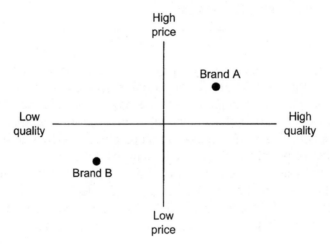

Figure 3.1 A simple positioning map

Repositioning

Sometimes marketers want to reposition their products and brands in the marketplace. There may be several reasons which lie behind the repositioning decision. For example, the current position may have become too competitive as other brands have sought to position in the same market segment. Alternatively, sometimes repositioning stems from a desire on the part of the organization to move its brands upmarket to be seen as more fashionable or higher quality and so on. Finally, repositioning may be part of a total re-branding exercise to take advantage of emerging new segments and/or changes in customer needs.

Marketing in practice: example

One of the most successful repositioning exercises in recent years has been the repositioning of the brand Lucozade.

Lucozade is essentially a glucose-based drink product. Originally it was positioned as a pick-me-up tonic for the sick person or invalid. Gradually, however, based on a planned repositioning strategy, the brand is now positioned as an energy drink targeted essentially at the young energetic person with a healthy lifestyle. This almost complete reversal of positioning has kept the brand up to date and relevant to today's market and it is now one of the most successful brands in its category. In this case, repositioning was achieved through a mixture of product and packaging redesign; sales promotion, but perhaps above all, above the line advertising and the use of influentials and celebrities in the marketing of the brand.

Extending knowledge

As we said, you should be able to gauge for yourself the extent to which you understand the processes of segmentation, targeting and positioning. If you feel it is necessary, having completed this section of the unit, you can extend your knowledge by consulting G.A. Lancaster *et al.* (2002) *Essentials of Marketing*, 4th edition, Chapter 4.

The context for the marketing mix

Planning the marketing mix, then, stems from the earlier stages and decisions in our planning process shown in Figure 2.1 with, as we have seen in this unit, targeting and positioning strategies in particular playing perhaps the key role in this respect. In addition, however, a range of what the CIM refer to as '*Contextual Factors*' in their syllabus for this subject must be considered in marketing mix decisions. According to the context, marketers will then apply the marketing mix tools and techniques in different ways. Amongst the most important contextual factors affecting marketing mix decisions are the following:

- o The product's life cycle and its stages.
- o The type of organization and its objectives, for example small and medium sized enterprises (SMEs), voluntary and not-for-profit organizations.
- o The type of customers/markets, for example FMCG markets, b2b markets, large or capital based projects, services markets.
- o Whether or not the context is purely domestic versus marketing in international markets.
- o More recently, but increasingly importantly, the extent to which we are marketing in the 'virtual marketplace'.

These, then, are the most important of the range of different contextual settings in which marketers operate and plan decisions. And it is indeed important to recognize that to a large extent, these different contextual settings will determine the appropriateness or otherwise of the different mix elements and how they are combined. The Chartered Institute are right, then, in stressing the need to understanding the context for marketing mix decisions.

Study tip

As already explained, each of the contexts above and their implications for the marketing mix are considered in detail in Unit 9.

Marketing in practice: case study

'Calling Middle England'

The importance of effective segmentation and targeting in marketing success is illustrated by the recent contrasting fortunes of two of the United Kingdom's largest retailers, Marks & Spencer (M&S) and ASDA, with regard to the clothing parts of their business.

Put simply, M&S has in recent years struggled to hold its share of sales in the UK clothing market. From a position of market dominance not too many years ago M&S has found itself struggling to hold this position against increasingly aggressive competitors. In 2004, one of the fiercest of these competitors, the supermarket chain ASDA – part of the US Walmart group – eventually superseded M&S as the United Kingdom's largest (by volume) marketer of clothing products.

Much of the success of ASDA and many of the problems of M&S in this market are accounted for by differences in the effectiveness of each company with regard to market segmentation and targeting.

As might be expected, the market for clothing products is highly segmented. Beginning with the obvious segmentation of male versus female, the clothing market then segments into a potentially bewildering myriad of sub-segments based on variables such as age, income, social class, geodemographic and life style factors. Moreover, if anything, the complexity of segmentation in this market has increased in recent years. Today, any company in this market who does not understand the different segments and their needs, will as a result, struggle to target their customers effectively and find it difficult to develop marketing mix programmes which are integrated and cohesive.

The evidence would appear to suggest that ASDA clearly understand their target customers needs when it comes to clothing and has used this to develop an effective and coherent marketing mix.

The ASDA clothing brand 'George' comprises of a range of competitively priced clothing products that appeal to customers looking for value for money clothing with style and reasonable quality. ASDA is not appealing to the highly fashion conscious clothing buyer; nor is it targeting those clothing buyers who want something very expensive or unique. Its clothing products are well made, up to date, easy-care and affordable. The products themselves are supported by very competitive pricing, effective in-store merchandising, and of course the promotion and reassurance of the George brand itself.

Above all, the marketing 'fits' the ASDA shopper profile and needs, and the marketing mix is consistent and integrated.

Marks & Spencer, on the other hand, have struggled to segment and target their customers. In order to overcome this, M&S have undertaken a number of initiatives designed to respond to the increasing fragmentation of the market. Initiative have included, for example: The introduction of more fashionable ranges designed to appeal to the more fashion conscious buyer; a range of more sporty/leisure garments targeted at customers with more active lifestyles, and ranges designed to appeal to customers looking for something 'a little bit special' and not minding having to pay a little more. But why, you might think haven't these initiatives succeeded, after all they would appear very much to reflect the underpinning concepts of market segmentation and targeting with M&S simply, and one might think rightly, responding to a new more segmented market?

In fact, although some of M&S's segmentation and targeting initiatives have been successful, many of them appear to have been less so. There may have been several reasons for this, but perhaps one of the main ones has been, that, in trying to meet the needs of so many segments, all within the same store environment. M&S have actually ended up losing sight of their 'real' target customers and their needs.

Under the stewardship of a new chief executive, M&S appear to have realized this and have vowed to return to a strategy of targeting the so-called 'Middle England' with a platform of value for money quality and style.

The real question, and the one that may determine the future of M&S then, is whether there still is a sufficiently large 'Middle England' segment out there.

Summary

In this unit you have seen that:

o The marketer must understand the range of marketing tools available for developing marketing plans.
o The main marketing tools are normally referred to as the 'marketing mix'.
o The main marketing mix elements are product, price, place, promotion, process, physical evidence, people and customer service.
o Each of these marketing mix elements in turn is comprised of several sub-elements. For example, the promotional element of the marketing mix can be sub-divided into, for example, advertising, sales promotion, sponsorship and so on.
o The marketer must combine the mix elements in such a way that they are integrated and consistent.
o Two of the most important determinants of marketing mix decisions are 'Segmentation, Targeting and Positioning' strategies and the 'Context' in which the marketing mix decisions are made.

Examination preparation: previous examination question

Previous examination question

Attempt Question 1a of the examination paper for June 2004 (Appendix 4). For Specimen Answer Examination Question 1a June 2004, see www.cim.co.uk.

Further reading and bibliography

Brassington, F. and Pettitt, S. (2003) *Principles of Marketing*, 3rd edition, FT Prentice Hall, Chapter 1, pp. 25–29, Chapter 5, Chapter 8, pp. 328–334.

Dibb, S., Simkin, L., Pride, W. and Ferrell, O.C. (2000) *Marketing Concepts and Strategies*, 4th European edition, Houghton, Mifflin, Chapters 8, 9 and 10.

Kotler, P., Armstrong, G., Saunders, J.A. and Wong, V. (1999) *Principles of Marketing*, 2nd European edition, Prentice Hall, 1999, Chapters 11 and 12.

Lancaster, G., Massingham, L. and Ashford, R. (2001) *Essentials of Marketing*, 4th edition, McGraw-Hill, 2001, Chapter 8.

unit 4
the marketing mix: product

Learning objectives

Learning outcomes

By the end of this unit you will be able to:

o Identify and describe the product element of the marketing mix.

Knowledge and skills

By the end of this unit you will be able to:

o Demonstrate awareness of products as bundles of benefits that deliver customer value and have different characteristics, features, levels (3.4).

o Explain and illustrate the product life-cycle concept and recognize its effects on marketing mix decisions (3.5).

o Explain and illustrate the principles of product policy: branding, product lines, packaging and service support (3.6).

o Explain the importance of introducing new products, and describe the processes involved in their development and launch (3.7).

Study Guide

This unit covers the first of the elements of the so-called 'marketing mix', the elements of which you were introduced to in Unit 1. Remember we stated that the marketing mix comprises those tools or ingredients, which the marketer uses to develop marketing plans and programmes. You will also recall that the original four elements of the marketing mix comprise the elements of Price, Place, Promotion and the focus of this unit, namely Product. Since first proposed by Neil Borden, these four original elements of the marketing mix have since been extended to include the further three Ps of People, Process and Physical evidence. In discussing the key elements of the marketing mix in this and the units which follow, we will obviously discuss the elements individually and in some detail. It is vital, however, for you to remember that ultimately each of the individual elements of the mix must be co-ordinated and integrated so as to provide a cohesive and balanced overall mix of the elements in marketing strategy. This is something, therefore, that we shall stress throughout our discussion of the individual mix elements.

Having noted the importance of combining and co-ordinating the marketing mix, this unit introduces what many consider to be the most critical element in the marketing mix, for without products there would be nothing to market and hence no need for other marketing mix decisions. You will consequently learn about different categories of products and the notion of the product mix. We examine the notion of products and bundles of benefits that deliver customer value together with the related notion of different levels of product, from the core product through to the potential product. One of the most vaunted and widely used concepts used in marketing is introduced in this unit, namely the so-called 'product life-cycle concept' underpinned as it is by the product adoption process. The important areas of branding and packaging in product management are considered, together with the increasingly important augmented product-level element of service support. Finally, we consider the key area of new product development explaining its importance and the processes involved.

Because of the importance and scope of product decisions this is in fact one of the longer units in the coursebook and as such we would expect you to take about 8–10 hours to work through this unit plus about the same amount of time on the exercises.

Study tip

Because of the length of this unit, it might be a good idea to tackle it in two or three study sessions.

Study tip

Much of what we have to say about product decisions in this and the subsequent unit on new products applies to both physical or tangible products and service products. Where this is not the case, or where we feel it would be appropriate to distinguish between products and services, we shall highlight this. However, for the purpose of this unit in particular we will tend to concentrate on physical products. Service products and the issues and problems they give rise to with regard to their marketing are discussed in more detail in Unit 9 where we discuss marketing in context. Let's start by having a look at what is meant by a product or service.

What is meant by a product or service?

 ## Activity 4.1

In your own words describe what you think these are in terms of customers and in terms of those who offer them to customers, then compare your answer with the one shown in the debriefing.

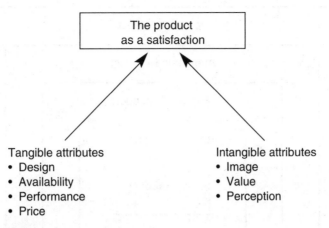

Figure 4.1 Product dimensions

Marketing people should consider this broad view of the product or service in order to present customers with satisfactions that have been identified as being appropriate to their needs. The marketing mix creates the product or service in this broader sense, and marketing efforts should be devoted to delivering something that matches defined customer needs and wants. These needs and wants are determined through the medium of marketing research.

What we have just explained relates to the product or service in its broadest context, and this is sometimes referred to as the extended product. In effect, it considers the product as all marketing effort and not merely a single physical object. Services too can be regarded as products, for example a special non-interest-bearing bank account for young persons who receive full-time education. To consumers, products or services represent need satisfactions.

 Key definition

A product – Is anything that can be offered to a market for attention, consumption, acquisition or use.

The five levels of product

In addition to considering the tangible and intangible attributes that relate to a product, it is useful for the marketer to think of the product as comprising a number of levels. These different levels are shown in Figure 4.2 and discussed below.

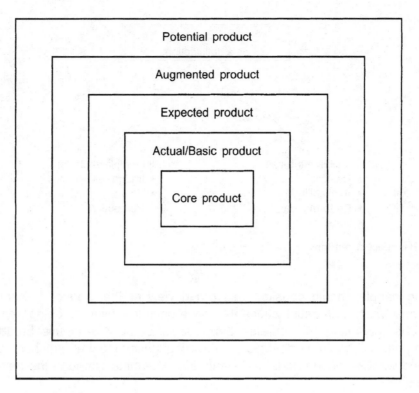

Figure 4.2 The five levels of the product

Extending knowledge

For further information on the basic anatomy of a product see, for example, F. Brassington and S. Pettitt (2003) *Principles of Marketing*, 3rd edition, Prentice Hall, Chapter 7.

Level 1 – the core product

This level of product is the most fundamental level and consists of the core benefit(s) which the product or service provides. So, for example, in the case of a car this might be, say, transport.

Level 2 – the actual or basic product

This level of product comprises the features offered in a product. It could include, for example, the design of the product, its packaging, its quality levels and so on.

Level 3 – the expected product

This level of product is a set of attributes that the buyers normally accept and agree to when they purchase the product. Clearly, where these attributes exceed the buyers' expectations we have satisfied customers, where they do not come up to the customers' expectations we have dissatisfied customers.

So, for example, when a customer purchases a car he expects it to start, accelerate, steer, stop and so on. Much less obvious, however, are the 'psychological expectations' of buyers such as expectations with regard to the extent to which a product will confer, say, status or credibility for the purchaser.

Level 4 – the augmented product

The augmented product includes those aspects or elements of a product which support the core and actual product features. So, for example, we could include customer service, delivery and credit, after-sales support and so on. In many ways, this is where a product can meet and exceed the customers' desires beyond their expectations referred to in Level 3. Today's competition mainly takes place at the augmented product level. Product augmentation requires the marketer to look at the buyers' total consumption system. On the other hand, the marketer has to realize that the product augmentation strategy will inevitably cost money, and the augmented benefits can soon become expected benefits by the customer.

Marketing in practice: example

Dell supply computer systems direct to customers. A key target market for Dell are small businesses, often operating from home. Dell have recognized that many of their target market customers are interested in a 'full package of services' involving much more than simply buying the hardware and software. Dell therefore offer customers an augmented product package of services including on-site delivery and installation, 24-hour helplines and troubleshooting services and packages of hardware and software designed specifically to meet the needs of individual customer requirements. As much as anything, Dell recognize that customers are purchasing 'peace of mind' and back-up expertise as much as the computer itself.

Many products are essentially marketed at the augmented product level. In other words, it is this level of the product, which is used to distinguish the offering from that of competitors, thereby bestowing a competitive edge. So, for example, many computer companies distinguish their product offerings on the basis of, say, the level of after-sales service including on-site and off-site warranties. It can be these aspects of the product offering which are most influential in customer choice of supplier.

Level 5 – the potential product

The fifth level of the product is the potential product, which encompasses all the augmentations and transformations that the product might ultimately undergo in the future. This level is important because it raises the possibility of future product improvements in order to keep the product competitive.

Some products have much more potential than others. For example, products which embody developing technologies where constant improvements are being made. However, all products have some further potential and the marketer must be creative in looking for and seeking to develop such further potential for products and brands.

Marketing in practice: example

One of the most successful marketers of recent years has been James Dyson with his range of household electrical products. His most successful product in this range was and still is his range of Dyson vacuum cleaners. Despite tremendous competition and against all the odds, Dyson successfully launched his new and innovative vacuum cleaner to a tremendous market reception. With its innovatory features together with skilful use of patented designs, many marketers would have rested on their laurels and not put much effort into developing a very successful product further unless and until they had to. However, Dyson's continuing success has been based on the fact that Dyson has always looked ahead to how the product might be further augmented and transformed to provide the next generation of vacuum cleaners. In doing so, Dyson has not only attracted new customers but has kept competition at bay. It is perhaps the potential of the company as much as the potential of the product with respect to ideas for how to improve the product in the future that has been the key reason for success.

Functional, physical and symbolic issues

Another useful concept in looking at the anatomy of a product is to consider the product/service portfolio from the point of view of the benefits related to functional, physical and symbolic issues.

It is important to think of products from the consumer point of view as comprising a bundle of benefits, which the customer is seeking to obtain from purchase of a product or service. So, for example, in purchasing a car the customer is seeking the benefit of convenient transport. In addition, however, the customer may also be looking for psychological benefits of status or perhaps a feeling of safety from choosing a particular model. Marketers have long known about the importance of distinguishing between features and benefits when marketing and selling products. So, for example, if we are marketing a two-speed drill for use in the home, the marketer needs to sell the benefits of, say, a wide range of possible applications and uses, which stem from this feature of having a two-speed motor. Advertising and promotion in particular need to identify and stress the benefits of the product or service rather than the features. We would go so far as to suggest that the distinction between features and benefits with regard to the product or service underpins the marketing concept and the idea of looking at the business through the eyes of the customers and their needs. We can, however, take this distinction between features and benefits of the product/service portfolio and identify the functional, physical and symbolic issues associated with benefits related to products.

The functional benefits related to the product/service portfolio relate to the core and actual product levels in our earlier discussion of the five levels of the product. As we pointed out, the product must be functional and fill the essential core needs with regard to what the customer is actually looking for when they buy the product or service. So, for example, nobody would buy a camera that did not reproduce images. Similarly, no one would buy a toothpaste, which did not care for one's teeth. It is essential, therefore, that first and foremost the product or service fulfil these functional needs.

In fulfilling functional needs, the physical attributes of the product are important. So, for example, decisions with regard to the appearance of the product, the materials it is made from and the design and packaging all need to relate to the functional benefits desired from the product. In addition to these physical attributes, however, it is important for the marketer to understand the symbolic issues of the product. Symbolic issues may derive from and be related to many aspects of the product. Ultimately, as you would expect, given the marketing concept, symbolic issues, their nature and importance derive from the perceptions and needs of the customer. Symbolic issues are essentially socially or psychologically driven. So, for example, alcoholic products such as drinks have strong symbolic connotations associated with aspects such as hedonism, excess, virility, sexual attractiveness and so on. In other words, a product is much more than its physical and functional attributes. A lot of marketing, and again particularly as evidenced in the promotional element of the marketing mix, centres on symbolic issues of the product. These symbolic issues can be linked to brand attributes in order to position products and brands in markets. The marketer needs to be aware of the symbolic connotations of products and brands and in particular needs to understand the customer's perception of these symbolic issues. Understanding of these can provide the marketer with important insights into the behaviour and perceptions of customers, which can in turn be used to develop more effective marketing programmes. These symbolic issues of the product are considered in more detail later in this unit when we turn our attention to branding.

 Activity 4.2

Consider the following products and services and then write down what you consider to be the need satisfactions to the buyers of each:

o A housewife who has ordered some made-to-measure curtains for the living room.
o A buyer for a large multiple grocery chain who has just placed a long-term order with a yoghurt producer to manufacture and supply a range of products under the grocery chain's own label.
o An 8-year-old child who has just purchased an ice cream cornet from the ice cream delivery van.
o A 17-year-old who has just purchased his first motorcycle.
o A newly married couple who have just purchased their first home.
o A couple who have just completed their weekly shop at the local supermarket.

Compare your answers with those shown in the debriefing.

Product and service classifications

Now that we know that products and services have many intangible as well as tangible attributes, we can consider products and services in identifiable groups. We can use a formal classification system whereby we can ascribe to each group a customer view of products and thereby assess why and how they might be purchased.

We can distinguish between consumer and industrial goods and services. Industrial goods and services are those purchased by manufacturers, who use them to make products and services that are in turn sold to make other products or services. Consumer goods and services are sold to the ultimate user. We shall now examine each category in turn.

Consumer goods

These goods are split into a number of categories and sub-categories.

Convenience goods – are our first category here. These are simple items whose purchase requires little effort on the part of the purchaser, for example routine items like bread, detergents, toothpaste, shampoo and so on. A primary aim of manufacturers of such goods is to attempt to predetermine the purchase decision by promoting it as a branded product, so the consumer looks for a certain brand rather than merely going for a generic (non-branded) product.

Convenience goods are further classified into *staple* and *impulse* purchases. Staple goods are those consumed by most people every day, for example fruit and vegetables, and here product differentiation tends to be minimal. Impulse purchases, on the other hand, mean that there is no preplanning in their purchase, and here supermarket displays (or merchandising) are often designed to promote such sales.

Activity 4.3

List three examples each of staple and impulse purchase convenience goods.

Shopping goods – include major durable or semi-durable items. They are generally more expensive than convenience goods and their purchase is less frequent. Much preplanning goes into their choice in terms of searching for information and price comparisons. For instance, the purchase of a new bedroom suite will call for extensive consideration of the relative merits of different bedroom suites on offer, and consumers will consider price along perhaps with credit terms, delivery arrangements and guarantees. The quality of sales staff in stores is basic to the success of marketing shopping goods. Promotional strategies aim to simplify the decision process for consumers by ensuring that they have a high level of brand awareness even before purchase planning begins.

Shopping goods can be further classified as *homogeneous* or *heterogeneous*. This rather technical terminology simply means that homogeneous goods are not really exclusive. In terms of their market appeal, they are broadly similar to each other in both their technical performance and price, examples being refrigerators and washing machines. Certain brands in this category attempt to differentiate themselves from other brands through image or technical or design superiority. Heterogeneous goods, on the other hand, tend to be non-standard, and price is often of secondary importance to the customer after image. Here behavioural factors play an important role in the purchasing decision.

Activity 4.4

List three examples each of homogeneous and heterogeneous shopping goods.

Speciality goods – are the next category, and their purchase is characterized by an extensive market search and a reluctance to accept substitutes once the purchase choice has been made. Consumers of such goods are usually prepared to pay a premium price for the prestige associated with the product or service, and it is important that companies marketing such products create and preserve the correct image. Examples of such products are expensive perfume brands, designer label clothes, expensive 'West End' type restaurants and exotic cars.

Activity 4.5

List three examples of speciality goods.

Unsought goods – are those the customer has not considered buying before being made aware of them, and the promotion of such goods is often done through the so-called 'hard sell', which has served to dent the image of marketing in general and selling in particular. Unsought goods often satisfy a genuine need that the consumer did not recognize existed, and it might be said that double glazing is sometimes an example of this in that it helps to obviate condensation and assists in insulating the home from heat loss. However, consumers rarely recognize this until they have been approached by someone selling double glazing.

Activity 4.6

List three examples of unsought goods.

Consumer services

Many products purchased these days are in the form of customer services rather than, or perhaps sometimes in addition to, physical products. The service sector of many economies has been the fastest growing sector and indeed in many economies such as the United States, most parts of Western Europe, and many parts of the Middle and Far East are now predominantly service economies. Remember, we discussed the growth of services marketing in Unit 1 when considering the wider range of applications for marketing. A key issue in services marketing is the extent to which there are any special characteristics of services (compared to their physical product counter-parts) which in turn give rise to special considerations and issues in their marketing. In fact, there are special characteristics when it comes to services and they do require different approaches with regard to their marketing because of these differences. This is of sufficient importance that these special characteristics and differences are in fact part of the Fundamentals syllabus. We shall therefore be considering the marketing of services in much more detail in Unit 9. At this stage, then, it is sufficient to introduce you to the five basic characteristics of services, which give rise to differences in their marketing. These basic characteristics are as follows.

Perishability
Unlike physical products, services cannot be stored. If, for example, a hotel room is not occupied for a night, the revenue-generating capacity of that room for the hotel owner is lost for ever.

Intangibility
Unlike physical consumer products such as, say, a computer or a battery, service products can often not be touched or even seen let alone smelled or tasted.

Variability
Sometimes also referred to as heterogeneity, this characteristic means that service products tend to be more difficult to ensure consistent and repeatable product aspects such as quality.

Services are produced and delivered by people. This makes them much more difficult to control and replicate than their physical product counterparts.

Inseparability

Associated with the people, element of services referred to above, usually service products are produced and consumed simultaneously, that is consumer and service provider are inseparable at the point of consumption. After all, it would be very difficult to have a tattoo done without the tattooist and customer being present.

Non-ownership

Again, unlike most physical products, the service customer often does not obtain ownership. After all, it would be strange to talk about 'owning' a haircut or 'owning' a hotel room, apart from of course occupying it for a few hours or days. With many service products we simply do not take them home like we do with physical products.

These characteristics and their implications for the marketing of services will be considered in more detail in Unit 9.

Industrial goods

Only certain goods within this classification are directly essential to the manufacturing process, as will be seen in the classifications that follow.

Installations – are critical and usually expensive items. They are the major items of plant and machinery required for the production of an organization's products. Their purchase is often critical to the economic well-being of the company, for it often commits the company for a long time into the future. Purchase is often the result of a very extensive search process, and although price must be viewed as important in such a decision, it is rarely the single deciding factor. Much emphasis is placed on the quality of sales support and advice, and subsequent technical support and after-sales service.

Accessories – are goods that are usually less expensive than installations, and their depreciation is normally over fewer years. Although their purchase is important, it is not as critical as for installations. Accessories include ancillary plant and machinery, office equipment and office furniture.

 Activity 4.7

List two examples of installations and two examples of accessories.

Raw materials – account for most of the time and work of a typical purchasing department. Quality, consistency of supply, service and price are important considerations here.

 Activity 4.8

List three examples of raw materials.

Component parts and materials – include replacement and maintenance items for manufacturing machinery. They should not be confused with 'accessories', because they include those products that facilitate or are essential in the manufacturing process but do not form part of the finished products. Examples are adhesives and packaging materials.

Activity 4.9

List three examples of component parts and materials.

Supplies – are sometimes called the convenience goods of industrial requirements. They include such items as office stationery and cleaning materials. Their purchase is often routine and undertaken by less than senior employees. Most supplies tend to be homogeneous in nature, and price is usually the major factor in purchasing decisions.

Activity 4.10

List three examples of supplies.

Industrial services – Like their consumer services counterparts, the market for industrial services too has grown considerably over recent years. Many companies now find that it is less expensive to employ outside agencies, with their attendant specialist expertise, than attempting to carry out these functions themselves. As long as suppliers can match the standards required by the company, this makes sense, as the company can then concentrate upon its own areas of expertise in producing and marketing its products. Maintenance and catering are examples of such specialist services. Management consultancy, which is often required on an *ad hoc* basis, is also an example of such a service. An important aspect of industrial services is the service component, which is attached to physical products. In industrial markets in particular the service component, and hence the augmented level of the product described earlier, is particularly important. Business customers often look for high levels and certainly effective levels of service such as, for example, technical support and advice, installation and maintenance, and after-sales service. They also look for high levels of service in other components of the mix including, for example, delivery. In many ways and perhaps surprisingly, industrial products are often marketed on their service-level component more than their physical attributes such as design, performance, materials and so on. Industrial services have the same special characteristics as consumer services and hence many of the considerations in their marketing are also the same.

Activity 4.11

List three examples of industrial services.

The product mix

The product mix is sometimes called the product assortment, and it consists of all the products or services that a company offers to its customers.

The three considerations under this heading are:

1. Length of product mix
2. Breadth or width of product mix
3. Depth of product mix.

Before we consider each of these headings, we should understand that consistency among different products in the product mix is a prerequisite to successful marketing. In other words, decisions upon one product should not be taken without having due regard to other products in the product assortment. For instance, it would be unlikely that Rolls-Royce Cars would consider producing a family saloon car, because of the detrimental effect this would have upon their image as producers of one of the most prestigious makers of car in the world.

Length of product mix

The length of a company's product mix is the total number of individual products or services in the entire product mix. The length can be stretched downwards or upwards (depending upon where the company's products are located in the eyes of customers in terms of being up-market or down-market) or the stretch can be in both directions (termed a two-way stretch). Such line stretching happens when the company decides to increase its present product line.

Activity 4.12

Consider why a company might engage in:

1. Downwards line stretching
2. Upwards line stretching
3. Two-way line stretching.

Breadth of product mix

The breadth or width of a company's product mix relates to the number of product lines that the company possesses. For instance, a company producing coffee might have ground coffee in one product line, instant coffee in another and coffee beans in the third.

Depth of product mix

The depth of a company's product mix refers to the number of products in each product line. In the coffee producer example, it might be that the instant coffee line consists of powdered coffee, granulated coffee, premium blend granulated coffee and Brazilian blend granulated coffee.

In considering the structures that have been described, their organization is sometimes referred to as the product manager type of structure where a product (or products) manager is in charge of a product line and a brand manager is in charge of a specific product (or brand) in that line.

However, the terms are not altogether clear because quite often the term 'product manager' is interchangeable with the term 'brand manager'. In industrial goods marketing, the term 'product manager' is more prevalent, whereas in the marketing of FMCG the term 'brand manager' is more common.

Product life cycle

This concept is based on the idea that a new product enters a life cycle once it is launched in the market. It has a birth (introduction) and a death (decline). By thinking of a product in this manner, it is possible to devise different marketing strategies for relevant stages in the product's life.

This theory is perhaps an oversimplification, because in reality very few products will fit into the theoretical curve, so there is a danger of taking the concept too literally.

Figure 4.3 shows the course of the product life cycle from the developmental pre-introduction stage to decline. A profit (and loss) curve is superimposed on this figure.

During the development phase there are of course no sales, but the product is picking up costs of development, including marketing-research costs. The introduction phase witnesses a slow growth as the product 'catches on'. Once it has caught on, sales grow rapidly and the product becomes profitable. The product then matures as the market reaches saturation. In fact, the terms 'maturity' and 'saturation' are sometimes used interchangeably, although some authors say that saturation follows maturity. This phase tends to be longer than Figure 4.3 infers. Decline is the final phase, when the product eventually drops out of the market, usually at the point when losses begin to be incurred.

The product life cycle is influenced by the nature of the product itself, changes in the macro environment, that is outside the control of the company, and changes in consumer preferences and competitive actions. These factors also influence the time span of the life cycle, which can range from a few weeks to many decades.

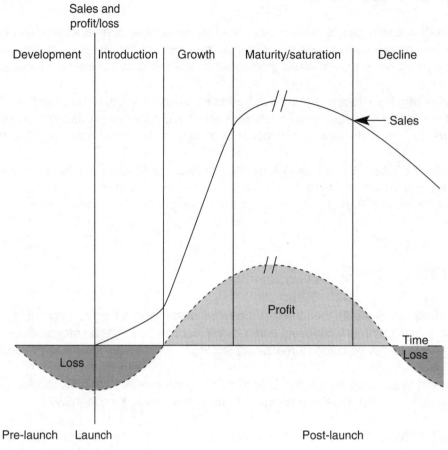

Figure 4.3 The product life cycle

Marketing in practice: example

The so-called 'WAP'-enabled mobile phones have been in the market for approximately 3 years. Although the growth in sales of these products has varied enormously in different markets around the world, in many markets, for a variety of reasons, despite a predicted (or perhaps hoped for by their marketers) massive take off in sales, in fact take up of this technology and the products based on it has been relatively slow. While all products have life cycles, they are notoriously difficult to predict.

Characteristics of the different product life-cycle stages

It can be useful to the marketer to understand the essential characteristics of each stage of the product life cycle. Kotler *et al.* (2002) has usefully summarized the characteristics of each stage and these are shown in Table 4.1.

Table 4.1 Characteristics of each product life-cycle stage

Development	Introduction	Growth	Maturity	Decline
No sales	Low sales	Rapidly rising sales	High sales	Declining sales
High cost of R&D	Negative profits	Rising profits	High profits	Declining profits
Test market	Innovator customers	Early adopters	Middle majority customers	Laggard customers
	Few competitors	More competitors	Competitors start to decline	Smaller number of competitors

Understanding these characteristics is useful because it helps the marketer to develop strategies for the different life-cycle stages. These different strategies are now discussed.

Strategies at different life-cycle stages

Development – of course takes place before the product launch and here marketing research in the form of testing out the product's acceptance takes place. Some companies attempt to ensure secrecy during this phase in order that competitors cannot pre-empt the product's launch, while others use this period as a time for informing the public that the new product is forthcoming.

Introduction – is when the new product is launched, and the goal here is to create awareness. This usually calls for a disproportionate level of marketing expenditure relative to sales revenue, and it must be regarded as an investment in the product's future. Promotion tends to be informative at this stage, and the principal aim of selling is to communicate the product's benefits to customers. Pricing is considered later, but for innovative products a skimming strategy is often employed at this stage. These pricing implications are dealt with in Unit 5. If indeed the product is innovative, then it is likely that it will be only available in a limited number of outlets at this early stage (termed 'selective distribution', which is dealt with in more detail in Unit 6).

 Activity 4.13

> Think of a new product that has not been long on the market that you feel is in the introductory phase of its product life cycle.

Growth – is where competitive products usually enter the market and there is less product distinctiveness. Rising sales generally mean more profitable returns, and company or product acquisitions sometimes feature at this stage. Promotional expenditure still features highly, but the type of promotion moves from informative advertising to advertising to achieve brand superiority. In FMCG examples, finding shelf space is important, and every effort is made to persuade retailers to stock. In non-FMCG examples, suppliers are often in competition with each other to acquire dealerships and distributive outlets. During the growth period, a company must attempt to optimize the product's price. At the end of the growth period, prices are sometimes reduced because the full effect of economies of scale can be passed on to customers. As the growth period tends towards maturity, market shares will begin to stabilize and a hierarchy of brand or market leaders will probably have emerged.

 Activity 4.14

Think of a product that you feel has passed through its introductory stage and is now in the growth phase.

Maturity – is where most products are situated, and much marketing activity is devoted to this stage. The major characteristics here are that sales continue to grow, but at a much decreased rate; attempts are made to differentiate and redifferentiate products; and there is increased brand and inventory rationalization among retailers and distributors.

Promotion tends to reinforce brand loyalty, and there is a need for sustained promotional activity, even if only to retain existing customers. Distribution strategies too are designed to retain outlets. 'Price wars' are common, and the aim of price cutting is usually to attempt to increase purchases sufficiently to offset any revenue losses.

Saturation – follows maturity, and this period sees some marginal manufacturers retiring from the market when faced with severe competition and reduced margins. As prices begin to fall in battles to retain market share, profits begin to fall correspondingly. In some cases, the major thrust of promotional effort moves away from consumers to distributive intermediaries in that maximum display at point of sale is regarded as being important to support brands, so 'below the line' activity features more strongly than 'above the line' (dealt with in detail in Unit 7). Many marketing writers do not recognize this as a separate phase and simply view it as the tail end of the maturity phase.

 Activity 4.15

Think of three products that are in the maturity or saturation phases of the product life cycle.

Decline – is where consumer preferences may have changed or innovative products may have displaced existing products. Characteristics of this period are intensified price cutting and producers deciding to abandon the market. Some firms find it worth extending the product's life cycle well into decline, while the number of competitors is falling. During this period the attention of management is likely to move from active marketing to strict cost control as the main means of maintaining profitability.

Examples of products that are at the decline stage of their life cycles, again in the context of the United Kingdom, would include cassette recorders, heated hair rollers, and black and white televisions.

Activity 4.16

Think of a product that you feel has now reached the decline stage of its product life cycle. Chart how long it has taken this product to reach the decline stage.

Applications of the product life cycle

The ability to accurately identify the transition from one stage of the product life cycle to another is a key issue for marketing management. Such prediction requires the use of marketing research and market intelligence. Once these are in place, marketing management has the basis for long-term marketing planning, with appropriate strategies duly budgeted to meet changing conditions.

Normally, an extension of the product life cycle can be found by finding new uses for the product or by finding new markets, but such extensions should not call for too many product modifications. It should also be remembered that although Figure 4.3 shows the maturity/saturation as a short continuum, in fact this period can last for months, years or decades, depending upon the nature of the product being considered.

The product life cycle and marketing mix stages

We have already considered the fact that marketing strategies and hence, by implication, the marketing mix will need to be modified in each stage of a product's life cycle. We can now consider this in a little more detail. Below is outlined in indicative terms the likely focus and thrust of the combination of the marketing mix elements in each of the stages of the product life cycle.

In the introductory stage

Spending on the promotional element of the mix will be high compared to sales. This is necessary to create awareness and interest (see Unit 7).

Within the promotional mix the emphasis will tend to be on advertising backed by special sales promotions to the trade. Selling will emphasize missionary selling.

The product element of the mix is likely to be basic, with few (if any) variations or added features.

Distribution and logistics (place) will centre on securing initial channels of distribution and ensuring that products are in stock to coincide with the launch plans.

Price may be set either to skim or to penetrate the market according to circumstances (see Unit 5).

Marketing in practice: example

In 2002, Jaguar launched their new version of the S-type Jaguar. The launch was accompanied by extensive promotional activities involving newspaper and magazine advertising, stands at leading international motor shows, and special sales promotions to the trade. Jaguar took great care to ensure that products were in stock to coincide with the launch plans and the overall objective was in creating substantial trade and customer awareness and interest.

In the growth stage

Spending on promotion will still be heavy to expand the market and strengthen competitive position.

Product quality may be improved, together with the addition of special features, styling and so on. The product mix may be widened.

The emphasis in place will be on securing new channels of distribution. If price skimming has been used in the introductory stage, prices will be reduced to bring in the next price-sensitive layer of the market.

Marketing in practice: example

Marconi PLC remains at the heart of the ever-growing global communications and IT market. Central to Marconi's strategy to remain successful in this market the company is focusing, among other things, on constantly improving product quality and features. Marconi works together with key customers to provide reliable network foundations for the core of the Internet. Close liaison with customers such as Cable and Wireless, UUNET Technologies and Level 3 Communications, Marconi offers a broad portfolio of solutions designed to facilitate further growth in the marketplace and is constantly widening its product mix.

In the maturity stage

Promotion will be aimed at trying to maintain market share. The emphasis is likely to be on sales promotions aimed at both trade and consumer. Advertising is likely to take the form of reminder advertising.

Further product modifications may take place to try to maintain sales. Further features and alternative product variations may be added.

Distribution decisions will stress the importance of ensuring that costs are kept to a minimum compatible with desired levels of customer service.

Price, although needing to be competitive, may be less price elastic owing to brand loyalty.

Marketing in practice: example

In the European package holiday destination market, Spain, one of the first countries to develop resorts and package holidays for European and particularly UK travellers, has in recent years peaked in terms of its market share. The Spanish tourist agencies and government have responded to this maturity stage of sales by improving and updating their product. Many Spanish tourist resorts have moved further up-market in quality and have developed further product modifications such as, for example, all-inclusive holidays, activity holidays and villa/self-catering as opposed to hotel holidays. Early signs indicate that through these activities linked to effective sales promotion and pricing policies, the Spanish tourist industry is managing to maintain market share during what many would argue is the maturity stage of their life cycle in the holiday market.

In the decline stage

At this stage of the product life cycle, both the total market and for many brands their market share will gradually be eroded. Those customers still buying the product will tend to be core customers that have bought the product or brand for a long time and still remain loyal. Any new customers buying at this stage will come from the laggards group of adopters, that is those who do not seek market innovation and older members of the community who tend to be behind in current developments. Competition will be intense but will gradually reduce as companies leave the market. Some competitors may attempt to regrow the market and/or capture market share by introducing product improvements or technological advances.

Promotion will tend to be reduced to minimum levels. Emphasis within the promotional mix will again tend to be on sales promotion.

Unprofitable products in the range will be phased out. Similarly, unprofitable/marginal outlets will be phased out. Price elasticity will be high, so that prices and company margins may be cut to maintain sales and dealer loyalty. Trying to maintain sales as long as possible is essential. The organization may seem to cut costs by, for example, reducing the number of product features. Price should be carefully monitored, but remember at this stage the product may be a cash cow and prices should be kept steady, if possible, so as to maximize this cash flow.

Marketing in practice: example

The Royal Mail continues to earn much of its revenue from the delivery of letters. However, for a variety of reasons, some cultural, some technological and some commercial, postage of letters between individuals and organizations has been in decline for many years now. Many argue that the art of letter writing is now dead or at least dying. Although to some extent perhaps this continuing decline is inevitable, the importance of this element of their overall business has meant that Royal Mail has, over the years, tried at least partially to stem the decline by promoting, for example, the value and enjoyment of letter writing between individuals. Notwithstanding this, and despite the fact that some will still continue to write and send letters thereby remaining core customers for this part of Royal Mail's activities, Royal Mail has sought to diversify into other activities which will help maintain its business in the future while at the same time trying to manage the decline stage of this area of their business.

Activity 4.17

Reflect on the examples of products and services in different stages of the life cycle, which we have asked you to consider so far in this unit. Try to establish the extent to which the marketing mix for these different products and services corresponds to the indicative use of the mix suggested in this unit for each stage of the life cycle.

Criticisms of the product life cycle

Needless to say, the concept of the product life cycle, particularly as a planning tool for marketers, is not without its limitations. Indeed, the concept of the product life cycle has many critics. The main criticisms of the product life cycle have been as follows:

- o The stages are not always easily defined. Identifying where one stage ends and another begins, therefore, is often difficult and dangerous in terms of basing marketing plans upon the identification of each stage.
- o As we shall see shortly, not all products go through each stage. For example, fad products such as 'cyberpets', the children's toy. We shall consider different possible shapes for the product life cycle in the next part of the unit.
- o The life cycle is not inevitable or a given, but rather strategic decisions can change the cycle. In other words, product life cycles may be a function of strategies and not the other way around. For example, the repositioning of a product can have an impact on the length of the stages.
- o The length of life cycles differs enormously and therefore makes the concept difficult to use. So, for example, the life cycle varies between different industries. In electronics, for example, life cycles are relatively short. Whereas in more traditional industries such as ship-building life cycles can be extremely long.

Product life-cycle patterns

It has been suggested that the product life cycle can take a number of shapes, depending upon the type of product or market being considered. Certain patterns are suggested in Figure 4.4.

In example (a), sales grow rapidly after the initial launch, followed by a sharp drop as the novelty wears off. Eventually, this decline will be arrested and the product will enter a relatively long period of sales stability as late adopters (see the next section on the product adoption process) purchase and early buyers purchase again and become replacement buyers. A good example of a product that has evidenced this shape of life cycle, being at the maturity stage for many years without disappearing from the market, is the 'mini' car first produced by Austin.

In example (b), we see a truncated pattern, which shows that sales grow steeply from the start. Here we find products for which there is a large market appeal and for which there is little perceived risk. A good example of a product with this truncated pattern would be the video recorder market in the United Kingdom.

Example (c) shows a rapid growth followed by a rapid decline, with little maturity. In this category, we see fad products. The 'cyberpet' was given earlier as an example of a fad-type product. And indeed many children's toys fall into this category. Having said this, some children's toys such as the Barbie doll exhibit product life-cycle patterns similar to those shown in Figure 4.4(b).

Example (d) shows a pattern with a relatively short introduction followed by rapid sales growth, a short maturity and then decline, only to be followed by a repeated process once the product goes so far down the decline curve. This type of cycle is typical for seasonal or fashion products. Skiing holidays would be a good example of this type of life-cycle pattern, or sales of Christmas cards.

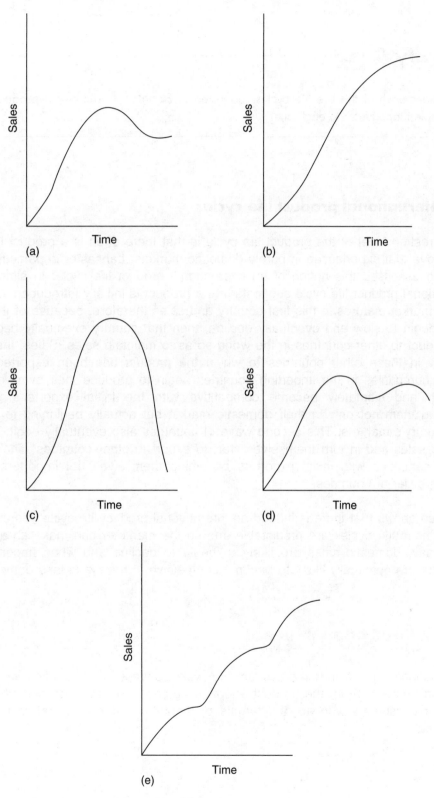

Figure 4.4 Different patterns of the product life cycle

In example (e), we see a scalloped pattern as sales pass through a number of mini life cycles. Such mini life cycles might be new adaptations of the original product that add value or represent an updating in styling. A good example of a product exhibiting this type of life-cycle shape is the market for televisions, where manufacturers and marketers are continually adapting the product with new features in order to extend the life-cycle curve.

 ## Activity 4.18

Consider each of the five life cycles suggested in Figure 4.4. Think of a product or service example that equates to each one.

The international product life cycle

An interesting facet of the product life cycle is that there often is a product life cycle over and above that experienced in purely domestic markets. Lancaster in particular has identified and assessed this notion of an international product life cycle. In simple terms, the international product life cycle suggests that a product is initially introduced in one country. As the market matures in this first country and sales therefore, because of the product life cycle, begin to slow and eventually decline, then that country eventually begins to export the product to other countries in the world so as to maintain sales. Sales, therefore, begin to grow in these other countries to which the product has been exported. Eventually, though companies in the importing countries begin to produce their own versions of the product, and ultimately become competitive with the initial exporter's products and replacing them not only in their domestic market but actually beginning to export to the first country's markets. This second wave of countries also eventually begin to experience slowing sales and in turn themselves start to export to other countries. The process then simply continues with initial exporters becoming themselves net importers in a sort of pecking order of countries.

Evidence shows that there is indeed an international product life cycle. Moreover, to some extent these life cycles are predictable and so the marketer can make an assessment of when, say, domestic sales are likely to begin to decline and when imports from other countries are eventually likely to become competitive in the marketer's domestic market.

The product adoption process

It is essential to consider the product life-cycle concept in conjunction with the product adoption process. From the product adoption process we can learn something about the users or consumers who are the targets of marketing efforts. Its nature is described in Figure 4.5.

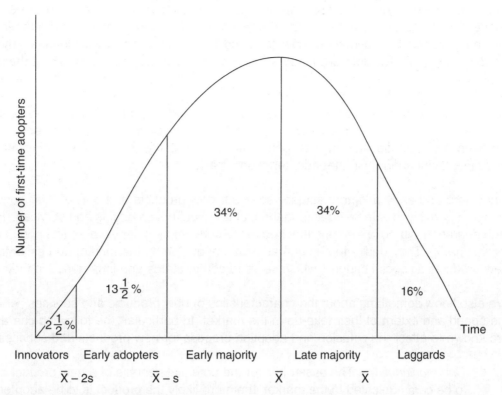

Figure 4.5 The product adoption process

The rate at which the product moves through the adoption categories is the function of a process called the diffusion of innovations. It should be specifically noted that this measure is for first-time adopters only; once the product has been purchased, successive purchases do not count in this theory. In other words, what we are looking at is the extent to which each adopter category successively influences another towards adoption. Each of the adopter categories is now discussed in turn.

Innovators are likely to be younger, better educated and relatively affluent, with a higher social status than other customers. In terms of personal characteristics they are likely to be broad-minded, receptive people, with a wide range of social relationships. Their product knowledge relies more upon their own efforts to gather objective information than on company literature or sales people.

Early adopters possess many of the characteristics of innovators, but tend to belong to more 'local' systems. Although their social relationships are less broadly based, they tend to be opinion leaders and are highly influential within their particular group. As such, they are a major target for marketers, whose aim is to have their product accepted as quickly as possible.

The *early majority* group is slightly above average in socio-economic terms. They rely heavily on the marketing effort for information and are clearly influenced by the opinion leaders of the early adopter category.

Late majority adopters are more likely to adopt innovations because those innovations have become generally accepted by previous groups. Social pressure or economic considerations are more influential in this group than innate personal characteristics.

Laggards make up the cautious group. They tend to be older, with a relatively low socio-economic status. The innovator group may be considering another newer product before laggards have entirely adopted the original innovation.

Needless to say, innovators and early adopters are extremely important to the success or failure of new products. The marketer, therefore, needs to understand who are the innovators and early adopters in a market, how to reach these categories of customers, and how to influence them. Fortunately, we actually know a lot about the characteristics of these groups of adopters.

For example, with regard to the characteristics of innovators and early adopters we know that they tend to come from higher income and socio-economic groups; that they tend to be more extrovert and cosmopolitan in their personalities and lifestyles and their behaviour involves more risk-taking than their later adopter counterparts.

Innovators and early adopters actually seek out new products and part of their consumption pleasure is involved with being among the first to try out new products and services. There is a high degree of symbolic element attached to the consumption of new products and innovations for this group. They desire to be seen as being innovators in the market and essentially wear new products as social badges, which serve to confer status and importance in their eyes.

We also know something about the characteristics of new products and services, which affect the speed and extent of their take-up in the market. In particular, the following characteristics are known to affect the diffusion and adoption process for new products and services.

- o *Communicability* – The easier it is for the potential benefits of a new product or service to be communicated to the market, the more likely the product is to be adopted. So, for example, if a new product can be shown to, say, reduce costs to the customer substantially, and where these cost savings can be readily communicated and understood, then the quicker and more extensive would be the acceptance of the new product. With many products, however, the potential benefits are sometimes difficult to communicate to the customer because, for example, they are technical in nature or perhaps they provide entirely new benefits which the customer therefore has to be educated about. In some respects, the relatively slow take-up of DVD products so far in the United Kingdom is partly because of the difficulties of communicating the relative benefits of this new technology.
- o *Trialability* – The easier it is for a customer to try a new product either on a limited basis and/or before making a major commitment to purchase, again the more likely that product is to be adopted. Adopting a new product or service after all can represent a substantial risk to a customer. So, for example, the customer risks whether the product will be satisfactory or not, or perhaps whether the new supplier will continue to be in business and so on. Anything the marketer can do, therefore, to reduce such perceived risks by making it easier to trial the product before making a purchase or long-term commitment is likely to help adoption. Allowing customers to use a vehicle through an extended test drive period when launching a new car is an example of making it easier to trial a product. Similarly, the use of samples through, say, direct mail shots is another good way for the marketer to make it easier for the customer to try out a new product.
- o *Relative advantage* – Remember that customers are buying benefits when they purchase products or services. In the case of encouraging the adoption of new products, the marketer must ensure that the target market understands and appreciates the relative advantages of the new product compared to existing/established products available in the market. Remember there is a risk element for the consumer with regard to adopting new products, therefore the consumer must feel, or rather the marketer must be able to persuade the customer to feel, that the relative advantages offered by the new product are enough to overcome these risks and the inbuilt inertia which is normal for customers. We know therefore that new products which only offer marginal extra advantages to customers and certainly those which are essentially 'me too' products which offer no advantages are unlikely to be adopted.

Activity 4.19

Consider the 'home personal computer'. Analyse how this product has spread through a market with which you are familiar and the different groups of consumers who have adopted it at varying stages of diffusion.

Activity 4.20

Consider Figures 4.3 (The product life cycle) and 4.5 (The product adoption process). They are quite similar in shape. Do you feel that there is a relationship between the two?

As marketers, we are also interested in consumer behaviour as it relates to new products. Figure 4.6 shows a sequential model of the adoption process for an innovative new product. We shall use this model again in Unit 7 when we look at promotion tools. First, let us consider the elements of the model and its relationship to the product life cycle.

Figure 4.6 The adoption process

It is the task of the marketer to create awareness and then to guide the consumer through subsequent stages of the process. Without awareness, consumers cannot even begin to consider it as a solution to need-related problems. To be worthwhile, innovative products should always be problem-solving in nature as far as the consumer is concerned.

Awareness (Figure 4.6) can come about by word of mouth communication or from the marketing efforts of the company. The individual is exposed to the innovation and becomes aware of its existence.

Interest is aroused and information will be sought.

At the *evaluation* stage, the consumer weighs the relative advantages of the new product against those of existing products and perhaps against directly competing products if these have been launched.

115

The consumer decides to make a trial through a test run or by purchasing a small amount. For this reason many new FMCG products are sold initially in 'trial sizes' or are distributed as free samples. If a trial cannot be made, the likelihood of adoption will decrease.

At the *adoption* stage, the consumer decides whether or not to adopt, that is begin to buy and use, the product on a regular basis.

Post-adoption confirmation comes when the product has been adopted and the consumer is seeking assurance and reassurance (unconsciously) that a sensible decision has been made. New information has been accepted and prior information has been rejected. Often, after an important purchase, a phenomenon called 'post-purchase dissonance' is present; this is a feeling of unease that the goods purchased may not represent good value. The product itself may be perfectly acceptable, yet the consumer may feel that the purchase was not as good as it could have been. Despite these uneasy feelings, consumers frequently rationalize and reinforce their purchase decisions and will not voice dissatisfaction and thus appear poor judges to their peer-group colleagues. With this in mind, companies should attach as much importance to after-sales service and general customer care as they do to making the sale in the first place.

Activity 4.21

Think of a major product you have purchased. Remember how you purchased this product and the formal and informal information sources you consulted. Now try to match your various stages of purchasing behaviour to the elements of the adoption process in Figure 4.6. Did you have any feeling of post-purchase dissonance afterwards?

Packaging

It is open to discussion whether packaging should come under the product heading or under promotion. That it is an inseparable sub-component of the marketing mix is without doubt. If it is viewed in terms of product protection, then it is considered as part of the product, but if it forms part of a product's display on, say, the shelves of a supermarket, then its function must be regarded as coming under promotion.

It is increasingly recognized that packaging has now become so important in competitive marketing and customer choice that it is often referred to as being the fifth 'P' of the marketing mix. There is no doubt that recently packaging has become a very effective and potent marketing tool, especially as an increasing number of products are sold on a self-selection basis at supermarkets. We have also seen the growth of the so-called 'copy cat' packaging where, often, unscrupulous companies attempt to mislead customers by making their packaging similar to the market leaders.

The first consideration under packaging is 'outers' or outer containers. Industrial products are usually packed in plain simple boxes, principally for protection while the goods are in transit. However, for consumer products, outers can sometimes form part of a product's display, especially when it is sold in small shops or other convenience outlets. The example of potato crisps comes to mind here, where the outer has a serrated round hole. The retailer presses the serration through and sells individual packets of crisps from the bulk box.

For consumer goods in particular, the package around the goods themselves forms part of the communications process. This is most important for goods that are sold in self-service outlets.

Here the goods themselves must form part of the selling process, and if the goods in the package are not prone to attractive display, for example canned foodstuffs, then the package must attempt to 'sell' the goods. Sometimes the packaging is referred to as the 'silent salesman' in this respect. A fuller discussion upon the implications of this is found in Unit 7, which deals with promotion.

Exam hint

Remember, the examiners will often ask for, and will almost certainly be looking for even where they do not specify, the use of relevant examples to show that you understand and can apply the fundamentals of marketing. In the case of packaging, it is relatively easy to collect examples for potential use in the examination in the process of your everyday shopping and consumption behaviour. This is because packaging is so easy to observe and experience. Keep your eyes open, then, for examples of new/innovative packaging. In particular, look out for packaging which you feel is particularly good and which is particularly bad. In terms of good packaging, you are looking for packaging which, for example, makes the product stand out, easy to handle and use, or has some other consumer benefits such as storage, reuse and so on. In terms of bad packaging, you are looking for packaging which, for example, does not stand out, is not easy to handle and use, or is in some other way inconvenient or dysfunctional.

The principal considerations under the heading of packaging are:

- Size and range of sizes.
- Protection and preservation.
- Convenience for the customer.
- Information in terms of instructions for use or contents.
- The relationship between packaging (it is sometimes termed the 'silent salesperson') and promotion.
- Ease of handling for the intermediary.
- Innovation opportunities.

 ## Activity 4.22

Think of an industrial product. Consider the functions of packaging in relation to this example. Then think of a non-food consumer product and consider again the functions of its packaging. Finally, think of a processed food item for sale in a typical supermarket and consider its packaging functions.

Developments in packaging design

Packaging has in recent years been one of the most innovative areas of marketing. The development of new packaging materials and new packaging technologies have added considerably to the armoury of tools with respect to the marketer's decisions in the use of packaging design. For example, toothpaste packaging is now much more user-friendly than it was only a few years ago. Cans are much easier to open with their ring-pull designs than their potentially dangerous can opener predecessors. In addition to these technical changes in packaging, packaging has also been one of the areas which has felt the greatest effects of an increasing concern with the environment and 'green issues'. Packaging is increasingly recyclable. Indeed in some countries there are very stringent regulations indeed concerning this aspect of packaging. In Germany, for example, all packaging must be recyclable and there are substantial fines for it not being so. Related to this, there is a movement towards 'less being more' in packaging. Consumers do not want to feel they are paying excessive amounts for packaging apart from, for example, where it is desired for, say, gift giving purposes and so on.

International aspects of packaging

Perhaps surprisingly, packaging is one of the elements of the product where there are substantial implications with regard to marketing products in different parts of the world.

In some countries, for example, there are very stringent regulations concerning packaging design. In Germany, for example, even though it is part of the European Union (EU), regulations relating to the recyclability of packaging are much more stringent than in other parts of the EU. In some parts of the world, the package in which a product arrives is as valuable to the user as what the package contains. Tins, cardboard boxes, plastic bottles, glass jars are all examples of packing which can serve an important secondary use in some countries. Clearly, such secondary uses are often not the major concern and responsibility of the marketer of the original product, but the marketer should not neglect what can be important cultural differences with regard to the secondary uses of packaging. Finally, the marketer needs to consider that in many parts of the world certainly expensive and luxury packaging which would be the order of the day in many developed economies is simply not affordable, even though there may be a substantial demand for the product contained in such packaging.

Branding

It is a moot point whether branding and brand management is part of the product or promotional element of the mix. In fact, it is both. As we shall see, brands perform a strong communication role in marketing and are often supported by heavy spends on promotion. Most, however, consider branding to be part of the product management element of the marketing mix and so we shall consider the importance of the brand and the elements of managing brands in this unit.

Irrespective of where in the mix we think branding lies, there is little doubt that building and managing successful brands is one of the most important areas and issues in contemporary marketing. There are many reasons for this but among some of the most important are the following:

o Brands represent one of the most important and powerful of ways for a company to create and maintain a differential advantage.
o Brands represent ease of choice and psychological comfort for consumers.
o Related to the above, prestigious brands confer status and legitimacy for some consumers.
o Successful brands are a major company asset not only in marketing but in financial terms.
o Successful brands give the marketer substantial power and leverage when dealing with intermediaries with regard to, for example, securing shelf space.

Together, these factors have made brands and brand management one of the hottest issues in marketing over the decade of the 1990s and if anything, this trend is set to continue with an even greater momentum during the first decade of the new millennium. But what are some of the key issues in the brand area of product management, and in particular what makes for successful management of this element of the product? First, we need to establish what a brand is.

What is a brand?

In its most prosaic sense a brand, or perhaps more accurately branding, is an approach to distinguishing one supplier's product(s) from another supplier's product(s) in the marketplace. This is best illustrated by the fact that one of the decisions regarding building and managing brands relates to the basis of such distinctions. Again, in its simplest sense a brand is often distinguished through its name. So, for example, in the cola market we have of course Coca-Cola, Pepsi-Cola, Virgin Cola and so on. In addition, or alternatively, brands may be distinguished through, for example, their appearance such as, say, their packaging. Finally a brand may be distinguished through, for example, its image which in turn may comprise of a combination of factors including design, after-sales service, company reputation and so on. Certainly, brands are often and usually physically distinguished from their competitor brand counterparts, but actually a brand is much more than simply the physical characteristics of a product. In essence, a brand represents a product which has a set of values that meet certain of the customer's psychological needs leading to a perception of added values and feelings of confidence on the part of customers. It is these added values and the psychological and perceptual effects they have on customer choice that constitute the essence of what a brand is.

The importance of brands in customer choice

It is now recognized that in many markets, and not just as initially felt in the market for FMCG, brands and brand values are among the most important influences on buying decisions and customer choice. There are many reasons for this, but Peter Doyle has suggested the following are among two of the major reasons.

First, Doyle believes that in markets now characterized by a wealth of alternative offerings, the task of choosing between competing products has simply become too difficult, time-consuming and expensive for most buyers. In addition, the customer is subjected to an enormous variety of competing claims and advertising and selling messages. Reputable brands allow the customer to choose with confidence and reduce the risks, therefore, associated with choice and the complexities thereof.

The second reason according to Doyle, we have already touched on, is that brands are strongly associated with, and bought, for emotional, psychological and status reasons as well as function. It is in fact the brand and the brand image which conveys as much functionality, in a psychological sense, as the product itself. Most colas refresh so why is Coca-Cola the world's leading brand in this market? Most watches tell the time accurately so why do some choose a Rolex or a Tag Hauer? As we have moved into the twenty-first century, of course, these psychological and emotional reasons associated with brand values reflect the fact that in many societies consumers have moved from merely buying products and services to fulfil basic physical needs and requirements to buying products to satisfy higher needs such as self-actualization and esteem.

We can see, then, the importance and relevance of branding in customer choice and company success, but what are the elements of developing and managing successful brands and in particular what are some of the key decisions that the marketer must consider?

Elements of branding and brand management

Among the major elements of branding and brand management decisions are the following:

○ *Branding versus no branding* – Perhaps an obvious decision but the marketer must decide whether or not to brand the organization's products and services. The alternative is to market products unbranded and therefore essentially as commodity items. As you would expect from our discussion above, increasingly marketers are opting to brand their products hoping to build better value and hence stronger market positions. However, some products are difficult to brand in the sense of being difficult to distinguish in any way from their competitive counterparts. Examples would include many raw materials, industrial commodities and so on. Even here, however, an element of branding can be introduced through developing a corporate approach to branding establishing a corporate image. Some marketers, of course, do not brand their own products but rather leave the branding element to their distributors. So, for example, in many markets we have retailer brands as opposed to company brands.

○ *Brand names* – If a marketer decides that branding is the best option, then brand names must be selected. Brand naming is in fact a quite surprisingly complex and technical area of brand management. There are, for example, legal issues to be considered with regard to ensuring that no other manufacturers' brand names are infringed; there are language problems and issues when it comes to international marketing; and finally, related to language issues there can be cultural issues associated with the choice of brand names. Although some of the mistakes made by brand namers in the past are potentially amusing or perhaps insulting depending on one's view, such as the Slovakian pasta brand 'Kuk & Fuk', for the marketer such brand naming mistakes are horrendous. In choosing a brand name, ideally, the name should have the following characteristics:

  – It should be distinctive
  – It should be legal
  – It should be protectable
  – It should be user-friendly
  – It should match the desired image of the company and the positioning of the brand.

When it comes to naming, there are also strategic aspects to consider. In particular, the extent to which individual as opposed to company branding will be used. So, for example, some organizations rely principally on company's brand name establishing this as the dominant brand identity across the range of their products. Examples would include Heinz and Mercedes Benz. At the other extreme, companies such as Unilever and Proctor & Gamble prefer a strategy of individual brand names and identities for each of their products. Other companies adopt a middle-ground approach either using both company and individual brands such as, for example, Kelloggs, or using range branding where groups of products, for example product lines, are marketed under their own brand family names.

Marketing in practice: example

'What's in a name?'

As the importance of brands and branding as a key element in effective marketing has been recognized, more and more companies are paying careful attention to the names they give to their companies and individual brands. Brand naming is now big business and is taken seriously by most companies. An indication of how seriously companies now take the naming of their companies and brands is the amount of time and money that companies often spend nowadays on renaming long-established brands. Because, in the past, brand names have often been decided on quite straightforward bases such as a combination of the founders' names, for example Mattel, or perhaps on the basis of the functional attributes of the product or service such as Duracell, often not much thought has been given to the actual name so long as it is pronounceable, distinctive, and not protected, that is belonging to someone else. Clearly, because of this, many companies arrive at a point where they feel that the brand names originally given to their companies or products are no longer appropriate. Over the past 2 or 3 years, then, there has been a spate of companies changing brand names, sometimes at substantial cost and nearly always at substantial risk.

Examples of companies who have made changes to corporate and brand names in recent years include, for example, the Post Office with its change to 'Consignia'; Ciba-Geigy/Sandos with the change of its name to 'Novartis'; BT Cellnet changing its mobile phone brand name to O_2 and Guinness and Grand Metropolitan post-merger selecting the name 'Diageo'. As already mentioned, changes to corporate and brand names such as these examples often involve considerable expenditure. Changing company and brand names often entails considerable design changes to reflect the new brand or corporate identity. Company livery, company logos, company promotional material and even employee uniforms may be changed. In addition, of course, establishing the new brand name can involve the need for substantial marketing and promotional expenditures. By far the greatest potential issue, however, with changing a long-established brand or corporate name is how the market or more specifically customers will react. In the case of long-established corporate and brand names, often customers will have strong feelings and even affections for the old brand name even if sometimes these affections emerge when the old brand name is ditched. Ditching the old corporate or brand names in this situation can give rise to considerable hostility and antagonism on the part of customers towards the company and its new brand names. In many cases, a brand or corporate name is often associated with perceptions of the very heritage and core values of the company, at least so far as the customer is concerned. Although it is only a name, changes to corporate and brand names can result in customers abandoning the company and its brands particularly if in the past they have been brand loyal. A good example of this is that, given earlier, of the Post Office changing its name to 'Consignia' in 2001. This caused such an adverse reaction from customers that eventually, despite substantial outlays in the new brand name, and company executives being wheeled out to defend and explain the change, the company had to admit that it had made a mistake and reverted to its original Post Office brand. Obviously, then, brand names are more than just a name. As already mentioned, corporate and brand names become synonymous with brand values and customers derive considerable meaning and assurance from strong brand names. Considerable care and research therefore should be given to any proposed changes in corporate and brand names. The company should consider how customers will respond to any proposed changes and to ensure that any new names should be congruent with the company's brand values. Obviously, sometimes companies should change their corporate or brand names perhaps to reflect new values or changes in direction. For example, a company may want to distance itself from its previous heritage or as in the case of Diageo, may want to signal the formation of a new company formed as in this case through merger. Under no circumstances, however, should corporate or brand names be changed simply or on a whim, or just for the sake of it.

There is no doubt that an effectively researched, planned implemented change to a corporate or brand name such as that of the recent name change of the industrial arm of the De Beers Diamond group Debid to the new name 'Element 6' can be extremely successful but great care needs to be taken in what appears to be 'simply a change of name'.

In conclusion, what's in a name? – Everything.

Establishing and supporting successful brands

Although decisions regarding whether or not to brand, naming brands and generic or individual naming brand strategies are important, perhaps the most important element of branding and brand management is how to establish, build and support successful brands. Needless to say, this is not an easy process and will often require considerable skill, investment and patience on the part of the marketer. The following, however, are some of the key steps in building and supporting successful brands.

- ○ Establish target market and customer needs with respect to what constitutes important aspects of brand choice and values.
- ○ Determine the brand values to be established in relation to these needs and considering competitor offerings and brand perceptions.
- ○ Position brands so as to occupy important value positions in the market with regard to customer needs and perceptions which can be defended.
- ○ Ensure that brand values are communicated to customers.
- ○ Ensure that brand values are supported over time.
- ○ Monitor changes in company and competitor brand positions and update brands as appropriate.

As already mentioned, it is not easy to build successful brands from scratch. Many of the market-leading brands today have taken many years to develop to this position. Moreover, the often dominant position of the leading brands in a marketplace can make it very difficult and often impossible to displace them. This may seem surprising given our earlier discussion of the product life cycle in this unit. After all, the life-cycle concept seems to suggest that brands in particular have finite lives. In fact, the lesson here is that the effective marketer can, through careful attention to revitalizing, repositioning and rationalizing brands keep even the longest established brands fresh and exciting.

 ## Activity 4.23

> Try to find a good example of a brand which has been long established and yet is still successful in today's marketplace. In what ways have the marketers of this brand maintained its successful position in its market.

Service support

Alongside branding, perhaps the other major emerging issue with regard to consumer choice has been that of the service support element of the product part of the marketing mix. In some ways, in fact, many of the reasons for the emergence of brands as an important element in customer choice also underpin the growth in importance of service support. As with branding, customers are now looking for more than simply basic functional products to satisfy their needs and requirements. They are looking for value in the product over and above its basic functional performance. They are looking then for additional elements of back-up and service from the marketer which add value to the product and generate higher levels of customer satisfaction, generating brand loyalty and leading to long-term relationships with customers.

Service support, of course, lies at the augmented, and to some extent potential, levels of the product outlined earlier in this unit. Some products of course comprise services only, but even here additional levels of service support over and above that of, say, competitors can be a primary reason for customer choice and loyalty. The marketer therefore must consider whether or not to offer additional levels of service support, what these service support elements will comprise of and how to distinguish service support offerings from competitors.

Service support can be provided in a number of ways. Examples would include:

o Technical support
o Marketing support (e.g. in the case of supplying to intermediaries)
o After-sales support.

Within these general approaches to offering service support there are any number of specific examples of ways in which product support can be provided. So, for example, technical support can be offered through technical sales support staff or through perhaps a telephone enquiry service. Marketing support can be provided through, for example, promotional tools or perhaps even through financial support systems such as the provision of credit facilities to customers. Finally, after-sales support again can be provided through, say, customer helplines or even through support systems such as return and exchange policies.

Service support, then, is an important element in customer choice in contemporary markets. We shall return to service support in our Unit 8 when we consider the role of people, customer care and service as an element of the marketing mix in its own right.

The importance of new product development

Activity 4.24

Think about the product concepts and tools you have covered already. Consider how useful these are in planning marketing activity:

o In the short tactical term (say 3 months)
o In the longer strategic term (say 1 year or more).

Although, as we have seen, it is possible to extend the life cycle of products, the very concept of the life cycle suggests that eventually many products will mature and decline. Innovation through new product development, therefore, is important to the survival of an organization. There are many examples of organizations that have suffered by not keeping up with the times. With new technological advances changing the way we live and the sophistication of consumer requirements, products can quickly become obsolete and services can become unnecessary. Recent examples of these include Betamax videos and 45-rpm records.

As a company's products progress along the life cycle, it is important that new products are developed to keep the company profitable.

As already stated, then, new products are the key to a company's survival, but this is probably the most risk-laden area of a company's activity. Not only can large sums of money be lost, but product failure can also damage a company's reputation. Needless to say, the prime objective of new product development strategy is to launch a successful product, but it is also essential that any strategy is also designed to reduce risk throughout the stages of development.

In consumer markets, new products appear on a regular basis.

Activity 4.25

Think of four new consumer products that have appeared over the last 12 months.

Exam hint

The fact that you have developed these examples here will help you to remember them in the examination. Remember that examiners like to see real examples quoted in examination answers, as it demonstrates that you can apply what you are writing about through a practical illustration. There are a number of definitions for various types of new products or services.

Innovative products

Innovative products are by definition new to the market. They provide completely different alternatives to existing products in existing markets. To a certain extent 'technological break-throughs' are less common now than, say, when the first television was developed. Nowadays it tends to be more a matter of refinement of existing products. However, in the field of medicine and the development of drugs, breakthrough products still appear from time to time.

Marketing in practice: example

One of the best examples in recent years of an entirely new product is the drug 'Viagra' developed by the Pfizer company. Originally developed with a view to treat heart and blood-pressure problems, Viagra was found to be effective in the treatment of patients with erectile dysfunction. There was simply no other product like this on the market and within a few months of its launch it had accumulated substantial sales throughout the world. Protected as it is through patents, there is no doubt, however, that this will be the first of ultimately a generation of products of this type in the marketplace.

Replacement products

Replacement products are new to consumers, but replace existing products rather than providing a total innovation. This type of product is more common nowadays because research teams tend to be commissioned to work upon product refinements rather than upon 'blockbuster' innovations. Even the digital audio tape (DAT) is a replacement product, although its development could be regarded as a breakthrough.

Imitative products

Imitative products is the category in which most new products fall. Once a firm has successfully launched an innovative or replacement product or service, others will follow. They are sometimes termed 'me too' products. Not all companies have the resources to develop new product ideas and they are happy to let others complete costly market development before launching their new product. If the innovative company is able to secure some kind of patent or copyright, then imitators will have to seek permission from the innovator before they can copy the product or idea. This is known as licensing. However, not all innovations are patentable and new products will quickly find imitators.

Relaunched products

Relaunched products are the final category, and this is where a product can be successfully relaunched via a different marketing strategy (perhaps by changing the emphasis of the product benefits). It is then categorized as a new product even though its physical characteristics may not have substantially altered.

Key definition

New product – Is anything that customers perceive to be new in terms of features of the product, its packaging or appearance, its uses or its benefits.

Activity 4.26

Think of a product that fits each of the categories just described.

For new product development to be successful, it should be managed effectively. In practice, there are a number of ways in which this is done.

Product managers

Product managers emerge where a company assigns the task of new product development to product (or brand) managers. This has already been discussed in Unit 3, but the problem is that such people are normally so taken up managing their existing products that they do not have the inclination to produce more than simple modifications to the brands under their control.

New product managers

New product managers report to a senior product manager. This is perhaps a better method than the first one, but the problem, again, is that such managers tend to relate more to line extensions and modifications of products than to totally new products.

New product committees

New product committees exist in most large companies. They change in terms of their membership structure and meet on an *ad hoc* basis. Their function is to review new product ideas and approve or reject them.

New product departments

New product departments exist in some large companies, usually under a manager who has authority across other line managers. The function of such departments is to generate and screen new ideas and to work with the research and development department through to conducting final product testing and commercialization. Sometimes individuals who work on specific products and see them through from inception to implementation are called 'product champions'.

New product venture teams

Such teams are brought together from a number of different parts of an organization's operations. They tend to be found in large, high-technology, multinational companies. Their sole responsibility is to develop a specific product or business within a predetermined time and budget allocation.

Marketing in practice: example

Both 3M – Minnesota, Mining and Manufacturing – and the Dupont company have made use of venture teams in their new product development programmes. Dupont, for example, use venture teams to take new products from concept to commercialization and launch. In the past, members of Dupont's venture teams have been allowed to invest in the new products they have been developing, the idea being to increase commitment and motivation to successful development and launch. Both of these organizations have open and flexible approaches to new product development seeking to foster an environment of creativity and entrepreneurism. As a result, both companies are acknowledged as successful innovators with new products as diverse as 'Post-it notes' and 'Teflon'.

The process of new product development

The product or service is of course central to all marketing activity. Without it no other marketing activity would take place. The sale of the product or service provides revenue, and it is the medium through which a company fulfils the marketing concept. It is therefore essential that any new product development programme should be conducted in a professional manner.

The first attempt at formalizing a theory about the process of product development was done by the American firm of management consultants, Booz, Allen and Hamilton. In 1968, after they had conducted a study, they concluded that it took 58 new product ideas to produce one successful product. They repeated the study in 1981 and found that companies had in general found out how to handle the product prescreening and planning processes more effectively, because it was found that it then took only seven new product ideas to produce a successful product.

From their findings we now have a generalized formal product development programme that incorporates a number of stages. Not all stages will be relevant for all products, but as a general guide it is useful (Figure 4.7).

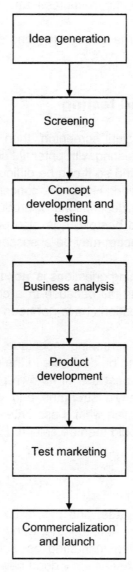

Figure 4.7 Stages in new product development

Idea generation

Idea generation can spring from formal research and development departments, or from production departments, which might see ways of modifying and improving the product. Marketing is of course important as a source of ideas through the marketing research process and indeed from the company's sales people, who are in constant touch with the marketplace.

It is the task of senior management to create an idea-oriented environment in the company and create a climate that encourages the generation of new product ideas.

Screening

Screening is meant to reduce the pool of ideas to a manageable number through the identification of the most potentially worthwhile ideas, and a number of questions must be answered:

- Is there a real consumer need?
- Does the company have the resources and technical competence to market and manufacture the product?
- Is the potential market large enough to generate profits that correspond to what the company expects?

Concept development and testing

If the product idea passes the initial screening, then the company can begin to refine and develop the product concept for testing with potential consumers. At this stage, the product or service will still be only an idea and so it can be difficult, particularly with service products, to assess possible customer reaction. However, concept testing is now well developed and refined. It is possible to produce descriptions of products indicating what the product is and the central benefits that it would bestow. It is also possible to use pictorial descriptions of physical products so that the concept may be assessed.

If the answer to any of the screening questions is 'no', then no further work need to be done. It is a fact that many new products fail because in a company's enthusiasm to develop such products, these very obvious questions have not been asked.

In order to develop an effective screening technique, the company must isolate a series of factors that research has shown to be desirable in the marketplace. The firm should of course develop products that make the best use of its own production and marketing strengths. An internal appraisal of the company's strengths and weaknesses, together with input from marketing research, should establish what these criteria should be. Products that best satisfy the various screening criteria should then be selected for further development.

Business analysis

'Business analysis' is the next stage, and this is concerned with financial rather than with practical matters. Demand is estimated, together with costs and profitability. All costs should be taken into account here, including marketing as well as costs of production. It is at this pragmatic stage that a number of seemingly good new product ideas are discarded.

Product development

'Product development' is the stage when costs can rise phenomenally. Up to now, time and energy will have been expended perhaps commissioning a market-research survey, but these are likely to be small by comparison with this stage. By this stage the company should have tried to minimize the risk and isolate potentially valuable new product ideas. During this product development stage the company develops a prototype product in order to confirm its potential. Once this is satisfactory, the company must again turn to the marketplace to obtain feedback on the product's suitability in terms of performance and customer attitude. Prototypes should correspond as closely as possible to the envisaged production model so as to obtain accurate customer reaction.

At this stage, it is now a matter of 'fine-tuning'. It is also an opportunity to abandon the product if market reaction is negative. It is important that correct decisions are taken now, because, although it may be frustrating and appear wasteful to abandon a product at this stage, the costs and potential damage to the company's reputation will be greater if the product is launched and subsequently fails.

If this stage is successful, the firm should then have the confidence to go ahead with the product launch. This decision is critical and requires considerable business analytical skills, because if full-scale production is undertaken, then costs of setting up production facilities will greatly add to the final cost. Many companies go to this final full-scale production phase, depending upon the nature of the product to be marketed. Many FMCG go through the next screening process.

Test marketing

Test marketing is the final check on whether or not the new product can be marketed appropriately. When a company enters a test market, it is fairly well committed to launching the product, and the test's real purpose is to look at the product's appropriateness in a geographically controlled situation. The objective of a test market is to investigate the appropriateness of proposed marketing strategy and tactics, to refine them, and then predict the effects of such strategies in terms of market potential.

In the United Kingdom, test marketing is made a little easier by the existence of independent television areas that divide the United Kingdom conveniently into well-defined regions that can be used as test market areas. They are appropriate when television advertising is a component of marketing strategy. In other parts of the world there are not such discrete independent television areas with well-defined regions and hence test marketing in other countries can be more difficult with respect to the selection of test areas. The chosen area for a test market should be as closely representative of the final total market as possible, and if this was not to be the case, the whole objective of testing would be lost. Sometimes companies run two test markets at the same time, which offer opportunities for experimentation by varying the marketing mix in the two markets simultaneously to try to find the best balance within an optimum budget.

Test marketing is obviously an attempt to establish whether or not a new product is viable. For this reason, test marketing is principally used to gauge the response to a proposed new product, and in particular to try to forecast potential sales and profits. However, test marketing can be used to specifically assess a particular part of a proposed or amended element of the marketing mix such as new or improved packaging, different pricing levels, special promotional deals and so on.

In industrial markets, where the number of customers might be quite small, testing can be done by initially marketing to a few cooperating customers, who will provide feedback before full-scale production is commenced. This is more correctly termed a 'product placement test'.

Marketing in practice: example

Using product placement to evaluate new products is becoming increasingly popular. It is recognized that a lot of test marketing has in the past been unrealistic and hence potentially misleading with regard to reflecting real-life reactions to new products and, particularly, customer attitudes to a new product when it is purchased and consumed in the normal context in which a customer would consume or use the brand. When Red Bull, the energy drink, was being market tested in the United Kingdom it was felt to be important to evaluate consumer reactions to the product by analysing how customers used and responded to the product in 'normal drinking situations'. Testing, for example, was therefore carried out using friends in bars to try to create an atmosphere similar to one in which this type of product would normally be consumed.

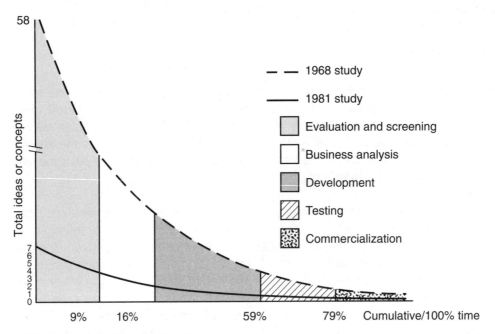

Figure 4.8 Decay rate of new product ideas

It has been known for competitive companies to attempt to 'sabotage' a test marketing programme by creating artificial conditions in the test area for the duration of the test, for example they might conduct an intensive promotional programme of their own with a view to depressing sales of the product being test marketed. For this reason, test markets should be as unobtrusive as possible, which is why many FMCG manufacturers confine their activities to test towns rather than television areas. Such towns are in concentrated areas of population, with their own newspaper, and tend to be separated geographically from other urban conurbations.

Commercialization and launch

Commercialization is the final stage, where many ideas have been filtered out and a viable proposition has been selected. Production, financial and other commercial criteria have been examined and a suitable product, acceptable to the marketplace, is ready to be launched. Even after all the preceding stages, success cannot be guaranteed at this stage, and a facet of the earlier Booz, Allen and Hamilton study found that even at this juncture only one in two products would be successful. All that can be said is that with a sequential examination of the criteria just described, then the risk of ultimate product failure is reduced.

Figure 4.8 describes the decay curve as the stages are passed through as first put forward by Booz, Allen and Hamilton, and Figure 4.9 shows the relationship between costs and the stages of product development outlined before.

Information and communication technology and new product development

Obviously, much new product development in itself is underpinned by developments and the applications of new technology, in as much as new products often incorporate new technology. In addition to this aspect of technology and new product development, however, developments in ICT are also affecting the new product development process.

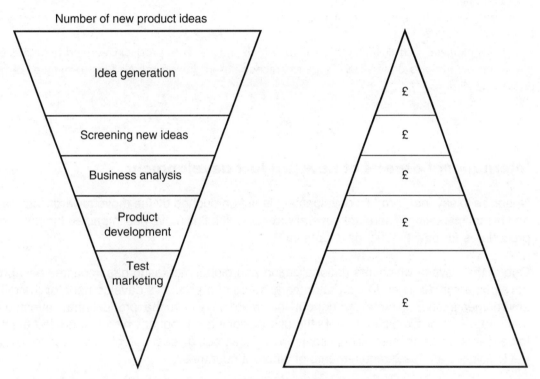

Figure 4.9 The relationship between cost and the stages of product development

The interactive nature of the Internet allows the marketer to involve and encourage customer participation in product design and also speed up the design commitment. In particular, net technology allows a much more flexible approach to the process of new product development while at the same time involving the customer in the process. The following represent some of the ways in which this flexibility and customer involvement are achieved.

o The customer can be involved in very early stages of product specification and design. The database can be used to identify key customers and their requirements. This can then be followed up with communication to selected customers so as to gain information about their particular needs and the implications of these for the product concept.

o Product concepts and proposed technical solutions to customer needs can then be interpreted into the design process and again the design options evaluated directly and immediately with customers.

o Finally, as the product is further developed, customer needs can be integrated with technical solutions by using intranet, extranet and Internet communications to integrate tasks, synchronize design changes and capture customer response as

131

the projects evolve. Applications of new technology to flexible product development include motor vehicle design, software product development and specific 'one-off' products.

Marketing in practice: example

Many market research companies are now providing research services for new product development based on developments in ICT. Examples of companies offering such services together with their website addresses, if you want to explore these further, are shown below:

Pegram Walters: www.aqr.com
Gfk Research: www.procongfk.com
Harris Polls: www.harrisinteractive.com

Harris, for example, has developed 'BuildUp' which is a software product designed to help clients develop new products or services. Guinness recently used this program to test a number of new packaging designs.

International aspects of new product development

Needless to say, new product development is not untouched by the move towards international and global marketing. There are several ways in which this move has impacted the process and procedures for new product development.

One of the ways in which internationalization and global marketing has impacted new product development is the need to plan at an early stage of a product's development for the different environments and markets throughout the world in which the product may eventually be marketed. So, for example, it is of little use designing a product which is intended eventually to be marketed on an international scale which does not, at least potentially, meet, for example, the legislative and user requirements of different countries.

Related to the above, very often a key aspect of new product development these days is the design of standardized products which can be marketed in the same form or at least a very similar one, throughout the world without major changes to design and production, etc. Ford had this idea in mind with the concept of producing a 'world car'. This was essentially a design concept for a product based on a notional that most of the key components of the car, such as chassis design, suspension, drive units and so on, would be standardized but could be readily varied to meet the needs of individual different markets and regions throughout the world. In this way, Ford hope to reduce both the development and production costs whilst at the same time remaining responsive to different market needs.

Finally, as an aspect of the impact of international factors on new product development is the fact that, due primarily to the increasingly high costs and risks of developing new products, many companies are entering into some form of joint arrangement and ventures with their competitors in other parts of the world. Sometimes this takes form of full-blown mergers but often it involves factors such as joint development programmes on, say, research where the research costs are pooled and the responsibility shared with an agreement as to how to treat the outcome of any successful research. In other situations, product development and marketing is based on contractual arrangements such as franchising which facilitates the marketing of a new product throughout the world which may not otherwise be possible if the marketer responsible for developing the new products had to bear the full burden of such a venture.

Marketing in practice: case study

'Fancy a cuppa!'

One tends to associate innovation and new product development with hi-tech companies and markets such as computing companies, engineering companies and so on. However, most industries have to innovate in order to keep their products competitive, even those industries which one would perhaps initially think of as being relatively staid and stable with little or no product innovation and development.

A good example of an industry which has experienced substantial product innovation and development is in fact one of the longest established industries or markets in the world, namely the tea industry/market. Tea, of course, has been drunk for thousands of years, allegedly having its origin in China. Since then tea has become one of the world's most popular beverages, with, for example, 175 million cups of tea per day being consumed in the United Kingdom alone. Despite this phenomenal popularity of tea, needless to say, over the years, like any other product, tea has faced substantial competition from other products, or in this case beverages. The tea marketers' products are constantly being threatened not only by other hot beverages such as coffee, chocolate and so on, but also by a whole range of cold beverages such as cola products and increasingly even bottled waters. Against this background of extreme competition, the tea marketers have had to develop new and improved products as a way to combat this competition. Below are just some of the product innovations which have been used over the years by the tea makers as an element in their competitive marketing strategies.

1953 – Joseph Tetley introduces the tea bag which serves to revolutionize the making of tea.
1985 – PG Tips introduces tea bags on a string 'PG Tags' to help make the use of tea bags easier.
1989 – The introduction of the round tea bag by Tetleys, supposedly to suit the habit of brewing tea in a mug.
1996 – PG Tips introduces a pyramid shaped tea bag which is claimed to allow more flavour to be released.
1997 – Tetley launches the drawstring tea bag designed to reduce messy drips from conventional tea bags.

This list of product innovations may seem to encompass what appear to be relatively minor innovations involving, for example, shape, minor features and so on. However, we should not underestimate the costs and risks associated with many of these apparently 'minor' developments. Not only have they often involved substantial investment on the part of the companies involved but also, and especially for a product as long established as tea, even seemingly small changes to how the product is brewed or consumed can be risky.

More recently, the tea marketers have continued their product development strategies by launching entirely new teas onto the market including instant granule teas, decaffeinated teas, fruit infusion teas, organic teas and most recently of all, therapy teas which are normally black teas blended with natural herbs.

We can see then that what at first sight may appear a very conservative market with regard to product innovation and development is in fact extremely dynamic. All marketers are faced with the imperatives of the product life cycle and intense competition which makes continued product development and improvement a necessity rather than a luxury.

Continuous product development and improvement in this market has helped make us all 'fancy a cuppa'.

Source: www.tetley.co.uk.

www.pgmoment.com.

Summary

In this unit you have seen that:

o Product decisions lie at the heart of the marketing mix tools.
o Products can be usefully viewed as a collection of tangible and intangible attributes that combine to provide bundles of benefits underpinning customer satisfaction.
o It is useful to distinguish between the different levels of a product ranging from the inner-most core product or basic benefits through to the augmented and potential product levels.
o Another useful concept of the anatomy of a product is to consider the functional, physical and symbolic issues associated with product benefits.
o Useful concepts in managing products include the notion of the product mix which in turn is based on product lines and individual product items.
o The product life cycle suggests that products have finite lives and pass through definitive and identifiable product life-cycle stages.
o Different strategies exist for different phases of the product life cycle, and the curve of the product life cycle itself can assume a variety of shapes.
o The product adoption process consists of a number of discrete adopter categories that each behave in a different way to a new product offering.
o Packaging, branding and service support elements have become very important elements of the product area of the marketing mix.
o New product development is a key activity in the management of the product element of the marketing mix.
o There are a number of definitions and types of new products with regard to their degree of newness and a variety of approaches to managing new product development effectively.
o The new product development process encompasses a series of stages from idea generation to commercialization and launch which should be conducted in a systematic manner.

Examination preparation: previous examination question

Attempt Question 4 of the examination paper for December 2003 (Appendix 4). For Specimen Answer Examination Question 4, December 2003, see Appendix 4 and www.cim.co.uk.

Bibliography

Brassington, F. and Pettitt, S. (2003) *Principles of Marketing*, 3rd edition, FT Prentice Hall, Chapters 9 and 20.

Dibb, S., Simkin, L., Pride, W. and Ferrell, O.C. (2000) *Marketing Concepts and Strategies*, 4th European edition, Houghton, Mifflin, Chapters 1 and 22.

Kotler, P., Armstrong, G., Saunders, J. and Wong, V. (2002) *Principles of Marketing*, 3rd edition, Essex, England: FT Prentice Hall.

Lancaster, G., Massingham, L. and Ashford, R. (2002) *Essentials of Marketing*, 4th edition, McGraw-Hill, Chapters 6 and 12, Appendix 1.

unit 5
the marketing mix: price

Learning objectives

Learning outcomes

By the end of the unit you will be able to:

o Identify and describe the pricing element of the marketing mix.

Knowledge and skills

By the end of this unit you will be able to:

o Explore the range of internal and external factors that influence pricing decisions (3.8).

o Identify and illustrate a range of different pricing policies and tactics that are adopted by organizations as effective means of competition (3.9).

Study Guide

This unit covers the second key element of the marketing mix and the only one that generates revenue for the company.

In a profit-making organization, and perhaps surprisingly in many not-for-profit ones too, pricing decisions are central to the effectiveness of a company. For obvious reasons prices have a major impact on levels of profits. However, pricing is more than simply an accountancy exercise – indeed it is a vital element of marketing plans. For example, price helps to position a product/ service in a market and ultimately in the mind of the customer.

All too often, marketers shy away from attempting to understand some of the key inputs to pricing decisions and instead leave it to accountants. For example, many marketers do not understand the different types of cost in producing a product or how to conduct a breakeven analysis. Similarly, some do not understand the relation between price and demand, and factors such as 'price elasticity'. Where this is the case, the marketer is unable to make informed and profes- sional pricing decisions and instead is at the mercy of the accountant and the economist. The intention here is not to turn you into instant accountants or economists but simply to help you understand the contributions and jargon of these disciplines in helping make pricing decisions.

We would expect it to take you about 3 hours to work through this unit and suggest you allow a further 3–4 hours to undertake the various activities suggested. Other than your notebook and writing equipment you will not need anything further to complete this unit.

The role and importance of price in marketing

Study tip

Because pricing decisions are among some of the most visible parts of a company's marketing strategy, in that prices need to be communicated to potential customers, you will be able to observe and reflect upon pricing approaches and strategies in your everyday role as a consumer. Look out for examples of pricing strategies used by marketers in your everyday life. Look, for example, at things such as special offer pricing, price-lining and loss leaders when you do your own shopping. Do not worry if at this stage these terms mean nothing to you; we shall explain these and others in the unit and then you can observe them in the real world.

As consumers, we all know what is meant by 'price' of a product or service. In simple terms, price is the monetary value placed upon a product/service by the marketer, and we must pay it in order to acquire or use the product or service. A 'price', however, can take several forms, depending upon the circumstances. For example, in the case of a credit card we pay an annual 'fee' and a monthly 'rate of interest'. At the end of the month, we may pay a landlord 'rent'. An agent may charge us 'commission'. All these are variations on the word 'price'. In the case of many not-for-profit organizations, there is no price as such for the product. For example, the customer may instead be required to give up his or her time, or perhaps his or her vote, as opposed to paying over a monetary sum.

Immediately, therefore, we can see that even the word 'price', which we all take for granted as knowing what it means, is more complex and varied than we might at first imagine. In addition, price plays a vital role in marketing. Some major roles of price are as follows:

- As mentioned earlier, price is the major basis for generating revenue and, where relevant, profits in an organization.
- Put simply:

    - Revenue = price × quantity
    - Profit = revenue − costs

- Prices connect customers and suppliers at the point of exchange.
- Prices send signals to customers about factors such as product quality, exclusiveness and so on. There are powerful behavioural and psychological aspects to the price element.
- Price is also used as a powerful competitive weapon in markets, sometimes to drive other competitors out of business, prevent new ones entering, and forcing those that remain to follow prices that have been laid down.

Activity 5.1

As we have already seen, there are various terms for the word 'price'. Using your experience and knowledge, look for as many different examples that mean the same thing as price used by different industries, for different products and so on.

A good idea would be to look through newspapers and magazines in addition to keeping your eyes open when you next go shopping.

Perspectives on pricing decisions

Broadly we can distinguish between three different approaches to pricing decisions each with its own distinct perspective and emphasis. These three approaches correspond to the three disciplines, concepts and techniques of the economist, the accountant and the marketer. Each of these would individually suggest a different approach to pricing decisions.

Exam hint

In the past, comparing and contrasting the approaches and perspectives of these three disciplines has been a popular area for questions on the Fundamentals paper. We shall therefore continue by outlining each perspective and the contributions of these three different disciplines to the pricing decision.

The economist's perspective

Pricing is viewed as the mechanism/signal whereby demand and supply are brought into equilibrium. The operation of this mechanism varies according to market structure, ranging from perfectly competitive markets to imperfect competition and monopolistic market structures.

The economist looks at price on the assumption that companies are 'profit maximizers'. The major contribution of the economist to price planning in marketing is the notion surrounding the relationships between demand and price.

The accountant's perspective

The emphasis is on recovering costs to make a profit, often expressed as a required rate of return. This emphasis on costs means that the accountant stresses the importance of identifying and classifying different costs.

The major contribution of the accountant therefore to planning pricing decisions is this analysis of costs together with techniques such as breakeven analysis. The major disadvantage of the accountant's perspective is that there is a tendency to ignore demand and market considerations.

The marketer's perspective

The emphasis is on the effect of price on competitive market position, including sales, market share and sometimes profit levels. However, price is seen as being only one factor affecting market demand.

The marketer stresses the importance of 'value' rather than just price. The marketer's approach to pricing is essentially based on pricing 'at what the market will bear'.

Although these are three different perspectives on price, each has something to contribute to informed pricing decisions. This means, therefore, that the marketer can and should draw upon each of these perspectives when making pricing decisions. We can see this more clearly by examining the considerations or inputs to pricing decisions.

Activity 5.2

Before we look at inputs to pricing decisions try to find out how prices are set in your own company and who is responsible for setting them. We can use this information later in the unit when we look at pricing methods.

Inputs and information for pricing decisions

Before we look at approaches to making a pricing decision and, in particular, how to structure these and specific methods of pricing, it is important to ensure that you understand what the key inputs or considerations are in any pricing decision made by the marketer. The key considerations in most pricing decisions are now outlined and discussed. We can think of these considerations as the 4Cs, namely: Costs, Customers, Competition and Company considerations.

Costs and prices

As mentioned earlier, information on costs is the key contribution of the accountant to setting prices. In most companies, costs determine the lower limit to the prices a company can charge. The following represent some of the information and analysis on costs that we need when setting a price on a product for the first time:

- ○ Total costs
- ○ Average costs
- ○ Fixed costs
- ○ Variable costs
- ○ Marginal cost
- ○ Relation between volume and cost: 'scale economies'
- ○ Relation between experience and costs: 'experience curves'.

Some definitions might be useful before proceeding.

Key definitions

Total cost – The sum of all fixed costs and variable costs times the quantity produced.

Average cost – Total cost divided by number of units produced.

Fixed costs – Costs that do not vary with the number of units produced or sold.

Variable costs – Costs that vary directly according to the number of units produced or sold.

Marginal cost – The addition to total cost of producing one additional unit of output.

Scale economies – The potential reduction in average costs as a result of increasing output/sales.

Experience curves – The potential reduction in average costs as a result of learning/experience based on cumulative output.

By providing this type of analysis and information on costs the accountant plays a key role in contributing to pricing decisions. In addition, a variety of tools of analysis provided by the accountant can be useful. Perhaps the best example of such a tool is breakeven analysis. But before we look briefly at breakeven analysis you should undertake the following activity.

Activity 5.3

Examples of types of cost

Preferably using your own organization, explore and list examples of various kinds of cost:

1. Fixed costs
2. Variable costs
3. Neither of the above.

When you have completed this activity, you should look at the debriefing for examples of different types of cost.

Using this concept of different costs enables the accountant and the marketer to explore some of the relationships between costs and prices. Two of the most useful tools of cost analysis are the related notions of 'contribution' and 'breakeven'.

Contribution

Contribution is calculated in the following way:

$$\text{Selling price} - \text{variable cost} = \text{contribution}$$

As the term implies, contribution is the amount, if any, which is left after deducting variable costs from a selling price and which therefore 'contributes' to covering fixed costs. By calculating contribution, the marketer can assess if it would be worthwhile, at least in the short run, to sell a product at less than total cost. As fixed costs by definition would be incurred irrespective of how much is produced or sold, then we might decide that if we can cover variable costs, we should continue to produce the product. In the long run, of course, all costs must be covered.

Breakeven analysis

The breakeven point represents the level of output at any given price where total revenue is exactly equal to the total costs of production and marketing. The breakeven quantity (BEQ) can be calculated in the following way.

$$\text{BEQ} = \text{fixed costs/contribution}$$

Activity 5.4

Contribution and breakeven calculations

Calculate:

1. The contribution and
2. The breakeven point.

from the following information:

Selling price = £20.00

Variable cost = £10.00

Fixed costs = £100 000.00

Compare your calculations with those shown in the debriefing.

Breakeven analysis can also be done graphically. An example using the same information as in the previous activity is shown in Figure 5.1.

Not only is Figure 5.1 easy to interpret, but we can also use the chart very simply to examine the effect on breakeven quantities of different prices.

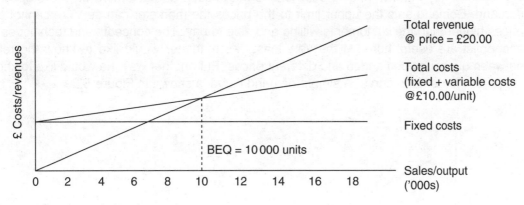

Figure 5.1 A simple breakeven chart

Activity 5.5

Revised breakeven calculations and breakeven chart

Using the information from the previous activity calculate the effect on breakeven point of:

1. Increasing the selling price to £25.00
2. Reducing the selling price to £15.00.

Compare your calculations to those shown in the debriefing.

Sketch out the effect of (1) and (2) above on our simple breakeven chart. Compare your sketch with that shown in the debriefing.

We can see then how the accountant can make a valuable contribution to pricing decisions by providing information and analyses on costs.

However, as we shall see later, it is dangerous to base pricing decisions on cost information alone. As mentioned earlier, costs set the lower limit to the prices the marketer can charge. The upper limit is determined by demand or customer considerations. We shall now turn our attention to this second input to pricing decisions.

Customers (demand) and prices

Our second key input to pricing decisions is information on customers or, more specifically, demand. Demand sets the upper limit to the prices the marketer can set. We cannot charge prices higher than the customer is willing and able to pay. The concepts and techniques of the economist are useful here. At the very least, the marketer would like to know the relations between quantities demanded and different prices. Put another way, he would like to know the shape of the demand curve. A simple demand curve is shown in Figure 5.2.

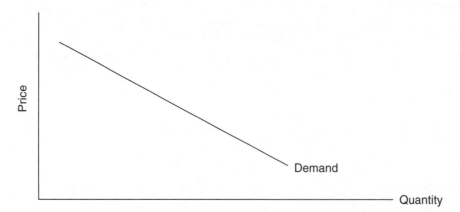

Figure 5.2 A simple demand curve

We can immediately see that even the simple diagram of Figure 5.2 gives the marketer valuable information for pricing. The shape of the demand curve shows how much will be demanded at any given price, and the effect on demand of changes in price. This second piece of information is referred to as 'price elasticity' and indicates how sensitive demand is to changes in price.

Key definition

Price elasticity of demand – Percentage change in quantity demanded/percent change in price.

In simple terms, the steeper the demand curve, the less sensitive demand is to changes in price, that is relatively price 'inelastic'. Similarly, the flatter the demand curve, the more sensitive demand is to changes in price, that is relatively price elastic.

Examples of products which are relatively price inelastic are those where either the customer has no option but to purchase, such as car insurance, electricity and other energy forms, water and so on, or where the customer has developed a high degree of brand loyalty to a particular supplier which serves to desensitize the customer to changes in price. Incidentally, this highlights the value of effective branding in markets.

Examples of products which are relatively price elastic are those where there is considerable choice and discretion in product selection on the part of a customer and/or where brand loyalty is relatively low. Many undifferentiated products and commodities such as flour, salt and bread and so on fall into this category.

Information on the demand curve can be gleaned from market research including customer surveys and test marketing. You should note that the shape of the demand curve and therefore price elasticity is influenced by many factors. Three of the most important of these factors are: the marketing strategies of the company; the product life cycle and the marketing strategies of competitors. We shall look at competitors as our third input to pricing decisions, so let us briefly consider the first two factors.

Pricing and the consumer's purchase decision-making process

As we have seen, all marketing decisions should be based on an understanding of the customers and their needs. This is as true for pricing therefore as it is for any element of the marketing mix. The marketer must therefore understand the consumer's decision-making process and in particular some of the factors related to price and pricing which a customer might consider when deciding to make a purchase. Some of the more important of these factors are outlined below.

- *Competitors' prices* – A consumer is likely to shop around for a product and will consider the competitors' offering and pricing structure.
- *Discounts offered* – Discounts offered often will have an effect on the buying decision process – an extra 10 per cent off the price may induce trial.
- *Quality and image of the product* – The consumer will consider the price in relation to the perceived quality and image of the product and packaging and often the distribution outlet. Many consumers are happy to pay a higher price for Marks & Spencer food as they believe that the quality of the product is guaranteed to be of a certain standard.
- *Disposable income and lifestyle* – Consumers will need to consider their disposable income and lifestyle when considering the price of a product and making purchases.
- *Personal objectives or utility* – The consumer will have their own set of objectives for purchasing a product – it may be for a gift, a personal treat, a necessity, something to make them feel good and so on. These considerations will have some impact on the purchase decision related to the price. For example, a person may buy a more expensive bottle of red wine to take to a dinner party with friends and a cheaper one for a Friday night in front of the television.
- *Value for money* – The perceived value of the product will often be a prime consideration, especially for essential items such as food products.

143

> o *Personality and culture* – A person's personality may have some bearing on the purchase decision related to price. A person may be more thrifty or generous which will have some bearing on their perceptions of the pricing and purchasing of products. There may be cultural differences in the perception of prices and product, for example in certain countries a very expensive gift of jewellery is given as a wedding dowry.
>
> o *Perceived risk* – A consumer may consider the purchase of a product in relation to perceived risk. So, for example, the consumer may well prefer a higher priced security alarm for the car, considering this to be more effective than the lower priced product.
>
> o *Previous experience and loyalty* – Experience about a product which has been purchased previously will inform the decision and loyalty towards that product.

We can see therefore that 'getting inside the customer's head' with respect to their purchase decision-making process and the factors which affect it can be very useful in providing insights for effective pricing decisions.

Marketing in practice: example

Often marketers have misconceptions and therefore misunderstand how customers perceive and interpret prices and the role of price in the purchase decision-making process. This can lead them to wrong pricing decisions. In particular, many marketers perceive prices, or more specifically low prices, to be the most important factor in customer choice and hence competitive success. This is particularly the case in b2b marketers. Some years ago Alcan were looking at ways to reduce prices in the very competitive supply of raw materials to the canning industry. To their surprise, however, when they approached customers about how they might respond to lower prices, they found that price was not as important in the purchase decision-making process for their customers as they had always thought. Far more important to customers were issues such as reliability of delivery, consistency of product quality and technical and after-sales service. Rather than trying to build market share through lower costs and prices, then, Alcan set about trying to achieve this through improvements to the areas of the marketing mix which were most influential in the customer's choice process.

Price elasticity and marketing strategies of a company

The marketer can and does attempt to influence price elasticity through marketing strategies. Very often the marketer will try to 'desensitize' the customer to price, that is make the customer less sensitive to price in the purchase decision. For example, the marketer may attempt to create brand loyalty through other elements of the mix. Most marketers would like to alter the slope of the demand curve so that demand for their products is less sensitive to price.

We have already touched on the fact that price sensitivity and therefore price elasticity is lower where brand loyalty exists in a market. Similarly, and related to this, where a company has strong relationships with its customers, again, demand is less likely to be price sensitive. The marketer therefore must consider ways of decreasing the customer's sensitivity to price, and branding and relationship marketing represent two major approaches. Evidence suggests that prices can be as high as sometimes a factor of two compared to competitors where strong brand loyalty exists.

Pricing and the product life cycle

We discussed the product life cycle in Unit 3. In general terms, price elasticity varies in each stage of the life cycle.

Question 5.1

See if you can gauge how price elasticity might change in each stage of the product life cycle. Figure 5.3 has four diagrams showing different degrees of price elasticity. Examine them carefully and then write down which stage of the product life cycle – introduction, growth, maturity or decline – each diagram corresponds to. Then compare your answers to those shown in the answer.

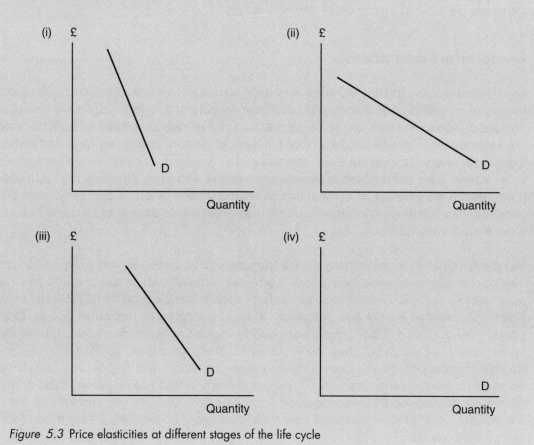

Figure 5.3 Price elasticities at different stages of the life cycle

Partly because of these differences in price elasticity at various stages in the life cycle, together with other considerations in the life-cycle stages, such as differing degrees of competition, size of market and so on, it is very often necessary to have differing pricing policies for each stage of the product life cycle. These are shown in Table 5.1.

Table 5.1 Pricing and the product life cycle

Introduction stage	Growth stage	Maturity stage	Decline stage
Skimming policy with high prices, but low profit margin due to high fixed costs	Reduce price to penetrate market further	Price to match or beat competitors	Cut price if not repositioning
Penetration policy to enter the market and gain a high share quickly or to prevent competitors from entering		Retain higher prices in some market segments	Some increases in prices may occur in the late decline stage

Both skimming and penetration pricing policies together with their advantages and disadvantages are discussed in more detail later in the unit.

Competitors and prices

Our third input to pricing decisions is information on competitors. In all marketing decisions, it is important to assess competitors, both existing and potential. This is especially true of pricing decisions. The extent and nature of competition in a market obviously affects the prices the marketer is able to charge, and the price elasticity of demand, which we have just considered. In markets where competitors are numerous and aggressive, and where new competitors can enter easily, price competition is likely to be intense and price elasticity high. On the other hand, where the number of competitors is limited and/or where a company is much more powerful than its competitors, the marketer may enjoy some degree of monopoly power, and price elasticity will be low.

Monopoly power in a market may derive from several sources. So, for example, a company can gain a degree of monopoly power from, say, control over resources and raw material supplies in a market. Diamonds occur only in certain parts of the world and any company, which controls this supply has potentially at least a degree of monopoly power. Monopoly power may also stem from government and/or regulatory restrictions. So, for example, to some extent, although recently deregulated in many countries, airlines may have some degree of monopoly power due to government protection and regulations, which prevent competitors from entering markets. Finally, and many would argue, perhaps the only defensible monopoly is where the monopoly power stems from superior performance on the part of a company which in turn generates very loyal customers and makes it very difficult for other competitors to enter.

Throughout the world most countries have legislation to protect the customer from the worst excesses of monopoly power.

Marketing in practice: example

In the United Kingdom unfair trading and the abuse of monopoly power fall within the remit of the Office of Fair Trading and the legislation enshrined in the Monopolies Act. In America, if anything, unfair trading legislation is probably more stringent than anywhere else in the world. In recent years, one of the America's most successful companies, Microsoft has attracted the attention of the anti-trust legislators and lawyers with regard in particular to its use of marketing and pricing tools. Although this case is still ongoing, already Microsoft has been forced to reconsider some of its approaches to marketing in order to take account of this attention.

Extending knowledge

Click on the following website to extend your knowledge on how government legislation affects the marketer and the consumer with regard to pricing strategies.

www.oft.gov.uk

Related to this, a number of factors have also tended to increase competition in markets throughout the world. So, for example, the World Trade Organization promotes world trade without barriers; many governments have acted to deregulate markets and in the United Kingdom, for example we have seen a continuing trend towards privatization even in public utilities. Finally, increasing global competition and the ubiquitous Internet, of course, have meant more and more competition between companies.

The marketer must carefully assess the prices competitors are charging and/or are likely to charge, and how they may respond to the marketer's own pricing decisions.

Activity 5.6

Try to find examples of the following:

1. Markets characterized by intense competition between companies and brands.
2. Markets where, although competition is intense to some extent, marketers have been able to lessen the effects of competition by effective marketing, for example by building, say, brand loyalty.
3. Markets where there are few or no competitors and the marketer enjoys a degree of monopoly power.

Compare your findings with those shown in the debriefing.

Company considerations and prices

This fourth major input to pricing decisions encompasses a number of considerations. All marketing decisions, but again particularly pricing decisions, should reflect and be consistent with company objectives and marketing strategies. So, for example, the pricing decision will probably be different if the company objective is growth as opposed to short-term return on capital.

Similarly, pricing decisions should reflect wider considerations, such as company resources, target markets and positioning, and desired company/corporate image. It is important to stress that the pricing decision must be consistent and planned in conjunction with the marketing mix. Finally, pricing strategies will obviously differ where price is used as a major element of competitive strategy as opposed to where it is used in a more passive way in the marketing strategy. Some companies decide to be price leaders, others price followers.

Activity 5.7

We have seen that pricing decisions should reflect company and marketing objectives and strategies. For each of the following, indicate whether you think a higher or a lower price would generally be appropriate:

The ABC company wishes to achieve rapid market growth	Higher/Lower
The XYZ company wants quick returns on capital employed	Higher/Lower
The LPT company wishes to promote a quality image	Higher/Lower
The NYZ company is targeting socio-economic groups D/E	Higher/Lower

Communicational aspects of pricing

Another major consideration in pricing decisions is the fact that prices have an important communicational role as regards customers and potential customers. In other words, the price set for a product sends signals to customers about the company and its products. This is why we have suggested that pricing decisions must be in line with target markets and positioning, and desired company/corporate image. Pricing decisions therefore need to be closely linked, as already mentioned, to other areas of the mix, but particularly to the promotion elements. So, for example, pricing may be linked to promotional objectives so as to encourage trial of a new product.

Another area where price has a strong communicational aspect is in relation to price as an indicator of quality. Rightly or wrongly, but certainly in the absence of experience or, say, objective information about a product offering, customers will often use price as an indication of the quality of a product offering. This means that, then, contrary to what many companies appear to believe and certainly practise, it is possible to price a product too low where the price acts as a deterrent to potential customers, and particularly new ones, because of suspicions regarding the quality of a product. Economists have long known about this phenomenon as it gives rise to an unusual backward-sloping demand curve.

Other considerations/information in the pricing decision

Although these are the four major considerations in pricing decisions there are often many other factors that will need to be taken into account when setting prices. The marketer will need information on these before making a decision.

 ## Activity 5.8

Before proceeding, try to list as many other factors not already encompassed in our discussion that might need to be taken into account in pricing decisions.

Structuring pricing decisions

As with any other decision-making process, pricing decisions are likely to be most effective when they are taken in a planned and systematic way. Pricing is not something that is best done as an afterthought during the marketing of a product.

You will find different suggested frameworks for structuring the pricing decision according to the particular textbook you consult. In other words, there is no one way to structure this decision. However, Figure 5.4 represents a logical and acceptable way of structuring the process.

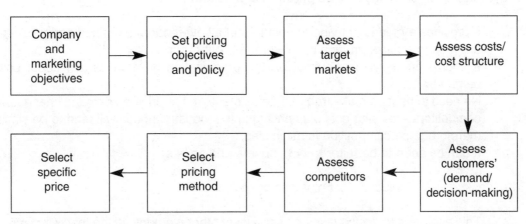

Figure 5.4 A structured approach to pricing decisions

Extending knowledge

Because there are so many alternative ways in which the structure of the pricing decision can be described, it would be a good idea to have a look at alternatives.

One of the most useful contributions to structuring the pricing decision is that suggested by A.R. Oxenfeldt in 'A Decision-Making Structure for Price Decisions' (1973) *Journal of Marketing*, 37, January.

We have already looked at some of the key steps in our structured approach to pricing decisions. In particular of course the 4Cs. We now need to look at the two remaining steps in this framework, namely selection of a pricing method and selection of specific prices. We also need to say a little more about pricing policies. We shall start by discussing pricing methods, followed by the considerations in setting specific prices, and finally look at pricing policy.

Selection of a pricing method

Earlier we looked at the perspectives and contributions of the accountant, the economist and the marketer with respect to pricing decisions. To a certain extent the legacy of these different perspectives can be seen in the different methods of pricing. The three major categories of pricing methods are cost-based methods, competitor-based methods and demand/market-based methods. We shall now examine each of these in turn.

Cost-based methods

As you would expect, cost-based methods of pricing primarily reflect the accountant's approach to pricing. Additionally, as you would expect, these methods set prices primarily on the basis of costs. There are several alternatives for cost-based pricing but the major ones are:

- o *Full cost/cost plus pricing* – One of the simplest and most widely used methods of pricing. Usually a standard percentage is added to the total cost of the product to arrive at a price.

The strengths of full cost/cost plus pricing are as follows:

- o It provides a means of trying to ensure that all overheads (e.g. fixed and product costs) are met. In addition, it tries to allow for a profit return on top.
- o It should be easy to calculate, as the organization is more certain about cost than demand.
- o No need to have to make frequent adjustments to the price as demand changes. Where competitors are using cost plus pricing in the industry, prices will tend to be similar and therefore price competition is minimized.
- o It can be seen to be fairer to both buyers and sellers.

The weaknesses of full cost/cost plus pricing include:

- o This approach to pricing takes no account of other elements in the marketing mix, that is product, place and so on.
- o It does not reflect consumers' perceptions. If a consumer perceives a product as cheap, it is often associated with poor quality.
- o Being a cost-based pricing strategy, it ignores other factors such as the going rate for similar products. It does not consider different segments and so on.
- o It does not consider the 'needs' and 'wants' of customers. Similarly, this method does not consider competitors' prices.
- o It may be difficult to identify direct costs and overheads for each item.
- o It does not consider the elasticity of demand for the product.
- o This method only works if the price actually brings in the expected level of sales.
- o *Marginal cost pricing* – Here the distinction between the variable and fixed costs comes into play. With this pricing method, the marketer assesses whether or not a contribution to fixed costs can be obtained. Hence marginal cost pricing can lead to prices that are less than full cost.

Marginal cost pricing overcomes some of the major weaknesses of full cost/cost plus pricing, for example it allows prices to reflect demand conditions to a greater extent. However, it is still primarily of course cost based and hence is not really marketing oriented.

In general, cost-based pricing methods are inward looking and neglect marketing considerations.

Competitor-based methods

Sometimes companies base their pricing decisions largely on competitors' prices. You should note that this does not mean charging the same prices as competitors; it may be more or less than major competitors. Such pricing is predominant in oligopolistic markets. A larger company may act as the price leader, with smaller companies following this lead. This pricing method is sometimes called 'going rate pricing'.

The advantages of competitor-based pricing include the fact that it is relatively simple, and, of course, takes into account competitor considerations. However, one of the disadvantages of this pricing method is that it is essentially passive in approach, especially when following rather than leading competitors on price. The major disadvantage of this approach to pricing, however, is that it does not reflect differences in company cost structures, objectives, resources, and marketing strategies.

A particularly good example of where competition and therefore competitor-based methods of pricing can come to predominate in a market is in the pricing methods used by many of the larger UK supermarkets. Although some companies do try to avoid it, competitor-based pricing is so predominant now in this market that price wars are the order of the day and margins have been severely depressed.

Demand/market-based methods

Obviously, these are the most marketing-oriented methods of pricing. Predominantly, prices are set with demand and market considerations in mind. There are several alternative methods available to the marketer that are demand/market based according to circumstances. Some of the most frequently encountered methods are as follows.

When pricing new products, or 'Pioneer pricing' as it is sometimes referred to, the marketer may choose between *market skimming prices* and *market penetration prices*.

 Activity 5.9

In your own words, write down what you think is meant by, first, market skimming and, secondly, market penetration pricing.

As you probably guessed or knew, market skimming is where the marketer charges a high or premium price for a new product, effectively skimming off the cream of demand.

 Activity 5.10

Can you assess the circumstances, which would tend to suggest price skimming for a new product?

The advantages of a market skimming pricing policy are as follows:

- It allows for quick recovery on investment in the new product such as R&D costs and so on
- It may confer a prestigious/quality image to customers
- Higher prices are likely to appeal to innovator groups
- It allows for flexibility in reducing prices should the initial price result in too few sales. It also allows for reduced prices for later stages of the product life cycle to appeal to the mass market.

151

Among the disadvantages of a market skimming pricing policy are:

o It may encourage competitors to enter the market more quickly.
o It results in lower levels of sales and hence fewer economies of scale and experience curve effects, that is costs are higher.
o It may attract attention from regulatory bodies, or consumer groups where 'profiteering' is suspected.

Many marketers have used price skimming as their approach in markets and many will no doubt continue to do so. We have seen in Unit 4 that the innovators in markets in particular want to be among the first to purchase new products and are willing and able to pay higher prices to achieve this. Many new electronic consumer products are priced in this way therefore. For example, when they were first launched, CD players were extremely expensive compared to their prices today. Similarly, the new generation of DVD-based players are also an example of a price skimming strategy at work.

As you also probably guessed market penetration pricing is the setting of low prices in order to gain rapid market share.

Activity 5.11

Can you assess the circumstances which would tend to suggest penetration pricing for a product?

The advantages of a market penetration pricing policy are as follows:

o It should produce larger sales volume
o This should lead to an organization gaining a large slice of the market
o It can prevent competitors from entering the market.

The limitations of a market penetration pricing policy include:

o It is often difficult to raise price after this policy has been used
o It is less flexible than using a skimming policy
o It may not be appropriate due to the costs of R&D and competitors' positions.

Recently, the petrol retailers in the United Kingdom have launched their new low-sulphur petrol products, which are aimed at a cleaner environment, at penetration prices. By pricing these products at slightly lower prices than their other existing products in the range, the companies are hoping to switch customers to these cleaner fuel products.

Perceived value pricing – is perhaps one of the most marketing-oriented ways of setting prices. The price is set on the perceived value of the product to the customer. It is in fact a variation on 'price at what the market will bear'. The marketer uses other elements of the mix – product, promotion and so on – to build up the perceived value of the product or service in the mind of the customer. Prices are then set to reflect this value.

Perceived value pricing is also related to our earlier price as an indicator of quality. This approach to pricing is particularly useful when pricing products for organizational markets or more expensive consumer products where the usage takes place over a long period of time such as a car. Mercedes use this approach very successfully in pricing their products. The perceived value of their products is heightened through stressing the quality and engineering aspects embodied, but, in addition, Mercedes, probably with some justification, stress the lifetime value of their cars, not the least of which is affected by their claims for low depreciation costs.

Activity 5.12

Think back to a purchase you made in the past where:

1. You got 'very good value for money'
2. You got 'very poor value for money'.

Reflect on what each of these meant for the prices you paid.

Psychological pricing – has to do with the strong behavioural forces at work in the pricing of products and services. For example, we know that price is used by consumers as an indicator of quality. Similarly, high prices can bestow 'prestige' on the purchaser and this is known as 'Prestige pricing'. Some marketers believe that ending the price with certain numbers can influence buyers, for example pricing a product at £9.99 instead of £10.00. This is known as 'odd' pricing. Similarly there is some evidence that rounding prices up from say £9.99 to £10.00 adds to an image of quality in the mind of the customer. This is known as 'even' pricing.

Psychological, and particularly odd pricing, is used extensively in retailing with regard to consumer products. Even pricing tends to be used where connotations of quality are important in determining product and brand choice and is often used in pricing expensive restaurants or theatre tickets.

Activity 5.13

Next time you go shopping make a note of examples of 'odd' and 'even' pricing.

Promotional pricing – is perhaps more of a tactical than a strategic approach to pricing, but price is potentially a very powerful tactical weapon. This approach to pricing is based on temporary changes in price, usually though not always reductions, in order to boost sales. Examples include:

○ *Cash rebates* – A variety of different types of these, but as the term implies they all involve offering some cash reduction or payback to customers. They may be related to, for example, purchasing in quantity or perhaps for buying at particular times of the year. Some holiday package companies are beginning to use systems of cash rebates to tempt customers to book early.

○ *Special event pricing* – Again, a variety of different types, but this is where special prices are linked to one-off events. So, for example, many companies offered special prices and promotional deals during the 2000 Sydney Olympics.

○ *Loss leader pricing* – Used extensively in retail marketing settings, this approach to pricing involves setting very low prices on certain selected products as an attraction to draw customers into the store.

○ *Low interest deals* – Obviously, this type of pricing weapon is particularly useful where a customer is likely to want extended credit on a product. So, for example, it is used extensively in marketing cars or other high value consumer products where payments are spread over a period of time.

153

○ *Other promotional deals* – Many sales promotion offers are effectively price offers including some of the ones we have discussed above. But, for example, 'two for one' offers, 'buy one get one free' offers (bogofs), '20 per cent extra' offers and so on – all widely used by marketers – are in fact really promotional pricing offers.

Marketers need to be careful how they use promotional pricing. Excessive use can lead to an image of 'inferior' products, and/or customers can come to expect low prices.

 Activity 5.14

When you are looking for examples for odd/even pricing also make note of any special promotional pricing you observe.

Product mix/product line pricing – Much of our discussion of pricing to date in this unit has centred on making pricing decisions for individual products. However, most companies produce and market a mix of products, and very often there are interrelations between the products in this mix with respect, for example, to costs of production, marketing costs or customer demand. Very often therefore the marketer must set prices that reflect these interrelations so as to maximize sales and profits.

There are many examples of such product mix/product line pricing in marketing. Here are just two:

1. Cheap razors to sell higher priced razor blades
2. The use of 'price points' in retail sales of clothing, for example shirts at £15.00, £20.00 and £25.00.

 Activity 5.15

Complete your list of examples of pricing in practice by making note of any examples you come across exemplifying product mix pricing.

Selection of specific prices

So far we have considered what might be called pointers to setting prices. For example, we have looked at inputs to pricing, broad approaches or methods of pricing and so on. However, the outcome of all these deliberations and considerations should be the setting of a specific price on a product or service. Of course the earlier steps in pricing procedure should serve to direct and constrain the selection of the final price. This narrowing of the price range from which to select the final price is intentional and indeed is part of the process of a structured approach to pricing. But in this final stage the marketer will still have some flexibility with regard to the specific price selected. This flexibility is needed to reflect the marketer's assessment of any final considerations in setting the price. Examples would include the state of the economy at the time of pricing, any special seasonal factors, unusual competitor activity and so on. We should remember that marketing managers are also paid to use their expertise and experience in making decisions as well as following systematic frameworks.

Price adjustment policies

Having set prices, often companies will need to adjust their basic prices to account for various customer differences and changing situations. Companies therefore need to establish price adjustment policies. Three examples of price adjustment policies are as follows:

1. *Discount and allowance pricing* – This is where the basic price is adjusted to reward customers for responses such as early payment, large or off-season purchases. These can be in the form of cash discounts, quantity discounts for bulk purchases and seasonal discounts for products bought out of season. Trade-in allowances and promotional allowances are price reductions given to encourage purchase.

Marketing in practice: example

Discount and allowance pricing are particularly prevalent where the customer is replacing an expensive durable product which still has some life, or more specifically value, left in it. One of the best examples of a product of this kind is of course a motor vehicle. For understandable reasons, a key factor in competitive marketing in the car market is the trade-in allowances which customers are offered for their existing vehicles when considering purchasing a replacement. In the United Kingdom, Dixons, a major new and used car distributor, uses trading allowances and promotional campaigns related to these very effectively. So, for example, sometimes customers may use a vehicle which has very little, if any, real value left in it to cover the total deposit on a replacement vehicle.

Source: www.findspot.com/dixons-car-dealer.htm.

2. *Segmented/differential pricing (price discrimination)* – Companies will often adjust their basic prices to allow for differences in customers, products, location, time/season and so on. Essentially, the company sells its products at two or more prices, even though the difference in price is not always based on differences in costs. Examples may be where different prices are charged to different age groups, for example special prices for old age pensioners. Similarly, prices may be charged during different times of the day, for example telephone calls. Often known as price discrimination, this approach to price adjustments can be very effective in maximizing demand and company revenue. Care needs to be taken, however, not to alienate the customer groups being charged higher prices.

Marketing in practice: example

Segmented/differential pricing is particularly useful and therefore prevalent in services marketing. The marketing issues associated with services including the application of the marketing mix elements to these products are explored in more detail in Unit 9. As we shall see in Unit 9, the characteristics of service products give rise to an increased importance in matching demand and supply. Obviously, price is a key determinant in this matching process and hence is used extensively to achieve a match. Specifically in services marketing, the marketer will often charge different prices to iron out fluctuations in demand. For example, in the airline industry different prices are charged for customers flying at different times of the day, or in some cases the year, to ensure that aeroplanes do not fly with empty seats. Similarly in the hotel market, hotels offer different prices at different times of the week, and again the year, to ensure maximum occupancy.

3. *Promotional pricing* – Our earlier discussed example of promotional pricing is also an example of price adjustment procedures, and as we have seen, is where companies use price as a tactical rather than a strategic approach using temporary changes in prices to generate demand. Obviously, usually prices in promotional pricing are set below list price and sometimes below cost prices. The example shown earlier under promotional pricing can also be described as a price adjustment policy.

Marketing in practice: example

In the United Kingdom, evidence shows that by far the most effective method of promotional pricing is that of multiple purchase offers, for example 'bogofs', 3 for 2 and so on. It is estimated that nearly 60 per cent of consumers feel this is the most important promotional approach in their product and brand choice. Multiple purchase offers are followed closely by the so-called 'complementary offers' of promotional pricing where customers buy one product and get a related product free.

Overall policies for pricing

It is important that pricing decisions are taken within and guided by a policy for pricing. As with all policies in organizations, such a policy should serve to provide an indication of what is acceptable and unacceptable in decision-making and action. A pricing policy should encompass the following:

- ○ Responsibilities and authority for pricing decisions.
- ○ Discretion with regard to price discounts, special deals and so on.
- ○ Procedures for responding to competitor price changes.
- ○ Procedures for changing prices in the company.
- ○ Credit policy.

 Activity 5.16

If you are working for a company at the moment, try to establish what your company's policies (if any) are with respect to our list of pricing policy areas.

Pricing and the Internet

There is no doubt that one of the major areas of marketing affected by the growth of Internet marketing is that of price and pricing decisions. At its simplest, the effect of the Internet has been to provide the opportunities for customers to compare and contrast competitors' prices much more widely and easily than they have ever been able to do in the past. This has put extra pressure, particularly on non-Internet conventional suppliers of products and services, to be cost and hence price effective. Customers can and do shop around for the cheapest prices. Moreover, of course, many of the Internet suppliers of consumer products, because they do not have expensive retail premises and properties to support, can often undercut many of their more conventional competitors' prices. Because of this, as use of the Internet grows for things like home shopping, we can expect price competition to become even more important in the future. Companies, who because of their costs and so on cannot compete on price, will have no alternative but to withdraw from markets or more positively to develop strong brand loyalty and customer franchises again to desensitize customers to the price element of the mix.

Marketing in practice: example

The Internet banks such as Egg, Cahoot and Smile have been particularly successful in using the Internet to prompt customers to compare and contrast their prices, essentially their interest rates, with those of competitors. They understand that increasingly the Internet bank customer will shop around on the net to find the most attractive rates.

Marketing in practice: case study

'Don't stoop so low'

Although being competitive on price is vital, it is usually a mistake to use price as the main competitive weapon in the marketing mix. In fact, from the marketers perspective, price competition is the lowest form of competition and in many ways is a sign of marketing failure.

If price is the main competitive weapon, this means that we have not tried and/or managed to persuade the customer of the superior value of our total offering. In doing so then, we leave the customer with nothing else on which to choose between suppliers or brands than price. The most effective marketing 'de-sensitizes' customers to price persuading them instead to purchase on the basis is perceived superior value.

The European market for hair shampoo and conditioning products is amongst the most competitive markets in the world. With several major global companies including the likes of Proctor & Gamble (P&G) L'Oreal, Lever Faberge, John Frieda, Alberto Culver, and Johnson and Johnson all fighting for market share in what is estimated to be a £550 million market. Entry barriers to this market are surprisingly low, there are literally dozens of brands to choose from. Moreover, shampoos and conditioner products are frequently purchased products often bought at the same time as the grocery in supermarkets. This then is a market that would in many ways appear to very close to being a perfectly competitive market structure where price competition would predominate and the leading brands and market shares being those with the lowest prices.

In fact, some of the most successful and fastest growing shampoo and conditioner brands in this market today compete not on price at all but rather on the bases of superior quality and product performance and/or by focusing on the special needs of clearly identified segments of the market. So, for example, P&G's Nicky Clarke range of branded products (formerly owned by Wella) is very successful despite, or perhaps because of, its premium price. Alberto Culver has attempted to hold its market share not by competing primarily on price but by continuing to produce shampoos for specific hair types, for example Sunsilk. One of the industries original mass-market, shampoos has moved to producing products for specific uses such as a shampoo for 'removing frizz'.

Admittedly, there is still plenty of price promotion, slowly but surely, however, brand managers in this market are realizing that competing on price simply drives margins and profits down for everyone in the industry. In addition, once prices are reduced it is very difficult to increase them again. Finally, low prices detract from the image and positioning strategies for a brand, and make it that much more difficult to support brand development through R&D and promotion.

It really is possible to price too low.

Summary

- In this unit, we have seen that price plays a central and unique role in the marketing mix.
- The economist, the accountant and the marketer each have different perspectives on pricing, but each has something to contribute to the pricing decision. The major inputs to pricing decisions are the 4Cs of Cost, Customers, Competition and Company.
- The pricing decision should be systematically structured as a series of steps or stages.
- Pricing methods include cost-based methods, competitor-based methods and demand/ market-based methods.
- Pricing decisions should reflect company objectives and strategies.
- Pricing strategies may vary over the life cycle of a product.
- Two alternative pricing strategies for new products are price skimming and price penetration. A company needs to establish pricing policies, including responsibilities for pricing, credit policies and price adjustment policies.
- The growth of Internet marketing is increasing price competition and shopping around on the part of customers for low prices in many markets.

Examination preparation: previous examination question

Attempt Question 2 of the examination paper for June 2004 (Appendix 4). For Specimen Answer Examination Question 2 June 2004, see Appendix 4 and www.cim.co.uk.

Further reading and bibliography

Brassington, F. and Pettitt, S. (2003) *Principles of Marketing*, 3rd edition, FT Prentice Hall, Chapters 10 and 11.

Dibb, S., Simkin, L., Pride, W. and Ferrell, O.C. (2000) *Marketing Concepts and Strategies*, 4th European edition, Houghton, Mifflin, Chapters 18 and 19.

Lancaster, G., Massingham, L. and Ashford, R. (2001) *Essentials of Marketing*, 4th edition, McGraw-Hill, Chapter 7.

unit 6
the marketing mix: place

Learning objectives

Learning outcomes

By the end of this unit you will be able to:

o Identify and describe the place element of the marketing mix.

Knowledge and skills

By the end of this unit you will be able to:

o Define channels of distribution, intermediaries and logistics, and understand the contribution they make to the marketing effort (3.10).

o State and explain the factors that influence channel decisions and the selection of alternative distribution channel options, including the effects of the new ICT (3.11).

Study Guide

This unit covers our third key element of the marketing mix and encompasses the means and mechanisms whereby products and services are made available to customers.

Variously referred to as either distribution or (in the context of our 4Ps) 'place', this element for a variety of reasons has been perhaps a neglected area of marketing. However, as we shall see, and as no doubt you can appreciate, the place element is just as important as each of the other three elements of the mix, and is very much the responsibility of the marketer – though increasingly the management and planning of channels of distribution and logistics is a task for a specialist in this area. In fact, many organizations now employ such experts. While acknowledging that this is an increasingly specialized field and therefore it is not necessary, appropriate, or possible for you to become an expert in this area, we must add that the focus for the design and planning of distribution and logistics must be on the customer and his or her needs. Because of this and because of its central importance to effective marketing plans, it is vital that you at least appreciate the role of the marketing function in the design, operation and control of place.

We would expect it to take you about 3 hours to work through this unit and suggest you allow a further 3–4 hours to undertake the various activities suggested. Other than your notebook and writing equipment, you will not need anything further to complete this unit.

The role and importance of place in marketing

Study tip

As with pricing decisions, some aspects of a company's distribution strategy can be observed on an everyday basis in your role as consumer. As for pricing therefore, when you have studied this unit, you should look out for good examples to illustrate the use (and abuse) of some of the aspects of planning logistics and distribution you will cover in the unit. Where appropriate and feasible, as in earlier units, we shall also be asking you to explore this element of the mix in the context of your own organization.

Put simply, the role of this element of the marketing mix is to ensure that products and services are available to target customers in the 'right place' and at the 'right time'. However, there are other important aspects to the place element. For example, the marketer's product and services also need to be available:

- In the 'right quantities'
- In the 'right condition'
- With the 'right degree' of advice, installation and after-sales service.

If place is badly planned, these requirements to be 'right' will not be fulfilled, and as a consequence all the other possibly perfectly planned efforts of the marketer, such as an excellent product, a competitive price and an exciting advertising campaign, will be to no avail. Indeed companies have often gone out of business and new products failed because of problems with distribution and logistics.

Another way of illustrating the role and importance of place in marketing is to consider some of the things that can go wrong and the implications for the marketer and the company. Here are just some examples:

- 'Nobody could be persuaded to stock the product.' Perhaps the marketing implications of this are obvious.
- 'Most of the retailers who carry the product are out of stock.' Customers go elsewhere, become angry and brand disloyal.
- 'At the moment our retailers are carrying too much stock, owing to our unwillingness to deliver in smaller quantities.' Retailers go elsewhere, become angry and supplier disloyal.
- 'Ten per cent of our products are being damaged in transit.' Customers, distributors and our own board of directors become angry.
- 'Our competitors will now deliver direct to the customer's home.' We have lost 10 per cent market share.
- 'The costs of our distribution are much too high, owing to ineffective warehousing and delivery.' We have lost 10 per cent of our profits.

We could go on citing examples of the types of problem companies can have with a badly planned place element, but it should now be obvious to you that ineffective management in this area has a major impact on levels of customer satisfaction and levels of company sales and profits. Put another way, effective management of place is now recognized as being a major factor in competitive marketing strategy and company success.

Activity 6.1

Try to recall any 'bad experiences' you have had as a customer or a potential customer for a product/service in the past, which perhaps on reflection have been due to badly planned and managed distribution.

Reflect on the effect of this experience at the time with regard to your attitudes towards the product or brand and its supplier.

A heightened and changed role for place

Everything we have said so far about place underlines its importance in marketing. In recent times, though, this importance has increased, bringing with it a changing role for place in marketing and the development of new techniques and approaches to its management. We can briefly explore the reasons for these changes.

The high costs of distribution/potential for savings

Until relatively recently, distribution and logistics have been neglected areas for potential cost savings. This is perhaps surprising, given that costs associated with distribution and logistics account for 30 per cent or more of a product's total cost. Somewhat belatedly but now increasingly, companies are recognizing rapidly that these potential cost savings represent significant opportunities for improving profits.

The potential for competitive advantage

We have already noted the impact (both good and bad) of place and its management on customers. Effective distribution and logistics designed to increase customer satisfaction can have a tremendous effect on sales and market share. Customers, in fact, now demand levels of service from distribution unheard of even 5 years ago. In addition, as we shall see later, some of the trends in industrial manufacturing and production, such as 'just in time' management, have resulted in a premium for those marketers who can plan their distribution logistics to meet the increased demands placed on them by such developments.

Improved techniques for planning and managing place

Partly as a result of the recognition of the potential for cost-saving and competitive advantage, significant strides have been made in recent years in the tools and techniques for managing place more effectively. In addition, as mentioned earlier, we now have specialists in this area of marketing. The concept of place has moved from looking at individual elements of the distribution network such as channels, to viewing and planning distribution as a complete interrelated system in which the whole process of moving products and services into, through and out of the organization is planned.

With these points in mind we can now turn our attention to planning the place element of the marketing mix.

Broadly there are two key and interrelated areas in planning the place part of the mix. In fact because they are interrelated, they should ideally be planned together. However, we shall discuss each area of planning separately before looking at them as two sub-elements in a total system. The two areas are:

1. Planning marketing channels
2. Planning physical distribution/logistics.

We shall start with channels.

Marketing channels

 Definition

A marketing channel – Comprises individuals and organizations that together ensure the flow of products and services from producer to customers.

The use of the word 'channel' is appropriate in that in itself it indicates a pipeline and flows through it. In fact, perhaps the easiest way to understand the notion of a marketing channel is to use a simple diagram. See Figure 6.1.

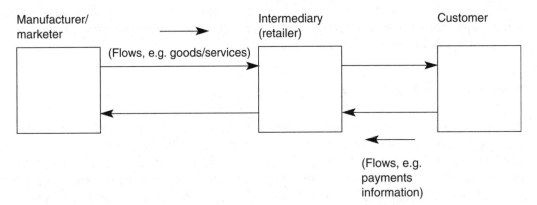

Figure 6.1 A simple channel of distribution

As an example, Kelloggs manufactures its range of breakfast cereals, packaging its various products in sizes suitable for the target market. From its production plants, the company's different products are delivered directly to retail outlets throughout the world based on pre-negotiated contracts and according to customer demand. Through these retail intermediaries, Kelloggs' products are then made available to final customers, with these customers being required to make payment there and then. Information on demand including, for example, responses to new products or special promotional deals can be fed back via the retailer direct to Kelloggs' marketing and production teams. Payment to Kelloggs is made by the intermediaries on pre-negotiated terms. The retailer provides stocking and assortment functions for Kelloggs with promotional and other marketing tools often being shared between both parties. Information about the customer and demand is fed back by the retailer to Kelloggs and can be used to adjust marketing tactics and to help develop new products.

Activity 6.2

Using Figure 6.1, list what you think are the key elements of a channel of distribution.

Not all channels look like the one shown in Figure 6.1. Some are longer, with more intermediaries; some have different types of intermediary; some are shorter. Often different flows, outward and inward, occur. In fact, these elements of the channel are decision areas. The marketer must plan the configuration of the channel using these elements as variables. The key decision areas, therefore, in planning a channel of distribution are as follows:

1. Channel length, that is the number of intermediaries or 'levels' in the channel.
2. Types of intermediary (if any) in the channel.
3. Channel/market coverage, that is the number of intermediaries at any one level.
4. Respective tasks, responsibilities and terms for various channel members.

Channel length

In Figure 6.1, there is only one intermediary level between the producer/marketer and the final customer. The channel, therefore, is relatively short and is in fact a 'one-level channel'. A 'two-level channel' has two sets of intermediaries, a 'three-level channel' has three sets and so on.

 Activity 6.3

What do you think a 'zero-level channel' is?

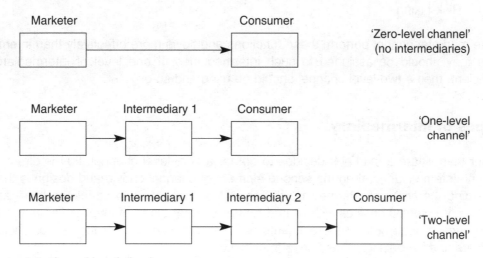

Figure 6.2 Channel length/levels

Examples of markets where the various channel lengths tend to predominate include:

○ Zero level (direct): For example mail order books/records, direct flight bookings, Internet sales and bookings of various kinds.
○ One-level channel: Many FMCG fall into this category, for example branded foodstuffs, clothing, DIY products, cars.
○ Two or more level channels: Many smaller companies tend to use two or more level channels, as their size means that they have to deal through, for example wholesalers.

Generally speaking the longer the channel, that is the more levels, the further the marketer is from the final customer, and therefore the less control the marketer can exert. In addition, each level of the channel will normally wish to make a profit; hence either final prices to the customer are increased and/or profit margins at each level are decreased. This would seem to imply that the shorter the channel, the better. In fact it raises the question as to why a marketer should use intermediaries at all instead of direct marketing.

Activity 6.4

On the basis of your own experience/knowledge try to list any reasons why the marketer might use intermediaries in distributing products and services.

Ultimately, a decision to use intermediaries at one or more levels in a channel is based upon their superior effectiveness in performing the required channel functions and flows. We have already seen a little of the flows involved in channels in Figure 6.1, but examples of other functions and flows required to be performed in channels include:

○ Storage and movement of products
○ Transfer of ownership/title
○ Promotion
○ Negotiation
○ Risk-taking.

If the marketer cannot perform these functions and flows more effectively than intermediaries, then they should be assigned to such intermediaries. If one level of intermediaries is not sufficient, then a two-level channel should be used and so on.

Types of intermediary

Other than where a marketer decides to opt for a zero-level channel, that is direct marketing with no intermediaries, then the second element of channel choice and design is the decision regarding the types of intermediary to use in the channel. With variations there are literally dozens of potential choices with regard to the different types of intermediaries but the major categories of intermediaries are agents and brokers, distributors and dealers, wholesalers, retailers and increasingly these days franchisees.

Agents and brokers are often used in international and export marketing. Effectively, agents perform a sales function for the marketer and rather than taking legal title or even physical possession of products and services, they act on behalf of the manufacturer to bring buyer and seller together.

Distributors and dealers are used in many markets, but in particular are found in b2b markets and in consumer product areas such as computers and motor cars. Distributors and dealers are usually independent companies but who are closely allied to the supplying marketer. They effectively serve to add value through their special knowledge and/or additional services offered to customers such as delivery, after-sales service and so on. In some cases, distributors and dealers may be afforded the status of 'exclusive dealerships' in that they are granted the exclusive right to sell a company's products in, say, a designated geographical area. The rules and regulations pertaining to exclusive dealership agreements are quite complex and the marketer can run foul of competition policy if care is not taken in the design and operation of such agreements.

Marketing in practice: example

In the European Union, there has been considerable controversy over some of the dealership arrangements between manufacturers and independent dealers of cars. It was suggested that some of these dealership arrangements effectively prevented customers from securing the best deal when purchasing a particular model. So, for example, some dealers, supported by their manufacturing suppliers were refusing to service models purchased in another country by a customer. Similarly, they were refusing to fulfil warranty obligations. At the time of writing, although these and other issues concerned with the practice of dealer and distributor networks in the European motor industry were under review, steps have already been taken to open up the market to more competition through new legislation pertaining to the operation of these activities.

Wholesalers generally do not deal with final customers but with other intermediaries, normally retailers. The wholesaler essentially performs a bulk buying, storage and bulk breaking set of functions in the channel. Wholesalers act as independent intermediaries in the channel and take legal title to goods as well as physical possession.

Retailers of course sell direct to consumers and are the most frequently used intermediary for most types of consumer goods and certainly FMCG. Some smaller retailers purchase from wholesalers but the larger retailers with their huge purchasing power normally deal direct with manufacturers. In many markets, large retailers effectively control the channel and the marketing of many products and services meaning that effectively they are in charge of many of the marketing mix elements of the products they market and in particular pricing and many of the promotional decisions.

In recent years, one of the major growth areas has been franchising arrangements. Examples of products which are marketed through franchise channels include, for example, Kentucky Fried Chicken, The Body Shop, Dynarod, Benetton and of course the best-known franchise operation of all, McDonalds. We need not concern ourselves with all the different types of franchising here and certainly not with the detailed issues of their establishment and administration. Essentially, though, all franchising is based on a contractual arrangement between the owner or originator of a product or service and an essentially independent franchisee. In return for a licence to produce and market the product or service, together with advice and help on aspects such as production, delivery, and on selling and marketing of the product or service, the franchisee pays usually an up-front payment followed by royalties on sales.

 ## Activity 6.5

If you are currently working for an organization or company try to find out what sorts of intermediary (possibly at various levels in the channel) are available/used to distribute the types of products or services that your company markets.

Channels/market coverage

This third element of channel planning and decisions relates to the number of intermediaries to be used. So, for example, the marketer has to decide whether distribution will be, say, on a national basis or only in selected regional locations. Another aspect of market coverage would be the number of intermediaries and/or outlets to be covered within a particular region. So, for example, the marketer can decide to cover all the outlets in a region or only selected ones. Market coverage, then, is often referred to as distribution intensity. There are three major categories of possible market coverage, namely intensive, selective and exclusive.

Intensive distribution as the term implies means that the marketer goes for the maximum market coverage so this might, say, encompass national distribution as opposed to selected regions with all outlets covered in each region. Intensive distribution is particularly appropriate where products have to be easily and widely available because, for example, they are regularly purchased convenience products such as, bread, newspapers, cigarettes, milk and so on.

Selective distribution, again as the term suggests, is where the marketer uses a smaller number of intermediaries and/or outlets than the maximum available. So, for example, the marketer may select only certain distributors or retailers so as not to swamp the market. Selective distribution is often used for shopping-type products such as electrical goods where the customer needs some help in selection and therefore only certain intermediaries may have the necessary skills and training.

Exclusive distribution is where the marketer uses a very small number of intermediaries and may relatedly cover only selected areas of the market. Needless to say, exclusive distribution is used for products which are either in themselves exclusive due to, say, price such as Rolex watches, and/or where the product or service is specialized and requires specialist support and knowledge from the intermediary. Exclusive distribution is therefore often used in the marketing of expensive capital and/or technical products in b2b markets.

Question 6.1

Which of the following products would probably be best distributed on an intensive, exclusive or selective basis?

Compare your answers with those shown in the debriefing.

- o Rolex watches
- o Cigarettes
- o Mid-priced hi-fi systems
- o Toilet rolls
- o Haute couture fashion.

Respective tasks, responsibilities and terms

This fourth and final element of channel design and planning encompasses decisions regarding who does what in the marketing process. So, for example, decisions need to be made as to, say, who will be responsible ultimately for determining prices. Similarly, decisions need to be made regarding who will undertake and be responsible for delivery and after-sales service. It is very important to establish and agree wherever possible the respective tasks, responsibilities and terms for the various members of the channel. It is often disputes about these areas that give rise to major channel conflict. Sometimes, particularly where the different members of the channel effectively operate independently, it is almost impossible to secure agreement between the respective members with regard to who does what.

These then are our four major elements of channel design and planning but what factors affect decisions about these elements and therefore the overall plan for the channel itself?

Factors affecting channel choice and design

Many factors affect channel choice and design with regard to making decisions about the four major components of channel design just outlined. Ultimately, the marketer should try to design the channel so that it is most effective and efficient in performing its functions. However this is difficult because there are often conflicting considerations with regard to effectiveness and efficiency when assessed from the point of view of the marketer, intermediaries and customers.

Some of the major factors influencing channel choice include, for example,

- o Organizational objectives and resources
- o Marketing objectives and strategies
- o The target market and in particular whether it is local, national or international
- o The characteristics of the product, for example whether it is bulky, dangerous, fragile, perishable and so on
- o The level of expertise and specialist knowledge required when dealing with customers for the product or service
- o Customer needs and requirements with regard to, e.g. delivery, after-sales service, credit and so on
- o Customer purchasing habits and preferences, for example types of stores visited
- o Competitor considerations, for example channels used by competitors/opportunities for innovation and competitive advantage
- o Channel availability
- o Costs and profitability of channel alternatives
- o Degree of control
- o Legal/regulatory considerations.

We can see then that the channel choice and planning process is complex and multi-faceted. Many factors affect what is the most appropriate and effective channel and the marketer must make a careful assessment of these factors in arriving at channel selection and configuration.

The growth of direct marketing

In recent years there has been a trend towards shorter channels. In fact direct marketing, that is a zero-level channel, is increasingly being used. As the term implies in direct marketing, the marketer directly sells to the final customer.

 Activity 6.6

> List four examples of types of direct marketing. Then compare your list with the one shown in the debriefing.

As we saw earlier, direct marketing can only be justified where it is more efficient and effective than using intermediaries. A number of reasons explain the growth of direct marketing in most countries of the world.

Activity 6.7

Try to list four possible reasons for the growth of direct marketing. Then compare your list with that shown in the debriefing.

The reasons for the growth in direct marketing shown in the debriefing Activity 6.6 at the end of the book explain the reasons why marketers have been interested in using this form of distribution more and more in recent years. However, this desire and willingness to use direct marketing on the part of marketers, important though this is, is not on its own sufficient to explain the significant growth in this area in recent years. Equally important to the growth in direct marketing, therefore, have been two other factors, which have been equally significant in helping the growth of direct marketing. These two factors are, first, the advances in IT and particularly databases, and, secondly, developments and advances in direct response media. We shall now consider each of these a little more.

Information technology and direct marketing: use of databases

The advances in IT have enabled organizations to develop and use sophisticated databases to identify their customers, their behaviour and characteristics, and as a result, to market to them directly without the need for intermediaries. There is no doubt that the database is central to successful direct marketing activities. Increasingly, powerful and low-cost computer power has enabled companies to collect and store data on customers which can be used to, for example, determine appropriate segments and target markets, produce mailing lists, store information on customer responses to direct communications and so on. Information may be stored regarding transactions with customers in the past, but can also be bought in from, say, list agencies for targeting direct mail and other forms of direct marketing contact. The databases can be used to track, analyse and develop relationships with customers. Many companies are now using their databases to develop these relationships as a key part of their overall marketing and promotional strategy. We shall examine the use of databases in more detail in Unit 9 and the use of databases on customers in the development of relationship marketing, together with the meaning and implications of relationship marketing itself, in more detail in Unit 8 when we consider customer care. Databases now include information on customers from very many sources, which can be layered and amalgamated to give a comprehensive profile of customers. Examples of sources of information for databases that facilitate direct marketing include, for example: census data, postcode data, electoral role data, credit data, transactional data, vehicle ownership data and lifestyle databases.

Often database information is available from commercial databases and indeed there are some companies whose whole business is the provision of data including, for example, list companies which specialize in supplying information for direct marketing.

A good example of a company developing business opportunities through the provision of databases and database information is the Royal Mail in the United Kingdom. As you would expect, the Royal Mail's database centres around address and postcode information. But this information is also linked to huge amounts of other consumer information in their database. In this way, postcode addresses can be linked to, for example, purchasing behaviour variables and/or lifestyle information to provide insightful information for marketing decisions. Direct marketers in particular have found this and other similar databases useful.

Extending knowledge

You might want to look further at some of these database providers to see what sort of services they can offer. Needless to say, many of them can be accessed through their company websites. So, for example, information about the Royal Mail database services can be accessed through www.royalmail.com/mysolution.

In addition to these commercially available databases, many companies of course develop their own databases on customers. So, for example, many of the leading UK retailers have developed in-house databases. The use of loyalty card systems, mentioned earlier in our discussion of relationship marketing, has proved invaluable here. A good example of a company using loyalty cards and schemes in this way is the Boots company who use their Advantage loyalty card system to build a database which in turn helps them to develop effective promotional and other marketing campaigns based on a detailed knowledge of its cardholders and users.

As you would expect, the internally developed database has several potential advantages compared to its bought-in counterpart. In particular, there is greater potential for control, greater potential accuracy, and a tendency for the information in the database, perhaps for understandable reasons, to be more relevant to the marketer's activities.

Against these potential advantages of developing an internal powered database are the costs and complexity, not to mention the skills, required for a company to build and use its own database systems. Database providers are now very professional and bring high degrees of expertise and experience to the marketer. Further examples of information database services include, for example, the British Market Research Bureau, CACI and Nielson Audits. Again, remember many of these marketing databases can be accessed via the Internet. In their text *Principles of Marketing*, Brassington and Pettitt suggest that there are currently over 4000 companies offering database services in the United Kingdom with a further 20 000 throughout the rest of Europe.

To some extent, if anything, the problem that marketers face today is not lack of information and data, but rather a surfeit of it, leading to the potential for information overload. It is important to remember that information costs money and a substantial amount of money can be wasted building, accessing and using databases if great care is not taken in their design and operation. Examples of the sorts of potential problems which marketers must seek to avoid in their database systems include data which is out of date and/or inaccurate data which cannot easily be accessed and analysed, and above all, data which is not useful in helping to improve marketing decisions. Effective database design and operation therefore is extremely important and must be suitable for the purpose the marketer intends. In the case of direct marketing programmes, the following represents the types of information, which might be required for developing and executing a consumer goods direct marketing campaign.

- o Customer name
- o Customer address – and in particular postcode
- o Customer status, for example user, non-user, lapsed user and so on
- o Age
- o Income
- o Socio-economic group
- o Purchase history (where appropriate)
- o Geodemographic profile
- o Previous response profile (where appropriate).

Remember, these are just examples of the sort of information that might be contained in a typical database for a direct marketing campaign. Obviously the more information, the more accurate this information, and the more relevant to the marketing campaign in question, the better. Though again we need to remember that information costs money. The database should help to ensure that the direct mail campaign is aimed at the right target customers and that the content of the direct mail programme is designed with these target customers in mind. In doing so, there is likely to be a much higher response rate and of course a reduction in the number of customers feeling that they have been sent junk mail.

Another important aspect of information kept on databases that the marketer needs to consider is the issue of data protection. In 1998, in the United Kingdom, the Data Protection Act became law. This is a complex area of legislation but essentially the Act was designed to regulate how information held on databases could be accessed, analysed and used. It not only encompasses marketing activities but for obvious reasons marketers and particularly direct marketers are affected by the Act. Because the Act encompassed so many activities and was far-reaching, it has been gradually rolled out and was finally fully implemented only in October 2001. Any marketer accessing or holding information on databases must understand and comply with this important Act. Similarly, marketers who utilize this data for direct marketing activities must fully understand the implications of the Act.

Marketing in practice: example

An excellent guide to the Data Protection Act and its implications for the direct marketer is available from the Direct Marketing Association. Details of this can be accessed through the Direct Marketing Association website www.dma.org.uk.

Not surprisingly, the difference between an effective and an ineffective database with regard to the impact of direct mail and marketing campaigns can be significant. The marketer needs to ensure, therefore, that the database is kept up to date and clean. This helps not only to improve response rates but also to mitigate against some of the worst of the horror stories which have in the past been associated with some direct marketing campaigns. For example, some companies unfortunately send out direct mail shots to customers who are deceased. Or, for example, offering pregnancy testing services to pensioners.

Marketing in practice: example

A company which has made excellent use of direct marketing in its sales and marketing strategies is Slendertone. Using a comprehensive and well-designed database, Slendertone has used a wide range of direct response tools including, for example, direct mail, press and radio to achieve uninterrupted growth in market share.

Developments in direct distribution technology: electronic methods

Although direct marketing represents a zero-level channel, and therefore is legitimately a consideration in developing the place element of the mix, direct marketing campaigns also make use of promotional tools and media, indeed they are essential in the development and implementation of a direct marketing approach. Because of this, therefore, we shall also return to direct marketing, and in particular to some of the main tools used in direct marketing in Unit 7 covering the promotional tools of marketing.

However, there have been several major developments in the last few years with regard to the technology available for distribution which have in turn facilitated further growth and potential for more direct channels of distribution which you need to be familiar with. In particular, the growth in direct marketing in recent years has been underpinned by the development of direct distribution via electronic methods which in turn have given rise to a move towards convenience driven access such as home shopping. Of particular significance here, of course, is the Internet and the World Wide Web.

The Internet and the World Wide Web

The growth of the Internet and the World Wide Web represents probably the most significant development in direct marketing. The customer can now shop from home surfing the World Wide Web for products and services to buy on-line.

At first restricted in many countries by the incidence of PC ownership and by concerns about security, the Internet and the direct marketing which goes with it has finally taken off and there is no doubt that it will continue to grow in importance. In some ways, the Internet probably represents the most direct marketing channel possible; other than a service provider and perhaps an Internet search engine no intermediaries are involved at all in the channel. Hence, as we have seen in the previous unit, prices can therefore, potentially at least, be much lower than through conventional channels. Perhaps above all, however, the Internet represents one of the most convenient ways of purchasing for the customer. No longer does the customer have to turn out in inclement weather and struggle to find a parking space at the shopping centre; the customer can now not only shop, but shop around from the comfort of their homes. Although the Internet is growing rapidly as a marketing channel throughout Europe and particularly in the United Kingdom, many marketers have still not woken up to the potential and impact from a channel and marketing perspective. Even those companies that have developed websites have often not got to grips with the fact that in order to be effective, great care must be taken in the design of the website and, for example, its links with search engines, etc. Put bluntly, website and Internet marketing skills in general are poorly developed in many companies. Many companies make the mistake of thinking that a website is just another way of advertising or presenting information about the company and its products. Many companies and certainly many marketers who would never dream, for example, of designing their own advertising and copy content, are quite happy to design their own websites. As a result, and again to be blunt, many websites are unprofessional, underutilized and unimpressive. Marketers must realize that website design in all its facets requires specialized skills and knowledge and is far better left to experts in this area. Having said this, of course, this is not a reason for the marketer not understanding at least the basics of website design and Internet usage in marketing. Marketers are now increasingly appreciating how Web techniques such as 'chat rooms' and 'bulletin boards', for example, can be used in marketing.

Extending knowledge

Although, as we have said, marketers should leave the more technical aspects of website design and operation to the experts, by the same token the contemporary marketer must be familiar with the use of websites and the Internet for developing marketing programmes, including the area we are discussing here, namely direct marketing. You should take the opportunity therefore to learn as much as you can about Web-based marketing, the Internet and e-commerce. Two particularly good textbooks which you are advised to consult in this area are those by D. Chaffey, L. Mayer, L. Johnston and F. Ellis-Chadwick (*Internet Marketing*) and *Cybermarketing* by P. Bickerton, M. Bickerton and U. Pardesi which are in fact essential reading for this syllabus.

There is also a huge amount of information available on the use of the Internet and Web-based marketing on the following CIM websites:

> www.wnim.com
> www.connectedinmarketing.com

Although the growth of the Internet and the World Wide Web is, as previously mentioned, linked to developments in technology and, for example, the incidence of PC ownership, as you would expect this growth is driven by the fact that as a marketing channel the Internet offers several advantages compared to other channels, including other direct channels such as mail order, telemarketing and so on. Some of these advantages accrue to the marketer and some to the customer, but the real driving forces in the growth of this channel are those where the advantages accrue to both. Some of the advantages which serve to explain the growth of the Internet as a marketing channel include:

- ○ Convenience
- ○ Potential for lower prices to customers
- ○ Potential for customers to shop around
- ○ Potential for marketer to build databases based on customer visits, information provision and so on
- ○ Flexibility and speed, for example customer orders can be dealt with immediately, quick delivery and so on
- ○ Customers using/visiting websites already predisposed towards product, that is have already indicated interest
- ○ Websites potentially much more interesting than other direct promotional material, that is can include movement and sound.

In addition to PC ownership and the cost of access to the Internet, probably the major factor determining future growth of this area of marketing will be consumer attitudes towards security factors. A recent government survey in the United Kingdom indicated that worries about security among Internet users represents the major barrier to an increased growth in shopping via this channel. Some 70 per cent of regular Internet users expressed concern and said that it was the main reason for their not having bought anything through this channel. Certainly, there have been problems in some instances with, for example, protecting customers' information and interests, but perhaps as much as anything this is really a marketing problem, that is potential shoppers need to be convinced and persuaded about the levels of security in the Internet shopping systems.

Despite these concerns, however, the advantages of the Internet as a channel of distribution mean that it will certainly continue to grow in importance.

Other technology driven advances

Although the Internet probably represents the most important technological development affecting channels, it is by no means the only one. Again, we shall consider some of these developments in other units in the context of, for example, the promotional mix (in Unit 7). Specifically in the context of channels, however, and even more specifically in the context of direct marketing channels, other technological developments have had or are beginning to have a major effect. Two of the most important are introduced below.

Telemarketing

Although obviously the telephone is not a new technology, ownership is now so widespread in many countries that marketers have turned more and more to using the telephone as a way of directly selling, or at least communicating, to their customers. Both outbound, where the organization contacts a potential customer, and inbound, where the potential customer is encouraged to contact the organization, are used as in, for example, direct response advertising. As with direct mail and the Internet, telemarketing is both a promotional tool and a marketing channel. With telemarketing customers are contacted in their own homes or businesses with a view to creating some sort of response. Sometimes the response sought will be a direct sale, but more often the response sought will be to encourage interest and to generate sales leads and opportunities including the establishment of appointments, for example for a salesperson to visit. Because customers are being contacted in their own homes or premises and because calls are usually unsolicited, there are some who feel that this type of marketing is intrusive and even unethical. Certainly, telemarketing can be annoying to some customers and great care needs to be used in its application. In addition, there are industry codes of practice and regulations which govern the use of this tool. For telemarketing to be successful like direct mail, good lists are important. It is also important to ensure that company personnel making the calls are well trained and polite. Success rates in terms of, for example, generating appointments and certainly for generating sales are relatively low with often as many as 100 calls being required to generate only one or two successes. However, compared to other forms of promotion and channel arrangements, costs are also relatively low. It is likely that, despite some customer resistance to this method of direct marketing, usage of this channel will continue to grow.

Marketing in practice: example

Perhaps understandably, a company which has made extensive and effective use of telemarketing is the UK telecommunications company British Telecom. The company contacts existing customers on a regular basis via the telephone checking on whether customers are satisfied with their current level and range of services, advising them on how to reduce their telephone bills or make more effective use of the services they are currently subscribed to, and finally using the telephone to market new products and services to their existing customers. The company has also had a concerted campaign to recapture customers who have switched to other telephone service providers, again of course through telemarketing.

Admittedly, in the past, contacting customers particularly in their own homes via the telephone in order to sell them products has been viewed as a somewhat unprofessional approach to marketing. However, thankfully some of the worst excesses of the past have now been replaced by much more professional techniques of telephone selling.

In addition, of course, to the marketer contacting customers via the telephone, customers can also contact marketers. Sometimes this contact comprises an enquiry or even sometimes the placement of an order, but in addition customers contact companies in order to sort out problems, pay bills, make complaints and so on. Increasingly, organizations have discouraged face-to-face contact with customers as this is expensive on staff time and facilities. Instead, a major trend has been the establishment of the so-called 'call centres' which deal with customers, their enquiries, complaints and so on, in one central location. Many marketers claim that this improves customer service and helps develop better customer relationships because customers can often make contact via their own telephones, 24 hours a day, 7 days a week. In fact, the introduction and operation of call centres has in recent years been one of the most frequent causes of customer dissatisfaction and frustration. This is because, in the past all too often, call centres have been used more to reduce costs rather than improve customer service. Call centres or any inbound telemarketing service needs to be carefully designed and managed if it is to improve customer service and help develop better customer relationships. Having to wait several minutes before a reply or having to hold while they are re-routed through several sub-systems while often at the same time being subjected to 'musak' can be very annoying and frustrating to customers. The best telemarketers have developed effective systems for call centres and the management of inbound telemarketing operations so as to improve rather than detract from levels of customer service.

Marketing in practice: example

Partly prompted by the success and hence threat of its competitor, EasyJet, and its successful use of telemarketing, British Airways has responded by expanding and improving its facilities for telephone booking. This has facilitated the ease with which customers can enquire about and then book seats on its airline. Telephone enquirers now obtain a much quicker service than they have done in the past. British Airways predicts that an increasing percentage of its sales will come from a combination of direct response advertising and telephone contact thereby increasing response times while at the same time cutting costs.

An interesting development in the use of call centres in telemarketing is the use of what have become termed 'V-Reps'. This is where a customer contacts a call centre and is connected to a virtual call-centre operator – the V-Rep who can talk to and understand customers. Using state-of-the-art virtual computing technology V-Reps provide an almost 'human face' to the call-centre caller. In this way, instead of being asked to 'hold', for example, the customer can talk 'face to face' with a talking V-Rep. It is felt that the V-Rep approach is much more sympathetic and warm to the caller than simply talking to a telephone operator. In addition, of course, human beings who cost in the region of £30 per call and are also subject to the ups and downs of the normal human condition in dealing with callers can be replaced with cheap electronic replacements which cost as little as £1.50 per call, do not eat, sleep, drink or have off-days and can be programmed to be as attractive and amenable as is felt necessary. Increasingly V-Reps are being linked to company websites where a customer or 'caller' has the added advantage of actually being able to see the V-Rep on screen.

Marketing in practice: example

The brewing company Miller Brewing have a V-Rep called 'Bill the Brewmaster'. Bill is there to answer callers' problems or questions regarding anything to do with beer, its brewing and consumption.

Contact at www.millerbrewing.com

Coca-Cola have a V-Rep called 'Hank' who can be contacted at www.coca-cola.com

AT&T's V-Rep is 'Allie' found at www.allie.att.com

Ford Motor Company have 'Kate' as their V-Rep at www.ford.com/en/support

Ragu Pasta Sauce have 'Mama' as their V-Rep at www.eat.com

M-marketing

The 'M' here stands for 'Mobile'. Mobile marketing looks set to be one of the fastest growing and most exciting recent developments in marketing in recent years. Essentially, another form of telemarketing in as much as it is based on use of the telephone, as the term implies, mobile marketing centres on marketing through the mobile telephone. As with many of the channels discussed in this unit, M-marketing, although in part a channel of distribution, is more properly considered as a promotional tool and therefore this important area and development in marketing is considered in Unit 7.

Teleshopping/interactive TV

The growth of this type of channel and promotional method is underpinned by developments in communications technology. For example, cable and satellite television allied to digital technologies are giving rise to significant growth in home-based shopping via the television. Many of the cable and satellite companies offer channels specifically devoted to shopping but in addition, of course, conventional programming often now includes opportunities for teleshopping during the normal commercial breaks between programmes. Current developments such as 3D television and television linked directly through a modem to the Internet will only increase the use of this type of channel. Again, the underpinning reason for the growth of this channel is its convenience allied to an increase in satellite and cable systems and companies. There are those who believe that it is teleshopping via the Internet which represents the channel of the future as opposed to PC-based Internet usage. Certainly, the familiarity of the television as opposed to PCs for many people gives it a great advantage, but there is still a reluctance on the part of consumers to participate in television shopping. Teleshopping and particularly interactive shopping using the television linked to the Internet is growing throughout Europe and in many other parts of the world. Many of the cable and satellite operators have channels dedicated to teleshopping, an example being QVC on the cable and digital networks in the United Kingdom. The advantage of marketing products in this way is that there can be extensive and detailed demonstration of products to a live audience. Admittedly, many will watch simply as a form of entertainment but more and more customers are purchasing products using this form of marketing and distribution.

Extending knowledge

As you will appreciate, technology and particularly ICT is changing all the time. For this reason, you should try and keep as up to date as you can with recent developments in this area. In this unit, we have in fact considered some of the key developments in ICT as applied to the place element of the marketing mix, but you will find lots of examples and indications of emerging developments on the website:

www.wnim.co.uk

In addition you will find the following two websites provide excellent information on how these particular companies are using ICT in the place element of their marketing:

www.interflora.co.uk

Trends and developments in channels of distribution

Although it is impossible in what is one of the most dynamic areas of marketing to cover all the recent trends and developments in channels of distribution, the examiners will look for at least some appreciation of contemporary events. In addition to the problem of scope regarding trends and developments, at least some of these are country specific. For example, certain important trends in, say, retailing in the United Kingdom are not relevant to other parts of the world. However, with these caveats in mind it is possible to identify some broad general trends and developments in distribution which are affecting marketers on a broad scale.

Exam hint

As you know, the examiners will look for application and examples. Wherever possible try to find examples and applications of the key elements and concepts in the syllabus as they apply to your own country/situation. Remember that the basic principles (the fundamentals if you like) apply wherever you are.

Among some of the most significant trends and developments affecting channels of distribution are the following:

- ○ *The increased power of the retailers* – In many developed economies, and particularly in the United Kingdom, retailing has become very concentrated. The multiples are now very powerful and can often dictate terms to suppliers.
- ○ *The growth of own branding* – Related to the above, the power of the retailers has enabled them to market their own brands in direct competition with the suppliers' brands.

Marketing in practice: example

In many markets, in the past, retailers' own brands have essentially been cheaper versions of the manufacturer's branded version. Down-market packaging, fewer product features, more basic designs, all focused on selling the retailer's own brand products at lower prices, have been the norm with own brands.

More recently, however, many retailers have begun to develop and market what might be called real brands with distinct brand images and personalities and with 'real' brand values. These are designed to compete head-on with suppliers' own brands and on a value/quality basis rather than a low price basis. A good example of this are many of the own brands developed by the UK supermarket retailer, Sainsbury's. Among the 'real' own label brands are the 'Blue Parrot' range of children's food products, a 'Taste the Difference' range of branded food products and a range of products for the health conscious 'Be Good to Yourself'.

- ○ *The growth of 'vertical' marketing channels* – Vertical marketing channels are channels where the different levels and members in a channel are co-ordinated or managed by a single channel member so as to achieve efficient and effective distribution to target market customers. Vertical marketing channels also potentially reduce the inherent conflict between different levels and members in a channel. There are a number of ways in which vertical channel integration can be achieved. For example, one member of the marketing channel may simply purchase the operations of other members/levels of the channel. This is sometimes referred to as a *corporate* vertical marketing system (VMS). A retailer that purchases, for example, wholesaling and production facilities would be an example of a corporate VMS. Similarly, but this time working from the other end of the distribution channel, a manufacturer may purchase wholesaling and retailing facilities in order to con-solidate and co-ordinate this channel. A second approach to achieving vertical channel integration is known as an *administered* VMS. Here the different channel members remain independent with vertical integration and co-ordination being achieved on the basis of informal agreements between the members of the channel. Although channel members remain independent, normally one channel member will effectively control and administer the channel so as to optimize the operation of the channel as a whole. Often such control will fall to the largest and most powerful member of the channel. For example, in the United Kingdom the power and size of Marks & Spencer, the retailer, enables them to operate an administered VMS over which they have control. The third type of VMS for achieving vertical integration is the *contractual* VMS. Under this sort of system, the channel relationships and co-ordination are achieved through formalized agreements and contracts. A good example of this is the type of channel structure discussed earlier in the unit, namely franchising. As already mentioned, this has been one of the fastest growing types of channel arrangements in recent years. There are many reasons for this growth but there is no doubt that one of the main reasons is the fact that franchising offers the marketer (the franchisee) a substantial degree of control over channel arrangements and in particular the terms 'responsibilities' and 'activities' of the intermediaries.

o *The growth of 'horizontal' marketing channels* – This is where institutions at the same level of the marketing channel are combined under one management. For example, an organization may integrate horizontally by merging with another organization at the same level in a marketing channel such as the merger of a college with a university. Horizontal integration is done to achieve efficiencies and economies of scale in areas such as purchasing, promotion and so on. However, horizontal integration can lead to a decrease in flexibility and difficulties in co-ordination.

o *The growth of direct channels and the use of electronic methods* – These have been outlined earlier.

Activity 6.8

See if you can find examples of franchising arrangements in your own country and, where appropriate, preferably in your own area of marketing.

Note: You are not allowed to use McDonald's, Burger King or Kentucky Fried Chicken. (These are too easy!)

Physical distribution/logistics

Our second major element in planning the place decisions of a marketing mix is the planning of the systems and procedures for physically moving products and services from a marketer to the customer. This element is known therefore as physical distribution. In line with the increase in sophistication of planning place at the time of writing, the scope of planning physical distribution has widened to include all the physical flows of products and services into, through and out of the marketer's organization. This wider, and what was referred to earlier as a systems, approach to physical distribution is termed 'logistics'.

In examining physical distribution and logistics, we shall cover the following areas:

1. The importance of physical distribution/logistics
2. Key planning areas/decisions
3. Inputs to planning physical distribution and logistics.

177

The importance of physical distribution/logistics

Earlier we referred to the high cost of distribution and the potential for savings in this area. In most companies a large proportion of this cost and therefore potential for saving is associated with the physical distribution element of place. Perhaps this is easier to appreciate if we think of some of the functions and activities encompassed by physical distribution.

Activity 6.9

Before proceeding, see if you can write down what you think might be types of activity in physical distribution.

Much more important, however, for the marketer is again something we raised earlier in the unit that serves to underline the importance of physical distribution. This is the fact that physical distribution decisions have a major impact on levels of customer satisfaction (or dissatisfaction) and hence are a major source of potential competitive advantage.

This impact centres on levels of customer service, which are directly affected by the design and activities of the physical distribution system.

Activity 6.10

Before we proceed, see if you can write down any examples of elements of customer service that might be affected by physical distribution.

We can see that if a company can improve its level of service in areas such as this, it might increase sales and market share. This is especially true in markets where it is difficult to differentiate one's products and services in any other way.

In addition, particularly in industrial markets, many customers are operating just-in-time systems of production. In this situation, service delivery is crucial. In many industries, it is impossible to become a supplier unless one has a physical distribution system geared to supplying on a just-in-time basis.

Key planning areas and decisions

Our outline of the major activities in physical distribution, together with our discussion of the various areas of customer service affected by the physical distribution system, already points us to what are the key decision areas in planning physical distribution and logistics.

First of all we must decide the objectives for our physical distribution system. These objectives should be couched in terms of objectives with regard to desired levels and areas of customer service. These should be specified in advance, preferably in quantitative terms, for example 'All customer orders must be fulfilled within a maximum of 36 hours from receipt of order.'

Activity 6.11

Before you proceed, see if you can write down your own examples of possible objectives with regard to levels of customer service that might be desirable from your physical distribution system.

Once objectives for the output of the physical distribution system are set, then the system itself and its component activities can be planned to achieve the specified objectives. Key decisions would include, for example:

- ○ Inventory levels
- ○ Order-processing systems
- ○ Methods of transport
- ○ Warehousing: numbers and locations.

Inputs to planning physical distribution and logistics

We have seen that the design of a physical distribution system and its component activities should centre around meeting predetermined objectives with regard to the elements of customer service. Because of this, the first and most important input to planning physical distribution and logistics is 'information on customer requirements with regard to areas and levels of service'. Remember what we are looking for is at the very least to provide the minimum levels of service required, and preferably to use improved service levels as a basis for competitive advantage.

We should find out, therefore, what the customers' requirements are and what constitutes value in terms of service levels to the customer. For example, would the customer value speedier delivery? Would the customer value the ability to deal with special orders?

If customer requirements are the first and most important input to planning physical distribution and logistics, we should also remind ourselves that costs and profit to the company are also important. For example, most customers, if asked, would probably say they would value the ability to deal with special orders. However, improved levels of customer service usually cost the provider more. The real issue, therefore, is the extent to which this 'value' to the customer is sufficient to offset the potentially higher costs of providing it. Put simply, in designing the physical distribution system the second key input is 'cost'. We must carefully balance competitive advantage against cost. Most physical distribution systems are designed to provide pre-specified levels of customer service at minimum cost.

The third key consideration with regard to the design of the system is that it should be considered *as that*, that is 'a system'. It is no use minimizing costs in one area of the system, for example inventory costs, only to find that this is more than offset by a corresponding increase in costs elsewhere in the system, for example delivery. This is why in recent years much more emphasis has been placed on planning the whole of physical distribution and the channel element as a complete logistical system.

Our fourth input to the design of the physical distribution system is a consideration of 'competitors'. After all, every marketing decision should reflect the competitive situation. It is important to assess the levels and types of service being offered by competitors in the market.

The fifth and final consideration in the design of physical distribution is to remind ourselves that this is a very dynamic area of management and marketing. Changes in technology, techniques of production, and customer needs mean that physical distribution systems need to be constantly evaluated and, if necessary, updated and changed to reflect these changes and to remain competitive.

As we have seen so many times already in our discussion throughout the units, physical distribution and logistics planning has been enhanced and facilitated in recent years by developments in IT. There is no doubt that this area of distribution is complex due to the number of elements comprising the physical distribution and logistics system and the interrelationships between them. Cheap computing power has enabled the marketer to take account of these complexities and interrelationships, and design the total logistic system so as to provide optimum service at minimum cost.

Activity 6.12

Try to think of any changes in physical distribution over the last few years either in the industry in which you work or in an industry with which you are familiar. How have these affected marketing in the industry?

Marketing in practice: case study

'The party is set to continue!'

It is now over 50 years since Silas Tupper introduced the idea of selling his 'Tupperware' products through a team of agents organizing parties in the customers' own homes. At the time, an entirely new approach to distributing and selling products, Tupperware parties became one of the most successful channel arrangements in marketing history. Essentially, distribution and sales were achieved by appointing a series of agents who in turn would contact their friends and relatives to arrange a party in these friends' and relatives' homes to which further friends and relatives would be invited. The Tupperware agent would attend this party and demonstrate the products, the whole process being set in the convivial and friendly surroundings of a private home with people who knew each other. Obviously, the Tupperware agent would hope to secure sales at the party by taking orders and in turn the party organizer would receive a percentage of any sales made in the form of Tupperware products of their choice. Up until the mid-1970s, Tupperware parties were one of the most popular and successful ways in which customers purchased, in this case, plastic storage containers. Virtually every housewife would probably have attended at least one Tupperware party in their purchasing lifetimes.

By the 1970s, however, Tupperware parties began to decline in popularity. There were many reasons for this including the fact that there is simply less demand for the product due to improvements in competitive storage products and technologies. Some argued, however, that essentially, the whole notion of 'party selling' to people in their own homes was one which had become outdated, outmoded and irrelevant. In 2002, Tupperware parties became obsolete altogether. Is it the case, then, that party selling is obsolete in today's world? The answer is definitely no.

If anything, party selling has now begun to re-emerge as a way of direct marketing. An increasing number of products are once again now being sold through this at one time most novel of distribution channels. Examples of companies successfully using party selling include: Virgin Vie with their cosmetics range, Weekender clothes, and one of the most successful of all, the Ann Summers company with their party evenings selling exotic underwear and sex aids.

As a product, a million miles away from Tupperware, Ann Summers essentially uses the same principles for selling her exotic underwear and sex aid products as were once used to sell plastic boxes for storing pickles and so on. Almost exactly the same approach as originally used by Silas Tupper is used by the Ann Summers organization. If anything, given its success originally for Tupperware and more recently for Ann Summers, it is perhaps surprising that party selling is not used more widely by marketers. Perhaps it is viewed by some as being a little 'naff' or perhaps only some products can be sold and distributed in this way. Whatever, despite the demise of the Tupperware party there is no doubt that the party goes on.

Summary

In this unit we have seen that:

- Place decisions have a major impact on levels of customer satisfaction.
- Place costs a company a great deal.
- Place should be designed to provide pre-planned levels of customer service at the minimum cost for each level of service.
- The two broad and interrelated areas of planning place are planning marketing channels and planning physical distribution/logistics.
- In planning both these areas, the key considerations are customer needs, company objectives and costs, and competitors.
- Channels are one of the most dynamic areas of marketing these days with many changes taking place, often underpinned by developments and changes in technology, in particular the growth of more direct channels based on electronic and communication technologies.

Examination preparation: previous examination question

Attempt Question 4 of the examination paper for June 2004 (Appendix 4). For Specimen Answer Examination Question 4, June 2004, see Appendix 4 and www.cim.co.uk.

Further reading and bibliography

Bickerton, P., Bickerton, M. and Pardesi, U. (2000) *Cybermarketing*, 2nd edition, Butterworth-Heinemann.

Brassington, F. and Pettitt, S. (2003) *Principles of Marketing*, 3rd edition, FT Prentice Hall, Chapters 12 and 13.

Chaffey, D., Mayer, L., Johnston, L. and Ellis-Chadwick, F. (2000) *Internet Marketing*, FT Prentice Hall.

Dibb, S., Simkin, L., Pride, W. and Ferrell, O.C. (2000) *Marketing Concepts and Strategies*, 4th European edition, Houghton, Mifflin, Chapters 12 and 13.

Lancaster, G., Massingham, L. and Ashford, R. (2002) *Essentials of Marketing*, 4th edition, McGraw-Hill, Chapter 8.

unit 7
the marketing mix: promotion

Learning objectives

Learning outcome

By the end of this unit you will be able to:

○ Identify and describe the promotional element of the marketing mix.

Knowledge and skills

By the end of this unit you will be able to:

○ Describe the extensive range of tools that comprise a marketing communications mix, and examine the factors that contribute to its development and implementation (3.12).

Study Guide

This unit covers our fourth so-called 'P' element of the marketing mix, and encompasses the tools available to the marketer to communicate with customers and others about products and services.

Although essentially about communication, this particular tool of the marketing mix is normally referred to as promotion. This is a very wide area of marketing encompassing, as it does, decisions about advertising, sales promotion, personal selling, publicity/PR and direct mail. Because this is such a wide-ranging area of marketing, including factors as diverse as media selection for advertising through to recruitment and selection of the sales force and so on, we cannot hope to cover all the areas in promotion. Instead, a more realistic objective is to make sure that you understand the process of communication, the key elements of the promotional mix and how to plan these, and how to manage the individual tools of promotion.

We would expect it to take you about 3 hours to work through this unit and suggest you allow a further 3–4 hours to undertake the various activities suggested. Other than your notebook and writing equipment, you will not need anything further to complete this unit.

The role and importance of promotion in marketing

Study tip

If pricing and place decisions are readily observable elements of marketing activity in your everyday life, promotional decisions are even more so. Whichever part of the world we live in and whatever area of marketing we are familiar with, virtually all of us are exposed, as indeed is the objective, to marketing communications. Perhaps the most visible and obvious example of this is advertising. However, as we shall see in the unit and as no doubt you are probably aware, this is only one of the promotional tools to which each and everyone of us is exposed virtually in every day of our lives. Throughout this unit, and later when you have studied it, we will ask you to use your eyes and ears to observe and learn from what is going on with respect to marketing communications in the real world. You should be able to collect lots of examples of both effective and ineffective promotional efforts.

Marketing promotions or, as we shall alternatively call this area, marketing communications is an important tool of marketing for a variety of reasons. However, it is useful to highlight two major reasons that serve to underpin the vital role this element of the marketing mix plays.

The first reason why promotion is vital is quite simple. It is impossible to sell your products and services if nobody knows of their existence. Similarly, it can be difficult to market a product if customers have little information about your company. As we all know, even if the customers are familiar with both product and company, they may still require 'a little persuading' in order to be convinced that they actually need the product. All these are situations where, without effective marketing communication, making a sale is difficult. What we are talking about here are processes such as creating awareness, generating interest, heightening desire, and ultimately creating action in the form of a sale. Each in their own way, the various tools of promotion are aimed at fulfilling one or more of these functions.

This important communication role of marketing promotions is not just applicable to products and services but also to any other area where marketing tools and concepts are applied.

For example:

o Marketing 'ideas and causes' needs effective communications.
o Marketing 'people and celebrities' needs effective communications.

In short, everything that can be marketed needs to be communicated to customers. A company can have the best possible product for the target market, the most effective channels and systems of distribution, and a very competitive price, but if marketing communications are ineffective, all this can amount to nothing. In addition, ineffective marketing communications may result in substantial sums of money being wasted.

This brings us to our second reason for the importance of this area of the marketing mix. The second reason is that spending on promotional activities by companies and organizations is costly.

Last year in the United Kingdom, organizational spending on promotion amounted to several billion pounds. In some cases, a single promotional programme for, say, a new product launch can cost a company several millions. Clearly, it is not being suggested that all promotion necessarily costs a company so much, but there is no doubt that in contemporary marketing, where competition is intense, high levels of promotional spend are common and sometimes obligatory. Because of this, it is essential that the marketer understands the process of marketing communications, the range of promotional tools available and their characteristics, and how to plan promotion so as to have the greatest impact for any given level of spend.

As we did with place, perhaps another way of illustrating the role and importance of promotion in marketing is to consider some of the things that can go wrong if promotion is badly planned and executed, together with the possible implications for the marketer and the company. Here are just some examples:

- o 'We have just launched our new product and dealers did not have any brochures to give to customers who expressed an interest.'
- o 'Because we chose the wrong media for our advertising campaign, the target market is still unaware of the merits of our product.'
- o 'We have still not managed to overcome the damage to our company image from the pollution scare last year.'
- o 'Half our advertising spend is wasted. The problem is we are not sure which half.'
- o 'I don't know you, I've never heard of your product, I've never heard of your company, now what was it you wanted to sell me.'

We could go on citing examples of the types of problem resulting from badly planned and implemented marketing communications, but it should now be obvious to you that this area has a major impact on marketing effectiveness.

Activity 7.1

Try to recall any 'bad experiences' you have had as a customer or a potential customer for a product/service in the past that perhaps on reflection have been due to badly planned and managed marketing communications.

Reflect on the effect of this experience at the time with regard to your attitudes towards the product or brand and its supplier.

The process of communication

If the marketer is to manage the promotional element of the mix effectively, it is essential for him to understand the basic process and concepts of what is after all a communication process. For this reason, virtually every basic marketing textbook in this area starts by examining this process and the key concepts which underpin it.

Exam hint

Because this part of marketing communications appears to be a little 'theoretical', there is perhaps an understandable temptation to skip over this process and its concepts. However, not only is a basic understanding of the process and concepts of communication useful in very practical terms to the marketer, but, perhaps reflecting this usefulness, there have in fact been questions in the past in the Fundamentals paper on these aspects.

Communication is a vital part of all of our lives. We attempt to communicate with our husbands or wives, with our neighbours next door, or with our employees or managers. Nations attempt to communicate with other nations, often unsuccessfully. We are entertained, informed, often annoyed by communications. Whole industries are based on communicating. In short, communication and the need to manage it effectively is not something that is only relevant to marketers.

Key definitions

Communicate – To impart; to transmit; to receive; to administer. Hold intercourse; have common door or opening with.

Communication – Imparting; access or means of access; connection between places.

With such an extensive and varied scope for communication activities and meanings perhaps surprisingly we can distinguish a number of basic elements which, irrespective of the precise type of communication, make up the process. The elements in virtually all types of communication, and certainly marketing communications are shown in Figure 7.1.

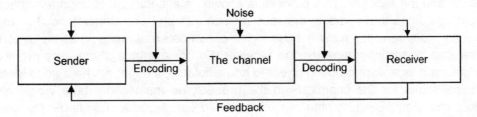

Figure 7.1 Key elements of the communications process

The sender (source, transmitter)

All communication requires that there be a sender from which the communication stems. This could be, for example, a broadcasting authority, the editor of a newspaper, an employer or in our case the marketer.

The receiver (audience)

Our second key element in the communication process is the party or person with which we wish to communicate. As we shall see, unless and until the intended audience receives the message, there is no possibility of effective communication. In many cases, the target audience for marketing communications is the customer or at least the potential customer. However, much marketing communication is also aimed at persons or parties other than the customer. For example, communications may be aimed at others who influence the purchasing process. Similarly, communications may be aimed at 'publics' important to the company, such as shareholders, local communities, and even politicians and governments.

The channel (media or medium)

If we have a sender and a receiver at either end of the communication process, then we also need a channel through which they can communicate. There are many types of channel of communication and these various types are very important to the marketer in planning marketing communications. A broad distinction can be made between 'personal' and 'impersonal' channels of communication. One of the most important areas in marketing communications is media selection and planning.

These are the first three basic elements of a communication process: a sender, a receiver and a channel. In addition to these three basic building blocks, we have a number of other elements that might be called 'technical aspects' in a communication process. These are aspects a communications engineer would perhaps be more familiar with, but, because they are endemic to the communication process, they are relevant to marketing communications.

Encoding

In order to transmit and share messages and information the sender must translate the message or information by means of a variety of signs and symbols appropriate for both the channel and the receiver. This process is known as encoding. It is important that the sender should use signs and symbols the receiver can interpret and understand. For example, the marketing communicator must not use words or symbols that make no sense or perhaps, even worse, can be misinterpreted by the receiver. So, for example, if we were promoting a new product such as a waterproofing agent to householders, it might not be a good idea to use the technical terms for the chemicals in the product, as most consumers would probably not understand them. Similarly, the marketer should use signs and symbols the customer can relate to: advertising messages for teenagers, for instance, might be very different to those we would use for the more mature end of the market. Encoding and its principles are particularly important when marketing crosses national frontiers, that is in international marketing. There are many examples of marketers making classic faux pas in their use of language and symbols in such markets.

 Activity 7.2

> Try to look out for and make note of any advertising and promotion for products you feel are inappropriate for the target market. This might be, for example, promotion for an imported product or service you feel the marketer has not got quite right for the intended market.

Decoding

Obviously, if there is an encoding process in communication, there must be a decoding process at the receiver's end of the process. Many of the comments with regard to the appropriate signs and language we made about encoding apply here. In the decoding process, the target audience tries to interpret and make sense of the messages that are being conveyed. We know that very often in the decoding process the intended message can become changed or distorted. The receivers will have their own perceptions and beliefs, which can cause changes and distortions.

Noise

Where the message received after transmission and decoding is not the same as that intended, or where the receiver has difficulty even receiving the message, we say there is 'noise' in the communication system. In fact, one source of such noise is the different perceptions and beliefs that can influence the decoding process referred to above. There are many sources of noise, however, in communication systems. For example, each and every day most of us are bombarded with dozens of selling and promotional messages. In this clamour for our attention by the marketer much of the information intended for us is simply lost. We suffer from what the communication specialists call 'information overload'. Two further sources of noise in the communications process are the encoding and decoding elements and in particular the use of signs and symbols used to encode and decode including, of course, the major one of language. Many marketers, particularly in international markets, have found to their cost that the words and symbols they have used to encode their messages to reach and influence the receiver of the marketing communications are decoded in an entirely different and often wholly inappropriate and unintended way so far as the marketer is concerned. So, for example, the Swedish marketer who used the brand name 'Krap' for his toilet paper products to be sold in the United Kingdom obviously was unfamiliar with the way this would be decoded by the target market. In fact, although at first sight amusing, mistakes such as this in the encoding and decoding process, and often much subtler ones, can be disastrous for the marketer and are much more frequently encountered than one might imagine and certainly hope for. Clearly, the marketer must understand the sources of noise in a communication system and how best to minimize this through careful planning.

Feedback

Our final basic element of a communication system is what is known as feedback – information from the receiver this time, as a result of the communication sent. Such feedback may be intended or unintended, voluntary or involuntary, personal/direct or impersonal/indirect. Such feedback serves a number of useful purposes in a communication system. But in particular, feedback enables the sender, for example the marketer, to ascertain the extent to which the intended message has been received and interpreted correctly. As importantly, it will also help to indicate the extent to which it has achieved the desired result. Perhaps the most obvious form of feedback in marketing communications is where the message is intended to create a sale, whether or not the customer has actually purchased. As we shall see, however, there are many possible objectives for marketing communications of which creating a sale is only one. The marketing communicator must ensure that feedback is planned for and obtained as a way of evaluating the effectiveness or not of marketing communications.

Activity 7.3

Try to think of ways in which the marketer can obtain feedback from customers regarding the effectiveness of marketing communications. Compare your list with that shown in the debriefing.

The tools of promotion: the promotion mix

Later in this unit we are going to look at the planning of marketing communications. Before we do this, we need to ensure that we are familiar with the major tools of promotion that are available to the marketer. The selection and combination of these tools in a communications campaign is referred to as the 'promotional mix'.

Key definition

Promotional mix – Is that combination of individual promotional tools selected by the marketer in order to promote a particular product to a particular target audience.

In fact, there are dozens of individual promotional tools from which the marketer may select. We may, however, group these tools into one of the five major sub-categories to represent the main constituents of the promotional mix. They are listed below and we shall discuss each in turn.

- ○ Advertising
- ○ Personal selling
- ○ Sales promotion
- ○ Publicity and PR
- ○ Direct mail.

Advertising

Perhaps the first promotional tool we tend to think of in marketing communications is advertising.

Key definition

Advertising – Any paid-for type of marketing communication, that is non-personal, aimed at a specific target audience through a mass media channel.

This definition encompasses a wide variety of different types and reasons for advertising. For example, advertising may be used in:

- ○ Advertising products and services: Ford cars, McDonald's restaurants.
- ○ Advertising ideas and issues: Greenpeace, Oxfam.
- ○ Advertising people: Jennifer Lopez, President Bush.

Types of advertising may include:

- o Trade advertising: 'B&Q warehouses for professional decorators'.
- o Consumer advertising: 'Robinsons Barley water – refresh your ideas'.
- o Corporate advertising: 'Shell: the caring company'.

In many markets, advertising constitutes the largest spend area for marketing communications, especially in consumer goods markets. Advertising has several advantages as a tool of marketing communications.

Activity 7.4

Make a list of what you feel might be the advantages of advertising as a promotional tool. When you have completed this list, compare it with that shown in the debriefing.

We can see some of the reasons why advertising is used so extensively by some marketers. There are, however, potential disadvantages associated with advertising, the main ones being the following:

- o Potentially high absolute costs.
- o Often difficult to evaluate effectiveness.
- o Persuasive value may be less than more personal promotional tools.
- o The very power of advertising means that sometimes adverts, as well as creating strong favourable attitudes and feelings among customers, can also create strong and even violent reactions of dislike, loathing and animosity towards the advertiser or brand.

Marketing in practice: example

Honda recently ran a poster campaign showing a speed camera in rainbow colours and using the tag line 'Happy Breaking'. The advertising Standards Authority received a number of complaints about this ad with suggestions that the ad condoned speeding and undermined the safety message that speed kills.

Accantia is an example of another company who received complaints through the Advertising Watchdog when it showed pictures demonstrating how its Lil-lets tampon brand was coated in a gel. The complainants argued that the ads were offensive.

Other companies and brands who/which have experienced negative responses to their advertising include:

Benetton's 'United Colours' campaign

The UK National Lottery 'Billy Connolly – Live a Lotto' campaign

French Connection's FCUK slogan and campaign

Yves St Lauren's 'Opium' campaign

Personal selling

Anyone new to marketing might not have first thought of personal selling as a tool of marketing communications. However, to the extent that personal selling and other tools in the promotional mix are substitutable one for another, this is a major promotional tool. In many industrial markets, spending on personal selling is the major promotional spend.

Key definition

Promotional spend – A paid-for type of marketing communication that normally calls for personal and often one-to-one contact between marketer and customer.

This definition encompasses a wide variety of different types of selling. For example:

- Telephone selling
- Technical selling
- Missionary (or pioneer) selling
- Retail selling.

Each of these types of selling can be found across a wide variety of markets and marketing situations, but below are some examples of situations and markets where each type tends to predominate.

Telephone selling – is used widely for home improvement products such as double glazing.

Technical selling – as one would expect is particularly prevalent in b2b markets involving products such as computers, machinery and even consultancy.

Missionary selling – is used widely for selling new products and/or in new markets. So this type of selling is often found in international markets where a marketer is selling for the first time.

Retail selling – perhaps self-explanatory, but many retail situations do not actually involve any selling as such, so retail selling tends to be associated with, for example, household appliances, cameras and electrical equipment, holidays and cars.

Activity 7.5

Make a list of what you feel might be the advantages of personal selling as a promotional tool. When you have completed this, compare your list with that shown in the debriefing.

Personal selling has many advantages. However, the potential disadvantages associated with personal selling are as follows:

- More difficult to vary spend in short term compared to other promotional tools.
- Cost per customer contact high.
- Depends on people and therefore potentially suffers from 'people problems'.

Sales promotion

Our third major category of promotional tools represents what is probably one of the fastest growing areas of spend in marketing communications. In some markets spending on sales promotion is equivalent to or greater than spending on either advertising or personal selling.

Key definition

Sales promotion – Any intermittent and/or short-term incentive designed to encourage purchase or sale of a product or service. Usually but not always impersonal in nature and usually non-media based.

This definition encompasses a wide variety of different types and reasons for sales promotion. For example, sales promotion may be aimed at:

o   Trade and intermediaries
o   The sales force
o   Consumers.

Types of sales promotion activity and tools include:

Premiums
Coupons
Self-liquidating offers
Buy-back allowances
Bargain packages
Giveaways
Dealer loaders
Discounts and cash allowances
Merchandising allowances
Exhibitions
Sales contests
Multiple purchase promotions, for example 3 for 2 offers
Loyalty cards
'Bogofs' (buy one, get one free)
Buy one, get a different one free
Free samples.

Obviously, many factors affect the choice of the most effective promotional tools, so, for example, multiple purchase promotions, buy one product, get a different one free, and extra loyalty card points are known to be very effective in prompting purchases and particularly heavier purchases by customers. Free samples, however, are probably more likely to be effective where the marketer wishes to encourage brand switching or brand trial.

In many markets, consumers have come to expect special promotional offers to accompany the brands they purchase and will not purchase or switch brands if these expected promotional offers are not made. The dilemma for the marketer, therefore, is that in some ways sales promotion can, over time, lose its ability to achieve the sales and marketing objectives set out for it. There is also some danger with regular sales promotions for a brand that the brand becomes 'devalued' to some extent in the mind of the customer with the image of the brand being cheapened. However, generally public perceptions of sales promotions are favourable in as much as they are seen as offering value for money and strong incentives to purchase, and brand choice.

Marketing in practice: example

With so much competition in most markets and with often huge spends on sales promotion activities by companies in order to support their brands and generate sales and market share, the planning and application of sales promotional campaigns is becoming increasingly sophisticated and innovative.

When Procter & Gamble (P&G) relaunched its Pantene hair care range in response to their competitor Unilever's launch of its Dove hair care range in 2001, it included a fully co-ordinated range of sales promotion activities involving activities such as consumer samples, a new website for customer competitions and a range of merchandising and trade deals and support. These activities were supported by a budget in the range of £10 million.

Extending knowledge

The range of types of promotional tools is probably more extensive in sales promotion than in any other area of the promotional mix. Because of this, it is impossible to list them all here, let alone discuss each of them. You are therefore advised to consult a good standard text on the various tools of sales promotion and their uses, relative advantages, etc. An excellent source of examples of the use of sales promotion in contemporary marketing can be found in Hugh Davidson (1997) *Even More Offensive Marketing*, 2nd edition, Penguin.

Question 7.1

What are:

1. Self-liquidating offers?
2. Giveaways?
3. Coupons?
4. Premiums?
5. Dealer loaders?
6. Buy-back allowances?

When you have completed this, compare your answers with those shown in the answer.

Publicity and public relations

Perhaps at one time this was the most neglected promotional tool, but recent years have witnessed an increasingly professional approach to managing this area of marketing communications.

Key definition

Publicity – Is any type of news story and information about an organization and/or its products transmitted at no charge through a mass medium. Public relations are activities designed to create understanding and goodwill between an organization and its publics.

Publicity and PR are often planned together, frequently using the services of a specialist publicity and PR agency. There are a wide variety of different types of activity in publicity and PR. For example:

- Press releases
- Company open days
- Press conferences
- Third-party endorsements.

Activity 7.6

Make a list of what you feel might be the advantages of publicity/PR as a promotional tool. When you have completed this, compare your list with that shown in the debriefing.

Some of the potential disadvantages associated with publicity and PR:

- Difficult to control media comments/reactions to publicity and PR.
- Difficult to assess impact, if any, on sales/profits.
- More difficult to control content and timing of communication.

Activity 7.7

Try to think of examples in recent years where companies have for one reason or another received 'bad publicity'.

Marketing in practice: example

Many would argue that one of the most effective exponents of publicity and PR in marketing is Richard Branson's Virgin organization.

Branson long ago recognized the potential advantages of effective publicity and PR. His PR and publicity 'stunts' include dressing like a bride and throwing 'a wedding party' for the national press at the launch of Virgin Brides, a supplier of wedding clothes. In part, at least Branson has used his well-publicized attempts at capturing hot air balloon records to keep his company name in front of global customers. Finally, Branson has not been slow to take advantage of the potential for bad publicity generated by his competitors with perhaps one of the best known examples of this being his very public court case which Branson won against British Airways and some of their marketing practices.

Direct mail

Direct mail is, of course, part of direct marketing which was discussed in Unit 6 as part of the place element of the marketing mix and is one of the main communicational tools used in direct marketing. We have stressed several times that this area of marketing has grown substantially in recent years and you are now familiar with some of the reasons for this. As a result, many marketers and marketing academics, including, for example, Kotler, now consider direct mail to be the fifth element of the traditional promotional mix. Certainly, direct mail can be considered as one of the most effective methods of communication especially when linked to a company database and loyalty scheme. This method is particularly useful in building consumer relationships and is very easy to control and evaluate. We shall be looking at these uses of database and loyalty schemes in building effective consumer relationships in more detail in Units 8 and 9.

Study tip

You will have no doubt noticed that often in a unit we will cross-refer to other units of the course. So, for example, in our discussion here of direct mail we have cross-referenced already to Units 6 and 8. In addition, of course, direct mail and its growth is related to developments in IT in marketing, which we have touched on in several units.

The point we are making here is that it is important, if sometimes difficult, not to compartmentalize the areas of study and the syllabus too much, even though for ease of study we have broken these down into individual study units.

Direct mail is usually a personally addressed marketing communication that is delivered direct to targeted respondents through the postal system. As already mentioned, its effectiveness depends on the accuracy and completeness of the list of addresses, together with the comprehensiveness of the information on the individuals or households to which the direct mail is being sent. Provided this database and the resulting mailing lists are effective, direct mail can be personalized and targeted very accurately. Most direct mail is aimed at generating enquiries and leads, and as already mentioned can be used to build relationships with customers. In part, the growth of direct mail has been a response to the increasing frustration and concern of marketers with regard to mass media channels such as television, newspapers and so on with respect to their cost-effectiveness in reaching target customers.

Although, at first sight, direct mail can appear relatively inexpensive compared to other forms and methods of communication such as TV advertising, in fact the return rates from direct mail, which can vary enormously but are often as low as 0.5 per cent, can make this an expensive way of targeting promotional activities. Nevertheless, its advantages mean that direct mail will continue to grow, especially in consumer markets.

Study tip

It is important to remember that, although the syllabus is divided up into distinct sections with sub-sections, the different parts of the syllabus are interrelated and in some areas often overlap substantially. So, for example, we have seen that direct mail, as well as being a promotional tool, is also a channel. You will recall in this respect that for this reason we discussed the growth of direct marketing, of which, of course, direct mail is a major tool, in our previous unit. We also discussed some of the developments in direct marketing, and in particular the impact of databases and new technologies such as the Internet. It would be useful now therefore to re-read our previous discussion of the growth of direct marketing, but this time considering it from the perspective of the promotional elements of the mix. We shall also be considering these elements further shortly in this unit, but again from the perspective of promotion this time.

These then are the four major conventional promotional tools available to marketers. It is important to stress, though, that virtually everything a company does, says or stands for potentially communicates something to the outside world. For example, the appearance of the employees of an organization can send signals to customers. Similarly, the state of, say, a company's vehicles can also communicate images. Even the other elements of the marketing mix contain signs and signals (planned or not) for customers and publics. Because of this, companies increasingly need to plan all the elements of communication so as to ensure consistency and co-ordination. Planning promotion should be looked on as planning a total package.

In addition, as we shall see, we have recently seen the growth of new promotional tools, and in particular the Internet which we shall consider later.

Managing/planning promotional strategies

In this part of the unit, we turn our attention to the issues, steps and procedures in planning marketing communications. As mentioned earlier, it is impossible to look at detailed issues in planning each of the elements of the promotional mix. For example, management of personal selling includes recruitment and selection, motivation and compensation, territory design, sales planning, sales training, the sales process itself and so on. We shall be looking briefly at the management and planning associated with each of our four major tools of promotion but the emphasis is on the management of the total promotional package. In doing so, many of the issues that will be considered at this level, such as setting promotional budgets, can also be applied at the level of planning each individual element of the mix.

In planning promotion we can identify a number of sequential but interrelated steps. The examiners will at the very least expect you to be familiar with and understand each of these steps. We shall consider each in turn.

Identifying the target audience

We saw earlier that the process of communication is about passing messages/information from a sender to a receiver. The starting point, however, in planning marketing communications is to identify who this receiver is to be, or, in marketing terms, who is the target audience.

In many cases, of course, the target audience will be the target market, that is customers. In other cases, the target audience may be intermediaries, the general public, shareholders and so on. Even this identification of broad target audiences is not sufficient to plan marketing communications effectively. For example, if the target audience for marketing communications is customers, we need to define these customers precisely. Parameters that might be useful if the target audience is customers might include customer characteristics (age, sex, etc.), customer attitudes (interested customers, disenchanted customers, etc.) and customer behaviour (regular customers, infrequent customers, etc.).

Especially where the target audience is customers, details on the profile of the target audience are very closely related to something we shall look at in a later unit and which you are already probably familiar with, namely market segmentation and targeting. At this stage, it is sufficient to note that the identification and profiling of the intended target audience for marketing communications are essential.

Setting promotional objectives

Having identified the target audience for our marketing communications, we must next determine what we wish to achieve with our promotional activities. There is a temptation here to think of promotional objectives exclusively in terms of sales and profits, that is all promotion is ultimately aimed at maintaining or increasing these sales and profits. Certainly, it is true that in many cases this is the ultimate objective of all marketing activities, including promotional activities. However, it is much more useful to think of promotional objectives in terms of the communication tasks that our promotion is designed to fulfil. After all, communication is what marketing promotion is about. In addition, not all promotional efforts are in fact aimed at increasing sales and profits. Finally, in terms of setting promotional objectives in terms other than sales and profits, it is important to remember that promotion is only one factor affecting sales and profits. Certainly in some cases, such as direct response advertising, it is possible to relate sales to promotion. More often than not, though, promotion works in tandem with other elements of the marketing mix with regard to its effect on sales and profits. It is preferable therefore to think of promotion in terms of its desired communication effects. In other words, we should set promotional objectives in terms of what we wish to achieve with the target audience identified in the first stage of planning.

A number of models have been developed to help the marketer consider what audience response is being sought as a result of promotional efforts. We shall describe some of the best known of these models in order to help you understand how they relate to the setting of promotional objectives.

Exam hint

Discussion of these various models has been a popular area for questions on the Fundamentals paper in the past. Collectively, such models are often referred to as 'response hierarchy models'. Do not be put off if you see this term used by the examiner. You now know what it means. These are discussed further below.

Response hierarchy models

As the term implies, these models are based on the notion that there are a number of possible responses to marketing communications on the part of the target market. Furthermore, the word 'hierarchy' suggests that there is an ordering or sequencing of responses, each one representing a 'higher level' of response on the part of the customer in the buying process. These notions will become clearer if we discuss some of the best known of these response hierarchy models.

The 'AIDA' model

One of the earliest but still widely used and discussed models that can be used to consider promotional objectives suggests that the buyer, or potential buyer, passes through four key stages in the buying process. Each of these stages corresponds to one of the initial letters of the AIDA mnemonic.

Question 7.2

What do the initial letters of the AIDA model stand for?

If you have not heard of this model before, turn immediately to the answer before proceeding. If you think you already know what the letters stand for, write down your answer and then compare it with the answer shown in the debriefing.

The initial letters of the AIDA model are meant to represent the various stages a customer passes through in the purchasing process. It suggests that the marketer must first gain the 'Attention' of the customer, and then create 'Interest', which can be translated into 'Desire', and the final stage of course is where the customer translates desire into 'Action' by actually purchasing the product or service.

These four key stages in the AIDA model are shown in Figure 7.2.

Attention → Interest → Desire → Action

Figure 7.2 The AIDA model

Although a simple, and still useful model, there is now general agreement that this particular response hierarchy model is probably too simplistic in as much as it does not consider a range of very important issues which are important to the marketer because they affect the purchasing process and the role of communication on this.

Some of these issues which are not considered are related to the influences on the consumer such as perceived risk, level of involvement, environmental issues such as the economy related to disposable income, the buyer's experience of the product recently, competitor strategies and so on. Because of this, many suggest that AIDA is in fact now very limited in helping us to understand the issues involved in planning effective promotion.

The 'innovation-adoption' model

This too is a well-known alternative model of the steps and stages en route to purchasing a new product, which, you may recall, we first introduced in Unit 3. The model simply proposes a slightly different view of the steps in the purchase process compared to the AIDA model.

Question 7.3

What are the stages the customer is said to pass through in the innovation-adoption model?

If you cannot recall the steps in this model turn immediately to the debriefing. If you possibly can, however, try to recall the steps in this model, write down your answer and compare it to the one in the debriefing.

This model was specifically developed for the process of purchasing new products. The first two stages are very similar to the AIDA model, in that it is suggested that the customer needs to be made 'Aware' of the new product or service followed by the development of an 'Interest' in the product. If the customer is sufficiently interested, then he or she will be prepared to 'Evaluate' the product in more detail, followed by 'Trial'. If the trial is satisfactory, the customer 'Adopts' the product or service and – provided the customer continues to be satisfied with the product or service – enters post-adoption confirmation and becomes a regular/loyal customer.

The innovation-adoption model is shown in Figure 7.3.

Awareness → Interest → Evaluation → Trial → Adoption → Post-adoption confirmation

Figure 7.3 The innovation-adoption model

Activity 7.8

Try to think of a product or service where customers might have conceivably passed through the steps described in the innovation-adoption model. Preferably try to think of an example where you yourself might have passed through these stages.

Hierarchy of effects model

Developed by Lavidge and Steiner in 1961, this model actually uses the term 'hierarchy'. Again, as is common to all of these models, the Lavidge and Steiner model (1961), is based on the notion that the customer passes through a series of hierarchical steps en route to making a purchase. This model posits six steps in the process as shown in Figure 7.4.

Awareness → Knowledge → Liking → Preference → Conviction → Purchase

Figure 7.4 Hierarchy of effects model

Perhaps more than the first two models described here, this model clearly links the sequence in the hierarchy to the major functions of the promotional tools and, in particular, to advertising. The first two, awareness and knowledge, relate to information or ideas; the second pair, to attitudes or feelings towards the product; and the final two steps, conviction and purchase, produce action – the acquisition of the product. Lavidge and Steiner suggest that this model can help to develop advertising objectives and campaigns. It is also a useful model for helping to measure the effectiveness of advertising.

The DAGMAR model

First proposed by Russell Colley, DAGMAR stands for the title of Colley's book, *Defining Advertising Goals for Measuring Advertising Results*, Colley, R. (1961) Association of National Advertisers, New York. Again, this model is based on the notion that promotion, or in the case of Colley, specifically advertising, must move the customer through a number of stages towards purchase. The model is shown in Figure 7.5.

Unawareness $\rightarrow$ Awareness $\rightarrow$ Comprehension $\rightarrow$ Conviction $\rightarrow$ Action

Figure 7.5 The DAGMAR model

Colley refers to these stages as a *marketing communications spectrum.* The successive levels of the spectrum are as follows:

o *Unawareness/awareness* – At this first stage of the spectrum we must move those customers who are unaware of the product through to a stage of awareness. Without this, of course, there is no possibility of moving to the next stages of the spectrum. Advertising, therefore, is specifically aimed at creating awareness.
o *Comprehension* – This next level in the spectrum is where the customer moves from simply being aware to understanding and appreciating what the product or brand is about. Clearly, marketing communications can play a key role in this process either through advertising or perhaps through the sales person and in-store information.
o *Conviction* – At this stage the customer is moving towards preferring the brand. Again, this may be based on a number of factors including important word-of-mouth communication.
o *Action* – As the term implies, it is here that the customer actually acts to purchase the product. It may be felt that advertising and other forms of marketing communication are irrelevant at this stage, but remember customers can always change their mind and may need that final impetus or persuasion to purchase.

Colley's DAGMAR model, like the other response hierarchy models, illustrates that marketing promotions move the customer through a series of steps or stages towards purchase.

In terms of setting promotional objectives, the value of such models is that they force the planner to consider what type of response is being sought from the target audience. Rarely can a single promotional campaign take a customer through all the stages in the buying process. More realistically, the promotional campaign will nudge a potential customer from one stage to the next or possibly through a couple of the stages. So, for example, an objective for a promotional campaign might be to make customers, who are already aware of our products and services, more interested in them. The promotional objectives for such a campaign, therefore, need to be expressed in terms that reflect this intended outcome for the promotional spend. An example of promotional objectives set in the context of the notion of response hierarchy models is shown below. For example:

The objective of the promotional campaign is to increase customer awareness in the target market from its current level of 10 per cent to 15 per cent over the 12 months of the promotional campaign.

We can see that setting objectives in this way helps in planning the next stages of the promotional campaign, for example message, channels and so on. In addition, setting objectives in this way facilitates the measurement and control of the effectiveness of our promotion.

Activity 7.9

Using the examples of the audience-response hierarchy models shown earlier in the unit, practise setting illustrative but realistic possible objectives for promotional campaigns.

Extending knowledge

Find out about these models if you can. You will find further examples in G.A. Lancaster *et al.* (2002), *Essentials of Marketing*, 4th edition, Chapter 9.

Determining the message(s)

Having identified the target audience and the response sought from the promotional campaign, the marketer can then begin to think about the message(s) that will be needed to achieve this. Very often the marketer will make use of specialist help from outside in formulating messages, in particular an advertising agency. Of special importance is the message content, where the marketer must determine what appeals or themes are going to be used. In promotional terms, we often refer to the identification of the 'unique selling proposition' (USP) as the basis for the message content.

Key definition

A unique selling proposition – Is a feature or quality of a product/service/company that sets the organization apart from its competitors in the marketplace and can be used therefore to differentiate the product/service/company to develop a competitive advantage.

Activity 7.10

Try to identify unique selling propositions in promotional messages being used in the marketplace. This can be for your own organization and its promotion of its products or for others. Examples of messages based on USPs are shown in the debriefing.

In addition to USPs as the basis for designing message content in promotion, the following are also used as the focus for message design:

- Fear
- Guilt
- Joy
- Pride
- Morality
- Humour.

Activity 7.11

See if you can find examples of promotional messages based on the types of appeal listed above.

Selection of channels

We saw earlier in the unit that messages and information are communicated through channels. There is a wide range of possible channels for marketing promotion, each with its own characteristics, advantages and disadvantages and so on. We often refer to these as 'media'. No doubt you can think of plenty of examples, including television, newspapers, magazines, posters, exhibitions and so on. Selection of channels should stem from the preceding stages of promotional planning, for example target audience selection.

Although there are dozens of types of specific media available in broad terms, the marketer must choose between one or a combination of personal channels, for example personal selling, and/or impersonal channels, for example advertising.

Extending knowledge

In addition to these planned/marketer-dominated channels of communication, we know that in many markets unplanned/non-marketer-dominated channels are very important. In particular, we know that personal influence through 'word of mouth' from, say, friends, relatives and so on, is very important in influencing customer attitudes and choice. You should try to find out a little more about word of mouth in marketing communications and how marketers may 'use' this concept. A good source is P. Kotler (2004), *Marketing Management*, 10th edition.

Setting the promotional budget

Perhaps one of the most vexed questions in planning promotion is how much to spend, that is the total promotional budget.

Question 7.4

List four common methods for deciding the total promotion budget. Compare your answers to those shown in the debriefing.

Of the four methods shown in the debriefing, the first three are probably self-explanatory. Each method has its advantages and disadvantages but by far the most analytical of the methods is the one that perhaps needs a little explanation, namely the 'objective-and-task' method.

In this method, the promotional budget is set up by means of the following steps:

- o Establishing specific communication objectives.
- o Establishing tasks required to achieve objectives.
- o Estimating costs of these tasks.
- o Calculating required budget on the basis of first three steps.

Exam hint

Setting promotional budgets is a popular area for exam questions on the Fundamentals paper. Make sure you are familiar with the common methods of budget setting and their relative advantages and disadvantages.

Determining the promotional mix

Having determined the broad division between personal and non-personal channels, together with the promotional budget, we must determine the allocation of this budget between the different elements of the promotional mix, that is personal selling, advertising, sales promotion, publicity and PR, and direct mail. Many factors affect what is the most appropriate mix.

Activity 7.12

List what you think are the most important factors affecting the choice of promotional mix. Compare your list with that shown in the debriefing.

You will see from the debriefing, and you probably already knew, that many factors affect what is an appropriate promotional mix in any given situation.

Exam hint

Make sure that for each of the factors listed in the above debrief you know and understand how they relate to decisions about the promotional mix. For example, you should know how the promotional mix varies over the life cycle of a product. Similarly, you need to know how 'push versus pull' marketing strategies affect the promotional mix. This is important, so to help you we discuss each of the factors below.

Factors affecting the choice of the promotional mix

Many factors will affect the choice of an appropriate promotional mix. Some of the most important of these factors are as follows.

Target market/customer type

Target markets or, more broadly, the type of customer being targeted will affect the choice of the promotions mix. This is most easily demonstrated if we consider the promotions mix for an industrial versus a consumer target market. For the industrial customer, it is more likely that personal selling will predominate in the promotional mix. This is because personal selling techniques are usually much more effective for industrial buyers as the products are often technical and the message can be tailored to the needs of the buyer. In addition, because there are likely to be fewer numbers of buyers in the market, mass advertising is rarely appropriate. What advertising is done will probably be only a small amount conducted in the trade press. Also useful in the promotional mix to industrial buyers will be sales promotions, and particularly techniques such as discounts for bulk purchase, free trials and so on. Personal selling also helps in this type of market because there are different members of the decision-making unit (DMU). Finally, often the industrial marketer has a smaller promotional budget which restricts the use of some of the more expensive promotional tools.

In the consumer market, on the other hand, advertising is likely to predominate in the promotional mix. Personal selling will normally be confined only to more expensive consumer products. Sales promotion and direct mail, however, will also be useful in this market, especially for encouraging brand switching, initial purchasing and in the case of direct mail, enquiries.

Marketing in practice: example

It is sometimes suggested that older customers and particularly the so-called 'grey' market customers represented by the over-50s are more sceptical about the claims made for products and brands in advertising. Long experience, it is suggested, has inured them to the attractions of sexy and exciting advertising. It is suggested, therefore, that more 'practical' down-to-earth promotional appeals and tools will work best with this target market such as special price deals. Harley Davidson, however, has shown that this target market is potentially just as strongly influenced through exciting advertising campaigns and their recent advertising has proved to be very effective in attracting an over-50s market which simply does not want to grow old.

www.harleydavidson.com

Characteristics and cost-effectiveness of the promotional tools

As implied in our discussion of the promotional mix in industrial versus consumer markets above, each of the promotional tools has its own characteristics and relative advantages and disadvantages compared to the other promotional tools. This means that some tools are much more appropriate and hence cost-effective in achieving certain objectives or reaching certain target customers. So, for example, advertising is much more appropriate where there are large numbers of geographically dispersed customers. It is, however, an impersonal form of promotion and, therefore, is inappropriate where customers require a high degree of personal contact and/or source credibility. Personal selling, on the other hand, although expensive from the point of view of the cost of each sales person, can be a very cost-effective way of communicating with customers, especially where products are technical or complex, and where therefore the customer requires clarification. Sales promotion is particularly useful for encouraging one-off purchasing and short-term interest in a product or service. If used excessively, however, sales promotion can cheapen the image of a product or company.

Company resources, objectives and policies

As already indicated, mass advertising at a regional, national and certainly international level, will often require substantial promotional resources. Some companies simply cannot afford to spend on advertising. Also, the objectives of the organization will affect the promotional mix and certainly the extent to which the different promotional tools will be used. For example, if a company aims to develop and launch new products and therefore is required to create extensive awareness, it is likely to use more advertising in its promotional mix. Companies whose objective is to steal market share will often concentrate more on sales promotion efforts. Finally, a company may have policies which restrict the use of certain promotional tools. So, for example, some companies will not use direct marketing because they feel that this does not fit with the overall image which they wish to project.

Availability of promotional tools

We sometimes forget that not all the promotional tools are as easily or widely available to all marketers throughout the world. So, for example, in some countries, direct marketing and, in particular, direct mail would be very difficult to use because mailing lists are simply not available. Similarly, mass advertising and in particular the media channels on which it depends are very poorly developed in some countries.

Product life cycle

We have already seen in an earlier unit the stage in its life cycle, at which a product is, has implications in the selection of marketing strategies. An important area of strategy affected by the product life cycle is, of course, the promotional strategy and, in particular, the promotional mix. So, for example, at the introductory stage of the product life cycle, advertising may predominate in the promotional mix in order to develop awareness. In the maturity and decline stages in contrast, emphasis on the promotional mix may switch to the use of sales promotion in order to try to extend the life and sales of a product.

Push versus pull policies

The overall communications strategy will of course affect every element of planning a promotional campaign including the choice of the promotional tools. Of particular importance, though, is the extent to which a company chooses to use a push versus a pull strategy.

○ *A push strategy* – Is where the communication messages are targeted at the channel intermediaries (trade channels) such as dealers, wholesalers, agents, distributors and retailers. Often with a push policy the producer promotes a product to the next member in the marketing channel, with this member in turn promoting to the next level in the channel and so on. This strategy should allow the trade channel members to facilitate the distribution of the products to consumers or end-users, thus 'pushing' the products to the consumers. A push policy often uses predominantly personal selling, but also may involve advertisements in the trade press and sales promotion techniques such as discount for bulk orders, dealer competitions for the best sales figures and so on. The idea of a push strategy is shown in Figure 7.6.

○ *A pull strategy* – Is where the promotion is directed at the end consumer or buyer in an attempt to get the customer to demand the product or service and hence 'pull' the product through the channel. The promotional objective is usually to generate increased awareness, build attitudes and provoke motivation within this group of buyers. With this type of communications strategy examples of promotional tools in the promotional mix would be, for example, television advertisements, direct mail and sales promotions such as 50 per cent extra free and so on. The idea of a pull strategy is shown in Figure 7.7.

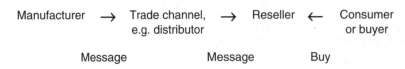

Figure 7.6 A push promotional strategy

Figure 7.7 A pull promotional strategy

Marketing in practice: example

As you will no doubt appreciate, many, if not most, promotional campaigns use a mixture of push and pull strategies combined and co-ordinated together so as to have the maximum impact.

Revlon recently launched a range of cosmetics for Black and Asian women branded as the 'Revlon Ethnic Shade' range. The launch was underpinned by a range of sales promotional strategies designed to encourage stocking and support the retailer in marketing the range including, for example, merchandising, point of sale material and special price promotional offers – the 'push' element of the campaign. At the same time, an extensive advertising campaign aimed at generating customer interest and demand was used with the American actress Halle Berry featuring as the face for this new Revlon product – the 'pull' element of the campaign.

Measurement and control of promotional effectiveness

As with all marketing activities, it is important to measure the impact of promotional programmes and the effectiveness of what we have seen can be a substantial spend. We also know, however, that measuring promotional effectiveness in terms of its effect on sales and profits is complicated by the wide range of factors that impact sales and profits. This is where setting objectives in communication terms comes into play. It is much easier to measure the impact of the promotional programme in terms of pre-specified audience response objectives, such as impact on, say, awareness. Measurement of the impact of the promotional programme is never easy but every effort must be made to ensure that the programme is cost-effective.

Managing/planning individual elements of the promotional mix

In addition to planning promotional strategies, the marketer must also plan, implement and control each of the individual elements of the promotional mix being used. In other words, if all four elements are being used, the marketer must plan advertising, sales promotion, publicity and PR and personal selling. As already emphasized, we cannot look at each of these individual elements separately. However, as you will appreciate, in the Fundamentals paper it is unlikely that the examiners will look for detailed knowledge of, say, sales planning. They may, however, realistically expect you to know a little about managing each of the promotional tools. Perhaps with the exception of the personal selling element of promotion, which raises special issues in terms of its management, at least some of the steps in the framework used here for planning promotion can be used to structure the planning process for each of publicity/PR, sales promotion and advertising.

In planning each of these elements, we can use the following steps from our framework:

- o Identifying the target audience.
- o Setting promotion objectives for each tool.
- o Determining the message/theme.
- o Selecting the media.
- o Determining the budget.
- o Implementing, evaluating and controlling.

Extending knowledge

You should ensure that you at least have a basic understanding of how to plan each of the major tools of promotion. A good basic textbook for this is G.A. Lancaster *et al.* (2002), *Essentials of Marketing*, 4th edition, Chapter 11.

Trends and developments in promotion

Just as in other areas of marketing, promotion has witnessed some interesting changes in recent years. Although the major promotional tools outlined so far in this unit still dominate, we have seen the increased use of the following promotional tools.

- ○ Corporate advertising
- ○ Sponsorship
- ○ Packaging.

We shall discuss the important promotional aspects of packaging in a little more detail.

Packaging and promotion

In Unit 3, we considered packaging as part of the product element of the marketing mix – in particular, in this context, its roles as protection and containment of the product itself. We also suggested, however, that packaging also plays an important promotional role and is sometimes said to act as the 'silent salesman'. If anything, this promotional role for packaging has become even more important in recent years. Many factors underpin this growth in importance including:

- ○ The growth of self-service
- ○ The proliferation of brands and branded products
- ○ Increased consumer affluence
- ○ Problems associated with differentiating the core product.

These and other factors have placed packaging and packaging decisions at the centre of many promotional programmes. Innovatory packaging can often lead to increased sales and market share, giving the marketer a competitive edge at least for a period of time until competitors catch up.

 ## Activity 7.13

Try to list examples of innovation in packaging that, at the time of their introduction, led to a competitive advantage for the marketer first using the packaging. Compare your list with that shown in the debriefing.

Whatever the examples on your list you will probably appreciate the powerful competitive edge that can be gained through packaging and some of the significant developments that have taken place in this area.

Decisions about packaging need to be taken by senior management and at an early stage in product development. Any proposed changes in packaging, however minor they may seem, should be carefully evaluated against customer perceptions and competitive activities. In the case of a new product, a 'packaging concept' should be developed and researched with both customers and distributors. Care should be taken to ensure that the packaging fulfils both its protective and promotional roles.

It is difficult and dangerous to be definitive about what constitutes 'good packaging'; after all, many factors from target market to the type of product affect this decision. With this in mind, though, effective packaging usually meets the following criteria from a promotional point of view:

- o It is distinctive
- o Related to the above, it is recognizable by customers
- o It fits with both product and corporate image
- o It is appropriate to the needs and perceptions of the target market.

Packaging must appeal not only to consumers, but also to resellers. Rising consumer affluence can mean that consumers are willing to pay a little more for the appearance and prestige of better packages.

If there is no real product difference between rival brands, it is essential that the packaging is used with the branding strategy to differentiate the product, for example the cat food Felix has a distinctive ring-pull opening top showing a cat's paw mark which reinforces the 'Felix' character used on the label and in the commercial television advertisement.

Decisions about packaging that must directly influence the promotional effect of the packaging include the following:

- o The pack should be *attractive and attract attention* in helping to promote the advertising and brand image – the logo should be clearly identifiable on the packaging. It should facilitate self-selection. Ferrero Rocher recently offered their individual chocolate products in a clear box shaped like a distinctive pyramid – the objective was to appeal to the mainstream audience while managing to break out of the sea of 'sameness'. The result was that this product was one of the fastest selling chocolate packs on the UK market during the Christmas period when it was launched.
- o *The shape and colour* should relate to the customer motivation and positioning of the product – such as the distinctively coloured tube packaging with resealable top and foil peel-back seal for Pringles crisps (a premium potato crisp product aimed at the trendy and affluent market).
- o *Social and ethical issues* as with all areas of marketing, it is important to conform not only to legal and regulatory requirements, but also to social and ethical issues. There is much criticism among some consumer groups regarding the 'wastefulness' of some types of packaging. Increasingly, 'green' consumers are looking for recyclable packaging and will make brand choices on this basis. In addition, packaging should not be misleading to consumers by, for example, making them think there is more of the product in the container than there actually is. Finally, several recent controversies over packaging show that care should be taken with regard to, for example, the promotional message used in the packaging. For example, some of the 'alcopop' products (fizzy drink-type products which are alcoholic) were criticized with regard to their labelling and packaging because it was suggested that some of the images and messages used in the packaging made them particularly appealing to under-age drinkers.
- o Packaging may be designed to *promote impulse buying*. For example, many confectionery products and counter line products are effectively marketed through packaging in this way.
- o Packaging should convey or *reinforce the promotional messages* related to sales promotion offers, sponsorship or tie-ups. For example, Walkers Crisps used their packaging to support a promotional campaign based on instant Spice Girls prizes.

    o As indicated above, the packaging should be integrated with all of the promotional elements and the marketing mix, for example Ferrero Rocher individual chocolates. The packaging echoes the quality statements made in the promotional advertisements, pricing strategy and product ingredient quality.

Information technology and promotion

Perhaps as you would expect, marketing promotions have been substantially affected by the advances in communication and IT within the past 10 years. Indeed, this has had a major impact for marketers planning the promotional mix for their products and services. Some of the key issues are as follows:

    o The growth of electronic communications such as the Internet, e-mail, fax and so on has allowed information to become more rapid and global.

    o The explosion in wireless technologies has led to a massive increase in mobile communications and as a result the growth of mobile marketing and advertising.

    o The increasing power of the computer has allowed the marketer to gather and analyse information about their customers more effectively. As we have seen, this is one of the major reasons for the increase in direct mail. As we shall see in some of the later units it has also enabled companies to develop loyalty schemes to build individual relationships with customers.

    o Digital technology is growing rapidly, with interactive digital television allowing two-way communications. The growth of satellite, cable and digital television has allowed marketers to target very specific target segments with their television advertisements such as pension plans for the over-50s advertised on the UK Gold channel (Sky). This will also offer marketers the opportunity to evaluate advertisements more effectively.

    o The increased use of the Internet and particularly websites as a promotional tool for individuals and companies has offered many marketers a further effective promotional tool, resulting in more control and evaluation of the communications. Remember we have already considered the impact of this on direct marketing and increases in direct sales.

It can be seen that there are a wide range of IT advances which have allowed the marketer to plan more interactive, two-way messages which ultimately convert into an increased knowledge about the consumer. This increase in information allows the marketer to tailor the messages to consumer behaviour, which should ultimately lead to more effective promotional strategies. In this part of the unit, therefore, we shall look at some of the reasons for the growth of the Internet as a promotional tool.

The Internet as a promotional tool

We have already considered the Internet from the perspective of the place element of the marketing mix, but of course the Internet is also a promotional tool in its own right. Moreover, and again as we have seen several times throughout different units, it is a promotional tool which is increasingly being used by marketers throughout the world. Some of the major reasons for the growth of the Internet for advertising and promotion include the following:

    o Internet advertising can be very dynamic compared to, for example, conventional print advertising with the use of powerful graphics and hence movement and sound where appropriate.

    o Given that consumers open websites voluntarily, even though sometimes a particular website is reached by accident, then at least some consumers are already predisposed to be interested in the product or service being advertised.

○ The marketer can measure the response at least to the website through the number of hits recorded for the site.

○ Dependent on the nature of the website and the advertising, the customer may often respond to the advertising immediately by placing an order.

○ Carefully designed websites can be used to encourage an element of two-way communication with a target audience with, for example, questions being used to prompt responses from the customer and/or being used to respond to customers' enquiries.

○ Compared to print and even television advertising, Internet advertising has a more insistent presence. Conventional advertisers are increasingly worried, for example, about customers simply 'turning off' literally or mentally when confronted with advertising. The Internet still has an element of novelty for many users.

○ Nominal costs for advertising on the Internet are substantially lower than when using conventional media channels. For many companies the cost of, say, television advertising, on a national scale, never mind an international, has become prohibitive.

○ Finally, much more information both in extent and detail can be provided through an Internet site, and again, the customer can to some extent pick and choose which elements of the information he or she wishes to receive.

The following are some of the major ways in which the Internet is being used by companies as a promotional tool.

Electronic store fronts

First, the marketer can use the Internet to create an electronic store front. This can either be done by buying space on a commercial on-line service or, as increasingly most companies do, opening its own website. The most basic type is a corporate website, which is essentially a way of handling interactive communication and enquiries initiated by the consumer. They are designed to allow the customer to find out about the company and its products and are linked to other forms of selling rather than selling the company's products directly. Increasingly, though, companies are creating true marketing websites designed to initiate or even complete the purchase process. These types of websites are marketer led, that is they are initiated by the marketer rather than the customer, often through conventional promotional activities such as advertising and direct mail activities.

Extending knowledge

No doubt you will have already visited company marketing websites in your role as a potential purchaser. It is a good idea, however, from time to time to visit a variety of company marketing websites with a view to assessing these sites in a critical way with regard to how effective you feel they are in terms of what they are trying to achieve in marketing terms. Wherever you can, then, from time to time you should visit websites of companies or products that interest you and make notes on the relative effectiveness of the website looked at from the point of view of a student of marketing. Obviously, there are literally thousands of websites you can visit. If you are not familiar with how to access websites you can visit one of the available search engines, examples include:

www.google.com
www.excite.com
www.yahoo.com
www.dogpile.com
www.metacrawler.com

On-line advertising

Companies are increasingly using the Internet for on-line advertisements. These take several forms and include, for example, classified advertisements in the on-line service providers' websites such as, for example, freeserve.com; advertising in commercial Internet news groups and an increasingly popular approach, pop-up ads which appear when Internet users are surfing on-line services or websites.

Marketing in practice: example

Some examples of companies with classified advertisements on freeserve's webpage include:

www.sainsburys.com
www.virgin.com
www.argos.com

Internet forums, news groups and bulletin boards

Obviously, the marketer is interested principally in commercial applications. Because forums, news groups and bulletin boards are normally accessed by individuals with particular interests they can be a very effective way of targeting certain groups of customers. For example, a marketer of health foods can target through these elements of the Web people who have a particular interest in health issues. The marketer in fact can achieve very accurate target marketing: continuing our example of health – the marketer of, say, slimming products can utilize diet forums, news groups and bulletin boards. This approach is useful because these types of Web activities attract consumers with common interests and often well-defined demographics and lifestyles.

E-mail and webcasting

Many customers are now familiar with and have access to, in one way or another, e-mail facilities. Companies can use the Internet to access customers via e-mail. Sometimes these will be company initiated based on, for example, electronic mailing lists or even better, customers who have contacted companies through the Web and registered interest in a company's products and services and provided their e-mail details. A variation on this is where a company signs up to a webcasting service. These services automatically download customized information to individuals' PCs in their homes and businesses.

Someone who subscribes to a webcasting service specifies the areas they are interested in and then the webcasting service automatically downloads information to the subscriber's desktop. So, for example, an individual can subscribe to, say, an entertainment webcast service or, say, a sports webcast service. They then receive information direct to their PCs in these areas. The on-line marketer can deliver Internet advertising on the webcast, selecting the webcast's and consumer targets who are likely to be most interested in their particular products and services. Most major commercial on-line services now offer webcasting to their members. As with much Internet advertising and promotion, however, the marketer must avoid causing antagonism by sending unsolicited e-mails to customers. Although there are various ways in which a customer or webcasting service can guard against this, there is no doubt that a major cause of resentment among Internet users is the transmission of 'junk e-mail' or 'SPAM' as it is often referred to.

Marketing in practice: example

Electronic marketing is increasingly attracting the attention of regulators to ensure that the electronic marketer does not abuse this technology. In 2002, the European Union introduced new regulations that applied to all businesses marketing goods or services over the Internet, by mobile phone or by e-mail. The regulations cover, for example, the use of SPAM in electronic marketing, the use of cookies and aspects such as using third-party mailing lists for marketing and electronic customer databases. Increasingly, the marketer will need to understand and take account of regulations governing electronic marketing, at least to the extent of seeking specialist advice when conducting electronic commerce.

Extending knowledge

Examples of currently available webcasting services which you may usefully look at to see what servicesw are offered and so on include the following:

www.placeware.com
www.audiovideoweb.com
www.perfectstream.tv
www.pointcast.com
www.ifusion.com

Clearly, then, the Internet has much to recommend it as a promotional tool, but as with its use as a channel, its use as a promotional tool is still primarily determined by access to and use of the Internet by customers. We have seen that this access is patchy throughout the world with the highest incidence of access to, and use of, being in countries like the United States, Japan and the United Kingdom. In some other parts of the world Internet access, particularly for home-shopping use, is still in its infancy. At the moment, therefore, the international marketer in particular is restricted to some extent. However, this restriction is to some extent offset by the fact that by definition at least in principle the World Wide Web is global.

Advertising and promoting via the Internet involves the same key considerations as in developing promotional and advertising campaigns through conventional channels. So, for example, the marketer still has to determine campaign objectives, identify the target audience, create the promotional message, develop budgets, implement the campaign and measure and evaluate performance. However, there are some aspects of Internet promotion and advertising which are very different and require different skills and expertise over and above those required for conventional promotional channels and campaigns. So, for example, messages need to be designed with search engines and Web access in mind. Similarly, there are several technical and regulatory website design conventions which need to be taken into account. Finally, things like security for customers and protection of data and information are important facets of designing websites and promotional messages on the Web. Again we would proffer the same advice with respect to using the Internet as a direct marketing channel, namely that unless the marketer is an expert in website design, including some of the technology aspects which underpin it, then developing websites for use in marketing is best left to the experts, albeit guided by, and in the context of, the marketing manager's objectives and requirements for the promotional and other elements of the marketing programme.

Having said this, more and more marketers are in fact becoming familiar with the intricacies and technicalities of website design and Internet usage for promotional purposes. A familiarity which no doubt will continue to grow as this increasingly important and powerful new advertising and promotional medium develops.

As a guide, some of the key decision areas in using the Internet and websites as a promotional tool are indicated below:

- The website should be designed as an active marketing tool rather than as a sort of trade directory listing of a company on the Internet.
- Communications objectives for the website must be set for each target audience, for example increasing awareness, encouraging on-line sales, educating the market, launching a new product, gathering information for a direct mail campaign and so on.
- It should be easy for customers to find the website.
- The website should offer the visitor a rewarding and rich experience.
- The website should be designed to 'fit' with the overall communication strategy, that is there should be consistency of message.
- There should be a good design and flow of information.
- Where appropriate, the website should ensure access to secure ordering systems.
- The website should offer added value, perhaps in the form of 'free downloadables' or links to mailed sales promotions.
- The site should be updated on a regular basis as necessary.
- The site should be evaluated and controlled with regard to its efficiency and effectiveness. Several commercially available website-tracking programmes can be purchased for this purpose.

This last point of evaluating and controlling websites is becoming more and more important as marketers and website designers develop more familiarity with the use of websites in marketing and how to evaluate them. Until now, relatively simple measurements such as click-through rates – registered when a person clicks on an advertisement – and impressions – a record of each time a viewer downloads an advertisement onto a browser – have been the standard measures for evaluating the response to Internet campaigns. However, it is increasingly recognized that these are extremely unsophisticated and hence potentially misleading measures of effectiveness. In particular, they reveal little or nothing about the nature of activity and consumer behaviour after the Internet site visitor has clicked or downloaded. Because of this there has been much activity in the development of tracking software and measurement services that provide more useful insights into the effectiveness of website campaigns. In the past, the technology underpinning website campaign tracking systems has been based on cookie-based applications, but it is now recognized that these are imperfect and often inappropriate. The more recent tracking systems are based on providing much more information about people visiting websites by collecting consumer information at the time of the visit. This information is then increasingly linked to subsequent consumer activity such as ordering profiles or even product usage information. A large number of companies, such as WCL, Mailtrack, Broadbase and Accrue, are now developing much more sophisticated tracking responses to opting e-mail and SMS marketing messages.

Study tip

If you have access to a computer through which you can also access the Internet, then visit several company websites and make your own assessment of how effectively you feel they have been designed from a promotional point of view. Obviously, to some extent, this assessment is personal and subjective but, for example, assess factors such as:

- How easy was the site to find?
- How interesting do you find the site in terms of making you interested in the company or its products?
- Related to the above, how creative is the promotional element of the site?
- How easy is it to find your way around the site and, for example, find further information?
- How tempted would you be to buy from the site?

If you can, make such visits and assessments a regular activity, perhaps even over and above any visits you make or already made in your role as a potential customer. Keep a record of what you feel are the best and the worst sites you visit which you can use as examples in possible examination questions.

Earlier in this unit, we asked you to visit some company websites to look at how they were using their websites in marketing. Remember, websites are used in many ways by marketers now and not just as promotional tools. A key issue, perhaps as with all promotional tools, is the extent to which a website is effective, in this case in promoting a company or its products. Needless to say this can be very difficult to assess. Certainly, it is easy to measure the number of visitors to a website but does this constitute effectiveness? There is a growing realization that nobody knows much about the way that consumers behave on-line. The most frequent measures for tracking the response to Internet promotional campaigns have been the use of click-through rates, which registers when a person clicks on an advertisement, and impressions, which record each time a viewer downloads an advertisement onto a browser. It is now realized that more sophisticated response tracking on customer behaviour on the Internet is required. Because of this, there has been a rapid increase in companies developing tracking software and bespoke services that can provide more powerful measures of the promotional effectiveness of website campaigns. The evaluation of IT-based communications, including Internet sites, is further explored shortly in the unit.

Extending knowledge

A detailed discussion of the design, application and evaluation of websites for promotional and other purposes in marketing is beyond the scope of this coursebook. You are, however, recommended at least to scan through a specialist textbook in this area. Two excellent textbooks are those given in the essential reading list for this syllabus, namely *Internet Marketing* by Chaffey *et al.* and *Cybermarketing* by Bickerton *et al.*

Websites are often thought of as just another selling device, but a website can be used much more actively, in particular to develop better relationships with a company's customers and publics.

Customer relations

A well-designed and operated website allows for very effective communication with customers. If customers can easily find the website and access information on it, and if they find that these visits are rewarding in the sense of offering more than simply information, the customer is likely to be favourably impressed with regard to the company and its offerings.

Media relations
The website can also be dedicated to developing media relations. This can be one of the most potent PR tools as, for example, reporters can access information which they may need at any time of the day or night, and if prepared carefully, in a format that is ready to use.

Investor relations
As the financial community is increasingly used to using the Internet, a corporate website can also be important for investors accessing information. This would include the annual reports being posted on the site.

Community relations
The website can also be used for developing community relations. This site could include information relating to the promotion of local joint projects, contributions to arts and culture, invitations to open days and educational pages.

We can see, therefore, that the strategic design and use of the website is growing in importance in today's marketplace and this must be considered as part of an integrated communications strategy.

The evaluation of websites and Internet marketing communications

As with all the marketing communications tools, it is vital that the marketer establishes clear objectives and standards for performance for what are often expensive elements of the marketing programme. These objectives and standards can then be used to evaluate the various tools. In the early stages of the application of some of the website and Internet marketing communication tools outlined, evaluation and control was not a strong point. However, this is now changing and evaluation is becoming more important and sophisticated. The following indicates just some of the ways in which the Internet and websites can be evaluated.

The most frequently used evaluation method for the Internet site is the analysis of what are known as 'hit records' for each file retrieved by the respondent or visitor.

Key definition

Hit – Is a downloaded file as recorded in a server log.

Although a broad measure of the number of people visit a site via a server, the hit record gives very little indication of the effectiveness of a website. Accordingly, some much more sophisticated software packages or Web-tracking programs are now available. Using such Web-tracking programs, a company can also identify and evaluate, for example, the following:

- Where the website visitor came from – based on their e-mail domain
- On what page the visitor started
- What pages were visited and in what order
- How long the visitor spent on each page
- What the visitor did on each page, for example complete a form, download a file, play a game.

Improvements in Internet site evaluation and control are being made all the time now.

Extending knowledge

An excellent source of further information regarding on-line marketing is Bill Eager and Cathy McCall's *The Complete Idiot's Guide to On-line Marketing* – don't be put off by the title!

Mobile marketing and advertising

Marketing in practice: example

Gossard, the UK lingerie-maker, recently developed a campaign involving sending text messages direct to consumers' mobile phones entitling them to receive a voucher which in turn could be used to receive £1 off on any Gossard g-string. Called the 'G4Me' campaign this was the first time that Gossard had used text messaging in its promotion. The 'G4Me' campaign co-ordinated with a television, press and poster campaign.

You were introduced to the term 'mobile' or as it is normally referred to M-marketing in Unit 6. The Gossard example above illustrates just one approach to this type of promotional marketing. From virtually nothing 2 years ago, mobile marketing and advertising have become one of the most exciting areas of contemporary marketing. You will recall that mobile marketing uses the mobile phone to reach customers. The rapid growth in this area of marketing therefore stems from, on the one hand, developments in mobile communications and particularly the so-called 'WAP' or wireless application technology developments. This has led to a growth in the wireless Internet reflected in turn in new generations of mobile phones which are based around these powerful wireless technologies. As a result, the marketer can now send much more information to customers via their mobile phones including sophisticated advertising and promotional messages. The second factor in the growth of mobile marketing, however, is, on the other hand, the changing lifestyles of today's consumers. Today's consumers lead increasingly busy and peripatetic lifestyles. They have a great desire and need to stay connected while at the same time being on the move. It is in this environment that mobile marketing and advertising is finding an increasing role. There are a number of types of M-marketing and the marketer can use these in different ways to develop promotional programmes and messages sent direct to potential target customers' mobile phones. Almost every mobile phone purchased now has a wireless in-built Web browser which allows customers to contact companies direct and vice versa. One of the types of mobile marketing that is attracting substantial attention is in fact the so-called 'push' variety, that is the marketer contacting the customer's mobile. Using the short messaging system (SMS) this type of mobile marketing is essentially a text-based system, very similar in fact to e-mail, in which short messages, normally around 80–100 characters, are sent to the target market's mobile phones. At one time, many carriers charged the mobile phone owner an additional fee to use SMS but now it is increasingly free and hence is expanding the opportunities for marketers considerably.

Mobile phone users are now not only familiar with and utilize text-based messaging systems but in fact this is now the major use of mobile phones. Customers are therefore much more receptive to receiving marketer sources texts to their mobile phones, although as with all 'unsolicited' marketing messages and promotions, care should be taken in targeting the right customers so as to not alienate them by filling their message screens and boxes with unwanted messages. The growth of the so-called 'permissions-based' marketing is useful in this respect, whereby the marketer first seeks permission from the mobile phone user to relay advertising messages to the customer about the organization's products and brands. The other approach to mobile marketing using text-based systems of course is the 'pull' variety whereby customers, again on the move, use their mobile phones to track and access information about marketers

215

and their products by tapping into the Web. Increasingly, customers are doing this while actively involved in the shopping process, calling up information on, say, competitors' prices and brands in the very act of considering product choice in the retail outlet.

There is no doubt that from a relatively slow start, mobile marketing is set to be one of the fastest growing areas of marketing communications and advertising. In Asia, in particular, mobile marketing and advertising is proving particularly successful mainly due to the fact that many of the Asian languages allow the marketer to get more information into their characters and therefore their SMS systems. At the moment, the predominant use of SMS systems means that to some extent mobile advertising is limited, particularly in terms of the information and detail that can be conveyed. However, already marketers are moving towards very innovative and creative new uses for M-marketing. One development, for example, has been the delivering of electronic coupons to customers' mobile phones, which they can then use in purchasing situations to receive discounts on products and brands.

Marketing in practice: example

Jiffylube International Inc. has recently used mobile marketing to deliver electronic coupons via a wireless website. Selected customers who receive this electronic coupon are eligible for a discount when they present the electronic coupon to distributors.

www.jiffylube.com

Another example of a creative use of M-marketing is the idea of electronically distributing tickets for concerts, movies, shows and so on, which have not sold, by mobile phone network suppliers as a promotional marketing tool to their customers thereby meeting the marketing needs of both ticket agencies and mobile phone companies.

Marketing in practice: example

Several companies have developed ticketing services of the type described above. GoZing has explored joint marketing efforts with several movie, concert and even holiday resort companies to give tickets away that otherwise would remain unsold.

www.GoZing.com

There is no doubt, then, that mobile marketing does indeed represent an exciting development, particularly in the promotional area of the marketing mix and we can expect this area to grow even faster in the future.

Other technological developments in promotion

As you will appreciate, we have only introduced some, albeit some of the major, developments in technology with respect to contemporary promotional techniques. We have concentrated mainly on developments in IT and promotion, and in particular the Internet and mobile marketing. However, with the rapid pace of technological change and development a number of other technological developments have affected and will continue to affect the promotional element of the marketing mix in important and far-reaching ways. In the context of the syllabus and of course from the point of view of your professional development as a marketer, therefore, it is important that you try to keep up to date with technological developments in the promotional and indeed the other areas of the marketing mix.

Marketing in practice: example

Marketers are being increasingly innovative in their use of new technology in promotion. Here are just some examples:

One leading UK departmental store is introducing store windows which 'talk' to customers as they pass by about products and offers in store.

One leading holiday company is using specially adapted technology to create crop circle designs in fields under the main flight paths into major airports featuring the company's logo.

Perhaps most bizarre of all is recent research which claims that new developments in scanning the human brain have discovered an area of the brain which triggers shopping behaviour. Some marketers believe that the next step will be to find out how to target and trigger this area of the brain through future commercials. Already researchers have linked brands and promotion that seem to stimulate activity in this area of the brain and which it is therefore suggested are more likely to make a sale.

Marketing in practice: case study

'To advertise or not to advertise: that is the (unresolved) question'

There has long been a debate among marketers about the effectiveness and power of advertising. Although most marketers have agreed that advertising has a role to play in the marketing and promotional mix in many companies, there are some marketers who, on the one hand, believe that advertising is entirely ineffective in getting customers to purchase products and hence is a waste of money and, on the other, some who believe that advertising is so powerful and effective as to be the essential communications tool in any promotional campaign. If anything, this polarized view about the effectiveness or otherwise of marketing is increasing.

Proponents of the ineffective viewpoint on advertising cite examples of companies and brands such as Body Shop, Pizza Express and Red Bull who have all to some extent abandoned, or in some cases never used, advertising in their promotional campaigns. Proponents of the viewpoint that advertising is the most effective tool, on the other hand, include those marketers who understandably have found their advertising campaigns to be demonstrably successful including brands such as Orange, Walkers Crisps, Tango and French Connection. What then could possibly explain such diverse viewpoints as to the effectiveness of advertising and hence the decision as to whether to advertise or not?

Some of the possible reasons to explain those who eschew advertising as a promotional tool are those companies who believe their brands are strong enough to sell on their own merits. These are often brands that are long-established and that have strong brand-loyal users. Advertising, it is suggested in this case only adds to company and hence eventually customer costs. Others believe that advertising demeans the product or company, or in some cases is unethical. Finally, we have those marketers who believe that their customers are essentially unaffected by advertising, relying instead on other sources of information in order to form attitudes towards products and services and on which to base their product choices.

As already mentioned, those who embrace advertising as the most effective and hence important promotional tool tend to be those marketers who have demonstrable evidence from their own experience that advertising has worked for them. Several examples of companies and brands in this category were listed earlier. Generally, marketers who have this view of advertising feel that consumers will rarely, if ever, purchase unadvertised brands and that by not advertising a company is at a serious disadvantage compared to competitors.

So, who is right about the 'to advertise or not' dilemma? The answer is probably neither. Sometimes advertising is the most effective and significant promotional tool in a marketer's armoury, particularly where the advertising is well planned and executed. On the other hand, there are some situations where advertising is either ineffective or inappropriate such as where customers want or need a personal demonstration, say, of a product or where perhaps customers are strongly brand loyal and will ignore advertising for other brands. There is no doubt that the extremely high costs of advertising should force the marketer to objectively consider its effectiveness and hence use. Essentially, though, in deciding whether to advertise or not the marketer must carefully consider how advertising fits into the overall promotional programme, its potential effectiveness as a communication tool and the extent to which advertising is consistent with the values and mission of the organization.

Summary

- o In this unit we have looked at the role and importance of communication in marketing.
- o We have examined the key concepts in and process of communication and their implications for the marketer.
- o We have established what the key ingredients in the promotional mix are.
- o You should now appreciate the key steps and considerations in planning marketing communications.
- o As in all of the areas of the marketing mix, developments in technology and particularly the growth of the Internet are having major effects.

Examination preparation: previous examination question

Attempt Question 5 of the examination paper for December 2003 (Appendix 4). For Specimen Answer Examination Question 5, December 2003, see Appendix 4 and www.cim.co.uk.

Further reading and Bibliography

Brassington, F. and Pettitt, S. (2003) *Principles of Marketing*, 3rd edition, FT Prentice Hall, Chapters 14, 15, 16, 17, 18 19.

Bickerton, P., Bickerton, M. and Pardesi, U. (2000) *Cybermarketing*, 2nd edition, Butterworth-Heinemann.

Chaffey, D., Mayer, R., Johnston, K. and Ellis-Chadwick, F. (2000) *Internet Marketing*, FT Prentice Hall.

Dibb, S., Simkin, L., Pride, W. and Ferrell, O.C. (2000) *Marketing Concepts and Strategies*, 4th European edition, Houghton, Mifflin, Chapters 15, 16 and 17.

Eager, B. and McCall, C. (2000) *The Complete Idiot's Guide to On-line Marketing*, Edinburgh, Scotland: Canongate books.

Holtz, S. (1999) *Public Relations on the Net*, AMA, New York.

Lancaster, G., Massingham, L. and Ashford, R. (2002) *Essentials of Marketing*, 4th edition, McGraw-Hill, Chapter 11.

Lavidge, R.J. and Steiner, G.A. (1961) 'A model for predictive measurements of advertising effectiveness', *Journal of Marketing*, p. 61.

unit 8

the marketing mix: people, service and customer care

Learning objectives

Learning outcome

By the end of this unit you will be able to:

○ Identify and describe the people, service and customer-care elements of the marketing mix.

Knowledge and skills

By the end of this unit you will be able to:

○ Explain the importance of people in marketing and in particular the contribution of staff to effective service delivery (3.13).

○ Explain the importance of service in satisfying customer requirements and identify the factors that contribute to the delivery of service quality (3.14).

Study Guide

In this unit, we shall look at the interrelated aspects of service and service quality in satisfying customer requirements and the ways in which the notion of customer service has expanded to encompass the broader area of customer care. Within these areas of service and customer care we shall look at the role that people, and particularly an organization's staff, play in service and customer care delivery. We shall look at why service and customer care have become increasingly recognized as critical factors in the success of a business, whether it is concerned with providing services or selling products. Service delivery, customer care and the all-important people element of an organization on which they are based have become the focus of a new approach for organizations providing products as well as services. In some ways for marketers, this is familiar territory. Many marketing pundits have long argued that the delivery of extra 'added value' through the service, customer care and people dimensions is a critical competitive factor in marketplaces that are becoming more crowded and more compe-titive by the day. In fact, we have already seen that it is these augmented product dimensions that are often the most important factors in choice for customers. As we saw in Unit 4, the augmented level of the product is sometimes the only way in which a company can differentiate itself from competitors. Increasingly, customers are looking for good service delivery and quality and will often, in addition, respond to high standards of customer care from the marketer. It is to these increasingly important areas of the marketing mix that we turn our attention in this unit.

The importance of service in satisfying customer requirements

Customers have become increasingly demanding in terms of what they require from the marketer. It is no longer sufficient for the marketer simply to provide a satisfactory product at a competitive price which is distributed and promoted in such a way as to make it readily available and known to the customer. Customers are demanding additional elements of service from the marketer. These additional elements can, as we have seen, be considered as part of the augmented product and can include any number of factors which the marketer can use to attract and hold customers. At one time, these elements might have been considered simply as product 'extras' including, for example, after-sales care, technical advice, complaint handling, repairs and maintenance and so on. But increasingly, service elements also encompass virtually every aspect of the marketing mix tools such as ordering systems and facilities, delivery services, credit and financial services for customers, enquiry lines and so on. There are many reasons for this growth in the importance of these service elements of the marketing mix including the fact that customers have come to expect high levels of service in increasingly competitive markets. From the marketer's point of view, however, service represents one of the most potentially enduring ways of obtaining an SCA. In time, even the best protected product designs and technologies can be copied, competitive prices matched and effective promotion and channel arrangements emulated. One of the most difficult elements of competitive strategy to match, at least in the short term, however, are those which deliver high levels of customer service. The reason why customer service is so difficult to copy is that effective customer service in turn demands a customer-care philosophy to be present throughout an organization. Building such a philosophy can take a long time and require substantial commitment from a company. Not only does it require effective systems and procedures, but above all it requires the right staff and attitudes in the organization. All factors take time to build. Originally, the service element of the marketing mix, and particularly the people element on which, as we have already said, effective service delivery is built, were considered to be a special and additional part of the mix for service products and markets only. Certainly, in our final unit we shall return to the additional elements of the mix in service contexts, but it is now recognized that all markets require good service delivery, strong service quality backed up by effective customer-care philosophies and systems, based on people. Because customer-service delivery is so strongly linked to the broader concept of customer care, it is to this area we now turn our attention. We shall start our next section in this unit by reminding ourselves how customer service and customer care relate to our discussion of the augmented and potential product levels.

The nature of customer care

Key definition

Augmented product – Refers to the extra elements aiming to provide additional customer satisfaction – helpful and well-trained sales people, range of products provided, guarantees of delivery and responsiveness to customer needs, having 'just the right' flavour, colour, price and so on.

Definition

Potential product – The potential product refers to the extra dimensions of customer care that companies could develop, no-quibble refund, return-anything policies; extra high quality decor or extra value provided in service encounters by, for example, music, flowers or entertainment in the service environment; and sensitivity to customer needs, and empowerment of staff to deal with them without referring to higher levels of management. These are all aspects of 'potential product'.

Study tip

As you have done in many of the preceding units, you should use your eyes and ears in your role as a customer to observe examples of both good and bad practice of the service or customer-care dimensions. You will be able to use these examples to help you understand the ideas and concepts outlined in the unit. In addition, of course, you will be able to use your examples in any possible examination questions in this area. An example will serve to illustrate this point.

In the United Kingdom, we can easily observe and contrast the traditional approach of retailers focusing on a more traditional approach to the product or service and those that have moved towards an augmented/potential product or service, with a very strong emphasis on customer-care dimensions. For instance, Boots the Chemist or Timpsons Shoes, although excellent retailers, are still, at the moment, operating fairly conventional marketing policies. On the other hand, companies such as Marks & Spencer have long offered high-quality facilities and excellent customer-care dimensions.

Customer care is a widely used term, yet definitions of precisely what it covers vary quite a lot. Sometimes the term is used interchangeably with 'customer service' – a more familiar term but one that has never acquired the same cachet. Customer service developed from a focus on 'order cycle' related activities into a much more general and all-embracing approach, which covers activities at the pre-, during- and post-transaction stages.

Activity 8.1

From your perspective as a customer for a particular product or service, list the most common reasons for feeling dissatisfied with the service you receive. Consider:

o How they might be improved
o Possible reasons why problems cannot be addressed.

Customer care is the preferred term when we are forced to consider activities outside the realm, beyond direct contact with the customer. One commentator describes it as 'the ultimate marketing tool', and a critical factor in the process of differentiating products or services, to develop a competitive edge. It calls for what some have called the management and identification of 'moments of truth' – contacts between companies and customers where a firm's reputation is at stake. Interaction is still a critical dimension, and the focus has moved away from specific activities to look in general holistic ways at customer satisfaction.

An important aspect of customer care is attitude, covering every aspect of customer/supplier relationships. Customer care is aiming to close the gap between customers' expectations and their experience. Customer care is also, by common assent, a policy and a set of activities.

Activity 8.2

Summarize what you take to be the main characteristics of the 'customer-care' concept. When you have completed your own summary, compare it to that shown in the debriefing.

An important point to remember about the customer-care concept is that it is not simply a matter of responding to what customers perceive to be shortcomings but also a matter of anticipating what is often referred to as the 'delight' factor, and the difference between this product and its competitors.

Customer care and corporate culture

Most commentators see customer care as necessitating a culture change within a business. It is not an adjunct to company strategy but a core value that must form the basis for all policy making and strategic thinking.

The difference between 'customer care' and the more traditional notion of 'customer service' seems to lie in the degree of centrality this is given within the process of formulating corporate policies, objectives and strategies. Often it is part of programmes that set themselves the task of transforming the operating procedures of a business under the rubric of a 'quality' or 'customer-orientation' programme.

Various descriptions of customer care, then, agree that customer-impinging activities in policies or as a guiding concept form the core element in the implementation of customer care within a company.

Most practitioners would agree that modern strategic marketing begins and ends with the consumer, yet customer care may well be overlooked in the pursuit of broader, more abstract objectives. It is important to be aware of the dangers in programmes with broadly *similar aims* and *overlapping objectives*, but slightly different *perspectives* and *priorities*.

Activity 8.3

Referring back to Unit 1, list the ways in which the customer-care concept is

- o Similar to
- o Distinct from

the marketing concept.

The marketing concept expresses a particular business philosophy and provides an analysis of the nature of consumption, consumers and markets today, placing a central importance on the formulation of strategies that take account of their characteristics. It is, in that sense, focused on consumers as they exist within their environments and as target groups.

The customer-care concept is a principle to guide the formulation of processes and practices within the organization that can unify and integrate the activities of all organizational members. In a sense, the customer-care concept expresses as a corporate mission the strategic objectives of a marketing orientation.

The importance of quality within the customer-care programme

Quality has been thought to be the critical differentiating factor between British firms and their successful foreign competitors and, as a consequence, the pursuit of quality has become a major preoccupation of British companies. A by-product of the attempt to compete with successful foreign firms making inroads into domestic markets was a modernization process, which led, in many cases, to cuts in investment, downsizing, wage cuts and so on – and also to poorer service to customers. Such was a consequence of the search for higher levels of productivity and output, greater commitment and flexibility from the workforce, and a broad 'culture change' in the organization concerned.

As many studies showed, perceptions of quality and service in British products fell significantly, and customer satisfaction levels were also poor, representing a sure recipe for disaster in a situation where foreign competition was meeting targets for quality improvement.

 Activity 8.4

Using a product with which you are familiar, compare those dimensions that differentiate a very good brand from a very poor brand. Use that list to derive a formulation of 'good quality'.

One of the main reasons for the success of Japanese and German competitors is an ability to create organizations dedicated to the pursuit of total quality, that is organizations focused entirely on the delivery of quality to customers. This seems to go hand in hand with a customer-care concept, to the degree that it makes very little practical sense to talk of one factor without the other also being given high priority.

Another reason for foregrounding customer needs has been the growing significance of services within the economies of advanced societies. Here the consumption of services has become more and more important over the past 20 years, as increasing affluence generates demand for the provision of people-based enterprises. In the 'Service Age', competition depends on quality being delivered, whether this is in catering and fast food, leisure provision, hospitality, entertainment or nowadays in medicine and other public services such as education.

Many universities, for example, have now included a customer-care element in their organizational mission statements. Once the preserve of the purely commercial organization, customer care and customer-care programmes are now being increasingly adopted in not-for-profit and public service sectors.

The total quality management (TQM) approach to such businesses uses customer care to deliver better service, or 'to meet customer requirements first time, every time'.

Customer care and TQM, then, are closely related and therefore we shall be considering TQM in more detail shortly. Quality programmes, however, cover many topics other than dealing with customers. Customer-care programmes focus on gaining deep knowledge of customers, and aim to identify their needs and improve care provided for them. Care is the outcome of this process, and 'satisfied customers' are the focus of customer-care programmes. The challenge is to maintain this emphasis throughout a quality process. While customer care should be focused on the way in which customers experience the delivery of the product or service, it is quality programmes that direct the processes constituting the services or products to which they are experiencing and responding.

A good example of a company which has put a lot of emphasis on customer care and TQM underpinned by effective quality programmes is Virgin PLC. This is a company which has put the concept and practice of customer care at the heart of all its businesses from mobile phones to airlines.

How quality programmes affect customer care, and what objectives TQM can have and what it can do, then, are clearly important issues for marketers interested in the implementation of customer-care programmes.

 Activity 8.5

Describe what you would expect to be the common elements in TQM and customer-care programmes. Compare the list you produce with the following sections.

The preceding section should lead you to identify the following core elements:

- An emphasis on process
- An emphasis on the details of the system
- The need to establish fundamental changes in attitude, focus and orientation
- The idea of a 'core philosophy' that transforms practice
- The derivation of the concept of quality for this particular product/service from customer perceptions, attitudes, expectations and needs.

Total quality management

Briefly, 'quality' in management can be defined as combining the satisfaction of customer needs with the achievement of company objectives. That the two are intimately and inextricably connected is an article of faith for all who discourse on the subject.

The following areas are connected, within the terms of this analysis, in systems aiming to achieve success and profitability by placing the customer at the centre of all enterprise activities through providing the right amount of the following:

- Quality
- Availability (at launch and afterwards)
- Service
- Support
- Reliability
- Cost/value for money.

By common assent, such programmes must be 'total', reaching forward to distributors down the chain, and back to suppliers in the case of manufactured goods, to ensure the quality of raw materials and the condition of the product that reaches the ultimate consumer. Hence, TQM.

Total quality management is now widespread throughout many companies. At first it tended to be the larger manufacturing companies such as Ford and IBM which practised TQM, but as mentioned earlier the recognition of the importance of value of TQM in an organization has meant that irrespective of the type of company, its size, or target market, TQM is increasingly practised.

The customer–supplier relation is very important indeed within the TQM philosophy. This relation is one of a long chain of such customer–supplier relations, with each customer being a supplier to someone further down the chain, so that it makes no sense to differentiate one role from the other. Rather than pursuing self-interest, and creating an adversarial relationship, the aim of TQM is to expand the pie the relation is concerned with dividing, in traditional terms.

The establishment of such programmes has been the foundation for some startling corporate success stories.

Marketing in practice: example

Some years ago Jaguar Motors were experiencing severe difficulties and loss of market share due to quality problems which Jaguar drivers were experiencing with their products. Detailed investigations, however, showed that this was due to large numbers of faults and quality problems in the components bought in from outside suppliers. Jaguar realized that they needed a completely new approach to relationships with their suppliers and in particular to the quality of the components supplied by them. After extensive work, Jaguar planned and implemented a TQM philosophy backed by effective quality control and testing systems so as to improve quality throughout the value chain resulting in significantly improved quality in their final products and a return to their former sales and market performance.

Quality and customer care

As with quality programmes in general, TQM gives central place to the customer. Satisfying them is the first principle of TQM, since they are the guarantee of the organization's continued existence. Gaining custom means winning a competition for the patronage of each individual or corporate buyer, and satisfying the particular needs of that individual is the competitive edge that wins survival and prosperity rather than extinction.

Customer-driven quality is recognized in the United States as a core value of the Malcolm Baldridge National Quality Award. The Baldridge Award encompasses awards for quality in different types of sectors or markets including awards for manufacturing companies, service organizations and even not-for-profit sectors such as education. The guidelines for its winners state 'Quality is judged by the customer'. This seemingly simple statement is in fact deceptively complex in its implications. All products and service attributes that contribute value to the customer and lead to customer satisfaction and preference must be the foundation for a company's quality system. Value, satisfaction and preference may be influenced by many factors throughout the customers' purchase, ownership and service experiences.

Activity 8.6

List as many companies as you can in which, in the course of business, there are avenues for gathering information about customer attitudes and beliefs regarding the company, or which provide readily accessible means to register either approval or dissatisfaction with the companies' service or products. Describe those companies that seem particularly good or particularly bad at these things.

Three principles guide customer–supplier relationships under TQM:

1. Recognition of the strategic importance of customers and suppliers.
2. Development of win–win relations between customers and suppliers.
3. Establishing relations based on trust.

These principles are translated into practice by:

o Constantly collecting information on customer expectations.
o Disseminating this information widely within the organization.
o Using this information to design, produce and deliver the organization's products and services.

TQM programmes require the following conditions to be fulfilled.

Total commitment from staff

This is another way of talking about a structural or a cultural change being essential for the achievement of a quality programme. Often these schemes are presented as 'a philosophy of life' or a 'total way of thinking' rather than just another technique for management. It is a peculiar feature of these systems that they have a religious, or messianic quality – advocates are spoken of as 'evangelists' or, more commonly, 'gurus'. It is perhaps unsurprising that the generation that toyed with transcendental meditation and flower power in the 1960s should focus on gurus of a different kind in the 1990s!

For this system to work, however, it is a practical necessity for all staff to participate. Those best placed to make quality work are the people who actually deliver products or services. Partial quality improvements will constantly face the problems created by those parts of the system that have not been reformed, when staff are trying to improve the quality of what they deliver to customers.

A customer orientation

As suggested above, each internal group in the quality chain is composed of a customer and/or supplier to other internal groups, and in some cases to the market. Although programmes can start at any point in this chain, even if the quality of the supply to a group is low, the group should aim to build up its own quality before addressing the shortcomings of its own supplier.

Note how a 'customer orientation' under TQM focuses not just on the external customer but on the customer–supplier relation that is a general feature of marketing processes. Customer-care programmes, although focused on external customers, are important influences on the way in which such processes are conceived and practised.

227

Defining customer requirements and obligations

From the viewpoint of an organization, customers can be thought of as an agglomeration of *requirements and obligations.* Customers may be external customers, employees, shareholders, top management, government and so on. Requirements will be fitted to resource constraints and the objectives of the organization, and must be realistic and obtainable. Obligations need to be clearly defined, and requirements need to be quantified and accepted by both sides as reasonable. If a customer-care programme is to be effective, the relations must be clearly specified on both sides.

An example of an organization which practises this wider view of the range of customers, or perhaps we might say 'publics', in addressing customer-care programmes is the Open University. The Open University has realized that customer care encompasses not just students but also their employers, tutors, local communities and even governments.

Activity 8.7

Explain:

- What effect focusing on customers and suppliers has on the formulation of strategy.
- The value of a 'win–win' relation in this context.
- The importance of trust in these relationships.

Measurement

This is extremely important for any quality programme and, in relation to customer care, measurements must be continual and ubiquitous. Required performance needs to be clearly specified in terms that can be measured, and mechanisms must be instituted to provide clear indicators that these have been achieved. These must be in place before programmes are instigated.

Customer-care programmes will require survey data on internal and external customers, on customer behaviour and on the degree to which customer needs are being satisfied. These should permit the application of techniques such as key ratio and trend analysis, and fit into a cycle of assessment, planning, implementation and monitoring.

Commitment from the top management

Top management needs to ensure that the programme is delivered, and also that it provides the cash pay-off from improved quality in customer service.

Adherence to standard processes and procedures

Processes and procedures that are developed and specified as an end product of a TQM customer-care programme are intended to be followed. Such directions are intended to reproduce proven consistent quality, and should specify administered processes, timing, responsibility and areas of expertise, and gathering of feedback data. When these directions are adhered to, the output remains consistent, processes are appropriately monitored and the data provides the basis for learning and consistent improvement.

Paying-customer objectives

The end product of any programme must be to satisfy the needs of the paying customer in order to accomplish particular commercial, financial or strategic objectives. To that end, all analysis within customer-care programmes, and the development of any processes and procedures within such programmes, must relate to these objectives. Examples of such objectives would be:

- Increasing sales and profits
- Lowering prices of service provision
- Improving customer perceptions of service
- Shortening waiting lists and giving priority to customer needs.

The *mission* of the organization, and the corporate values that underlie corporate objectives, must always be clearly and directly related to the formulation of such objectives. If they are not, then TQM programmes will not accord with the strategic direction that has been agreed.

Activity 8.8

Using the example of an organization with which you are familiar, identify those parts or aspects of its operational procedures, which seem likely to pose the most problems when TQM is being introduced. Why should managers or workers resist the introduction of TQM?

The idea of the activity is to make you think about the contrast between the ideals of TQM and the actual circumstances within many companies that might wish to introduce it. Who would lose, or consider that they would be likely to lose, when this system was brought in?

Customer care, a comprehensive approach to working with customers

The close relation between the 'customer orientation' that lies at the heart of marketing and the notion of customer care is readily apparent. Customer care can be seen as a perspective that focuses on working with customers at every stage of the planning and implementation process. This is important in marketing all types of product and service. It is a *service component* and, as such, shares the *characteristics* of service marketing. It is, for example:

- People-based
- Perishable
- Dependent on high customer involvement
- Based on perceptions
- Sensitive to images
- Heavily dependent on consumption context
- Delivered over time.

While marketing is, as we have seen, fundamentally based on customer orientation, it is possible, in the pursuit of marketing objectives, to lose sight of the things that will satisfy customer needs.

229

Following a marketing plan in the delivery of a service can result in customer-care shortcomings in the following ways:

o   *As a result of an unrealistic corporate mission* – When those in charge of the company are making promises the company cannot possibly deliver. When the company is aiming to deliver the wrong level of care to the customer, or when the company is, for example, turning customers away.

o   *As a result of poor information about customers and the market* – Ignorance of customer needs and consequent mismatch of care levels to needs can produce a lack of customer care. This may come about because the information system fails to identify those areas in which customer needs must be given priority, focusing instead upon general aspects of customer satisfaction. Business priorities, for example carrying out the processes of delivering a service, can be out of line with customer priorities. Tom Peters emphasizes this aspect of customer satisfaction constantly: good products or services are perceived as failing because customers' small but important needs (being able to get coffee in a hotel in the early morning; having a space on which to place food or small items that may be needed quickly in an expensive car) are neglected.

o   *Poor timing* – When information that has been gathered in the past about what it is that customers want is used for too long, a mismatch can occur. Customer priorities are changing, and it may be that, for example, selling on price or on functional product attributes becomes inappropriate as products become mature, competition increases and differentiation is more problematic. In addition, good marketing may seek to identify needs of which some customers may not be fully aware; in marketing a product to satisfy these needs we are adding even more value to a product, by raising customer awareness of the needs it can meet that they do not, initially, anticipate.

o   *Poor staff communication* – In the delivery of services particularly, it is vital that staff should be aware of the needs suppliers require them to satisfy. When staff are not fully trained, or perhaps inadequately informed of the aims of a marketing programme, they may well fail to deliver the appropriate levels of service. Local improvization will cause inconsistencies, and variations in the quality of product and service delivered will arise. Often staff will react to problems by falling back on a 'defence' of the systems they are operating.

o   *Poor staff motivation* – When staff are not properly informed, trained or committed to delivering customer care, they will be inadequately motivated. This will invariably be communicated to customers.

o   *Poor control* – Systems of control are essential to the establishment and maintenance of customer-care standards throughout an organization. When such systems are absent or inadequate, levels of quality of customer care will vary. In some cases such variation may well take the form of very damaging inconsistencies, which may well undo the effects of good practice taking place in other parts of an organization or at other times with the same staff or customers.

o   *Confused priorities* – When staff are following through the delivery of, for example, specific practical aspects of service delivery, such as progressing an order or carrying out a task for the customer, they may find that there are too many priorities for them to pursue effectively. Attention to marketing tasks, or attendance to customer relations, is perceived to be an 'extra' in some organizations, and is strongly at risk of being sacrificed.

o   *Organizational confusion* – Many structures do not effectively delegate responsibilities for marketing or customer care. In principle, it should be part of everyone's job, but, at the same time, it must be expedited, and responsibility for the establishment and delivery of the systems that promote these priorities must be clearly defined within the organization.

o   *Non-acceptance of marketing and customer care* – When staff are pressurized into delivering too many difficult practical aspects of their jobs – meeting efficiency or productivity targets, delivering increased levels of output – they may well feel that concerns over meeting customer needs are not something they should be greatly concerned about.

o   *Short-term emphasis* – This is even more the case when the feedback, or the benefits of satisfying such needs, arise in the long rather than the short term. In this case, distortions in the delivery of services or products may arise because only behaviour (satisfaction of needs) which brings short-term rewards to the supplier is being reinforced by positive feedback from the customer.

o   *Power conflict* – Inconsistencies will also occur when there are imbalances between the power at the disposal of different functions within an organization. Here, the level of care customers are offered varies according to which parts of the organization customers contact. When customers require to contact more than one part of the system, they are highly likely to experience inadequate service levels.

Activity 8.9

Think of the ways in which the implementation of a marketing plan can frustrate the delivery of customer care. For each of these areas, think of strategies in which problems could be overcome by modification or replacement of particular aspects of the marketing plan.

Your answer to the activity should bring out the contrast between the width of focus in these plans. Clearly, marketing plans often have implications for customer-focused activities, and may imply conflicting, or contradictory, aims, for example over price, quality, or assortment in the product range. The important point to grasp is that company policy requires that these issues should be confronted and resolved by creative tension between these objectives. They must inform each other, rather than be treated as separate and isolated.

Delivering adequate levels of customer care

Produce an adequate definition of the corporate mission

Without clear definition of corporate goals, the business will always be wasting resources and effort through lack of a clear focus and consistent goal. A mission statement has as one of its fundamental aims, however, the communication of purpose to each member of the organization – it must be easily understood by every participant – and it must also inform individuals how their roles within the organization contribute towards the achievement of this mission. It therefore has a key role in motivation, and if it is not clearly and effectively formulated, the chance of establishing a customer-care ethos or 'culture' within the organization is seriously diminished. The line between mission statements and customer care is so important that we shall return to this area again shortly.

Activity 8.10

Formulate a mission statement for:

o Yourself
o Your family
o The leader of your country.

What is a mission statement for? What is it supposed to accomplish? What are the difficulties in bringing together various and often conflicting aims, and making decisions about priorities and ultimate objectives? This activity should force you to think about the issues that are in play when objectives are formulated.

Use up to date and reliable information

Assumptions about what it is that customers want, and notions that it is 'obvious' which product attributes are most important to the customers, are all too common and frequent causes of dissatisfaction. Information about customers should come from customers, or from those who are closest to them in delivering a product or service. Information about competitive activity, about changes in market conditions and even about the performance and perception of the company itself, should come from sources that are in touch with the recent reality of the situation, and not dependent on remote or potentially partial individuals or organizations.

Unless the company places a very high priority on the gathering, analysis and dissemination of information to inform decision-making, and also engenders a culture in which information flows freely and is available in a form that can be readily used by decision-makers at all levels, it is difficult to see the organization developing the degree of openness and responsiveness that is such an integral part of the customer-care concept.

Use information to inform decisions and planning

Too much information is gathered ritualistically or simply because it seems like a good or useful thing to do. When information about customer needs is gathered, it must be used to make effective decisions, and placed at the heart of the planning process. If the information being gathered is not used in this way, the organization needs to ask why it is being gathered at all. An important part of this informational system are the mechanisms by means of which this information can be gathered, stored, analysed, disseminated and rendered into forms that decision-makers can relate to their particular concerns. Since customer care is essentially founded on 'listening' above all else, but also on 'measuring' and 'reacting', or learning from what our information can tell us about what customers think and want, decisions must be information based in the case of even the most experienced and able managers.

Activity 8.11

Describe what information would be needed by:

- A managing director
- A store manager
- A sales person

to meet the needs of customers in a store selling clothes to very large men. Are they the same, or are they different? Why?

How far can information be shared? How relevant is, say, economic data to a sales person? Should it be? How far can we take the process of 'flattening' an organization, and distributing skills across the workforce?

Act quickly

Information decays quickly. Failing to act on the basis of information that is available now and acting after the information has ceased to be relevant are equally damaging and inappropriate. Customer needs and standards change very quickly in some markets and when action is needed, it should be taken as quickly as possible.

Use written plans that are understandable and achievable, and provide motivation for staff

Written plans should aim to meet communication objectives. If they are written for staff to implement, they should aim to provide a basis on which practical actions can be taken, effects can be identified and measured, and staff achievements can be formulated. Plans are counter-productive if those who are required to live by them feel that they cannot realistically be met, or that meeting them engenders no commitment and offers no reward or sense of achievement if their challenges have been met.

There is another school of thought about the notion of written plans. Arguing against the (traditional) idea of management by objectives (MBO), one author says that the creation of such objectives actually inhibits progress and militates against the achievement of high-quality service and products. The objectives set have to be achievable, and so the 'ceiling' on quality is fixed in advance. Setting such targets becomes increasingly difficult, and has less effect as time goes on, since it depends on setting 'realistic' goals, which are also built on goals that have just been achieved. In that sense, written plans can provide a brake on potential improvement, or, as the quality movement refers to it, the 'continuous improvement process'.

It is argued that a system in which excellence, quality and responsiveness to customer needs are ingrained in the corporate culture is far preferable; in that case, striving for quality and seeking to find new ways to add value and satisfy customer needs become a constant, endemic feature of the operation of the organization, at every level, and in every process. Rather than planning for customer care, every employee sees it as a natural feature of the job. This does, of course, call for careful analysis of procedures, and specifications of what happens in every process, based on observation, description and analysis. In that sense, written plans and clear definitions of procedures are essential bases for any programme seeking to make beneficial change.

Produce regular progress reports on the implementation of the marketing plan

These must be reliable and detailed, and not simply reports on results. Constant attention to progress, adjustment as necessary to changes in conditions and new customer needs, and changes in perception, all require that the marketing plan being followed should form the background to what is done.

Make measurement central to the process of implementation

Scores and systems of measurement provide invaluable benchmarks of progress, and provide targets that can be seen to be met, or not.

Activity 8.12

Think of trying to improve the customer-care element of the service provided in a travel agency. Write down which aspects of service encounters can be measured, briefly indicating the kind of instrument used, for example a survey questionnaire. In addition, say which aspects would be difficult or impossible to measure – and why.

Compare your list with that shown in the debriefing.

Disseminate a marketing philosophy, but also assign clear responsibility for the marketing function.

If everyone's job has marketing aspects, trouble can occur if no one is actually responsible for making it happen. There must be clearly defined responsibilities here, as well as a core commitment to building it in the way in which the organization functions at all levels.

Activity 8.13

Describe what activities you believe to be required in order to establish customer care for:

- o A car salesroom
- o A supermarket.

Customer care within the marketing process

Marketing calls for a structured approach and applying information about customer needs in order to achieve strategic objectives; typical steps include:

- o Defining corporate mission, corporate objectives and strategies
- o Analysing the environment
- o Setting marketing objectives

- ○ Developing marketing strategies
- ○ Devising action plans
- ○ Measuring results
- ○ Reacting to results.

Within each of these steps customer-care issues arise and must be met. Often, consideration of these issues will materially influence the ways in which the objectives of the marketing process are pursued. We consider them in more detail in the following section.

Defining the business mission

While definition of what business the enterprise is in, who is being served and how this will be accomplished seem incontestably essential questions for anyone in business, the simplicity they propose as the foundation of business activity is difficult to achieve. As the size of an organization and its tasks increase, so does their complexity, and the possibility of being diverted from central issues.

In defining the business mission, looking at who our customers are, and how we see ourselves as serving their needs, we need to take a large number of factors into account. Initial explorations of what customers want may actually reveal that this cannot be met by what the enterprise has to offer – in which case markets have to be redefined.

Mission statements that fail to accommodate the establishment of customer loyalty and the promotion of customer care as primary aims are bound to fail. Likewise, it is essential that mission statements espouse and promote effective plans to maintain high levels of caring for customers within the operating framework of the enterprise.

A good example of where a company's mission statement explicitly recognizes the importance of customer care and incorporates this into the company philosophy is that of the Interflora worldwide flower delivery company. The aims of the Interflora organization, particularly as regards customer care, are encompassed in its mission statement which is as follows:

> *Our mission is to ensure that Interflora will always be the consumer's first choice for flowers and appropriate gifts. This means: recognizing and responding to our customers' changing needs; providing a seamless service to our customers; leading our industry in innovation and design; continual improvement in quality, service, processes and costs and enabling our employees and associates to give their best.*

The marketing audit

The marketing audit must attempt to identify and define factors within the external environment that promote customer satisfaction and generate loyalty. This calls for comparisons between different policies, evaluations of the different degrees to which they actually promote customer loyalty, and analysis of why differences occur.

The audit should also evaluate the performance of the different factors within the enterprise that promote customer satisfaction, and identifying sources of dissatisfaction should play a major part in the marketing process.

Action plans for the formulation of the marketing mix

Problems, from the point of view of customer care, arise when such plans focus on short-term objectives, particularly sales and the promotion of improved margins. These very often prove antithetical to the main objectives of strategies based on customer care, which aim for the long term, not just winning custom, but winning customers by promoting good ongoing relationships, and looking for substantial long-term profits by sustaining customer loyalty.

235

Action plans to formulate marketing operations

Problems here have to do with the efficacy and efficiency of marketing procedures, for example the cost-effective and efficient delivery of beer to a public house, rather than with the perception and response of customers to the end product, for example an unfavourable comparison between product delivered in natural, old-fashioned wooden barrels, and that delivered in modern, cost-effective aluminium kegs – with a consequent attribution of many undesirable product characteristics such as chemical taste, additives, poor quality and so on.

Results

When too much emphasis is placed on tracking sales and profit, rather than customer inventory movements, results may not be providing the most effective form of feedback for the organization to make long-term plans.

 Activity 8.14

Give an example of a customer-care issue at each of the six stages listed.

When this framework is followed, attention is effectively focused on the delivery of customer care. What is also required, of course, is a clear idea of what customers want from the organization. This requires a systematic approach to the gathering and evaluation of information about what may actually be a number of different types of customer, since the product portfolio of many companies extends over different types of market for the same type of product or, of course, different brands and product types.

Identifying customer needs and perceptions of the company

To use a strategy based on customer care successfully, two questions need to be answered:

1. What policy of customer care is most appropriate for our company?
2. How far should this policy affect our operations?

In order to succeed, knowledge of customer needs is vital. What expectations should the company aim to meet? In the real world, these expectations will be related to the way in which the company is perceived. There are, for example, limits to the expectations a reasonable person has, and these are related to the realities of what resources a company has at its disposal, and how these must sensibly be employed.

The customer believes minimum rights should be respected, independent of such constraints, for they are the *sine qua non* of customer care. All customers have the absolute right to:

o   A basic minimum level of customer care
o   Common courtesy from staff
o   Responsive and effective response to complaints.

Customers' requirements in terms of care are likely to vary according to the significance, as they perceive it, of each transaction with the supplier. When customers perceive a contact with the supplier to be important, they have higher expectations of the level of care they should receive.

Many products are bought as a package, of which customer care is a greater or smaller part. Among the factors that may be important are the following:

o Time taken
o The importance of the service element of the package relative to other elements at different times in the relationship
o How important it is for the customer to be in control
o The degree of dependency on the supplier
o The importance of the service to the customer
o The degree of risk that is felt to attach to the supply of the service
o The dependence of the service on staff or equipment
o Contact with staff
o Degree of control perceived in staff
o Contact with other customers
o Skill/expertise expected of staff
o Degree of routine in encounters
o Number and complexity of stages and service encounters
o Emotions anticipated and experienced by customers at different stages.

The mix of factors is also affected by the characteristics and experience of individual customers. As a consequence, different individuals will view the same service in different ways. What is new and potentially stressful for one individual is routine to another, perhaps experienced, user of a service or product.

Given this important element, it appears likely that the role of the customer in the 'service-production' ('servuction') system can be increased according to the experience or number of occasions in which the customer makes use of the service or buys the product.

Levels of customer care may well be influenced thereby. While customers invariably expect minimum levels of care, they probably also have a desired level, which is influenced by the degree of experience they have of the organization. The greater experience they have, the more likely that they will entertain a perception of the level of care they receive.

These perceived levels contrast with actual levels, that is the levels the supplier says are provided in terms of customer-care activities. Perceptions of the levels of care are the strongest influence on satisfaction levels.

It is extremely important to define the 'minimum' levels of care expected by the customers. In many aspects these can be quantified very effectively, for example time taken to respond to a request for a repairman. Regular users will have a clear idea of desired and minimum standards, but how these are perceived will obviously vary across a group of customers. It is important for the company to identify minimum and 'optimum' levels. This would avoid the wastefulness and potential harm created by overprovision of certain aspects of customer care, for example having staff who are constantly pestering customers with offers of help.

Identifying the bands within which customer-care levels must be provided is particularly important. It is known that experience with the company providing the service or product, or with a competitor, provides a benchmark against which expectations are formed and delivery evaluated.

Identifying and analysing customer requirements are based on:

o Choosing customers
o Researching and modelling needs
o Determining care levels
o Building flexibility in.

Activity 8.15

Briefly outline the issues and the problems that might arise if you were trying to collect information to determine customer requirements with regard to service levels for a wine bar in a busy city centre.

Compare your outline with that shown in the debriefing.

An outline of the practical steps in establishing a customer-care programme

It is very important to establish practical processes for achieving desired levels of customer care. Some of the most important practical steps are now summarized.

Identify customer needs and perceptions

This first step in establishing a customer-care programme illustrates, once again, that the start point is customer needs. We must clearly establish what these are and how our customer-care programme needs to be designed to meet them. We must also evaluate the perceptions that current and potential customers have with regard to the company and its standards of customer care.

Establish a mission statement

The mission statement was referred to earlier in the unit; the approach to customer care and its importance in the company must be a key part of this statement. We also need a widely accepted mission statement for the approach to customer care itself.

Set service-level standards and specifications

Clear standards must be set for levels of customer care and the key elements to be included. Examples include standards for courtesy, credibility, communication, responsiveness, empathy with customer and confidentiality.

Establish management processes and communicate this to all staff

There should be clear specifications of how jobs should be done with regard to achieving customer-care objectives. This should include, for example:

o Who does what, and when – formal allocations of tasks and progress reviews.
o Information flows and systems required to implement customer-care programmes.
o The motivation, monitoring and control of people in the customer-care programmes.
o Obviously, responsibilities, and information on processes and procedures to be followed must be communicated to all staff.

Define tasks according to time factors

These factors include timing of recurrent work, seasonal factors and so on. This process should be accurately and comprehensively catalogued, and the programme of customer care must create systems by which the work can be handled according to the objectives of satisfying customer needs, and by using resources efficiently and cost-effectively.

Establish a basic minimum level

Although customer-care programmes should be built around customer needs, wherever possible, levels of customer care should meet the highest standards. However, it is also important to establish a baseline for standards of customer care below which levels of customer care should not drop.

Ensure systems for effective response to complaints

Although the idea of a customer-care programme is to reduce complaints, and indeed to remove the need for them altogether, it is unlikely that all complaints can be removed in this way. The customer-care programme therefore must have clear systems and procedures for ensuring effective responses to customer complaints.

Marketing in practice: example

An interesting twist in the idea of customer-care programmes being either to reduce or perhaps ideally to remove complaints altogether is the notion that a good customer-care programme will encourage more complaints. This apparently strange approach to customer-care programmes with respect to complaints is based in fact, on the plausible notion that the company's most challenging customers are also the most valuable – valuable in the sense that these are the customers who are the most demanding and therefore could help encourage a company to raise its standards and/or that they are the most valuable in the sense that once satisfied they tend to remain loyal and indeed act as ambassadors for the company and its brands. A company that has taken just this approach to customer complaints in its CRM programmes is the Dell Computer Corporation.

Secure management commitment

As stressed several times already in this unit, it is important to ensure commitment to customer-care programmes. It is especially important that this commitment is established, throughout all levels of management, but especially at the top level of the organization.

Implement effective and continuous measurement and control systems

Again, we have stressed several times the importance of measuring and controlling the customer-care programme. It is pointless paying lip service to customer care, it must be supported by objective and rigorously enforced measurement and control systems.

Successful customer-care programmes

If programmes are to work, the following conditions must be met. Staff must be:

o   Clear about the programme and their role in it
o   Committed to the programme
o   Well trained in programme needs
o   Sufficiently resourced to carry out their roles
o   Sufficiently skilled to carry out their roles.

The programme must:

o   Provide clear benefits for the staff
o   Be reinforced by top management action, with effective implementation regimes, clear priorities, and sanctions and rewards.

Management must be:

o   Informed about progress and effectiveness of staff performance
o   Provided with regular and appropriate information
o   The process must support marketing objectives and facilitate the work of staff towards its achievement.

Benefits of an effective customer-care programme

There is a range of clear benefits of an effective, long-term customer-care programme which marketers and top management should appreciate. We have touched on several of these benefits already but again, to summarize, an effective customer-care programme provides the following benefits:

o   Helps to establish standards for customer care
o   Minimizes organizational confusion about what is required and why
o   Potentially offers a competitive edge
o   Helps to establish TQM quality control
o   Offers value added to customers
o   Promotes better understanding of customers
o   Can be very motivating to staff
o   Helps build customer relationships and improves customer retention.

Although all of these benefits are significant, the role of customer care in the last point in our list, namely building customer relationships and therefore improving customer retention, is, as we have already seen, now accepted by marketers as being increasingly important. Because customer-service delivery and the broader aspect of customer care are so powerful in helping build relationships and thereby retaining customers, customer service and customer care are vital aspects of relationship marketing. We shall return to this shortly in the unit.

Marketing in practice: example

For many customers, one of the most potent indications of whether a company has truly adopted the principles and practice of an effective customer-care programme is when they contact a company by telephone for some reason. This could be, for example, to make a general enquiry, to ask for details of a product or service, to pay a bill or of course sometimes to make a complaint. A substantial number of companies have now switched to using call centres to deal with these telephone calls from customers. Indeed, the call-centre industry is one of the fastest growing sectors in many economies. In the United Kingdom alone, for example, more than 500 000 are already employed in call centres and this does not include the increasing trend for marketers to base their call centres in developing economies.

Unfortunately, if the experience of many customers with call centres is to be believed, many organizations are still woefully weak in terms of their customer-care programmes. Customers complain about getting through various automated options, the length of time they are held on hold, the fact that they cannot leave a message for a return call and when they do get through, the attitudes of operators. Because of all this, put simply, most customers find call centres at the least frustrating and at worst a complete disaster. This will not change unless and until call centres are seen as being an aid to customer service and are actually customer centred rather than as they have been in the past, simply a method of saving costs. Some companies at least are beginning to recognize this and change their call-centre operations. Technology again is helping here with things like integrated voice-recognition systems for ensuring calls are channelled to the right department. In addition, companies are making better use of database systems on their customers to take details and profiles of a customer's purchasing history, for example, when they contact a call centre. Amongst the worst performers amongst call-centre services are the banks, insurance companies, the building societies, the utilities and government departments.

Service delivery, customer care and the extended marketing mix

We have already touched on the fact that the marketing of service products is different to marketing physical products. We suggested that one of the major differences for the services marketer is the three additional marketing mix elements of 'people', 'physical evidence' and 'process'. Although we shall consider these further in Unit 9, it is important that marketers understand the implications and the interplay between service delivery, customer care and these three additional marketing mix elements. Some of these are outlined below.

1. *People (internal staff)* – It is important that there is commitment from all staff to customer care and that they are motivated. The 'people' element is central to effective service delivery and overall levels of customer care and it is vital therefore that there is investment in staff in terms of training and development in order to achieve predetermined levels of service delivery and customer care. Employee selection and motivation become central considerations, not just for the personnel department now, but for the marketer. If an organization's staff are badly trained, poorly selected, demoralized and unmotivated they cannot support good customer-service delivery and they are unlikely to be interested in supporting adequate levels of customer care. More often than not, poor service delivery and customer care can ultimately be traced to weaknesses or problems in the people element of an organization's marketing mix. So, for example, staff should be guided into what represents an appropriate level of courtesy to customers. In order to ensure TQM, internal quality groups should be devised and managed. Many of the market leaders in different industries have recognized the importance of the people element in providing effective customer care and again reflect this recognition in their mission statements.

2. *Process* – Processes should consider the customers' needs and perceptions with regard to adequate levels of service delivery and customer care. There should be customer support systems, TQM systems and good communications. Specifications should be written to ensure specific responses to customer complaints, to ensure

minimal waiting times, minimize bottlenecks and so on. A good example of a company paying careful attention to the process element and its effect on customer care is McDonald's, which has designed its processes to ensure standardization with a view to minimizing waiting times, bottlenecks and so on.

3. *Physical evidence* – Elements such as good signage, staff uniforms, informative communications must be planned and implemented to ensure that effective customer-service delivery is maintained and a customer-care ethos is achieved. Again, Interflora is a good example here. Although Interflora consists of 58 000 florists effectively trading through their own trade association (which Interflora is), that is each business is an independent floristry business, elements of physical evidence are standardized throughout the world including, for example, the use of the Interflora logo, shop image, staff appearance and so on. Even Interflora's trademark depicting the Roman god Mercury serves to act as a common element of physical evidence, thereby forming a common bond between the worldwide network of florists, which comprise Interflora, while at the same time offering the customer the reassurance of a worldwide trademark.

In summary, then, the integration of these three extended marketing mix elements is important to maximize the benefits of customer-service delivery and customer-care programmes. In turn, and ultimately, these determine levels of customer satisfaction and the all-important levels of customer retention so important to relationship marketing.

Study tip

Look again at the mission statement for Interflora which we introduced earlier.

Service delivery, customer care and relationship marketing

Remember, for any organization, it is more efficient to keep customers rather than to keep finding new ones. We noted in Unit 1 that this is one of the key reasons for making relationship marketing so important. Put simply, a happy customer will come back for more. On the other hand, the evidence suggests that nearly 70 per cent of most people will go elsewhere if they feel they are receiving indifferent levels of customer service. There are clear links, then, between customer service and customer care and the important 'relationship marketing' concept. In particular:

o Organizations need to view any transaction as part of a long-term goal.
o If the customer is satisfied with the product/service they have received for the price they have paid, they are more likely to return.
o A short-term outlook with lower levels of customer service might make higher short-term profits, but in the long run is likely to be less profitable.
o Trust is particularly important in relationship marketing, and hence it should be an important component of customer service. If a customer trusts an organization they are more likely to return. We must not forget, however, that trust is a two-way process. Not only must the customer trust the organization not to take advantage of them, but the business must also learn to trust its customers.

Customer service, by underpinning better relationships between an organization and its customers, helps to transform exchange relationships into 'win–win' rather than 'win–lose' ones.

Service quality in services marketing: the SERVQUAL model

As you will appreciate the importance of adequate levels of service quality, the notions of effective customer care and relationship marketing apply to all marketers and products whether physical or service products and markets. However, some of the special characteristics of service products which are discussed in Unit 9 mean that sometimes what constitutes service quality, the areas that are important in service quality and how to measure and evaluate levels of service quality can be more difficult than for the tangible physical product marketer. For example, with a physical product it is relatively easy to objectively measure, say, the functional performance of the product. With an intangible service product, however, this can be much more difficult. Recognizing this, several models have been proposed with regard to the criteria for assessing service quality and the sorts of data which would need to be collected and interpreted in order to make this assessment. One of the most influential of the models in this area is that developed by Parasuraman and Zeithaml and Berry and referred to as the so-called 'SERVQUAL' model. The main ideas and elements of this model are outlined below.

The model identifies ten criteria or areas for assessing levels of service quality. Collectively, these encompass the possible range of customer requirements from the service experience from the customers' perspective. Five of these criteria relate to the quality of the 'process' between customer and service provider. They are listed below:

1. *Responsiveness* – To what degree the service provider reacts to customer requirements and needs.
2. *Courtesy* – The extent to which service provider staff are polite, friendly, considerate, pleasant and so on.
3. *Competence* – The skills and expertise of the service provider staff in providing the service properly.
4. *Communication* – The extent to which service staff listen to customers, explain to customers and suggest solutions.
5. *Tangibles* – The extent to which the tangible/visible elements of the service, staff appearance, premises, state of equipment and so on are satisfactory.

The second set of quality criteria in the SERVQUAL model relate to the quality of the 'outcomes' of the service experience. They are outlined below:

1. *Access* – That is how easy or otherwise it is for the customer to gain access to the service and its delivery.
2. *Reliability* – The consistency and dependability of the service.
3. *Credibility* – The extent to which the service provider is seen as being trustworthy and believable.
4. *Security* – The extent to which the service is seen as being free from risk or danger.
5. *Understanding* – The extent to which the service provider understands and adapts to the needs of customers.

The SERVQUAL model provides a comprehensive framework for identifying what are key criteria from the customer's perspective when evaluating and assessing the quality of services provision. In turn, of course, it suggests the key areas where a service provider has to perform effectively. Finally, and related to these first two aspects, the SERVQUAL model guides the implementation of quality programmes for services marketers together with systems of evaluation and control.

The model stresses that a company has service quality problems where there is a gap between what consumers expect and what they perceive they receive with regard to services quality. There are four possible bases for such gaps and therefore strategies for their removal.

243

First of all, a gap can exist because a company simply does not understand what customers want and what represents the key service attributes and levels of performance. They simply do not understand their customers' needs. Secondly, a company even if they understand customers' needs and requirements may be unwilling or unable to meet these. Thirdly, the service provider may understand customer-service requirements and attempt to meet these but fail to do so because service contact staff or quality support systems are ineffective. Finally, customers may have been led to believe too much about a service provider's quality performance. So, for example, the company may have oversold its promises thereby increasing customer expectations.

Marketing in practice: example

When Virgin Trains was first established, Virgin made several promises about the service standards customers could expect from the Virgin Train Service. These related to areas such as punctuality, reliability, cleanliness, safety and so on. As much as anything, some of the problems that Virgin Trains have experienced with regard to customer complaints about the service stem from the initial expectations which these promises encouraged on the part of customers. In some respects, at least in the short term, some of them were probably unachievable.

Service delivery, customer care and new technology

As we have seen throughout, technology is changing marketing and marketing practices. Of particular importance with regard to service delivery and customer care in this respect is the fact that many of the technological developments in marketing are meaning that relationships with customers often take place with no direct physical contact of any kind, but rather are relationships which operate via the ether of the Internet or perhaps some of the direct marketing channels such as direct response television.

Given that among the strongest relationships individuals have with other parties are those which are based on personal relationships involving direct contact, for example, and certainly direct communication, the less personal nature of some contemporary marketing in some ways makes service delivery and customer care more problematical. Rather than thinking about developing customer care through these personal relationships with customers, the marketer must think of other ways to ensure adequate levels of customer service and care and to develop long-term relationships with customers. Information on customers and particularly databases can be extremely useful here.

Databases and customer care

A customer database is a record system of information on customers. Increasingly, of course, these record systems are held on computer. This record system will include information such as customer purchases, expenditure, credit ratings, complaints and so on. This information obviously can help in developing effective marketing mix programmes, but is particularly useful in developing systems of effective customer-service delivery and customer care. The database can be central to a customer-care programme and in particular where relationships with customers are themselves based on the Internet, for example.

The database can help with customer service and customer care in the following ways:

- o The database can be used to keep a record of customer contacts and any complaints.
- o The database can be used to assess what customers want so that marketing programmes, for example, can be more closely targeted towards customers.
- o We can use the database to keep ahead of customers and their needs by, for example, forecasting their future requirements.
- o Data can be analysed to discover any patterns, for example product faults, customer profiles and so on, thereby making it possible to improve the customer's experience of the exchange process.

There is no doubt that access to comprehensive databases these days, together of course with the computer power to be able to interpret and make sense of the data held in these, has become perhaps the most important facilitating mechanism for developing and improving CRM systems. For this reason, establishing, maintaining and using database management systems is essential to CRM, so much so that some refer to electronic CRM or e-CRM, as it is more commonly referred to in the CRM area. We shall consider this aspect in more detail in Unit 9.

International aspects of service delivery and customer care

Clearly, companies which operate in international markets want to develop similar standards of customer-service delivery and customer care throughout their operations. Note how our Interflora example illustrates how a company-wide commitment to customer care throughout different markets in different parts of the world can help build the image of a company, develop more effective relationships with customers and serve as a standard for operating procedures for all staff. If a customer has a satisfactory experience with a company in one country, then it is much more likely that the customer will seek to use the same company when he or she purchases elsewhere in the world. On the other hand, if a customer experiences different levels of service and customer care from the same company in different parts of the world, this is likely to lead to the customer being apprehensive and anxious about using the same supplier. However, customer-care programmes, including the selection of the level of customer care necessary and appropriate, are among the most difficult areas of the marketing programme to standardize. There are several reasons for this, but among the most important are differences in cultural practice in different parts of the world with regard to what is expected in terms of customer service and customer care. Almost without exception, the American customer expects, and in America largely gets, extremely high standards of customer service and care. In parts of Europe, however, including the United Kingdom, customers may not expect, and in fact positively dislike, some of the elements of customer service and care which are considered normal in the United States. In designing customer service and customer-care programmes, therefore, the marketer has to consider these cultural differences and reflect them in the design of customer service and customer-care programmes. Notwithstanding this, though, the international marketer should try to ensure consistent approaches to customer service and care in different parts of the world. Again, people, process and physical evidence are all important here. In designing an international effective customer-care programme, many of the issues and steps for planning a purely domestic customer-care programme are to be found. In essence, and by way of reminding you of some of these issues and steps, the following should be considered:

- o Identify customer needs and perceptions for each market.
- o Establish a mission statement.
- o Set service level standards and specifications reflecting individual country requirements but guided by an overall customer charter which reflects the mission statement and outlines measurable criteria/standards to be attained.
- o Establish management processes and communicate these to all staff.

245

- ○ Define specific tasks as regards customer-care elements for each country.
- ○ Establish basic minimum levels of customer care.
- ○ Ensure effective response systems for identifying, tracking and responding to complaints.
- ○ Ensure management and staff commitment to programmes through, for example, effective training and remuneration programmes.
- ○ Ensure effective and continuous measurement of the customer-care programmes.

Marketing in practice: case study

'High levels of customer care and service – a commitment or just words?'

Although many companies profess and would claim to have a commitment to high levels of customer care and service, unfortunately sometimes this is no more than empty words.

A good example of a company that has made substantial real commitment to its customer-care and service programmes is that of the global communications and information technology company, Marconi.

Despite its recent problems, Marconi remains committed to a philosophy of high levels of customer care and customer service. Indeed, continuing commitment to this philosophy is seen as being one of the key thrusts in Marconi's future recovery.

Although there are many ways in which it is possible to assess the extent of a company's commitment to high levels of customer care and service, one of the prime indicators in an organization are the values of senior management, particularly as represented in the company's mission and vision statements. An examination of these will normally quickly illustrate a company's approach and commitment to customer care and service. Below are just some examples of the sentiments that Marconi express in their mission and vision statements regarding customer care and service.

Marconi believe in people saying what they mean and meaning what they say. The Marconi approach is about creating relationships with customers based on trust and respect.

Marconi care passionately about success not only for the organization but for their customers and the other stakeholders in the business.

Marconi tries to win customers by listening to them, understanding their expectations and then acting with speed and precision to fill these.

Marconi take responsibility to deliver each time, every time, whether for customers, shareholders, colleagues or communities.

The bottom line for Marconi is that customers can rely on Marconi because customers' needs and expectations are important to them.

Of course, these are only words which are easy to say or to write and might not mean anything in terms of real commitment to customer care and service. In the case of Marconi, however, the values and philosophy indicated above are translated into company-wide programmes for delivering high levels of customer care and service with total commitment from staff and comprehensive approaches to working with customers to deliver high standards of customer care and service.

Certainly in Marconi, it's not just words.

Source: www.marconi.com.

Summary

In this unit, you have learned about the importance and scope of customer service and the broader concept of customer care of which customer-service decisions form but a part. We have seen that:

o Customer service is an increasingly important element in customer choice and hence the marketing mix.
o Customer care is an all-embracing approach, which encompasses customer service but covers activities at the pre-, during and post-transaction stages of dealing with customers. Customer care needs to be part of the corporate culture.
o Total quality management is a key part of customer-care programmes.
o Adequate levels of customer service and care should be carefully related to marketing objectives and strategies.
o Customer service and care programmes need to be based on information about customer needs and requirements.
o The implementation of customer service and care programmes should follow a series of pre-determined steps and stages.
o There are substantial benefits to be gained by all parties from the establishment of effective customer service and care programmes.
o The extended marketing mix elements are particularly important when it comes to considering customer service and care.
o Developing programmes for international levels of customer service gives rise to additional complexities, but in particular the marketer must consider differences in cultural circumstances and factors in designing and implementing customer-care programmes in international markets.
o Effective customer care can also be problematical when using some of the newer technologies and channels to market to customers such as, for example, the Internet.
o There is considerable overlap and interrelationship between customer service and customer-care programmes and the increasingly important aspects of customer retention and relationship marketing.

Examination preparation: previous examination question

Attempt Question 7 of the examination paper for December 2003 (Appendix 4). For Specimen Answer Examination Question 7, December 2003, see Appendix 4 and www.cim.co.uk.

Further reading and bibliography

Brassington, F. and Pettitt, S. (2003) *Principles of Marketing*, 3rd edition, FT Prentice Hall, Chapter 18.

Chaffey, D., Maher, L., Johnston, L. and Ellis-Chadwick, F. (2000) *Internet Marketing*, FT Prentice Hall.

Dibb, S., Simkin, L., Pride, W. and Ferrell, O.C. (2000) *Marketing Concepts and Strategies*, 4th European edition, Houghton, Mifflin, Chapter 1.

Lancaster, G.A., Massingham, L. and Ashford, R. (2002) *Essentials of Marketing*, 4th edition, McGraw-Hill, Chapter 13.

unit 9
marketing in context: further and future issues

Learning objectives

Learning outcomes

By the end of this unit you will be able to:

o Identify the basic differences in application of the marketing mix involved in marketing products and services within different marketing contexts.

Knowledge and skills

By the end of this unit you will be able to:

o Explain the importance of contextual setting in influencing the selection of, and emphasis given to, marketing mix tools (4.1).

o Explain differences in the characteristics of various types of marketing context: FMCG, b2b (supply chain), large or capital project-based, services, voluntary and not-for-profit, sales support (e.g. SMEs) and their impact on marketing mix decisions (4.2).

o Compare and contrast the marketing activities of organizations that operate and compete in different contextual settings (4.3).

o Explain the global dimension in effecting the nature of marketing organizations in an international environmental context (4.4).

o Explain the existing and potential impacts of the virtual marketplace on the pattern of marketing activities in given contexts including the effects of ICT on the development and implementation of the marketing mix (4.5, 3.15).

o Explain the importance of measuring the effectiveness of the selected marketing efforts and instituting appropriate changes where necessary (3.16).

Study Guide

In many ways, this unit seeks to draw together some of the key issues and concepts that we have considered in previous units. We shall see that, although of necessity we have to consider the individual elements of the marketing mix separately, in practice, it is vital that the marketer ensures these individual elements are combined and co-ordinated in planned marketing programmes. Many factors influence what is an appropriate combination and use of the marketing mix elements in marketing programmes including the factors considered in Units 2 and 3 encompassing, for example: opportunities and threats, company strengths and weaknesses, and the selection of marketing strategies including the key elements of target marketing and positioning strategies. In addition, however, and again as introduced in earlier units, it is now recognized that the use and combination of the marketing mix elements is greatly influenced by the context in which these tools are applied. We explained that in addition to the product life-cycle stages context which we have already discussed in Unit 4, these contextual settings for marketing encompass in particular FMCG contexts, b2b (supply chain) contexts, large or capital project-based contexts, services contexts, voluntary and not-for-profit contexts, SMEs contexts and international contexts. We shall, therefore, compare and contrast the marketing activities and particularly the use of the marketing mix tools of organizations that operate and compete in these different contextual settings.

In this unit, we shall also take the opportunity to explore some of the more recent contemporary developments affecting marketing activities and marketing mix decisions. In particular, we shall draw together some of the main effects of ICT which have been considered throughout the units in the coursebook and which are affecting the development and implementation of the marketing mix in organizations (CIM syllabus area 3.15). In this same area we shall also be considering the existing and potential impacts of the so-called 'virtual marketplace' on the pattern of marketing activities in different contexts. Finally, we shall reconsider the important final element of marketing planning, namely the need to measure the effectiveness of our marketing efforts where appropriate instituting any appropriate changes where necessary (CIM syllabus area 3.16).

We would expect you to take about 4 hours to work through this unit and suggest you allow a further 3–4 hours to undertake the various activities suggested. Other than your notebook and writing equipment, you will not need anything further to complete this unit.

Study tip

Syllabus areas 3.15 and 3.16 are the only two of the CIM's syllabus topics to be considered out or order in the sequencing of the coursebooks coverage of the CIM syllabus. This is simply because it was felt that it was more appropriate to deal with these two particular syllabus topics in this final unit. Remember, though, that these two syllabus areas actually form part of Element 3 of the Institute's Syllabus for this subject namely: 'The marketing mix and related tools'.

The nature and importance of contextual settings for marketing

As you would expect in a marketing fundamentals programme much of what we have considered in the units of this coursebook with regard to the tools and techniques of marketing and their application, the basic principles of marketing, if you like, are the same irrespective of the type of organization or market. So, for example, the basic elements of the marketing

249

planning process, the importance of marketing objectives, effective segmentation, targeting and positioning and so on are the same for all organizations and markets. However, again as you would expect, there are differences with regard to the practice of marketing according to the context in which marketing activities take place. Of particular importance with regard to different contexts are the different types of markets and organizations in which marketing is practised and applied. This is particularly true with regard to the selection of and the emphasis given to the different marketing mix tools and their use and combination in different market and organizational settings. Suggesting this, however, raises the issue of what are the key types of marketing context, and in particular how can we classify these contexts into different types so as to be able to explore and discuss how the selection and emphasis given to the marketing mix tools may differ between these different contexts. Although there are various ways of classifying contextual settings, the following represent some of the key and accepted classifications of contextual settings with regard to marketing:

- ○ Fast-moving consumer goods
- ○ Business-to-business
- ○ Large or capital projects
- ○ Small and medium-sized enterprises
- ○ Voluntary and not-for-profit organizations
- ○ Services.

Study tip

You will note that these are the different contextual settings identified in the syllabus for marketing fundamentals. For obvious reasons, then, we have organized our discussion on the different contexts in this unit around these.

Fast-moving consumer goods

Our first contextual setting is that of FMCG markets. Consumer goods markets are markets where the customer is purchasing products and services for their own or perhaps for their family's use. The principal motives for purchase, therefore, are personal in nature. This type of customer, then, may be contrasted with those buyers who are purchasing primarily for their organizations or institutions and hence are b2b customers purchasing, for example, raw materials and components and so on in the supply chain and/or large or capital project-based products and services for organizational motives.

In fact, FMCG represent only a sub-element of consumer goods purchasing and marketing. FMCG contexts are where customers are purchasing products or services for personal reasons but products and services, which generally involve relatively low financial outlays, are bought frequently and are generally non-durable. They include, therefore, products such as toothpaste, confectionery, grocery products, some of the more frequently purchased electrical items such as, say, batteries, light bulbs and so on. FMCGs therefore may be contrasted with, for example, durable consumer goods such as refrigerators, cars, computers and even non-durable consumer purchases which involve large infrequent outlays such as holidays, houses and so on. We have to be careful, therefore, in discussing how the marketing mix tools may vary within the broad category of consumer goods as there are so many different types of consumer goods contexts. However, it is fair to say that within the consumer goods category, FMCG marketing involves probably the most distinct differences in the use and application of the marketing mix tools compared to, for example, our b2b and large or capital project-based contexts. Put another way, FMCG marketing lies at the extreme, if you like, of consumer goods marketing when it comes to the application of the marketing mix tools. Bearing this in mind, the following represent some of the key characteristics of the FMCG context and the implications for the application of the marketing tools.

As already mentioned, FMCG contexts involve marketing to customers who are buying generally low financial outlay products, bought frequently, and with little information search or alternative evaluation by customers. In this type of context, although again we find all sorts of different combinations of the marketing mix according to an individual company's positioning strategy and so on, as a generalization when it comes to the mix elements we might expect to find the following.

Aspects of the product element of the mix which are particularly important in FMCG contexts include branding, packaging, and logos and design. Branding and brand image in particular are important as these provide reassurance for a customer and facilitate relatively easy brand choice. With regard to the promotional element of the mix there is likely to be heavy emphasis on advertising rather than personal selling. Advertising will generally be aimed at the mass market and will again tend to stress brand image and persuasive advertising messages rather than detailed factual messages. The importance and role of price in FMCG marketing varies enormously across different products and markets, but value for money is likely to be particularly important and predominant in customer choice. Negotiation between buyer and seller regarding price is likely to be used infrequently in FMCG markets. Nor is tendering widely used, though the importance and prevalence of negotiation will depend upon the culture in a market. In some cultures, therefore, negotiation is the order of the day even for FMCG. The availability of credit and payment terms may be important facets of pricing in consumer markets generally, but are less likely to be important in the case of FMCG markets due to the relatively low outlays involved. Many FMCG products and brands have short product life cycles, often due to fashion influences or consumers simply becoming bored. New product development and innovation is important in FMCG markets then, if only by way of, for example, repositioning, repackaging and so on so as to keep customers interested. Distribution for FMCG will often need to be intensive and will normally take place through intermediaries and particularly, of course, retailers. Although relationship marketing, particularly through the brand element of the marketing mix, may still be important in FMCG markets, the degree of brand switching in this type of market often means that relationships are difficult to develop and maintain with customers. Finally, although we should not dismiss it entirely, customer service plays a less important role in FMCG marketing than it does in, for example, b2b markets, large or capital project-based marketing, or of course services marketing.

In planning the marketing mix in FMCG markets, as indeed in all marketing planning, it is important to understand the nature of the consumer buying decision process and the factors which affect this. With regard to this decision process and the factors which affect this for FMCG, a simple model is useful (Figure 9.1).

Problem recognition
↓
Information search
↓
Evaluation of alternatives
↓
Purchase decision
↓
Post-purchase behaviour

Figure 9.1 A model of consumer buyer behaviour

o *Need recognition* – This is the start point of the buying process for a FMCG. Purchasing is essentially a problem-solving process. So unless the consumer perceives there is a problem, then no purchasing will take place. The marketer therefore needs to understand the process of problem recognition and sometimes will attempt to prompt it. So, for example, advertising and promotion may be designed to convince customers that their current products and brands could be improved. Remember, in FMCG markets advertising and promotion are among the most heavily used elements of the marketing mix.

o *Information search* – Having recognized that they have a problem, the next step in the purchasing process is to search for information regarding products and brands which may offer a solution to this problem. Information search can be based on existing information in the consumer's memory, for example, but sometimes the customer will search for information from a variety of sources including friends, relatives, sales persons, magazines and other forms of marketer-dominated sources of information. Obviously, the marketer of FMCG must ensure that the customer is provided with sufficient information in order to make a decision and obviously will be concerned to ensure that this information causes the customer to prefer the marketer's product and brand offerings.

o *Evaluation of alternatives* – The information collected through the process of search will be used to evaluate the various alternatives on offer. Essentially this is the part of the process where the customer makes a choice. The marketer must understand how alternatives are evaluated and particularly the choice criteria in this process. Evaluation criteria are among the most important facets in the buying process affecting the selection of the marketing mix tools. Obviously, if customers are primarily interested in price in choice, then the marketing mix must reflect this.

o *Purchase decision* – This is the stage of the process where the customer actually makes the purchase choice. It may be felt that by this time the customer is beyond the reach of the marketer as the decision is made. However, the marketer can still influence the customer at this stage. So, for example, a customer may have decided on the product and brand to be purchased, but if this is out of stock due to, say, poor distribution, then the customer may still make a different purchase choice at this stage.

o *Post-purchase evaluation* – Having made the purchase the customer must then evaluate this. So, for example, the customer will assess if he or she is satisfied with the decision. We know that often customers will be anxious about whether they have made the right choice or not. Every effort, therefore, must be made by the marketer to assure the customer that they have. One way of doing this, for example, is to write to the customer assuring them that they have made the right choice and reminding the customer that, if they have any problems or worries about the purchase, these can be discussed with the supplier.

Study tip

The extent to which the customer will pass through each and every stage of this buying process varies considerably. It is useful to remember that there are three types of decision-making or purchasing situation. Extended decision-making involves all the steps in the purchasing process outlined above and is normally associated with expensive and/or risky purchases such as the purchase of a new car. The second type of decision-making is limited decision-making. Here, although the customer may pass through all the stages, they may only spend comparatively little time and effort at some of the stages in the process. So, for example, the customer may spend comparatively little time searching for information and/or evaluating alternatives. This type of purchasing decision-making often occurs where the customer has some experience of the product or service in question, or for other reasons is not prepared to spend a long time making the purchase. Finally, the third type of decision-making process is routine response behaviour. Usually associated with frequently purchased low-cost items, here the purchasing process is almost automatic. Very little time, if any, is spent searching and evaluating alternatives, rather the customer here goes straight from problem recognition to choosing, for example, a favourite brand. Most FMCG fall into the routine response behaviour.

What factors influence FMCG purchasing behaviour?

In addition to understanding the steps in the purchasing decision process for FMCG, the marketer must understand the factors affecting purchasing behaviour. The problem here is that potentially very many factors can come into play. However, some of the most important influences on FMCG buying decisions are as follows.

- *Personal factors* – These factors include factors such as demographics, for example age, sex, race and income. They also encompass situational factors such as, say, the amount of time available to the consumer when making the purchase decision. Finally, personal factors include the level of involvement and commitment the individual has when making the purchase.
- *Psychological factors* – Psychological factors include a whole host of factors pertaining to an individual's overall and purchasing behaviour. We know that some of the most important of these factors include: perceptions, motives, learning, attitudes and personality. Essentially, these factors operate internally but they can be influenced, or at least taken account of by the marketer. So, for example, we know that personality influences both product and brand choice. The extrovert personality is more likely to choose a different brand to the introvert.
- *Social/cultural factors* – These factors too are extremely important in influencing the purchasing process and product and brand choice. Among the most important social factors known to influence consumers are roles and family influences, reference groups, social classes, culture and sub-culture. We know, for example, that the choice of a newspaper is heavily influenced by social class as are products such as holidays, cars, cosmetics and so on. Social/cultural factors in purchase choice are important in many markets but are particularly so for the international marketer.

Marketing in practice: example

Nestlé adapt their coffee brand products to social/cultural factors in different parts of the world. In the United Kingdom where coffee and coffee drinking tends to have strong socializing overtones, coffee brands are advertised in social settings or situations such as friends gathering together for a drink. In Germany and France, however, although obviously there are still social aspects, culturally the emphasis in coffee choice and drinking tends to be on the taste of the coffee. These, then, are some of the major considerations which stem from the contextual setting for FMCG markets. We can now turn our attention to the b2b context.

Business-to-business

As you already know here the marketer is targeting other organizations or institutions as customers. Remember that the business-to-business market (or b2b as it is increasingly referred to) customer differs from the consumer market customer in as much as they are primarily purchasing for organizational purposes and motives rather than personal ones. As with FMCG marketing, and for that matter any marketing context, in planning marketing mix programmes the marketer can benefit from an understanding of the nature of the customer and in particular the buying process and the factors which affect this. As we suggested with FMCG marketing, then, it is useful, indeed essential, for the marketer to understand the behaviour of b2b customers. In achieving this understanding, the marketer can usefully address the following questions with regard to b2b buyer behaviour.

Who is involved in the buying process?

In contrast to FMCG markets, there are often many people involved in the buying decision-making process in b2b markets. Of particular importance are the different roles which these different people may play.

In order to help you understand these different roles better, we shall use the example of the purchase of a new piece of production machinery by a business customer.

- *Initiators* – These are the people who start the process of buying. So, for example, the buying process may be initiated by, say, the production department in the organization who feel that an existing piece of production machinery is near to the end of its useful life.
- *Influencers* – Influencers can affect the buying decision in different ways, for example technical people may have helped in a major or minor way to develop the product specification for the new piece of machinery.
- *Deciders* – These are the people who make the actual buying decision. In this case, the deciders might be, for example, the production director or even the chief executive.
- *Buyers* – These people have the authority to sign orders and make the actual purchase in the organization. They may also help to shape the specification but their principal role is in supplier negotiation and selection. In our case, and indeed in most situations, this is likely to be the purchasing department.
- *Users* – Users are the people who will be working with, or using, the product or service purchased. In our example, users are the machine operators. It makes sense for a purchasing organization to ask operatives what problems they have had in using a particular piece of machinery and what features of a proposed new piece of equipment would help them perform their jobs more effectively.

We can see, then, that buying behaviour in b2b settings can involve several individuals and roles which combine to effect what is essentially a group purpose. It is very important, therefore, for the marketer to identify the individuals and/or functions comprising this group and performing the range of roles outlined above. In marketing, we refer to the individuals/functions involved in the buying process as the DMU.

B2B marketers should be clear about the members of the DMU and direct their marketing efforts accordingly.

How do they buy: a model of industrial buyer behaviour

As with FMCG purchasing, purchase decisions in b2b markets can usefully be looked at as a series of steps or stages in a problem-solving process. These are shown in Figure 9.2.

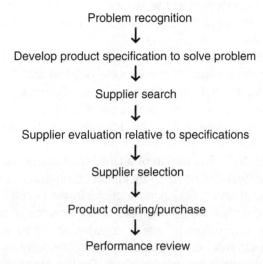

Problem recognition

↓

Develop product specification to solve problem

↓

Supplier search

↓

Supplier evaluation relative to specifications

↓

Supplier selection

↓

Product ordering/purchase

↓

Performance review

Figure 9.2 A model of business buyer behaviour

We can see that this process is very similar in nature to that described for consumer product purchasing. However, there are more steps in the process and the process itself is usually more formalized. Again, though, the marketer, by understanding the steps in the process, is able to develop appropriate marketing strategies for each stage. So, for example, it is important to know what product specifications have been set by the business purchaser and wherever possible try to influence this in favour of your particular products and services. Similarly, we need to understand again how purchasers search for products and suppliers and the criteria used to evaluate them.

Study tip

As with consumer product purchasing, not all industrial purchasing processes involve all of the steps or at least to the same degree. You will recall that we earlier distinguished between extended decision-making, limited decision-making and routine response types of purchasing in consumer markets. The industrial equivalents of these different types of purchasing processes are: new task purchasing, modified rebuys and straight rebuy purchases.

Why do they buy?

You will recall that we have already stressed the fact that a key difference between business and consumer buyers is the fact that business buyers buy in order to further their organization's objectives and plans. The motives for purchase, therefore, for the business buyer are somewhat different. Generally speaking, the business buyers' motives are much more rational than their consumer counterparts with, for example, little or no impulse purchasing. Similarly, because the business buyer is often interested primarily in costs and profit, price and negotiation on price and terms are likely to be much more important.

What factors affect?

If anything, the range of factors affecting business buyers is greater and more complex than for the consumer purchasing process. This is principally because, although individual and psychological factors are likely to be less important, the business purchasing process takes place in the context of an organization, thereby introducing several new factors into the buying process.

The most important factors affecting the business buying process which the marketer must seek to analyse and understand through marketing research are as follows:

○ *Environmental factors* – The range of uncontrollable factors which affect all marketers also affect their customers. These include political factors, regulations and laws, economic factors and technological factors. So, for example, new legislation may affect the specifications which customers need a supplier to meet. A good example of this is the car industry where engine component suppliers must meet increasingly stringent legislation regarding, for example, emission levels.

○ *Interpersonal factors* – The notion of a DMU means that very often relationships among the people in this unit can have a key influence on purchasing. So, for example, conflict between marketing and production functions in the purchasing organization may affect the choice of a supplier. As an example of the sources of such conflict, the marketer in an organization may prefer to use a supplier who can supply the latest technology, which may give the marketer's company an opportunity to develop a competitive edge over other companies in the marketplace. On the other hand, the production management of an organization may prefer a supplier who, though not at the cutting edge of technology, can supply products and services using tried and tested technology.

○ *Organizational factors* – The fact that purchasing takes place in the context of an organization means that the marketer must assess and understand things such as an organization's purchasing policies and systems. For example, some organizations may require suppliers to initially tender through a closed tender system for business. Among some of the best examples of such organizations are government or institutional buyers such as those that buy, say, defence-related products where closed tendering is the norm.

○ *Individual factors* – Finally, although business buying is by its very nature much more constrained and formal than its consumer counterpart, we must not forget that industrial customers are also individuals and are therefore affected by things such as their education and background, personal preferences regarding suppliers and their sales persons and so on.

These factors are likely to be particularly important where there is a strong professional network. Examples would include marketing products to the medical industry or to, say, the legal profession.

These differences in the nature of business buyers and the purchasing process allied to the different motives for purchase give rise to several differences when it comes to applying the marketing mix tools in b2b markets. These are outlined and discussed below.

The marketing mix elements in b2b markets

In b2b markets, the following are likely to be more significant in supplier and brand choice: quality assurance, delivery, speed and reliability, price and after-sales and technical service. The reliability of the product, together with the degree of back-up service being offered is a crucial part of the marketing mix in b2b markets. In terms of the promotional element of the mix, much more emphasis is likely to be placed on personal selling as opposed to the advertising element. As in consumer markets, however, sales promotion is used extensively in b2b markets and especially when marketing to distributors/intermediaries. Publicity too is a valuable promotional tool in b2b marketing and especially when launching new products. Finally, direct marketing can be a very effective promotional tool in b2b markets as mailing lists tend to be more accurate and the message can be tailored more closely to individual customer needs.

We have to be careful not to assume that b2b buyers products always buy on price. They are not. It is value that counts. However, obviously, price is always going to be a key factor in the marketing mix. Prices are much more likely to be negotiated in the b2b market and we may get different processes for pricing and particularly quoting prices, such as tendering. Finally, in b2b markets, although intermediaries are used, particularly in export and international markets, often distribution is direct.

Before we move on to discussing our other contexts for marketing, it might be useful to summarize our discussion of FMCG and b2b marketing by reiterating some of the key differences between these two marketing contexts and the implications of these for the use of the various marketing mix tools.

A brief summary of some of the suggested differences between marketing in FMCG versus b2b markets is shown in Table 9.1.

Table 9.1 FMCG and b2b markets compared

FMCG markets	b2b markets
Buyer/buying situations	
Individual/family	Group/organizational
Personal motives	Organizational requirements
Often unplanned/less rational	Planned/rational
Not specialist buyers	Trained/professional
Less informed	Well informed
Little power	Substantial power
Marketing mix product	
Often standardized	Often customized
Less technical	More technical
Less service	More service
Price	
Less important	More important
Rarely negotiated	Frequently negotiated
Few tenders/bids	Often tenders/bids
Promotion	
Emphasis on non-personal	Emphasis on personal
Place	
Less direct	Usually direct
Logistics important	Logistics vital

 Activity 9.1

Try to find an example of a product that is marketed in both business and consumer markets, for example a cleaning product, writing paper and envelopes, coffee and so on. Compare and contrast the ways in which this product might be marketed to each of these different markets, with particular respect to the use of the marketing mix.

Large or capital project-based contexts

A considerable amount of marketing activity centres around the marketing of large or capital project-based products. In fact, the marketing context here is essentially our b2b context already outlined and discussed. Many of the factors that affect the b2b marketer, then, including the complexity of the decision-making process, group influences and the motives for purchase also affect the marketer concerned with large or capital project-based products. However, marketing large or capital project-based products, if anything, heightens and emphasizes some of the differences we have described in the marketing mix elements between FMCG and b2b markets.

So, for example, in this context, personal selling as an element of the promotional aspect of the mix becomes even more important and critical. Most large or capital-based projects require substantial expertise and both technical and commercial skills on the part of the sales person. Although advertising and particularly corporate advertising and PR may still play a role, it is personal selling which will dominate. In addition, price negotiation again is even more important. After all, here the customer is considering substantial outlays which commit his or her organization to long time. Because of this, the customer will be concerned to ensure long-term continuity of, for example, service back-up from the supplier. Related to this, full contract or turnkey services may be expected by the customer whereby the supplier will undertake to make all necessary arrangements to, for example, plan, install, and service and maintain machinery and buildings and so on. The service element will be particularly important even though the customer may be specifying highly technical products. Distribution will almost certainly be direct in this marketing context.

Small and medium-sized enterprises

Although there is perhaps an understandable tendency to think of marketing being applied in large organizations, we should not forget that in many countries the smaller company is the predominant business unit. In addition, it is increasingly recognized that the small- and medium-sized new entrepreneurial business often represents the large multinational of the future. Many governments, therefore, are interested in helping SMEs to become established and eventually grow.

Until relatively recently, however, SMEs have been slow to take up and use the concepts and tools of modern marketing. To be fair, this has been due in part to a perhaps unwitting attitude in many textbooks, where the application of marketing is often only discussed in the context of the large company. If anything, however, the small company needs to be even more marketing oriented than its larger counterpart, and certainly there is nothing in marketing that the smaller organization cannot adopt. The basic concept and tools of marketing are essentially the same whether applied to the one-man business or the large multinational. However, it would be unrealistic to expect that these tools would be used in precisely the same way in both types of organization. The following are some of the considerations in applying marketing tools and in particular the marketing mix in SMEs. We first list some of the limitations inherent in most SMEs compared to their larger cousins, followed by the implications of these limitations for planning and applying some of the tools of marketing we have discussed so far in earlier units of the coursebook.

Financial limitations
Clearly, the absolute amount of finance available to the smaller business is often very restricted. In turn this means, of course, that extensive and expensive market research or advertising campaigns are out of the question. The smaller business simply cannot afford, for example, national TV advertising or a full test market, and you should therefore be careful to take account of this where appropriate in, say, mini-case questions.

Staff/specialist limitations
In the larger company, specialization is the order of the day. Marketing functions are broken down into more and more specialized areas, with specialist marketing, researchers, corporate planners, distribution specialists and so on. In the smaller business only one person may be

responsible for all these functions and, in the case of the one-man business, for all the other functions as well.

This means that the smaller business has much more restricted internal access to specialist marketing expertise, and may therefore have to make more use of outside help and advice for planning and control.

Competitive limitations

Clearly, many small businesses compete with larger ones. Again the small businesses simply do not have the resources to compete head on with their larger rivals. Particularly when it comes to competing on price, the smaller business is at a disadvantage, but also the smaller business, as we shall see, is often restricted in the range and types of market in which it can compete.

None of these limitations mean that the smaller business cannot be just as successful and profitable through the use of effective marketing as a large one. As you have already seen, the smaller business has a number of built-in advantages. However, the limitations do mean that a slightly different approach to the application of some of the marketing tools discussed in earlier units has to be adopted.

Activity 9.2

Before proceeding, see if you can think of any examples of how the application of the marketing tools might have to differ, owing to the limitations of the small business.

Market analysis and research

Although the elements of market analysis and research are similar for the smaller business, both finance and marketing expertise (as regards techniques of research) may be severely restricted. However, this does not mean that marketing analysis and research should not be carried out – indeed they are vital. Even without expensive and sophisticated marketing research, the smaller business can do much to improve its market intelligence. Here are some of the more useful sources and techniques for the smaller company.

The smaller business in particular must make the fullest possible use of secondary sources of data. In the larger business, the use of desk research is often the first step in analysing a marketing problem. In the smaller one it may be the only one.

Examples of useful sources of marketing research information for the smaller business include:

- ○ Internal sources: sales statistics, customer information, accountancy information, sales reports and so on
- ○ Central libraries
- ○ Yellow Pages and trade directories
- ○ Chambers of commerce, local authorities, banks
- ○ Local colleges/universities
- ○ Government sources.

In fact, in most countries government sources of information are likely to be the most important and potentially most useful sources of secondary information for the smaller business.

259

Syndicated research

Syndicated research occurs where a group of research buyers share the cost and fundings of research among themselves. Because of this, syndicated research is of particular relevance to the smaller business that cannot afford its own tailor-made research study but needs information over and above what is available from secondary sources. The majority of such syndicated research services are in fact conducted by the larger marketing research agencies, and the results are sold to anyone willing to buy it. In the United Kingdom, syndicated research services include:

- o Retail Audits (A.C. Nielsen Company)
- o Target Group Index (British Market Research Bureau)
- o National Readership Survey (Research Bureau Ltd).

Activity 9.3

These are examples of syndicated research organizations available in the United Kingdom. If you are not from the United Kingdom, see if you can find examples of similar syndicated research services in your own country.

In recent years, a number of market research companies have begun to produce specialized 'multi-client' research, in which a report is prepared for a limited number of companies that are prepared to commission and share the research between them.

Shared research

This type of research can be particularly cost-effective for the smaller company. Here some of the costs and field work are shared by a number of companies but the results are not. 'Omnibus' surveys are regular research surveys undertaken by the use of a predetermined sampling frame and methodology. A smaller business can 'buy a seat' on the omnibus by adding its own questions.

Omnibus research has the major advantage of low cost, as the field-work costs are shared by all participating companies. The number of questions that can be added to an omnibus is, however, generally limited to between six and ten and, because the respondents will be asked questions about a variety of products in the same interview, questions are best kept short and factual to avoid respondent fatigue.

Product decisions

Even in a small business, product decisions are still among the most important that the company will take.

Once again financial limitations will normally prohibit expensive research and development programmes, but the smaller business can develop ideas for new products from a number of sources. For example:

- o Customers
- o Competitors
- o Trade publications
- o Patent brokers
- o Product-licensing information services.

As with marketing research, government help is often at hand. For example, in the United Kingdom the Department of Trade and Industry will help with innovation or the introduction of new technologies.

Question 9.1

In addition to disadvantages in the area of new product development due to the limitations outlined here, small companies do, however, have a number of advantages in the area of new product development and innovation compared to the large company.

Write down what you think these advantages might be.

Pricing decisions

The small business must price its products so as to achieve long-run marketing and financial objectives. Again, the general consideration and approaches to pricing strategies are the same in the small as in the large business but the smaller company can tend to neglect one or two basic pointers, namely:

- As we have seen, prices should be related to the market and not solely to costs. Smaller companies often rely too heavily on cost-based approaches to pricing.
- Although the smaller business may have fewer overheads than its larger counterpart, underpricing is dangerous. The evidence suggests that more companies fail from underpricing than overpricing. The smaller business should be looking for ways in which to charge a premium price, for example for better delivery, after-sales service and so on.

Promotional decisions

It is in this element of the marketing mix that we can observe some of the greatest differences between small and large businesses. Once again these differences stem largely from the small business's limited financial resources. In the smaller business all the elements of a co-ordinated promotional mix – personal selling, PR and publicity, advertising and sales promotion – can and should be used. However, as previously noted, the smaller business simply has not the financial resources to undertake expensive promotional campaigns. Television advertising and some of the more expensive magazine and colour supplements are simply out of the question. Wherever possible, the smaller business needs to make use of more focused campaigns and media, together with the use of 'free' promotion that well-organized PR can bring. Below are listed some of the more appropriate forms of promotion and media for the smaller business:

- Local newspapers
- Local commercial radio
- Trade magazines and directories
- Yellow Pages
- Sponsorship of local events, sports teams and so on
- Exhibitions
- Press releases
- Direct mail
- Websites.

Place decisions

In terms of the place element of the promotional mix, the small business may find that it has to make more use of 'agents' and 'dealers' rather than employing its own sales force.

Marketing strategies for SMEs

There is now substantial evidence to show that marketing strategy is dependent on each firm's size and position in its industry. Understandably, large firms can implement certain strategies not affordable by small ones.

As far as the small business is concerned, a focus strategy is usually by far the most effective. Rather than trying to achieve lower costs or highly differentiated products, the smaller business is better focusing on specialist market segments where it can compete effectively.

This type of strategy is also called 'niche marketing', where the company concentrates on smaller, more specialized parts of the market that larger companies are likely to ignore. Such niche marketing allows both more efficient operations and the development of customer goodwill and loyalty.

Marketing in practice: example

Octagon Motor Sports is an example of a company that specializes in a particular segment of the gift market. The company offers days out aimed primarily at customers who want to buy their partners, for example, a day rallying or racing on a famous circuit. Customers can choose from driving Ferraris, supercars, single seaters and 4 x 4s. The company is targeting the specialized part of the market of customers who are looking for an adventure-based and high adrenaline gift experience.

www.octagonmotorsports.com

Question 9.2

In what ways, that is on what bases, might the SME choose to specialize in niche markets?

Voluntary and not-for-profit organizations

Marketing is increasingly being applied outside of the traditional profit-making sector. Hospitals, charities, museums and so on are all examples of voluntary and not-for-profit organizations using the tools of marketing. Often the marketing mix in such organizations is combined and applied in very different ways to their profit-making counterparts. Perhaps one of the most obvious differences in the marketing mix for these organizations is the absence of price in the marketing mix. Many do not actually set prices for their products and services, although of course there is always a cost and someone must pay for them. Very often the voluntary and not-for-profit organization will emphasize organizational or corporate image as opposed to, say, brand image in the promotional mix. Finally, many of these organizations 'sell' direct to the customer and hence have very different channels of distribution.

Obviously, voluntary and not-for-profit organizations primarily exist to achieve objectives other than the conventional business objectives of profit, return on capital and so on. This description, however, includes a very wide range of diverse types of organization, for example public organizations such as the army, local fire services, local authorities and so on, through to hospitals, charities, churches and religious causes, and political parties. Understandably, with this range of organizations we can expect to find differences in their approaches to marketing and their use of the marketing tools. However, most of the concepts and tools discussed in earlier units can be applied to these organizations. Some of the special characteristics of such organizations that need to be considered in developing marketing plans and programmes are the following:

o   Like services, the products provided by such organizations are often intangible and therefore are different when it comes to marketing them.
o   'Customers' may be more difficult to identify than in the profit-making organization. Very often there are several diverse groups that will need to be targeted. It is often more appropriate to define a target public or a range of stakeholders than target customers.
o   The marketing objectives of voluntary and not-for-profit organizations are generally set in terms of achieving a desired response, such as a financial contribution, increased use of the service, a vote and so on.

Activity 9.4

Write down what you think might be possible appropriate marketing objectives for the following voluntary and not-for-profit types of organization.

o   A national police force
o   A local charity
o   A church.

The following is a brief outline of how these characteristics of the voluntary and not-for-profit organization give rise to differences in the application of the tools of the marketing mix:

o   *Products* – Are usually intangible and may be an idea or service.
o   *Price* – Is often difficult to define and may often be associated more with the exchange of things such as time and effort to help a charitable cause or a political party rather than financial exchange.
o   *Place* – Is less concerned with the movement of goods and more with the communication of ideas. Marketing channels tend to be short.
o   *Promotion* – In some ways is the most important element of the mix for voluntary and not-for-profit organizations. All the promotional tools are likely to be used, although there may be less emphasis on personal selling.

Marketing in practice: example

Among one of the most effective not-for-profit organization marketers in recent years has been the Labour Party organization in the United Kingdom. There is no doubt that at least in part, the last two successes of the Party in general elections has been due to their understanding and application of marketing tools and techniques including, for example, effective marketing research and well-designed and implemented promotional programmes.

Services

We earlier suggested in Unit 3 that partly because of the growth and importance of services marketing but more importantly because of the suggested special characteristics of services which were outlined earlier, the marketing mix for service products needs to be extended to include an additional three marketing mix elements, namely the additional 3Ps of people, process and physical evidence. We shall look further at these three additional elements, therefore, in this part of the unit, but we shall also consider the application of our conventional 4Ps to services.

It would be useful to start by looking at the growth of service sectors and the distinguishing and special characteristics of service products. This will enable us to look at the issues that arise in planning marketing strategies for services, and in particular how these relate to the special characteristics identified. This will enable us to look at the combination of our marketing mix elements with services including our additional 3Ps.

The growth and scope of the service sectors

As you probably know, the service sector has been one of the fastest growing parts of many economies. Indeed, a considerable number of the developed economies of the world can now be termed 'service economies', in that the service sector contributes the greater part of economic activity. For example, currently in the United Kingdom the services have grown to account for some 65 per cent of total UK output, with a consequent decline in the relative proportion accounted for by manufacturing and agricultural industries. This trend has continued as economies continue to move towards post-industrial societies.

Activity 9.5

Thinking of your own experiences as a consumer of services, list as many specific examples of a service 'product' as you can think of before continuing.

Definitions and distinguishing characteristics of services

As is so often the case, virtually every marketing text offers a different, if related, definition of what constitutes a service. Unfortunately there is still no one accepted definition of the term 'service'. Nor, indeed, given the enormous diversity of types of service, should we expect one. For our purposes, we shall take what is perhaps one of the more concise definitions.

Key definition

A service – Is any activity or benefit that one party can offer to another that is essentially intangible and does not result in the ownership of anything.

Again, remembering the wide diversity of service industries and products, this definition underlines what are recognized as being some of the key distinguishing characteristics of services and which were briefly introduced in earlier units. Remember, it is these characteristics which it is suggested set them apart from their physical-product counterparts, and may give rise to additional and different considerations with respect to planning and controlling their marketing.

These suggested 'special' characteristics of services are therefore reproduced again below in order that we can consider them further:

- ○ Perishability
- ○ Intangibility
- ○ Variability
- ○ Inseparability
- ○ Non-ownership.

In order to explain these further we can compare and contrast services against physical products with respect to each characteristics. These are shown in Table 9.2.

Table 9.2 Services and physical products contrasted

Services		Physical products
High ◄————	Perishability	————► Low
High ◄————	Intangilibity	————► Low
High ◄————►	Inseparabality	————► Low
High ◄————	Variability	————► Low
No ◄————	Ownership	————► Yes

Now let us consider each of these characteristics in turn:

- ○ *Perishability* – Perhaps of all the suggested special characteristics of service products, this is one of the most difficult to appreciate. You will note that in Table 9.2 services are shown as being highly perishable compared to physical products. But how could, for example, the services of, say, an airline be considered to be more perishable than, say, fresh food and vegetable products?
  The reason is that, unlike most physical products, many services cannot be stored. For example, if an airline does not sell all the seats on a particular flight, then those seats, or rather the sales revenue the filling of them would have carried, has immediately and irreversibly gone.
- ○ *Intangibility* – Think about the last time you visited your local store or supermarket to shop. The products will probably have been on open display. You probably picked them up in your hands, felt the weight of them, perhaps even sniffed at them, before deciding whether or not to buy.
  Compare this with the choice of the services of, say, an insurance policy. You cannot touch, see or smell the product before choosing, although clearly you can make some assessment based on past experience, word of mouth, or even the location and décor of the insurance office. The intangible nature of most services gives rise to special problems for both suppliers and consumers.
- ○ *Variability* – In the production and marketing of physical products, companies have increasingly paid attention to ensuring consistency in quality, features, packaging and so on. More often than not the customer can be sure that every tin of Heinz baked beans he buys, even in a lifetime of purchases, will not vary. The provision of services, however, invariably includes a large measure of the 'human element'. Indeed, with many services we are purchasing nothing else but the skills of the supplier. Because

265

of this, it is often very difficult for both supplier and consumer to ensure a consistent 'product' or quality of service.

○ *Inseparability* – A key distinguishing feature of service marketing is that the service provision and provider are inseparable from the service consumption and consumer. For example, we cannot take a hotel room home for consumption; we must 'consume' its service at the point of provision. Similarly, the hairdresser needs to be physically present for his or her service to be consumed. As we shall see, this has implications for both channels of distribution and scales of operation.

○ *Non-ownership* – The final distinguishing feature of a service is that, unlike a physical product, the customer does not secure ownership of the service. Rather the customer pays only to secure access to or use of the service. Again the hotel room is a good example. Similarly with banking services, although the customer may be given a cheque book, credit cards and so on, they serve only to allow the customer to make use of what he or she is actually buying, namely bank services.

Marketing issues associated with services

Although the basic principles of a marketing concept and marketing management are essentially the same as for physical products, the characteristics of services give rise to a number of important issues when one considers marketing services.

 ## Activity 9.6

For the characteristics of services we have just outlined, try to assess what might be some of the marketing implications associated with each of them. For example, what do you feel might be some of the marketing implications of the fact that services are intangible and so on? When you have done this, compare your assessment with that shown in the debriefing.

The marketing mix and services

We can now look more closely at how the marketing mix may be applied to service products. We shall look first at our conventional 4Ps and then at our additional three mix elements in services marketing.

The service product

The 'product' element of the marketing mix for service products requires that decisions be made on the following:

○ The type and range of services
○ The quality and attributes of the services
○ Warranties, after-sale facilities and so on.

As regards product life-cycle management and new product development, all the tools and concepts of physical-product marketing apply, although, as mentioned previously, given the intangible nature of services, concept testing of new ideas for services takes on particular significance and can be extremely difficult to conduct.

Pricing of services

Again the basic methods of price determination and alternative pricing strategies, such as market skimming versus market penetration, apply equally to services. You will recall, however, that the perishability of services means that the careful matching of demand and supply is crucial. Because of this, we should expect to find that a much more flexible approach to pricing and margins is appropriate for services. We saw, for example, in Unit 5, where we considered pricing, that segmented/differential pricing is widely used in the pricing of services to try to ensure a matching of demand and supply.

You should also note that the intangible nature of service products also tends to heighten the use by customers of price as an indicator of quality.

Place and services
Remember that the perishable nature of service products stems from the fact that they cannot be stored. This means that with one or two exceptions physical distribution is not a key problem. As regards channels, we have also noted that inseparability demands that many services are sold directly by producer to consumer. However, some type of agent or broker is often used to market financial or travel services, for example, and increasingly franchising has become an important method of widening the distribution and market spread of many types of service, particularly in the fast-food market.

Promoting services
Once again we find that the intangible nature of service products raises special consideration for their marketing. You will recall that the marketer of service products needs to stress the benefits rather than the features of his service. So, for example, a college needs to promote, say, the job prospects for its graduates as much as the details of the courses it offers.

Personal selling is particularly important in the promotional mix for services. Often the customer is purchasing the personal qualities and skills of the service provider, so that an ability to develop close relationships and win customer confidence is crucial.

You should also note that some service providers are either reluctant, or prohibited, from advertising their services. This is the case, for example, in some areas of the UK medical profession, where the code of ethics in this service industry prevent the use of advertising.

Additional marketing-mix elements in service marketing
In addition to the conventional '4Ps' of the marketing mix outlined above, in Unit 3 we suggested that in the case of service marketing this list needs to be extended to include three further Ps, namely people, physical evidence and process.

> ### Study tip
>
> Turn back to Unit 3 and remind yourself of these three elements of the extended marketing mix for services.

These then are the 7Ps of the marketing mix for services. In fact, it is now increasingly recognized that all products have a service component; and indeed for many physical products, this service element is the most important in customer choice. Because of this, some of the notions of service marketing, including some of the mix elements, are now being applied to the marketing of physical products. For example, many forward-looking companies have developed total systems of customer care and quality, covering every aspect of their marketing and dealings with customers. We looked at such customer care and service elements in Unit 8.

Contemporary and further issues in the marketing context

As we have seen throughout the units of the coursebook, both marketing thinking and marketing practice continue to develop and change. Marketing takes place in a very dynamic environment. Moreover, it is through marketing activities that the opportunities and threats presented by these dynamics are responded to. In this penultimate part of the unit, we consider what are probably two of the most important developments affecting the context in which marketing and marketing mix decisions in particular take place.

The first of these developments underpins syllabus areas 3.15 and 4.5, namely respectively the continuing application of new ICT to marketing practice, and the existing and potential impact of the virtual marketing place on marketing. In fact, we have touched on some of the applications and implications of new technology as we have worked through the previous units. Here, then, we draw together and expand on the key strands of these developments and, in doing so, underline a gradual but increasing move towards the development of what many have termed a 'virtual' marketplace.

Our second key development related to contemporary and further issues in the marketing context is the increasing importance of the global dimension in marketing as companies continue to expand their planning and marketing horizons by focusing their attention on the global marketing setting.

The effects of ICT on marketing: The move towards the virtual marketplace

As already mentioned at several points throughout the units, we have noted the increasingly important effects of developments in ICT and marketing. There is no doubt that these developments are rapidly changing the face of marketing and particularly the development of marketing plans and the application of the marketing tools. We have already alluded to some of these effects with respect to each of the major elements of the marketing mix. Outlined below, however, in more detail are some of the most important issues which developments in ICT and a move towards a virtual marketplace are giving rise to.

Study tip

The following section mainly covers aspects of the effects of ICT on marketing not previously considered in earlier units. It should be considered and read in conjunction with those parts of earlier units which cover specific applications of ICT to the individual areas of the marketing mix.

The growth of electronic commerce (e-commerce)

One of the most important areas affected by advances in technology has been the growth of e-commerce. Often referred to as 'e-commerce' or alternatively 'e-business'. e-Commerce is a collective term to describe a variety of commercial transactions which make use of the technologies of electronic processing and data transmission.

Key definition

Electronic commerce – The use of electronic technologies and systems so as to facilitate and enhance transactions between different parts of the value chain.

This definition highlights the fact that, irrespective of the type of e-commerce, its purpose is to improve the transaction processes which are so central to marketing. e-Commerce would not have grown to the extent it has and will continue to do had it not offered enhancements to the process of marketing. Often these enhancements, as already stated, will be in the form of cost reductions for the marketer, but much more important are those enhancements which accrue to the customer. Put another way, the growth of e-commerce would not have been possible without the growth of the 'e-customer'. Remember, the marketing concept states that marketing is about identifying and satisfying customer needs. If customers, therefore, did not perceive a need for e-commerce, then the various e-commerce technologies would simply have withered and died. Finally, our definition points to the fact that e-commerce and the technologies which underpin it can, and do, relate to the total value chain including not only customers but also intermediaries, suppliers and other external agencies such as advertising and market research companies. In fact, again, as we shall see, the ability to link and co-ordinate all the members of the value chain is one of the major reasons for the growth of e-commerce. Furthermore, it is broad enough to encompass any electronic technology and system which can be used to do this.

e-Commerce encompasses many of the individually most significant developments in technology affecting marketers, which will therefore be covered shortly in this unit such as the Internet, EDI, the intranet and the extranet, the World Wide Web, database marketing and so on.

The first stages of the e-commerce revolution began over 20 years ago when companies began to use their computers for more effective delivery and supply systems. Initially, it was primarily in b2b transactions that this development took place, where effective customer and supplier relationships have always been felt to be particularly important. From manual systems of ordering and supply, gradually the computer enabled 'automation' of these processes to take place. This automation was built around the ability of the computer to exchange information electronically with regard to supply and delivery between customers and their suppliers. Eventually, this developed into fully automated systems of electronic data interchange (EDI) systems. Such EDI systems enabled, for example, an automatic order for, say, components to be sent to a supplier when the computer-based stock system in the customer's company monitored a minimum stock and reordering level. The required order would be sent via direct computer links to the supplier's computer, which would then automatically check the stock availability, delivery schedules and so on. At the supplier's end, the customer's order would be dealt with electronically and the order confirmed, invoice sent and so on, again electronically, back to the customer. Such EDI systems are now widespread in b2b markets, but perhaps more importantly, in the context of the development of e-commerce, this development together with advances in the facilitating technologies spawned a whole new approach to business and marketing incorporating new electronic ways of doing business.

Obviously, as already mentioned, given that e-commerce is a collective term for all electronically based systems and techniques of doing business, it encompasses a huge variety of specific technologies and applications each with their attendant advantages with regard to facilitating the marketing process. With this in mind, however, below are listed some examples of the advantages which e-commerce technology can give rise to and therefore some of the reasons for its rapid growth.

269

Some advantages of e-commerce

Remember again that the specific advantages to be derived from the application of a particular e-commerce technology depend upon that specific application. In general terms, however, some of the advantages underpinning the growth of e-commerce include:

○ Better communication between marketers and customers
○ Faster and more flexible transactions
○ Ability to reach and serve geographically disparate customers
○ Facilitates better control and co-ordination of all value chain activities
○ Improved relationships with customers
○ Related to above, increased customer retention and loyalty
○ Increased speed of doing business, ability to anticipate and react to increasingly rapid change.

Of course, many of these advantages are those that accrue to the marketer's organization. Needless to say, e-commerce has only grown to the extent that it has because it also offers significant advantages to the customer. Examples of advantages of e-commerce to customers include:

○ One-stop shopping
○ More convenient purchasing, for example from home
○ The ability to compare and contrast product offerings from different suppliers and therefore get the best value
○ Faster and more flexible purchasing
○ The opportunity to communicate directly with suppliers regarding, for example, needs, terms and complaints.

Examples of markets/products affected by e-commerce

Study tip

Note, the following examples are for illustration only. e-Commerce applications are now so widespread that it is not possible to list every specific application.

Some examples of areas of consumer marketing where e-commerce is being applied include:

○ Travel/holidays
○ Financial services – banking, insurance and so on
○ Music/entertainment
○ Food/wine
○ Books
○ Computer hardware and software
○ Event tickets
○ Restaurant bookings
○ Cars
○ Toys.

We can see, even from this illustrative list, that the range of industries and markets now affected by e-commerce is diverse and, moreover, the list is growing all the time. From its original b2b market usage, the effect of e-commerce and the technologies which underpin it are becoming more and more widespread.

Activity 9.7

Try to list other examples of products/markets where e-commerce techniques and activities are being used.

When you have completed your list compare it with the debriefing.

Clearly, e-commerce and new technology are having significant effects on marketing and markets, so let us now consider some of the e-commerce and new technologies further including the increasingly ubiquitous Internet, intranet and extranets.

The Internet
Probably the most significant e-commerce tool and technology is the Internet.

Key definition

The Internet – Is a network of computers which are linked together such that the computer user may communicate with the other computers in the network.

Originally developed so that academics and scientists in different geographical locations could communicate with each other quickly and easily, the Internet has now developed into a global network of linked computers through which individuals can perform any number of different activities. Using the Internet, an individual can investigate what is on offer to purchase from any company in the world which is connected to the network and is offering products and services on this network. Individuals can visit company websites, order products from virtual shopping precincts, book tickets for concerts, holidays and aeroplane flights, transfer information, ideas and money electronically and so on. From the point of view of the marketer the Internet offers the opportunity to reach customers anywhere in the world. Moreover, as we shall see, the Internet increasingly allows the marketer to communicate directly with individual customers, build up a powerful database on customers' needs and wants, and develop very effective relationships with customers. The Internet means that no longer does a company have to be large to operate in global markets. Increasingly, therefore, the Internet facilitates more and more competition. There is no doubt that the Internet is changing both consumer and therefore marketing practices and habits considerably. Increasingly, customers will shop for and buy products and services from home using their PCs. This has implications for virtually every facet of marketing such as product development, pricing, promotion and distribution. Marketing via the Internet is probably the fastest growing area of marketing now with the growth of the so-called 'dotcom' companies, and gradually we are moving more and more towards what can only be termed the virtual marketplace.

However, perhaps what many do not realize is that in fact it is probably the more established companies that have been responsible for the move towards this virtual marketplace in most countries. Indeed, the much vaunted so-called 'dotcom' companies have so far proved to be extremely disappointing in terms of their lack of success and profitability. There are many reasons for this perhaps, but one of the most important is probably the fact that customers generally feel safer using the Internet to deal with and buy from companies that have well-established brand names and long-established records of trading, albeit in the past using more traditional methods. For example, some of the major retail banks have been among some of the first and most successful protagonists of the virtual marketplace. Most conventional marketers in developed economies now at least have websites which customers can visit to find information, but increasingly these companies now have some facility for at least a degree of on-line shopping. Those companies that have seen the potential and the importance of the Internet now often offer all of their products for sale over the Internet, obviously combined with suitable methods of payment and delivery and distribution.

Study tip

If you do have access to the Internet try visiting a few company websites to find out how they are designing their Internet offerings and services. Make notes on those that impress you from a marketing point of view and those that do not. What are the differences between the two groups?

Perhaps an interesting phenomenon with regard to some of the early dotcom companies is the fact that some of these companies have moved from purely being Internet-based marketers to actually developing their own retail distribution outlets to market their products, that is the movement in this area is in two directions – many conventional retailers, and so on are becoming more involved in Internet marketing for their products and services, but at the same time some early virtual marketers are establishing more conventional marketing channels and techniques.

A good example of this is the dotcom company, 'Think Natural dotcom'. Originally an Internet marketer this company has been successfully selling health-related products through its website for 2 years. Partly as a result of this success, however, it has now negotiated a deal with Superdrug, a conventional retailer in this area, to include the stocking of many of its products and brands in Superdrug retail outlets throughout the United Kingdom.

This illustrates that increasingly we must think of on-line/virtual marketing and conventional marketing not as being dichotomous alternatives but as being a set of marketing approaches and techniques, which are increasingly being used together by companies. The Internet, then, is just another tool in the marketing process, albeit a powerful and increasingly important one. This, in turn, means that the Internet activities of a company's marketing must be planned as part of the overall marketing strategy and marketing mix of the company and not, as it so often has been in the past, simply be tagged on as an afterthought or an extra.

A further facet to consider with regard to the growth of the Internet and virtual marketing is that it is increasingly changing the conventional boundaries and structures of markets and the competition within them. The British Sky Broadcasting Group (BSkyB) is, as its name suggests, essentially a communications company primarily, of course, in television. But increasingly in the future, the growth of its interactive services may begin to transform this company into a potential major competitor for conventional retailers as it increasingly sells products and services through its Internet facilities to customers directly in their own living rooms.

Increasingly, therefore, no marketer in the future will be able to ignore the Internet even if – as is increasingly unlikely – their companies are not actually marketing via the net.

By providing direct links with customers, suppliers and distributors and by facilitating transactions, processes and information transfer, the Internet will radically transform the way marketing is done.

The Internet can be used in a vast number of ways for marketing purposes. It can be used as an external research tool to access market and competitor information. It can be used as a direct marketing channel and a home-shopping site. It can be used to raise awareness and support other communication tools for specific campaigns. For example, a leading manufacturer of white goods is currently about to use its Internet site as the main promotional tool when launching its new products because it is felt that the Internet can provide more crucial information which the customer will require before making a decision.

The Internet can also be used by organizations to communicate with other organizations in b2b marketing via e-mail. As the ownership of personal computers grows, mobility improves and the cost of Internet use declines, more consumers will also be contactable directly via e-mail instead of using mailshots.

The intranet

Key definition

The intranet – Is an electronic system of internal communication throughout an organization.

Similar to the Internet but operating within an organizational system, the intranet connects functions and activities within an organization thereby facilitating rapid and effective internal systems of communication. Intranets allow, for example, employees to access information from other parts of the company though obviously some of this may be restricted. This allows greater management of communication and can be used to advantage for relaying, say, information on important developments from outside an organization such as, say, competitor actions and so on. The intranet may also be used to advantage for internal promotional material such as company newsletters and so on.

The extranet

Key definition

The extranet – Is a system of electronic communication which connects members of a value/supply chain network together.

The extranet links together value chain companies such as material/component suppliers, producers, distributors and intermediaries, and in some cases customers. The development of EDI networks and marketing referred to earlier is an example of the extranet application. The extranet allows much closer and more sophisticated relationships to be developed between the members of the value chain, and the access and use of such information should allow for mutual economies and enhanced communication. This strategy also encourages trust and commitment between two organizations, such as a supplier and a customer. For example, the extranet may be used to allow a customer on-line access to some of its internal information sources. The extranet is used in a growing number of organizations where such access to information has helped in planning sales and logistics down the line. Obviously, there are some potential problems which relate to the level of investment required to allow for this system to work effectively. One must also consider the problem of access to information when one organization wishes to terminate the relationship.

Databases

Strictly speaking, databases are not a technology but rather bring a number of technologies together to increase and enhance customer information which a company can then use in its marketing. Databases, however, are so important in contemporary marketing, and particularly in the move towards the virtual marketplace, that we would consider further here.

Key definition

A database – Is a store of customer information which can be used to develop marketing strategies.

Remember that central to the marketing concept is the need to know your customers. Developments in information collection, storage and analysis are now making information one of the most important competitive assets a company can have.

A customer database can be built from many sources. So, for example, information can come from customer orders, subscription lists, guarantee return forms, loyalty cards, company sales persons, customer complaints, customer enquiries, traditional market research and outside companies that specialize in providing customer information. We can see from this list that information on customers can come from a wide variety of sources, both from inside and outside the organization. Coupled with the ability to store and manipulate large amounts of data, the plethora of customer data sources means that all too often it is possible to be overwhelmed by data. In order to avoid such information overload, while at the same time ensuring that valuable information about customers is not overlooked or lost, database management needs careful planning. The essence of successful database marketing requires careful attention to the following:

- ○ Specific objectives for the database, including types of information required and why
- ○ Effective systems for data capture including strategies for this
- ○ Appropriate systems for data storage including effective database maintenance
- ○ Effective systems of analysis and interpretation of data based around providing information for marketing decision-making.

Without careful attention to the objectives and uses to which the database is to be put, it is all too easy to collect data just for the sake of it. The marketer and the database planner need to work carefully together to determine precisely what data is required in the context of being useful for decision-making. Data capture involves systems for providing and collecting data for the database and encompasses many of the sources already mentioned such as market research, loyalty cards and so on. Companies have become much better at data collection with often very sophisticated methods for providing data. It is important to remember that there is considerable legislation relating to the collection and use of data on customers. The most important legislation is enshrined in the Data Protection Act of 1998 which covers both manual and computer systems, and protects customers' rights in several respects with regard to data on them. It is particularly important to build a database in such a way that valuable sources of customer data are not ignored. Many companies suffer from the fact that the different departments in the organization each have their own databases which are often never used by the rest of the organization. Increasingly, companies are using what is referred to as 'data warehousing' to deal with this problem.

Key definition

Data warehousing – Is the process of collecting all the data on customers and centralizing this into a single pool within a company.

Activity 9.8

List examples of the sorts of data on customers which functions other than the marketing function in an organization might generate in the course of performing their functional activities in an organization.

When you have completed your list, you should compare it with the debriefing.

Once the database is established, the next step is to use this data in order to improve our marketing. This involves ensuring that the data is analysed and manipulated so as to provide information for marketing decision-making. Again, developments in IT and computing power in particular have facilitated much more sophisticated analysis and interpretation of data for this purpose. Sophisticated statistical analysis and modelling techniques allow the marketing manager to look for important patterns of cause and effect between various data elements. This is sometimes called 'data mining'.

Key definition

Data mining – Is the process of analysing and manipulating data so as to provide new and more powerful insights into customer behaviour patterns in order to improve marketing decisions.

Such database analysis and manipulation has enabled the marketer to use database information in much more powerful ways in recent years including, for example, segmentation and targeting strategies, the development of relationship marketing strategies, customer retention and loyalty strategies, improved promotional and particularly direct mail strategies. Some of these applications of databases are considered in more detail later in the unit.

In managing the customer database, it is particularly important to ensure that the database is regularly maintained, or as it is sometimes referred to, cleaned. Obviously, customers and information on them is changing all the time. If the database contains inaccurate information, we run the risk of making the wrong decisions. For example, many companies waste money sending direct mail material to customers who have long since moved on. Worse still, there are examples of companies sending out marketing literature to customers on their database who are no longer living. Clearly, using inaccurate data at best wastes money, and at worst risks alienating customers or potential customers. It is not possible to describe in detail the techniques for ensuring clean databases, but many companies, for example, now reference their data against third-party lists to ensure its accuracy. Other companies use external consultants to ensure that the database is maintained. At the very least, companies should regularly check the information held on databases to try to ensure that the database is as up to date and accurate as possible.

Digital communications

Again, not a single technology but rather one which underpins several of the technological advances now affecting marketing, including, for example, many of the e-commerce developments. Digital technology developments, and particularly those which underpin recent developments in communications, are important enough to consider in their own right.

Digital technology is changing many facets of marketing activity and is set to change them even more in the future. This is particularly true in the area of communications. For example, digital technology is changing the face of television and therefore things like home shopping will increasingly be digitally based.

A growth area in the last few years has been the development of direct response television advertising (DRTV). This allows marketers to make very effective use of promotional campaigns which are designed to elicit an immediate response from the customer in the form of an enquiry or, more often than not, an order.

One of the most exciting developments in this area is the growth of interactive television which is based on the new digital technologies. Not only does this allow customers to shop from home but in the future will increasingly be used for access to the Web and associated activities such as e-mail services. There are those who believe that the television rather than the computer will be the interactive market of the future.

Similarly, we have seen the growth of multimedia including, for example, CD-ROMs and DVD systems, which are changing areas such as advertising and promotion in marketing and leading to the development of entirely new products, especially in the music and entertainment industries. Of course, marketers do not necessarily need to be experts in digital technology but they do need to recognize that increasingly marketing will make use of this technology, as indeed will the rest of the society.

Mobile marketing (M-marketing)

In Unit 6 we briefly mentioned the recent rapid growth in mobile or M-marketing as it is usually referred to, and in Unit 7 we explored what is the primary application of this development in marketing, namely the area of marketing communications or the promotional element of the marketing mix. To reiterate some of our earlier discussion of these aspects of M-marketing:

Related to developments in digital communications is the growth of wireless technologies, and the mobile technologies, and communications which are associated with them. Increasingly, the marketer, for example, will be able to communicate with customers and customers with marketers irrespective of where they are and what they are doing anywhere in the world. Although the Internet allows communication globally with customers, currently customers must have access to a computer. Admittedly, this can be a laptop computer but most Internet usage is in the home. In the future, wireless technologies will mean that, for example, the marketer and consumer will be able to communicate via a mobile phone. Already the new generation of mobile phones allows direct access to the Internet and facilities such as the sending and receiving of e-mails. There is no doubt that this application of technology and its importance to marketers will grow in the future and hence will be another contributory factor in the move towards a virtual marketplace.

Further examples of the effects of ICT

Remember, we are looking at the area of ICT and advances in these because they are fundamentally changing the process and application of many marketing activities. Indeed, this is the reason for including this area in the CIM's syllabus for this subject. We have already considered, therefore, some of the main effects of developments in ICT and particularly the growth of the Internet and the move towards the virtual marketplace. The effects of developments in ICT are so ubiquitous, however, that virtually every facet of marketing activity is being affected and in some areas transformed. Clearly, it is impossible to detail all the possible effects and implications in this area, but in addition to the effects already outlined, here are some more of the effects of ICT on marketing practice.

Application of the marketing concept

Developments in ICT are enabling marketers to apply the principles of the marketing concept to much greater effect than before. There are many reasons for this but essentially ICT and particularly the marketing research and database elements already referred to are enabling the marketer to understand and respond to customer needs and requirements much more effectively than ever before.

The marketing planning process

We discussed the impact of new technology and technological developments on the marketing planning process in Unit 2. We noted that virtually every element and step in the marketing planning process ranging from the marketing audit to evaluation and control is being impacted by developments in technology.

Study tip

It might be a good idea to remind yourself about the way that ICT is impacting the marketing planning process by looking at Unit 2 again.

Marketing research

Marketing research is in some ways perhaps the most obvious example of the potential for technological advances. The advances in IT have been very helpful to marketing researchers and in particular has made the often difficult process of international marketing research much easier. It has also made much secondary research far easier and economical. Below are some of the ways in which these advances in IT are being used in marketing research.

Secondary research

External secondary data sources are now available in a range of different technological formats in addition to print. Researchers can now access Internet-based sources and websites. On-line format allows the researcher to access and manipulate data with appropriate software; the data usually available on a subscription basis. Such sources are often very much more up to date than printed formats. A number of good universities have websites which provide an extensive listing of Internet-based information sources.

Internal secondary data sources, and particularly the databases referred to earlier, are also becoming increasingly powerful information sources. Remember, internal databases enable the market researcher to identify and analyse customer behaviour in some depth. Again, such information can be rapidly updated.

Primary research

Again, the use of IT can help the research in a number of ways.

For example, in terms of gathering information, quantitative data using a research instrument or questionnaire can be posted on the Internet on a particular site. It can also be e-mailed to potential respondents easily – so long as e-mail addresses are available. Quantitative information can also be collected via on-line scanners as an observation tool to assess purchasing behaviour. Scanners and electronic equipment can be used to monitor in-store traffic flows. Digital television will increasingly allow the researcher to gather further quantitative information directly from respondents. As regards qualitative information, chat rooms or discussion areas on the Internet are particularly useful.

Like many things to do with the Internet, the initial excitement regarding the potential for it as a new research tool has died down a little, with marketers becoming more realistic about what the Internet can and cannot do with respect to marketing research. Slowly but surely, market researchers are learning that using the Internet possibly requires new marketing research tools and certainly new attitudes and approaches to marketing research. Marketing research companies and marketing managers are only just beginning to learn how to use the Internet in this respect. But as they do so, this tool will become increasingly useful to marketers.

Extending knowledge

One of the leading research companies in the United Kingdom is National Opinion Polls (NOP). Recently NOP have linked their database technology with Web-based reporting systems that allowed clients to access and use results within 24 hours of data collection. NOP is also using its access to over 100 Internet cafés in the United Kingdom where it can combine, for example, demonstrations of new products with interviews with potential customers.

The potential for the Internet in marketing research then is huge, provided the marketer is careful and creative in using this new tool. Some research companies are beginning to use chat rooms and webcams to facilitate, for example, focus groups and in depth interviews on-line. Certainly on-line research will never replace some of the more conventional marketing research techniques; for example, it would be difficult to imagine how one could conduct, say, taste tests over the computer. But there is no doubting that the Internet offers many advantages even with conventional marketing research techniques. For example, a questionnaire can be posted on the Internet on a particular site, it can be e-mailed to potential respondents easily as long as e-mail addresses are available. Overall, we can certainly expect to see a continued growth in the use of the Internet for marketing research purposes.

Key definition

Chat room – Is an Internet facility whereby individuals can 'meet' in cyberspace to discuss issues with other Internet users. Often such chat rooms will be listed under topic/subject area of interest, for example fine wines.

Information technology developments are also helping in the analysis stage of market research. For example, during interviews, the responses can be entered directly into laptop computers which can ensure that the information is ready to analyse instantaneously. This can also be undertaken for telephone interviews. Increasingly powerful computer packages can be used to analyse the information effectively. There are now a number of different software packages that can also help to analyse qualitative data.

Promotional campaigns and the promotional mix

Advances in technology and particularly ICT developments have, and will continue to have, a major effect on the promotional elements of the marketing mix. Consider the following examples of uses and applications in this area of the marketing mix.

Advertising

Direct response television advertising has allowed advertising to achieve more than just awareness. Data can be captured and responses can lead to converts. The introduction of satellite television and digital technology has allowed for more sophisticated targeting via traditional advertising. The use of the Internet as an advertising window or banner advertising on other linked sites has been evident in the last 5 years. The use of the Internet as a vehicle for advertising is growing rapidly.

Activity 9.9

In what ways does satellite television allow for more sophisticated targeting with respect to advertising?

List any reasons you can think of and then compare your list with that shown in the debriefing.

Sales promotions

The sophistication of databases and the direct mailing of sales promotions has been very powerful for some organizations. The use of the website and the 'free downloadable program or screen saver' has allowed the marketer to become more creative.

Personal selling

As we shall see later in the unit, automated customer-handling technology has begun to erode some of the elements of personal selling. Indeed, some believe that new technology will mean that the role of personal selling will decline. Certainly, new technology and the growth of, for example, the use of call centres by companies can significantly reduce selling costs. However, and again as we shall see later, one has to be careful when diminishing the role of personal selling not to erode the service to the customer. New technology is certainly facilitating greater control over sales force activities in the field. The obvious examples are the use of mobile phone networks, e-mails through laptops and so on. Intranet technology, by allowing speedier and more flexible communication with sales staff, can, if used properly, increase sales force motivation and effectiveness in dealing with customers. Satellite and digital technology enables videoconferencing thereby allowing sales conferences to be held even when sales staff are globally scattered. Obviously, access to powerful and cheap computing enables very rapid analysis of response to sales data and sales performance which can be fed through to head office from a modem operated by each sales person at the end of the sales day.

Public relations (PR)

New technology is also affecting the PR element of the promotional mix. The use of the website as a relationship-building tool has been very effective for some organizations. For both internal (staff) and external audiences (customers, journalists, community, etc.) it has been easier to communicate using the intranet, the Internet and mobile technology. For example, internal newsletters can be communicated on the intranet and press releases to journalists can be e-mailed instantly with digital pictures using satellite technology. The Web is proving to be a particularly useful communication tool for crisis management such as disasters, accidents, tampering and pollution scares and so on when accurate and rapidly changing information to the public is crucial.

Direct mail

Advances in technology have had a major effect on the direct mail element of the promotional mix. In particular, of course, the growth in databases and a marketer's ability to increasingly improve both the accuracy and the complexity of information held on such databases is allowing the marketer to use direct marketing, and direct mail in particular, much more effectively. So, for example, the marketer can use the database to identify key target customers based on data regarding their purchasing habits, interests, and attitudes and opinions. By using databases in this way, the marketer is able to target the direct mail campaign to the right people thereby reducing the cost while at the same time increasing the response rate.

Extending knowledge

A detailed discussion of the design, application and evaluation of websites for promotional and other purposes in marketing is beyond the scope of this coursebook. You are, however, recommended at least to scan through a specialist textbook in this area. Two excellent text-books are those given in the essential reading list for this syllabus, namely *Internet Marketing* by Chaffey *et al.* and *Cybermarketing* by Bickerton *et al.*

Websites are often thought of as just another selling device, but the website can be used much more actively, in particular to develop better relationships with a company's customers and publics.

Customer relations
A well-designed and operated website allows for very effective communication with customers. If customers can easily find the website and access information from it, and if they find that these visits are rewarding in the sense of offering more than simply information, the customer is likely to be favourably impressed with regard to the company and its offerings.

Media relations
The website can also be dedicated to developing media relations. This can be one of the most potent PR tools as, for example, reporters can access information which they may need at any time of the day or night, and if prepared carefully, in a format that is ready to use.

Investor relations

As the financial community is increasingly used to using the Internet, a corporate website can also be important for investors accessing information. This would include the annual reports being posted on the site.

Community relations

The website can also be used for developing community relations. This site could include information relating to the promotion of local joint projects, contributions to arts and culture, invitations to open days and educational pages.

We can see, therefore, that the strategic design and use of the website is growing in importance in today's marketplace and this must be considered as part of an integrated communications strategy.

New product development

As with marketing planning, the impact of technological developments and ICT in particular on this area of marketing were discussed in earlier units.

Study tip

Again, you should refresh your memory about this area.

- o Remember, though, that we suggested that advances in technology are also helping to facilitate and improve the new product development process. The interactive nature of the Internet allows the marketer to involve and encourage customer participation in product design and also speed up the design commitment. In particular, net technology allows a much more flexible approach to the process of new product development while at the same time involving the customer in the process.

Electronic customer relationship management

As we have mentioned several times in this coursebook, an important development in both theory and practice of marketing has been the move towards the so-called 'relationship marketing'. Remember that we said that relationship marketing is based on the building of trust between the organization and its customers. Rather than viewing exchanges between the organization and its customers as one-off individual transactions, relationship marketing is based on the notion of building long-term transaction between both parties to the exchange. As such, CRM places increased emphasis on co-operation, co-ordination and communication between the members of the value chain. It also places much greater emphasis on the importance of developing customer loyalty and therefore retaining customers. Although effective relationship marketing requires, first and foremost, the right attitudes, philosophy and culture in an organization, the translation of these facets into effective relationship marketing programmes is increasingly being facilitated and based upon advances in technology. Not surprisingly, this is now usually referred to as electronic CRM or e-CRM.

The past 5 years in particular have seen an increasingly rapid movement from basic information systems to develop and manage customer relationship programmes to sophisticated electronically based relationship management programmes making use of the most up to date and powerful technologies of information and data management. For example, the use of both sophisticated databases and direct communications can enhance the relationship which can be built with a customer. The financial services sector and now many FMCG organizations are becoming more effective in using electronic methods to ensure that their relationship with their customers is more robust and effective in terms of securing mutual benefit. Indeed, they use technology and other marketing techniques to endeavour to build loyal customers with the intention of retaining them for a lifetime. Using the database, the marketer can, for example, develop loyalty schemes such as those used initially by many supermarket retailers, but now spreading into consumer durable goods marketing.

You will recall that relationship marketing was primarily initially used in b2b markets where it continues to grow. The extranet coupled with EDI systems, both outlined earlier in this unit, allows the different members of a value chain accurate and instant information which they may wish to use for planning purposes. This use of the extranet can be used to build and maintain very strong bonds between the members of the value chain and therefore can help to build customer loyalty and retention. The extranet not only allows for greater flow of information which facilitates cost economies, but it also communicates trust and commitment between customers and suppliers.

There are now many companies who specialize in ECRM management. Most of these companies use sophisticated information and database technology in developing and implementing ECRM systems for their clients.

Marketing in practice: example

'Software for Sport' is a company which, among its other activities, supplies CRM software and systems to football clubs. This application of ECRM shows in fact how far relationship management has come into marketing. At one time, many would have argued that CRM in general and ECRM in particular had little application in football, where, for example, someone is unlikely to switch from supporting one club to another, that is most fans are loyal to their favourite football clubs. However, the clubs have realized that unless they make efforts to retain even brand-loyal customers there are dangers in, say, people switching from watching their favourite club live to watching them on, say, Sky TV. They may also switch from one sport to another as newer sports, for example ice hockey, appear to be more exciting. In other words, even in this bastion of brand loyalty, companies cannot afford to become complacent about their relationships with customers. Software for Sports brings together information on, for example, season ticket holder data, club shop transactions, visits to club amenities and so on into a single database. By doing so, football clubs are able to build up information on fans and corporate customers to help them market their clubs and facilities. In addition to this software for databases some football clubs are also using smart card technology, which helps to improve the ticket application process and can be used to monitor data on season ticket holders.

There is no doubt that the way forward for modern CRM systems is the development of increasingly electronically based systems. Most of the modern CRM systems are based on sophisticated IT. Overall, this technology gives far greater market and customer knowledge based on sophisticated databases which in turn allow far higher levels of service and targeted marketing efforts to increase customer loyalty. However, there is a danger of the technology of ECRM systems becoming more important than what the system is designed to provide, namely improved customer relationships. In the past, too many companies have made the mistake of thinking that all they had to do was to design or buy in sophisticated data management systems and this would inevitably lead to improved CRM. This is a misconception about the true meaning of CRM and the role that technology plays in CRM systems. The systems must first and foremost be based on the requirements of customers and implemented through the right attitudes of management and staff. Certainly, ECRM systems are not of themselves a panacea for improving CRM.

Customer service and customer care

Finally, in our examples of applications and uses of technological advances in marketing, is the area of customer service and customer care. Examples of ways in which advances in technology are impacting this area include:

- o By effectively removing physical distance between customers and marketers, customer and company come closer together.
- o Improved databases facilitate the tracking of customer satisfaction and the following up of any complaints thereby potentially improving customer service.
- o The interactive nature of many of the new technologies allows customers potentially much greater involvement in the development of marketing programmes to satisfy their needs. Technological advances in IT facilitate the ease with which customers can evaluate and purchase products and services such as home banking and shopping and so on, all help to improve levels of customer service.

Automated customer-handling operations

An example of how new technology is affecting customer service is the growth of automated customer-handling operations.

Automated customer-handling operations have been in existence for a number of years now. Such systems enable the organization to handle large numbers of customer enquiries and complaints. Most of these systems are based on automated voice and push-button instructions when customers telephone the organization. By pushing a series of buttons in response to automated voice prompts, the customer is directed to the right department or person in the company and/or to the source of the information required.

As an example, Barclays Bank now allow customers to access information about their accounts 24 hours a day by telephone. The customer can access this information by keying in on the telephone their membership number and pin number, and by push-button technology they can, for example, access account balances, order cheque books, transfer money and so on. New technologies are allowing organizations to offer a level of service which might not have been available previously, and typically this is related to out-of-hours access to information and services.

Having said this, a company must be very careful to ensure that it is introducing new technology for the right reasons when it comes to customer care. We saw this in our discussion earlier in Unit 8 regarding the growth of customer call centres. We discussed for example that, in some cases, automated customer-handling operations and particularly call centres are introduced primarily to save costs for the company rather than with the objective of improving customer care. In addition, there is now an increasing concern that far from improving customer service, some of the automated customer-handling operations lack the human interface which many customers seek. In addition, the amount of time lost during what can be often long and laborious push-button processes can be very annoying to customers. Therefore, in considering technologies which enable a greater degree of automation in customer-handling operations, organizations need to be careful that such systems do not alienate their customer base and indeed erode levels of customer care rather than enhance them.

 Activity 9.10

Try to list any reasons that you can think of why many customers increasingly feel that automated customer-handling operations are annoying and frustrating.

Continuing developments in the application of new technology in marketing

As you would expect, with continuing developments in the technologies themselves, the application of new technology in various areas of marketing activity continues to develop and extend. For example, some retailers have recently introduced radio frequency identification (RFID) technology into their stores. This technology essentially comprises of inserting a tiny silicon chip no larger than grain of salt into every consumer product which, then, sends out a radio signal which can be read by a reading device. Using this technology the retailer is able to identify individually every single product on the supermarket shelf. Moreover these can then be scanned through the technology at the check-out. Not only does this potentially mean the demise of the check-out operator but it also enables the retailer to link individual products with individual customers thereby building up an enormous and detailed database on customers' buying activities. This can then be linked to customer information regarding, for example, personal details, address, credit card and so on and the information can be used to develop more effective marketing programmes. In fact, RFID technology is causing considerable concern amongst some consumer groups who consider it an invasion of privacy. However, RFID technology is typical of the way the use of technology in marketing is moving, with an emphasis on developing detailed databases about individual rather than even small segments of customers.

The whole area of e-commerce and the applications of new technology to commerce and marketing is now very much a hot issue. You can expect, therefore, to come across a considerable amount of information and reports on developments in this area in textbooks, newspapers, reports and, needless to say, on the Internet itself. You should be constantly looking for information in this area and particularly examples of developments and applications of technology in marketing. Finally, remember this is a huge area of study in its own right and therefore you should consider at least one of the textbooks recommended in this area in the CIM syllabus.

International and global dimensions

Our second major development in the context of marketing which, in turn, has given rise to major implications for the nature of marketing undertaken by organizations including their use of the various marketing mix tools is the increasingly important international and global dimensions of marketing practice.

Study tip

As you are no doubt aware, international and global marketing is an area of study in its own right. It is not possible but thankfully nor is it essential to encompass every facet of the international and global dimensions of marketing in this unit even if we confine ourselves to just examining the implications of the international and global context on the marketing mix tools. What follows, therefore, are just some examples of the ways in which international and global dimensions impact this area of marketing in order to illustrate the importance of these dimensions in contemporary marketing.

Extending knowledge

With reference to our study tip above, you are advised to consult a good basic text which covers the area of international marketing. We recommend G.A. Lancaster *et al.* (2002), *Essentials of Marketing*, 4th edition, Chapter 14.

Here, then, are just some ways in which international and global dimensions affect some of the areas of marketing, and particularly the elements of the marketing mix which we have discussed throughout the units.

International/global issues in products and packaging

The international and global marketer faces additional complexities and decisions when it comes to products and packaging compared to the purely domestic marketer. The STEP factors in particular are very important determinants affecting product and packaging decisions. To the extent to which these STEP factors are likely to differ between different countries, therefore, the marketer must take these into account in products and package areas of the mix. So, for example, when it comes to packaging design some countries are much more stringent with regard to recyclability regulations. Similarly, facets such as the product life-cycle stage for a product differ between different countries. Obviously, decisions about aspects such as product features, design, components and so on of a product will have to reflect individual country requirements. Perhaps one of the most significant issues facing the international marketer in this respect is the extent to which it is possible and desirable to standardize the product for different international markets. The other side of the coin being, of course, the extent to which the product needs to be modified or adapted to different countries. In fact, this standardization/adaptation issue runs throughout the marketing mix decisions for the international and global marketer, but it is particularly important when it comes to products and packaging. The main reason for this is that, on the one hand, standardization in the product and packaging areas of the marketing mix probably represents some of the largest potential cost savings available to a company. Put simply, the more a company can standardize its products, the more economies of scale it will gain. Offset against these gains, however, are the potential barriers to and disadvantages of product standardization. So, for example, consumers in many of the African markets simply don't want, can't use, or can't afford many of the features and design attributes of products marketed to the Western European or Northern American markets. So, for example, a much more basic washing machine or television is much more appropriate. Put simply, there can be major barriers to product and packaging standardization. The successful marketer must strike a balance between standardization and adaptation bearing in mind the costs of adaptation compared to meeting the needs of customers in individual markets.

When it comes to branding we have seen the emergence of global brands in recent years. Again this is a result of many factors, for example consumers are much more cosmopolitan these days and exposed to a much wider range of global influences. Within this environment, backed by the resources and efforts of the multinationals, global brands have flourished. All the advantages associated with effective brands and brand management outlined in the unit 'Product decisions' apply equally as much, if not more so, when set in an international/global context. Global brands allow consumers to buy their favourite brands with equanimity anywhere in the world giving them confidence and security. The marketer benefits through lower costs of brand support, although admittedly supporting global brands can and does require substantial investment and resources, particularly in advertising and promotion.

With regard to the new product aspects of marketing activities, increasingly, new products are being developed with global marketing in mind. It is much easier to build in requirements for adaptation to meet the needs of other markets at the early stages of product development rather than adapt them later on. This means that the marketer must be aware of factors in international markets which must be considered when thinking about product specifications for new products. In particular, any regulatory and legal factors must be considered. Needless to say, however, it is differences in buyer requirements which are likely to cause major changes to the product development programme. Returning to our standardization adaptation issue, many companies have attempted to develop new global products. So, for example, the Ford Motor Company have attempted to design and build a 'world car'. The basic concept of this product is to have a standardized core design for things like chassis, engines and so on, which can then be modified to meet the needs of individual markets or regions in different parts of the world. Understandably developing global products is not easy and requires, for example, global inputs from marketing research.

Pricing in international markets

The techniques, inputs to and strategies for pricing apply whether considering purely domestic or international markets. So, for example, the primary inputs include areas such as costs, demand, competitors, customer and company considerations. Pricing can be cost, demand or competitor based and pricing strategies can involve skimming or penetration. However, as in other areas of the marketing mix there are additional complexities and considerations when pricing in international markets. Some of these additional complexities and considerations are listed below:

- The marketer must consider any additional costs due to, say, tariffs and duties as a result of trading across international boundaries.
- Linked to the above, international marketers often face the issue of 'price escalation' for their products in international markets, that is there are forces which drive up prices such as tariffs, but also increased costs of transport and distribution.
- The international marketer also faces the problem of having to take account of different currencies and, related to this, changes in exchange rates. In some circumstances even small differences in exchange rates can have a major effect on profitability.
- The international marketer has to consider the terms and conditions which each party agrees to when considering price and delivery arrangements. So, for example, prices can be set at, say, a free on board (fob) price where the price includes delivery onto the customer's ship, say, for transport. On the other hand, a price may be set which includes carriage, insurance and freight (cif), that is all the costs to the customer's factory.

There is no doubt, then, that pricing in international markets is more complicated; however, as we move more and more towards global markets and free trading blocks some of these complexities may well reduce.

International aspects of channels and physical distribution

As with the price element of the marketing mix, and indeed each of the other elements of the mix, the underpinning principles, issues and management of channels and physical distribution are the same for both domestic and international markets. Again, as with price, however, these basic principles and decisions are made more complex when planning the place element for international markets. In addition, there are one or two considerations and complications which the international marketer faces in planning place which are simply not encountered when planning for purely domestic markets.

Some of the added complexities and considerations for international place decisions include the following:

o   Perhaps for obvious reasons, the distances involved for physical distribution are often much greater in international channels. This makes planning some of the logistical and physical distribution elements that much more important. So, for example, for products often travelling long distances, including by sea and by air, physical protection of the products during transit is much more important.

o   International channels involve several types of intermediaries often not found in purely domestic marketing. So, for example, we have export agents of various types, international forwarders and freighters, specialist government intermediaries and so on. The international marketer needs to be aware of, and be able to plan for and work with, a wider variety of types of intermediaries.

o   Linked to the points above, the international marketer must take much greater care over decisions such as responsibilities and payments between the different parties in the chain, for example who takes title to goods, and at what point in the channel.

o   Channel arrangements which are used satisfactorily in the domestic market simply may be unavailable in international markets. The United Kingdom, for example, has one of the most highly concentrated and developed retailing sectors in the world. Such channel arrangements are simply not available in many other countries and particularly developing ones.

o   Finally, and again as with all marketing decisions for international markets, the market, competitive and macro environment factors are often very different in international markets, which may have a major effect on the selection of channel and physical distribution arrangements. For example, even within Europe the competitive market structure for car distribution is very different across the different countries of Europe. In the United Kingdom, for example, car distribution is still very much controlled by the major car manufacturers with things like prices being more manageable from the manufacturer than in other parts of Europe due to different distribution arrangements.

International aspects of promotion

There are several additional considerations when considering the use of the promotional tools in international markets. Again, many of these are similar to those affecting the tools of Product, Price and Place already discussed. The main considerations are as follows:

o   Because many aspects of promotion, including areas such as message design, media availability, and more recently, technological considerations such as access to the Internet and communication technologies, are substantially affected by political, economic, social, cultural and technological considerations, and because these are often substantially different in other geographical areas of the world, it is vitally important to consider these differences when planning international promotional campaigns.

o   Having said this, international communications, again underpinned by developments in IT, are becoming more global in nature. It is now much more realistic to plan global promotion and communication campaigns in international marketing.

o   As in all of the areas of the marketing mix, a key consideration for the international marketer when planning international promotion is the extent to which it is possible and advisable to use standardized versus adapted promotional campaigns. Many factors affect this decision including, for example, the nature of the product, target market countries, the resources available, and perhaps above all, the similarity or otherwise of customer needs and behaviour. Overall, however, there has been a trend towards trying to standardize the tools of marketing by international marketers. This is particularly so with respect to at least some elements of promotional campaigns, and in particular elements such as brand names, corporate image and central messages

287

relating to company positioning and business missions. Companies like Coca-Cola and McDonald's have tried to build promotional campaigns which span the globe with only changes in language in advertising, and so on and media due to differences in availability. Obviously, standardization offers many advantages including:

- The development of a consistent corporate and brand image.
- The potential for economies of scale in the production of promotional material, for example advertising campaigns.
- The potential to appeal to what is an increasingly global customer.

These potential advantages, though, need to be compared and assessed against the individual needs and circumstances in particular markets.

International aspects of customer care

Clearly, companies which operate in international markets want to develop similar standards of customer care throughout their operations. Note how our Interflora example illustrates how a company-wide commitment to customer care throughout different markets in different parts of the world can help build the image of a company, develop more effective relationships with customers and serve as a standard for operating procedures for all staff. If a customer has a satisfactory experience with a company in one country, then it is much more likely that that customer will seek to use the same company when he or she purchases elsewhere in the world. On the other hand, if a customer experiences different levels of service and customer care from the same company in different parts of the world this is likely to lead to the customer being apprehensive and anxious about using the same supplier. However, customer-care programmes, including the selection of the level of customer care necessary and appropriate, are among the most difficult areas of the marketing programme to standardize. There are several reasons for this, but among one of the most important are differences in cultural practice in different parts of the world with regard to what is expected in terms of customer care. Almost without exception, the US customer expects, and in America largely gets, extremely high standards of customer care. In parts of Europe, however, including the United Kingdom, customers may not expect, and in fact positively dislike, some of the elements of customer care which are considered normal in the United States. In designing customer-care programmes therefore, the marketer has to consider these cultural differences and reflect them in the design of customer-care programmes. Notwithstanding this, though, the international marketer should try to ensure consistent approaches to customer care in different parts of the world. Again, people, process and physical evidence are all important here. In designing an international effective customer-care programme many of the issues and steps for planning a purely domestic customer-care programme are to be found. In essence, and by way of reminding you of some of these issues and steps, the following should be considered:

o Identify customer needs and perceptions for each market.
o Establish a mission statement.
o Set service level standards and specifications reflecting individual country requirements but guided by an overall customer charter which reflects the mission statement and outlines measurable criteria/standards to be attained.
o Establish management processes and communicate these to all staff.
o Define specific tasks as regards customer-care elements for each country.
o Establish basic minimum levels of customer care.
o Ensure effective response systems for identifying, tracking and responding to complaints.
o Ensure management and staff commitment to programmes through, for example, effective training and remuneration programmes.
o Ensure effective and continuous measurement of the customer-care programmes.

International implications of technological advances in marketing

Technological advances in marketing have affected many areas of international marketing operations. Once again, however, it is primarily developments in ICT which have had, or are having, the most profound and far-reaching implications. The speed with which information can be obtained and accessed, both by customers and by companies, has led to, for example, much greater and increasingly global competition. When a customer can access information and purchase products from anywhere in the world simply by clicking a button on their keyboard and entering the World Wide Web, obviously this means that companies are exposed to potentially global competition. As we saw in an earlier unit when we discussed the effect of the Internet in this respect, this means that the marketer must consider a much broader range of competitors and expect customers to shop for the best value and service.

Obviously, increased global competition because of developments in technology can be both an opportunity and a threat. In the case of developing and launching new products, technology, and again particularly IT, is presenting major opportunities and advantages for marketers these days. New technology can help cut the costs and increase the speed for developing and launching global new brands particularly through the use of new technology-based marketing research techniques.

New technology is also facilitating the ease of communication where companies have different operating divisions throughout the world. So, for example, marketing managers can be kept informed of company and market developments much more easily and intelligence on markets can be shared. In this sense, it is probably as much the intranet as well as the extranet which is presenting opportunities and advantages for the global marketer.

As already mentioned, ICT in particular is helping to facilitate at least pan-regional and in some cases global marketing, including the development of global brands.

Some companies are now launching pan-regional or even global websites. One example of a company which has just launched its first pan-European website is the Schweppes company with a website which gives details of bars throughout Europe, including their facilities, prices and so on. This website encourages customers who have visited a bar listed on the site to use 'word of mouse' to rate these and spread their experience and views about a particular bar to other members of the website. In effect, if you like, it is along the lines of a consumer guide to bars and drinking throughout Europe. In the future we can expect many more companies to use their international websites in similar ways to this, responding with pan-global technology to pan-global customers.

These then are some of the major additional considerations and implications with regard to the application and management of our various marketing mix elements in the context of international and global markets. Remember again we have only covered a small proportion of the issues in this area and again you are reminded therefore to read at least one, and preferably more, chapter from the texts recommended for this syllabus by the CIM.

Measuring and controlling marketing effectiveness and instituting appropriate changes

This final topic of this coursebook is the second of our two elements of the CIM syllabus to be considered out of order. It might be useful to explain why it was decided to cover this area as the final culminating topic of the coursebook.

Quite rightly, the CIM consider a fundamental area of marketing to be the measurement and control of the effectiveness of marketing programmes and plans and, related to this, the importance of instituting appropriate changes where necessary, hence the inclusion of these elements in the syllabus. But first why is evaluation and control so important to the marketing planning process and second when and where in this process should these elements be applied?

The importance of evaluation and control

Essentially, the process of monitoring and control comprises comparing actual performance against required or desired performance objectives and then taking any necessary action to correct differences between actual and required. Because of this, the control process in marketing stems from the marketing objectives and strategies of the company.

Without monitoring and control it is impossible to assess the extent to which marketing objectives have been achieved and the strategies have been effective. Given the potentially large costs and use of resources in implementing the elements of the marketing mix, it would be inadvisable not to assess how well these resources have been used.

In addition, we know that markets and organizations are dynamic. The environment changes, customers change, competitors change, even the company itself can change over time. This means, therefore, that marketing strategies and plans also need to change to reflect and cope with these external and internal changes. Monitoring and control of the marketing activities and performance facilitates the planning of such changes. Without monitoring and control there is a danger that marketing strategies become outmoded and no longer fit the market situation.

This, then, is the nature and importance of marketing evaluation and control but what about our 'where and when' question. Where and when in the marketing planning sequence does evaluation and control sit?

The place of evaluation and control in the marketing planning sequence
A clue to the place of evaluation and control is contained in our overview of the key steps in the marketing planning process shown in Figure 2.1 of Unit 2.

Study tip

You should turn back to Unit 2 at this stage and reacquaint yourself with the steps in the marketing planning sequence.

We can see that the monitoring and control process is shown as being the final stage of the marketing planning process, taking place after we have determined our marketing objectives and strategies, and implemented through the elements of the marketing mix. Obviously, it often only makes sense to evaluate marketing programmes when these programmes have had a chance to take effect (or otherwise) in the marketplace. In addition, although we also need to evaluate and control each of the marketing mix elements, as we have stressed, overall the marketing mix should be planned and implemented as a coherent and integrated whole and hence should be evaluated and controlled as such.

Perhaps you can appreciate now why we have left these elements of the syllabus until the last part of the final unit.

However, before we begin to remind ourselves of some of the key areas and techniques of marketing evaluation and control, it is important to examine two key caveats with regard to where evaluation and control fits in the planning sequence. First, the importance of ongoing, continuous evaluation and control including the pre-evaluation of marketing programmes. And secondly, the notion of evaluation and control as the first, as well as the last, stage of the marketing planning process.

The importance of ongoing, continuous evaluation and control, including pre-evaluation of marketing programmes

First of all, and notwithstanding that we have just stated that logically control and evaluation takes place at the end of the planning process, it is possible, and whenever so preferable, to control, evaluate and adjust marketing programmes, and certainly individual elements of the marketing mix as, and sometimes even before, they are implemented. Although our diagram of the marketing planning process shows control as the last stage, and despite this being the justification for dealing with this part of the syllabus last, in fact, evaluation, control and adjustment of marketing programmes and plans should be a continuous, ongoing process. In other words, marketing programmes must constantly be flexible and open to change in what is a complex, and often increasingly fast changing environment. The most pressing reason for changes to marketing plans is where they are simply not producing the results envisaged or required. Needless to say, where this is the case then the marketers control and information systems should flag this up as quickly as possible so that any necessary adaptations can be made. Waiting until the end of the planning period may, and often is, be simply too late. Although the most pressing reason perhaps it is not only shortcomings in performance or problems that may necessitate changes to ongoing marketing programmes, sometimes the marketer may need to adapt ongoing marketing programmes to take advantage of new marketing opportunities, for example the market has expanded much quicker than envisaged in our initial marketing plans. Opportunity or threat the marketer must be in a position to evaluate marketing plans and the elements of the marketing mix on an ongoing basis and be ready to make adaptations. Obviously, before making any changes, the marketer needs to evaluate and understand why changes may be needed and in particular the factors which are giving rise to the need to adapt our marketing plans. First of all are the external factors which can necessitate change/adaptation. Here are just some of the external factors which may underpin the need to adapt marketing plans.

External causes of need to adapt marketing plans, for example:

- o Changes in marketing environment – STEP factors, for example new legislation, a change in interest rates, changing attitudes and so on.
- o Competition – for example a new entrant, changes in competitor objectives and strategies and so on.
- o Customers – for example changes in tastes, needs, habits and so on.
- o One off unpredictable events – for example natural disasters, wars and so on.

We can see that a wide range of external factors can bring about a need to adapt marketing plans. In addition, however, internal factors too may necessitate changes to marketing programmes. Below are some examples.

Internal causes of need to adapt marketing plans, for example:

- o Changes in staff/leadership
- o Lack/loss of financial resources
- o Changes in overall company policy/objectives.

These examples serve to illustrate the need for ongoing evaluation and adaptation of marketing activities. But what about our suggestion that sometimes we can, and wherever possible should, evaluate and adapt marketing programmes even before they have been implemented. How is this possible? The answer of course is through limited trials of marketing plans before they are finalized and fully implemented. The best example of how this is done is through the techniques of test marketing. This, you may recall, involves trying out and evaluating marketing programmes on a limited scale usually, though not always, based on a limited, selected geographical area. Test marketing is widely used to evaluate the effectiveness of a proposed marketing mix, but can also be used to evaluate possible variations of variations on the different individual mix elements such as product variations, different prices, possible different promotional mixes and so on. According to the results from our test market, the marketer can adapt proposed marketing mix elements to give the most effective overall marketing programme for the selected target market. In addition to test marketing, marketers can also use the following to pre-evaluate and adapt proposed marketing programmes.

- o Customer surveys
- o Focus groups
- o Market hall tests
- o Laboratory tests.

Marketing evaluation and control as the first (as well as last) stage of the marketing planning process

The second aspect to stress with regard to the place of evaluation and control in the sequence of marketing planning is that, somewhat paradoxically, evaluation and control besides being the final stage in the marketing planning process is also amongst the first. This is because the results of the evaluation and control process should feedback into and hence influence the next round of the marketing planning process. This iterative feedback element of the control process underpins the nature and purpose of control in as much as it forms the basis of the adaptation process which it informs. Again we can see this in our marketing planning framework introduced in Unit 2. The marketing audit, a key element of the evaluation and control elements for marketing serves to help delineate and guide marketing objectives and strategies through, for example, the PEST and SWOT analyses then feedback into the start of the marketing planning process.

Key areas and techniques of marketing evaluation and control

The key areas and techniques of marketing control were introduced in Unit 2. To remind you they are shown again below:

1. Customer feedback/customer tracking, for example:

   (a) Customer surveys
   (b) Customer complaints
   (c) Sales-force reports
   (d) Customer panels.

2. Sales analysis and control, for example:

   (a) Sales volume/value
   (b) Sales trends
   (c) Breakdown of sales by product, customer, sales person and so on.

3. Market share analysis and control, for example:

   (a) As per sales analysis above, but based on percentage of market.

4. Profitability analysis and control, for example:

    (a) Analysis of costs and margins
    (b) Net profits
    (c) Return on capital.

5. Strategic control. This is the most wide-ranging and comprehensive of control techniques used in marketing, covering the control of the strategic planning process itself. One of the most comprehensive and wide-ranging approaches to strategic control is the use of a full marketing audit. The scope and nature of the marketing audit is outlined below.

Marketing audit

Probably the most comprehensive and far-reaching approach to marketing evaluation and control is the full marketing audit. Kotler *et al.* (1999) proposes the following coverage for the marketing audit

o   *The marketing strategy audit* – This encompasses evaluating the key marketing objectives of the organization together with an assessment of the major competitive strategies being pursued. These are assessed with regard to continuing relevance, feasibility and effectiveness.
o   *Marketing structures audit* – This part of the audit evaluates the effectiveness of existing marketing organization structures and systems and will encompass areas such as responsibilities and authority, co-ordination and communication, structures and systems.
o   *Marketing systems audit* – Auditing marketing systems encompasses areas such as planning and control mechanisms including budgeting, resource allocation and measures of marketing effectiveness.
o   *Productivity audit* – Here, specific measurement criteria are used to assess marketing performance encompassing areas such as profitability, sales effectiveness and market share measures. Detailed analysis can be applied to assess the relative productivity of, for example, products, market segments, individual customers, distribution channels and so on.
o   *Marketing functions audit* – 'Functions' here relates to the elements of the marketing mix. This part of the audit, then, encompasses an assessment of products, pricing, distribution and logistics, promotional and, where appropriate, the additional functional elements of marketing associated with services, that is the extended marketing mix with the additional three Ps of People, Process and Physical evidence.

The marketing audit should be carried out on a regular basis and certainly at least every year. Some suggest that the audit should be carried out by external auditors in order to increase objectivity and provide fresh perspectives on marketing issues and performance. If carried out by internal staff, inevitably the expertise of personnel from functions other than marketing and encompassing the other key functional areas of the business such as production, accountancy, personnel, research and development will be required. This means that ideally the marketing audit should be a team effort. In addition, the audit should be seen as a mechanism and in fact a crucial step in adapting future marketing plans and programmes. It should not therefore be seen or interpreted as a means to admonish and discipline marketing or other functional staff for ineffectiveness or poor performance in marketing. Where it is necessary, this should be a separate and quite a distinct process and not part of the marketing audit process.

Note that the marketing audit is seeking to establish more effective bases for competing in the marketplace. Certainly, often these bases will be primarily marketing in nature, for example effective advertising or packaging, say, but often companies compete using skills and resources in other functional areas of the business, so, for example, research and development, admittedly through new products, may be a major means of achieving competitive success. What the marketer must do, therefore, in conducting the internal audit is to establish what the critical resources, skills and processes in the context of the particular markets the company operates in are and the objectives it wishes to achieve in these. In addition, the audit should help highlight those resources and competencies which may be difficult for competitors to imitate and hence, provided they are valued by customers, can be used to develop an SCA.

Information for marketing evaluation and control

As we have seen, the whole process of marketing but especially effective evaluation and control requires up-to-date, accurate and pertinent information. Some of the developments in ICT such as improved databases have helped considerably in this respect in recent years. Obviously the marketer needs access to effective marketing information and decision systems. It is impossible – and perhaps dangerous – to specify all the areas and types of information that might form part of the evaluation and control process. In fact, the marketing information and decision system should be company- and even product brand-specific reflecting the individual needs of the marketing decision-maker. At the risk of generalizing, then, finally in this unit are suggested some of the possible sources and types of information that might be used to undertake a marketing audit for evaluation and control purposes.

- Sales figures breakdown by, for example, product type, customer type, intermediaries or channels.
- Allocation of resources including human to different aspects of the service.
- Forecast versus actual budgets and targets.
- Customer profiling from, for example, market research reports/customer database.
- Market trends developments and predictions from, for example, industry reports.
- Market trends developments and predictions from, for example, industry analysts.
- Profit by, for example, product type, customer type, channel type from accounts department.
- Competitor analysis from, for example, market research reports, intelligence-gathering activities.
- Size and structure of industry and its future policies from, for example, government reports, trade association reports and magazines.
- Customer satisfaction/changing needs from, for example, tracking studies, focus groups, customer service department, sale force.

Marketing in practice: case study

'More than just a number – getting to know your customers'

Literally, billions of pounds, euros, dollars, yen and so on have been spent by companies in recent years to develop and implement CRM strategies. Much of this spend has been on electronic systems and technologies for improving customer relationships including, for example, database, the Internet and marketing automation technologies designed to make it easier to identify customers and their needs. However, many companies have found that, to say the least, their spends on electronic systems for improved CRM have not produced the results in terms of improved relationships that they had hoped for. There are several reasons for this.

First is a misunderstanding of what CRM and particularly the technologies which often underpin CRM systems are all about. So, for example, some companies have felt that simply by purchasing or developing 'sophisticated' software and databases they would 'automatically' improve customer relationships. Effective CRM, though, is much more than having extensive database systems. Databases can only provide the start point for effective CRM. Much more important are the right staff attitudes in an organization towards customer relationships and in particular a desire to improve customer service.

Related to the above is the fact that perhaps surprisingly, at least at first glance, many customers do not in fact want a relationship with the marketer, they simply want good service. Customer relationship management systems and the technologies which underpin them must be designed with this in mind.

Finally, often customer relationship systems and again particularly elements such as databases are not designed and implemented so as to facilitate improved customer service as a means of developing better customer relationships.

An example of a company that has successfully negotiated some of these reasons for the often disappointing results of CRM programmes is that of the Britannia Building Society in the United Kingdom.

In designing and implementing its CRM system, Britannia were quite clear that the system should be built around improved customer service. They took the trouble therefore to identify what service items and levels customers were interested in and valued. The CRM system was then designed to deliver these service items and levels. Britannia also placed great emphasis on effective training and motivation of employees regarding the importance and purpose of CRM in the company. Persuading their staff to develop the right attitudes to improving customer relationships, again through effective service. Finally, Britannia were careful to ensure in their selection and use of the technology and database systems which underpinned their CRM activities that the CRM system improved customer service at key customer and interaction points including branches, telesales units and call centres. This has allowed Britannia Building Society to make their customers feel that they are being treated as individuals rather than as simply a number.

Summary

- In this unit, we have explored the importance of contextual setting in influencing the selection of, and emphasis given to, the marketing mix tools.
- We have explained the differences in the characteristics of various types of marketing context and their impact on marketing mix decisions.
- We have compared and contrasted the marketing activities of organizations that operate and compete in different contextual settings.
- We have seen the effects which ICT and the move towards a virtual marketplace are having on the development and implementation of the marketing mix.
- We have seen that marketers that operate in an international and global context need to take account of this with respect to the use and application of the different marketing mix tools.
- Finally, we have seen the importance of completing the cycle of the marketing process by evaluating and controlling the effectiveness of our marketing efforts and instituting appropriate changes where necessary.

Examination preparation: previous examination question

Attempt Question 5 of the examination paper June 2004 (Appendix 4). For Specimen Answer Examination Question 5, June 2004, see Appendix 4 and www.cim.co.uk.

Further reading and bibliography

Bicke, P., Bickerton, M. and Pardesi, U. (2000) *Cybermarketing*, 2nd edition, Butterworth-Heinemann.

Brassington, F. and Pettitt, S. (2003) *Principles of Marketing*, 3rd edition, FT Prentice Hall, Chapters 22 and 23.

Chaffey, D., Mayer, L., Johnston, L. and Ellis-Chadwick, F. (2000) *Internet Marketing*, FT Prentice Hall.

Dibb, S., Simkin, L., Pride, W. and Ferrel, O.C. (2000) *Marketing Concepts and Strategies*, 4th European edition, Houghton, Mifflin, Chapters 7, 20 and 21.

Jobber, D. (2001) *Principles of Marketing*, 3rd edition, McGraw-Hill, Chapters 14, 20 and 21.

Kotler *et al.* (1999) *Principles of Marketing*, 2nd European edition.

Lancaster, G.A., Massingham, L. and Ashford, R. (2002) *Essentials of Marketing*, 4th edition, McGraw-Hill, Chapters 12 and 14.

appendix 1

guidance on examination preparation

Preparing for your examination

You are now nearing the final phase of your studies and it is time to start the hard work of exam preparation.

During your period of study you will have become used to absorbing large amounts of information. You will have tried to understand and apply aspects of knowledge that may have been very new to you, while some of the information provided may have been more familiar. You may even have undertaken many of the activities that are positioned frequently throughout your coursebook, which will have enabled you to apply your learning in practical situations. But whatever the state of your knowledge and understanding, do not allow yourself to fall into the trap of thinking that you know enough, that you understand enough, or even worse, that you can just take it as it comes on the day.

Never underestimate the pressure of the CIM examination.

The whole point of preparing this textbook for you is to ensure that you never take the examination for granted, and that you do not go to the exam unprepared for what might come your way for 3 hours at a time.

One thing is for sure: there is no quick fix, no easy route, no waving a magic wand and finding you know it all.

Whether you have studied alone, in a CIM study centre, or through distance learning, you now need to ensure that this final phase of your learning process is tightly managed, highly structured and objective.

As a candidate in the examination, your role will be to convince the Senior Examiner for this subject that you have credibility. You need to demonstrate to the examiner that you can be trusted to undertake a range of challenges in the context of marketing and that you are able to capitalize on opportunities and manage your way through threats.

You should prove to the Senior Examiner that you are able to apply knowledge, make decisions, respond to situations and solve problems.

Very shortly we are going to look at a range of revision and exam preparation techniques, and at time-management issues, and encourage you towards developing and implementing your own revision plan, but before that, let's look at the role of the Senior Examiner.

A bit about the Senior Examiners!

You might be quite shocked to read this, but while it might appear that the examiners are 'relentless question masters' they actually want you to be able to answer the questions and pass the exams! In fact, they would derive no satisfaction or benefits from failing candidates; quite the contrary, they develop the syllabus and exam papers in order that you can learn and then apply that learning effectively so as to pass your examinations. Many of the examiners have said in the past that it is indeed psychologically more difficult to fail students than pass them.

Many of the hints and tips you find within this appendix have been suggested by the Senior Examiners and authors of the coursebook series. Therefore, you should consider them carefully and resolve to undertake as many of the elements suggested as possible.

The Chartered Institute of Marketing (CIM) has a range of processes and systems in place within the Examinations Division to ensure that fairness and consistency prevail across the team of examiners, and that the academic and vocational standards that are set and defined are indeed maintained. In doing this, CIM ensures that those who gain the Professional Certificate in Marketing, Professional Diploma in Marketing and the Professional Postgraduate Diploma in Marketing are worthy of the qualification and perceived as such in the view of employers, actual and potential.

Part of what you will need to do within the examination is be 'examiner friendly' – that means you have to make sure they get what they ask for. This will make life easier for you and for them.

Hints and tips for 'examiner friendly' actions are as follows:

o   Show them that you understand the basis of the question, by answering *precisely* the question asked, and not including just about everything you can remember about the subject area.
o   Read their needs – how many points is the question asking you to address?
o   Respond to the question appropriately. Is the question asking you to take on a role? If so, take on the role and answer the question in respect of the role. For example, you could be positioned as follows:
o   'You are working as a Marketing Assistant at Nike UK' or 'You are a Marketing Manager for an Engineering Company' or 'As Marketing Manager write a report to the Managing Partner'.

These examples of role-playing requirements are taken from questions in past papers:

o   Deliver the answer in the format requested. If the examiner asks for a memo, then provide a memo; likewise, if the examiner asks for a report, then write a report. If you do not do this, in some instances, you will fail to gain the necessary marks required to pass.
o   Take a business-like approach to your answers. This enhances your credibility. Badly ordered work, untidy work, lack of structure, headings and sub-headings can be off-putting. This would be unacceptable in the work situation, likewise it will be unacceptable in the eyes of the Senior Examiners and their marking teams.
o   Ensure the examiner has something to mark: give them substance, relevance, definitions, illustration and demonstration of your knowledge and understanding of the subject area.
o   See the examiner as your potential employer or ultimate consumer/customer. The whole purpose and culture of marketing is about meeting customers' needs. Try this approach – it works wonders.

○ Provide a strong sense of enthusiasm and professionalism in your answers; support it with relevant up-to-date examples and apply them where appropriate.

○ Try to do something that will make your exam paper a little bit different – make it stand out in the crowd.

All of these points might seem quite logical to you, but often in the panic of the examination they 'go out of the window'. Therefore, it is beneficial to remind ourselves of the importance of the examiner. He or she is the 'ultimate customer' – and we all know customers hate to be disappointed.

As we move on, some of these points will be revisited and developed further.

About the examination

In all examinations, with the exception of Marketing in Practice at Certificate level and Analysis and Decision at the postgraduate Diploma level, the paper is divided into two parts:

○ Part A – Mini-case study = 40 per cent of the marks
○ Part B – Option choice questions (choice of three questions from seven) = 60 per cent of the marks.

Let's look at the basis of each element.

Part A: The mini-case study

This is based on a mini-case or scenario with one question, possibly sub-divided into between two and four points, but totalling 40 per cent of marks overall.

In essence, you, the candidate, are placed in a problem-solving role through the medium of a short scenario. On occasions, the scenario may consist of an article from a journal in relation to a well-known organization: for example, in the past Interflora, EasyJet and Philips, among others, have been used as the basis of the mini-case.

Alternatively, it will be based upon a fictional company, and the examiner will have prepared it in order that the right balance of knowledge, understanding, application and skills is used.

Approaches to the mini-case study

When undertaking the mini-case study there are a number of key areas you should consider.

Structure/content

The mini-case that you will be presented with will vary slightly from paper to paper and, of course, from one examination to the other. Normally, the scenario presented will be 205–400-words long and will centre on a particular organization and its problems or may even relate to a specific industry.

The length of the mini-case study means that usually only a brief outline is provided of the situation, the organization and its marketing problems, and you must therefore learn to cope with analysing information and preparing your answer on the basis of a very limited amount of detail.

299

Time management

There are many differing views on time management and the approaches you can take to manage your time within the examination. You must find an approach to suit your way of working, but always remember, whatever you do, you must ensure that you allow enough time to complete the examination. Unfinished exams mean lost marks. A typical example of managing time is as follows.

Your paper is designed to assess you over a 3-hour period. With 40 per cent of the marks being allocated to the mini-case, it means that you should dedicate somewhere around 75 minutes of your time to both read and write up the answer on this mini-case. Some students, however, will prefer to allocate nearly half of their time (90 minutes) on the mini-case, so that they can read and fully absorb the case and answer the questions in the context of it. This is also acceptable as long as you ensure that you work extremely 'SMART' for the remaining time in order to finish the examination.

Do not forget that while there is only one question within the mini-case, it can have a number of components. You must answer all the components in that question, which is where the balance of time comes into play.

Knowledge/skills tested

Throughout all the CIM papers, your knowledge, skills and ability to apply those skills will be tested. However, the mini-cases are used particularly to test application, that is your ability to take your knowledge and apply it in a structured way to a given scenario. The examiners will be looking at your decision-making ability, your analytical and communication skills and, depending on the level, your ability as a manager to solve particular marketing problems.

When the examiner is marking your paper, he or she will be looking to see how you differentiate yourself, looking at your own individual 'unique selling points'. The examiner will also want to see if you can personally apply the knowledge or whether you are only able to repeat the textbook materials.

Format of answers

On many occasions, and within all examinations, you will most likely be given a particular communication method to use. If this is the case, you must ensure that you adhere to the requirements of the examiner. This is all part of meeting customer needs.

The likely communication tools you will be expected to use are as follows:

- ○ Memorandum
- ○ Memorandum/report
- ○ Report
- ○ Briefing notes
- ○ Presentation
- ○ Press release
- ○ Advertisement
- ○ Plan.

Make sure that you familiarize yourself with these particular communication tools and practise using them to ensure that, on the day, you will be able to respond confidently to the communication requests of the examiner.

By the same token, while communication methods are important, so is meeting the specific requirements of the question. This means you must understand what is meant by the precise instruction given. *Note the following terms carefully*:

- o *Identify* – Select key issues, point out key learning points, establish clearly what the examiner expects you to identify.
- o *Illustrate* – The examiner expects you to provide examples, scenarios and key concepts that illustrate your learning.
- o *Compare and contrast* – Look at the range of similarities between the two situations, contexts or even organizations. Then compare them, that is ascertain and list how activities, features and so on agree or disagree. Contrasting means highlighting the differences between the two.
- o *Discuss* – Questions that have 'discuss' in them offer a tremendous opportunity for you to debate, argue, justify your approach or understanding of the subject area – *caution*, it is not an opportunity to waffle.
- o *Briefly explain* – This means being succinct, structured and concise in your explanation, within the answer. Make your points clear, transparent and relevant.
- o *State* – Present in a clear, brief format.
- o *Interpret* – Expound the meaning of, make clear and explicit what it is you see and understand within the data provided.
- o *Outline* – Provide the examiner with the main concepts and features being asked for and avoid minor technical details. Structure will be critical here, or else you could find it difficult to contain your answer.
- o *Relate* – Show how different aspects of the syllabus connect together.
- o *Evaluate* – Review and reflect upon an area of the syllabus, a particular practice, an article and so on, and consider its overall worth in respect of its use as a tool or a model and its overall effectiveness in the role it plays.

Source: Worsam, Mike (1989) *How to Pass Marketing*, Croner.

Your approach to mini-cases

There is no one right way to approach and tackle a mini-case study, indeed it will be down to each individual to use their own creativity in tackling the tasks presented. You will have to use your initiative and discretion about how best to approach the mini-case. Having said this, however, there are some basic steps you can take.

- o Ensure that you read through the case study at least twice before making any judgements, starting to analyse the information provided, or indeed writing the answers.
- o On the third occasion read through the mini-case and, using a highlighter, start marking the essential and relevant information critical to the content and context. Then turn your attention to the question again, this time reading slowly and carefully to assess what it is you are expected to do. Note any instructions that the examiner gives you, and then start to plan how you might answer the question. Whatever the question, ensure the answer has a structure: a beginning, a structured central part of the answer and, finally, always a conclusion.
- o Keep the context of the question continually in mind: that is, the specifics of the case and the role which you might be performing.
- o Because there is limited material available, you will sometimes need to make assumptions. Don't be afraid to do this, it will show initiative on your part. Assumptions are an important part of dealing with case studies and can help you to be quite creative with your answer. However, do explain the basis of your assumptions within your answer so that the examiner understands the nature of them, and why you have arrived at your particular outcome. *Always ensure that your assumptions are realistic*.

    o Only now are you approaching the stage where it is time to start writing your answer to the question, tackling the problems, making decisions and recommendations on the case scenario set before you. As mentioned previously, your points will often be best set out in a report or memo type format, particularly if the examiner does not specify a communication method.

    o Ensure that your writing is succinct, avoid waffle and respond directly to the questions asked.

Part B: Option choice questions

At the Certificate level, Part B is comprised of six or seven more traditional questions, each worth 20 per cent. You will be expected to choose three of those questions, to make up the remaining 60 per cent of available marks.

Realistically, the same principles apply for these questions as in the case study. Communication formats, reading through the questions, structure, role-play, context and so on – everything is the same.

Part B will cover a number of broader issues from within the syllabus and will be taken from any element of it. The examiner makes the choice, and no prior direction is given to students or tutors on what that might be.

As regards time management in this area, if you used about 75 minutes for the mini-case you should have around 105 minutes left. This provides you with around 30 minutes to plan and write a question and 5 minutes per question to review and revise your answers. Keep practising – use a cooker timer, alarm clock or mobile phone alarm as your timer and work hard at answering questions within the time frame given.

Specimen examination papers and answers

To help you prepare and understand the nature of the paper, go to www.cim.co.uk/learning-zone to access Specimen Answers and Senior Examiner's advice for these exam questions. During your study, the author of your coursebook may have on occasions asked you to refer to these papers and answer the questions. You should undertake these exercises and utilize every opportunity to practise meeting examination requirements.

The specimen answers are vital learning tools. They are not always perfect, as they are answers written by students and annotated by the Senior Examiners, but they will give you a good indication of the approaches you could take, and the examiners' annotations suggest how these answers might be improved. Please use them.

Other sources of information to support your learning are available through www.cim.co.uk/learningzone. This gives you access to links to many useful case studies and a range of contemporary resources related to the syllabus and study areas, and will also be very useful to you when you are revising.

Key elements of preparation

There are three important elements to talk about when preparing for your examination:

1. Learning
2. Memory
3. Revision.

Let's look at each point in turn.

Learning

Quite often students find it difficult to learn properly. You can passively read books, look at some of the materials, perhaps revise a little, and regurgitate it all in the examination. In the main, however, this is rather an unsatisfactory method of learning. It is meaningless, shallow and ultimately of little use in practice.

For learning to be truly effective it must be active and applied. You must involve yourself in the learning process by thinking about what you have read, testing it against your experience by reflecting on how you use particular aspects of marketing, and how you could perhaps improve your own performance by implementing particular aspects of your learning into your everyday life. You should adopt the old adage of 'learning by doing'. If you do, you will find that passive learning has no place in your study life.

Below are some suggestions that have been prepared to assist you with the learning pathway throughout your revision:

- o Always make your own notes, in words you understand, and ensure that you combine all the sources of information and activities within them.
- o Always try to relate your learning back to your own organization.
- o Make sure you define key terms concisely, wherever possible.
- o Do not try to memorize your ideas, but work on the basis of understanding and, most important, applying them.
- o Think about the relevant and topical questions that might be set – use the questions and answers in your coursebooks to identify typical questions that might be asked in the future.
- o Attempt all of the questions within each of your coursebooks since these are vital tests of your active learning and understanding.

Memory

If you are prepared to undertake an active learning programme, then your knowledge will be considerably enhanced, as understanding and application of knowledge does tend to stay in your 'long-term' memory. It is likely that passive learning will only stay in your 'short-term' memory.

Do not try to memorize in parrot fashion; it is not helpful and, even more important, examiners are experienced in identifying various memorizing techniques and therefore will spot them as such.

Having said this, it is quite useful to memorize various acronyms such as SWOT, PEST, PESTLE, STEEPLE, or indeed various models such as Ansoff, GE Matrix, Shell Directional and so on, as in some of the questions you may be required to use illustrations of these to assist your answer.

Revision

The third and final stage to consider is 'revision', which is what we will concentrate on in detail below. Here just a few key tips are offered.

Revision should be an ongoing process rather than a panic measure that you decide to undertake just before the examination. You should be preparing notes *throughout* your course, with the view to using them as part of your revision process. Therefore, ensure that your notes are sufficiently comprehensive that you can reuse them successfully.

For each concept you learn about, you should identify, through your reading and your own personal experience, at least two or three examples that you could use; this then gives you some scope to broaden your perspective during the examination. It will, of course, help you gain some points for initiative with the examiners.

Knowledge is not something you will gain overnight – as we saw earlier, it is not a quick fix; it involves a process of learning that enables you to lay solid foundations upon which to build your long-term understanding and application. This will benefit you significantly in the future, not just in the examination.

In essence, you should ensure that you do the following in the period before the real intensive revision process begins:

- o Keep your study file well organized, updated and full of newspaper and journal cuttings that may help you formulate examples in your mind for use during the examination.
- o Practise defining key terms and acronyms from memory.
- o Prepare topic outlines and essay answer plans.
- o When you start your intensive revision, ensure it is planned and structured in the way described below. And then finally, read your concentrated notes the night before the examination.

Revision planning

You are now on a critical path – although hopefully not too critical at this time – with somewhere in the region of between 4 and 6 weeks to go to the examination. The following hints and tips will help you plan out your revision study:

- o You will, as already explained, need to be very organized. Therefore, before doing anything else, put your files, examples, reading material and so on in good order, so that you are able to work with them in the future and, of course, make sense of them.
- o Ensure that you have a quiet area within which to work. It is very easy to get distracted when preparing for an examination.
- o Take out your file along with your syllabus and make a list of key topic areas that you have studied and which you now need to revise. You could use the basis of this book to do that, by taking each unit a step at a time.
- o Plan the use of your time carefully. Ideally, you should start your revision at least 6 weeks prior to the exam, so therefore work out how many spare hours you could give to the revision process and then start to allocate time in your diary, and do not double-book with anything else.
- o Give up your social life for a short period of time. As the saying goes 'no pain no gain'.

○ Looking at each of the subject areas in turn, identify which are your strengths and which are your weaknesses. Which areas have you grasped and understood, and which are the areas that you have really struggled with? Split your page in two and make a list on each side. For example:

Planning and control	
Strengths	**Weaknesses**
Audit – PEST, SWOT models	Ratio analysis
Portfolio analysis	Market sensing
	Productivity analysis
	Trend extrapolation
	Forecasting

○ Break down your list again and divide the points of weakness giving priority in the first instance to your weakest areas and even prioritizing them by giving them a number. This will enable you to master the more difficult areas. Upto 60 per cent of your remaining revision time should be given over to that, as you may find you have to undertake a range of additional reading and also perhaps seeking tutor support, if you are studying at a CIM Accredited Study Centre.
○ The rest of the time should be spent reinforcing your knowledge and understanding of the stronger areas, spending time testing yourself on how much you really know.
○ Should you be taking two examinations or more at any one time, then the breakdown and managing of your time will be critical.
○ Taking a subject at a time, work through your notes and start breaking them down into sub-sections of learning, and ultimately into key learning points, items that you can refer to time and time again, that are meaningful and that your mind will absorb. You yourself will know how best you remember the key points. Some people try to develop acronyms, flowcharts or matrices, mind maps, fishbone diagrams and so on, or various connection diagrams that help them recall certain aspects of models. You could also develop processes that enable you to remember approaches to various options. (But do remember what we said earlier about regurgitating stuff, parrot fashion.)

Figure A1.1 is just a brief example of how you could use a 'bomb-burst' diagram (which, in this case, highlights the uses of advertising) as a very helpful approach to memorizing key elements of learning.

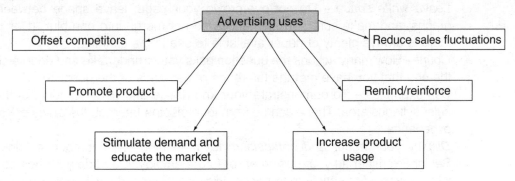

Figure A1.1 Use of a diagram to summarize key components of a concept
Source: Adapted from Dibb, Simkin, Pride and Ferrell (2001), *Marketing Concepts and Strategies*, 4th edition, Houghton, Mifflin

   o Eventually you should reduce your key learning to bullet points. For example: imagine you were looking at the concept of Time Management – you could eventually reduce your key learning to a bullet list containing the following points in relation to 'Effective Prioritization':

     – Organize
     – Take time
     – Delegate
     – Review.

   o Each of these headings would then remind you of the elements you need to discuss associated with the subject area.

   o Avoid getting involved in reading too many textbooks at this stage, as you may start to find that you are getting confused overall.

   o Look at examination questions in previous papers, and start to observe closely the various roles and tasks they expect you to undertake, and importantly, the context in which they are set.

   o *Use the specimen exam papers and specimen answers* to support your learning and see how you could actually improve upon them.

   o Without exception, find an associated examination question for the areas that you have studied and revised, and undertake it (more than once, if necessary).

   o Without referring to notes or books, try to draft an answer plan with the key concepts, knowledge, models and information that are needed to successfully complete the answer. Then refer to the specimen answer to see how close you are to the actual outline presented. Planning your answer, and ensuring that key components are included, and that the question has a meaningful structure, is one of the most beneficial activities that you can undertake.

   o Now write the answer out in full, time constrained and written by hand, not with the use of IT. (At this stage, you are still expected to be the scribe for the examination and present handwritten work. Many of us find this increasingly difficult as we spend more and more time using our computers to present information. Do your best to be neat. Difficult handwriting is often off-putting to the examiner.)

   o When writing answers as part of your revision process, be sure to practise the following essential examination techniques:

     – *Identify and use the communication method* – Requested by the examiner.
     – *Always have three key parts to the answer* – An introduction, middle section, that develops your answer in full, and a conclusion. Where appropriate, ensure that you have an introduction, main section, summary/conclusion and, if requested or helpful, recommendations.
     – *Always answer the question in the context or role set.*
     – *Always comply with the nature and terms of the question.*
     – *Leave white space* – Do not overcrowd your page; leave space between paragraphs, and make sure your sentences do not merge into one blur. (Don't worry, there is always plenty of paper available to use in the examination.)
     – *Count* – How many actions the question asks you to undertake and double-check at the end that you have met the full range of demands of the question.
     – *Use examples* – To demonstrate your knowledge and understanding of the particular syllabus area. These can be from journals, the Internet, the press or your own experience.
     – *Display your vigour and enthusiasm for marketing* – Remember to think of the Senior Examiner as your customer, or future employer, and do your best to deliver what is wanted to satisfy their needs. Impress them and show them how you are a 'cut above the rest'.

Review all your practice answers critically with the above points in mind.

Practical actions

The critical path is becoming even more critical now as the examination looms. The following are vital points:

- o Have you registered with CIM?
- o Do you know where you are taking your examination? CIM should let you know approximately 1 month in advance.
- o Do you know where your examination centre is? If not, find out, take a drive, time it – whatever you do don't be late!
- o Make sure you have all the tools of the examination ready. A dictionary, calculator, pens, pencils, ruler and so on. Try not to use multiple shades of pens, but at the same time make your work look professional. *Avoid using red and green as these are the colours that will be used for marking.*

Summary

Above all, you must remember that you personally have invested a tremendous amount of time, effort and money in studying for this programme and it is therefore imperative that you consider the suggestions given here as they will help to maximize your return on your investment.

Many of the hints and tips offered here are generic and will work across most of the CIM courses. We have tried to select those that will help you most in taking a sensible, planned approach to your study and revision.

The key to your success is being prepared to put in the time and effort required, planning your revision, and equally important, planning and answering your questions in a way that will ensure that you pass your examination on the day.

The advice offered here aims to guide you from a practical perspective. Guidance on syllabus content and developments associated with your learning will become clear to you as you work through this coursebook. The authors of each coursebook have given subject-specific guidance on the approach to the examination and on how to ensure that you meet the content requirements of the kind of question you will face. These considerations are in addition to the structuring issues we have been discussing throughout this appendix.

Each of the authors and Senior Examiners will guide you on their preferred approach to questions and answers as they go. Therefore, where you are presented with an opportunity to be involved in some activity or undertake an examination question either during or at the end of your study units, do take it. It not only prepares you for the examination, but helps you learn in the applied way we discussed above.

Here, then, is a last reminder:

- o Ensure you make the most of your learning process throughout.
- o Keep structured and orderly notes from which to revise.
- o Plan your revision – don't let it just happen.
- o Provide examples to enhance your answers.
- o Practise your writing skills in order that you present your work well and your writing is readable.
- o Take as many opportunities to test your knowledge and measure your progress as possible.

- ○ Plan and structure your answers.
- ○ Always do as the question asks you, especially with regard to context and communication method.
- ○ *Do not leave it until the last minute!*

The writers would like to take this opportunity to wish you every success in your endeavours to study, to revise and to pass your examinations.

Karen Beamish
Academic Development Advisor

appendix 2
assignment-based assessment

Introduction: The basis to the assignments and the integrative project

Within the CIM qualifications at both Professional Certificate and Professional Diploma levels there are several assessment options available. These are detailed in the outline of modules below. The purpose of an assignment is to provide another format to complete each module for students who want to apply the syllabus concepts from a module to their own or a selected organization. For either qualification, there are three modules providing assessment via an assignment and one module assessed via an integrative work-based project. The module assessed via the integrative project is the summative module for each qualification.

	Entry modules	Research & analysis	Planning	Implementation	Management of Marketing
Professional Post-Graduate Diploma in Marketing	Entry module	Analysis & Evaluation	Strategic Marketing Decisions	Managing Marketing Performance	Strategic Marketing in Practice
Professional Diploma in Marketing	Entry module	Marketing Research & Information	Marketing Planning	Marketing Communications	Marketing Management in Practice
Professional Certificate in Marketing		Marketing Environment	Marketing Fundamentals	Customer Communications	Marketing in Practice
Introductory Certificate		Supporting marketing processes (research & analysis, planning and implementation)			

Outline of CIM 'standard' syllabus, (The Chartered Institute of Marketing, September 2003)

The use of assignments does not mean that this route is easier than an examination. Both formats are carefully evaluated to ensure that a grade B in the assessment/integrative project route is the same as a grade B in an examination. However, the use of assignments does allow

309

a student to complete the assessment for a module over a longer period of time than a 3-hour examination. This will inevitably mean work being undertaken over the time span of a module. For those used to cramming for exams writing an assignment over several weeks which comprises a total of four separate questions will be a very different approach.

Each module within the qualification contains a different assignment written specifically for the module. These are designed to test understanding and provide the opportunity for you to demonstrate your abilities through the application of theory to practice. The format and structure of each module's assignment is identical, although the questions asked will differ and the exact type of assignment varies. The questions within an assignment will relate directly to the syllabus for that particular module, thereby giving the opportunity to demonstrate understanding and application.

The assignment structure

The assignment for each module is broken down into a range of questions. These consist of a core question, a selection of optional questions plus a reflective statement. The core question will always relate to the main aspects of each module's syllabus. Coupled with this are a range of four optional questions which will each draw from a different part of the syllabus. Students are requested to select two optional questions from the available four. In addition, a reflective statement requires a student to evaluate their learning from the module. When put together these form the assessment for the entire module. The overall pass mark for the module is the same as through an examination route, which is set at 50 per cent. In addition, the grade band structure is also identical to that of an examination.

Core question

This is the longest and therefore most important section of your assignment. Covering the major components of the syllabus, the core question is designed to provide a challenging assignment which not only tests the theoretical element but also permits application to a selected organization or situation. The rubric on the front of the assignment will give clear guidance in respect of word limits, therefore pay close attention to them and the overall requirements of CIM in relation to the use of appendices. However, the appendices should be kept to a minimum. Advice here is that they should be no longer than five pages of additional pertinent information.

Optional questions

There are a total of four questions provided for Professional Certificate and Professional Diploma levels of the syllabus from which a student is asked to select two. Each answer is expected to provide a challenge although the actual task required varies. The rubric on the front of the assignment will give clear guidance in respect of word limits, therefore pay close attention to them and the overall requirements of CIM in relation to the use of appendices.

These are designed to test areas of the syllabus not covered by the core question. As such, it is possible to base all of your questions on the same organization although there is significant benefit in using more than one organization as a basis for your assignment. Some of the questions specifically require a different organization to be selected from the one used for the core question. This occurs only where the questions are requiring similar areas to be investigated and will be specified clearly in the question itself.

Within the assignment there are several types of questions that may be asked, including:

o *A report* – The question requires a formal report to be completed, detailing an answer to the specific question set. This will often be reporting on a specific issue to an individual.

o *A briefing paper or notes* – Preparing a briefing paper or a series of notes which may be used for a presentation.

o *A presentation* – You may be required either to prepare the presentation only or to deliver the presentation in addition to its preparation. The audience for the presentation should be considered carefully and ICT used where possible.

o *A discussion paper* – The question requires an academic discussion paper to be prepared. You should show a range of sources and concepts within the paper. You may also be required to present the discussion paper as part of a question.

o *A project plan or action plan* – Some questions ask for planning techniques to be demonstrated. As such, the plan must be for the timescale given and costs shown where applicable. The use of ICT is recommended here in order to create the plan diagrammatically.

o *Planning a research project* – While market research may be required, questions have often asked for simply a research plan in a given situation. This would normally include timescales, the type(s) of research to be gathered, sampling, planned data collection and analysis.

o *Conducting research* – Following on from a research plan, a question can require student(s) to undertake a research gathering exercise. A research question can be either an individual or a group activity depending upon the question. This will usually result in a report of the findings of the exercise plus any recommendations arising from your findings.

o *Gathering of information and reporting* – Within many questions information will need gathering. The request for information can form part or all of a question. This may be a background to the organization, the activities contained in the question or external market and environmental information. It is advisable to detail the types of information utilized, their sources and report on any findings. Such a question will often ask for recommendations for the organization – these should be drawn from the data and not simply personal opinion.

o *An advisory document* – A question here will require students to evaluate a situation and present advice and recommendations drawn from findings and theory. Again, any advice should be backed up with evidence and not a personal perspective only.

o *An exercise, either planning and/or delivering the exercise* – At both Professional Certificate and Professional Diploma levels, exercises are offered as optional questions. These provide students with the opportunity to devise an exercise and may also require the delivery of this exercise. Such an activity should be evidenced where possible.

o *A role-play with associated documentation* – Several questions have asked students to undertake role-plays in exercises such as team-building. These are usually videoed and documentation demonstrating the objectives of the exercise provided.

Each of these questions related directly towards specific issues to be investigated, evaluated and answered. In addition, some of the questions asked present situations to be considered. These provide opportunities for specific answers relating directly to the question asked.

In order to aid students completing the assignment, each question is provided with an outline of marking guidance. This relates to the different categories by which each question is marked. The marker of your assignment will be provided with a detailed marking scheme constructed around the same marking guidance provided to students.

For both core and optional questions, it is important to use referencing where sources have been utilized. This has been a weakness in the past and continues to be an issue. There have been cases of plagiarism identified during marking and moderation, together with a distinct lack

311

of references and bibliography. It is highly recommended that a bibliography be included with each question and sources are cited within the text itself. The type of referencing method used is not important, only that sources are referred to.

The reflective statement

This is the final aspect to each module assignment. The purpose of the reflective statement is for each student to consider how the module has influenced him or her as an individual and reflect upon their practice. A shorter piece of work than for other aspects at 500 words Professional Certificate or 750 words Professional Diploma, it is also more personal in that your answer will often depend upon how you as an individual have applied the learning from the module to your work and other aspects.

A good reflective statement will comprise a number of aspects, including:

o   Details of the theoretical aspects that you found beneficial within the module, and their reasons. If you have found particular resources beneficial state this and the reason.
o   How these concepts have affected you as a practitioner with examples of application of concepts from the module to your work and/or other activities.
o   How you intend to progress your learning further after completing the module assessment.

When looking at the reflective statement your tutor or an assessor will try to award marks for your demonstration of understanding through the module together with how you have applied the theoretical concepts to practice. They are looking for evidence of learning and application over time, rather than a student simply completing the question because they have a deadline looming. The result of this marking tends to be that students who begin to apply the module concepts early often achieve higher marks overall.

Integrative project structure

The integrative project is designed to provide an in-company approach to assessment rather than having specified assignments. Utilized within the summative module element of each level's syllabus, this offers a student the chance to produce a piece of work which tackles a specific issue. The integrative project can only be completed after undertaking other modules as it will rely on information in each of these as guidance. The integrative project is approximately 5000 words in length and was introduced from September 2002 at Professional Certificate level. It was introduced from September 2003 at Professional Diploma level with the commencement of the new syllabus. The integrative project is marked by CIM assessors and not your own tutors.

The professional certificate level assignments: Marketing fundamentals

Divided into four elements, Marketing Fundamentals forms the basis of many other aspects within the Professional Certificate level. The assignment for the module draws much of its content from the marketing mix element – Element 3 (the marketing mix and related tools). For each of the four elements, a sample question is given together with an evaluation of the type of answer that would be expected at this level.

Element 1: The development of marketing and market orientation

Within the first element of the module, the aspects of the element cover the role of marketing within an organization and a marketing orientation. Therefore, the element also has to consider the consequences of marketing actions on wider society. As such, a question covering this element would include:

Your manager has asked you to prepare a briefing paper evaluating the marketing orientation of your organization in comparison with THREE key competitors. This is to form part of an overall presentation he/she will be making to senior management. Your paper should incorporate recommendations relevant to the organization.

In order to answer this question it will be necessary to identify a range of competitors and select the three most appropriate for the exercise. Other aspects that could be undertaken here include research into people's perspectives of the marketing orientation of the organization and an evaluation of a diverse set of competitors. A typical answer would include:

o The reasons for selection of and a background to the organization chosen as a basis for the question.
o An evaluation of the overall market(s) which the organization operates in, together with identifying a range of competitors.
o These competitors should be briefly evaluated, with three key competitors selected. This is best done using a table for layout. The reasons for selecting these competitors would be given.
o Each of these competitors would then be considered in more detail, providing an interpretation of their marketing orientation. Reasons for the findings should be given and sources of evidence where available.
o To provide a comparison, information needs to be gathered to provide a picture of the selected organization's marketing orientation. This may be in the form of primary research, drawn from existing data or a range of other methods. The organization's orientation should then be compared with each of the three key competitors identified.
o Finally, recommendations should be made on the basis of information drawn from the findings. These should not be of personal opinion but based upon the evidence found.
o As a briefing paper was requested, this is the format which is to be followed.

Element 2: Marketing planning and budgeting

The second element of the module draws on aspects of marketing planning. This covers a wide range of aspects although questions will usually centre on planning itself. In order to create an effective answer to a marketing planning question, a wide range of aspects will be incorporated, as in the example question:

You have been working in the Marketing Department for nearly two years and your Manager has asked you to help in the induction programme for a newly recruited graduate. Your Manager has asked you to put together a briefing paper to be used as the basis of a training section within the induction which details the stages of the marketing planning process and demonstrates how the marketing plan is an integral part of the corporate plan.

This question could seem simple at first glance. However, the phrase 'details the stages of the marketing planning process' requires an answer which reflects all aspects of the element. A typical answer will involve:

- o Selection of an organization on which to base the assignment. This provides a foundation upon which the discussion of marketing planning can be built.
- o The next stage is to identify the marketing planning process and the stages in a marketing plan. Use of marketing planning models would assist an answer here, shown diagrammatically if possible. This is also the appropriate point to cover the links between the marketing plan and corporate plan. The relationship and interdependency between each needs to be shown. Examples of your selected organization's marketing planning process would illustrate this point.
- o Within the question the aspects of a marketing plan should be considered. This includes macro- and micro-environmental analysis, marketing audits and marketing research. In addition to this, aspects of segmentation and how this is applied in your chosen organization would be beneficial.
- o A key aspect of the answer will be the issue of a budget. The process of setting and managing budgets needs to be identified, illustrated through the use of a budget in your selected organization.
- o The briefing paper is for a new recruit. Therefore this context needs to be remembered in any answer.

Element 3: The marketing mix and related tools

This element is the most detailed and comprehensive within Marketing Fundamentals and therefore represents the highest percentage of the module's syllabus. Questions drawing on this element as a basis will relate to both the standard and extended marketing mix together with the use of ICT to support marketing activities.

Your organization has recently taken over the running of a public-sector service and as part of the integration process your Manager has asked you to help bring their two marketing assistants up to speed. It has become obvious that their knowledge of some of the more commonly used marketing models is a little patchy. Therefore you are to prepare a presentation which covers the use of the extended marketing mix within your organization, together with supporting tools enabling marketing mix activities to be more effective.

This assignment requires a presentation suitable for the audience given here. In addition, the element covers a wide range of aspects. There have been a number of devolved public services now delivered by the private sector and therefore identifying a suitable example should not be a complex issue. Due to the situation given an overview will be required to provide a picture of the marketing mix as a concept and in action within the organization.

- o The first aspect of an answer to the question would be to set the scene, giving information about the organization and its activities. This needs to include the details of the ex-public service.
- o The next stage of the assignment would be to move into the presentation. This should be prepared using ICT with a handout provided and a disk supplied with the answer.
- o The marketing mix should be covered. This needs to include the extended marketing mix. Reference to the marketing mix in not-for-profit organizations (part of Element 4: Marketing in context) would help draw the new employees into the sphere of activities through providing a reference point.

- Examples of the marketing mix in action within the organization should also be part of the presentation, in addition to the benefits of using ICT within the organization to assist marketing mix activities.
- The presentation should be concluded with an effective summary and reflective activity. This could include any of the following: a quiz, a question and answer session, a memory test, the setting of future objectives plus a range of other aspects.

Element 4: Marketing in context

The final element of the Marketing Fundamentals module refers to the different contexts and applications of the marketing subject. Traversing across for-profit and not-for-profit, business-to-consumer and b2b, on-line and off-line sectors, marketing has different applications of the same concepts in order to create the right mix of activities. Therefore the questions relating to this section will do the same.

> Your Managing Director has donated some 'man-hours' to a local charity to enable them to become more market orientated. You have been assigned the task of spending an afternoon with a representative of a charity of your choice to explain the basic marketing concepts and to demonstrate the use of some of the more common marketing tools. The charity is considering raising funds using both on-line and off-line methods, rather than the street collection boxes they currently use. Part of your time is to be spent in the production of a guide covering the use of marketing in different contexts.

This would be both a challenging and an interesting question to answer. Selecting a charity of your choice, the task here is to evaluate their current marketing activity and present recommendations covering both marketing in a range of contexts and situations plus an evaluation of marketing using on-line methods. A typical answer would need to include the following:

- A background, the charity and reasons for selection would be beneficial. This could be included in the guide itself as an introduction, thereby creating the answer as a guide.
- An evaluation of the marketing mix and its application to the not-for-profit sector should be covered. Being a charitable organization, this should cover the extended marketing mix. The marketing mix concept then needs to be related to the charity. A pictorial representation would be beneficial here.
- Consideration of the differences between on-line and off-line methods need to be incorporated into the guide. In addition, terminology needs to take into consideration the audience for the guide; that is non-marketers.
- The guide should be printed and submitted as an answer to the question.

Assignment regulations

There have been a number of changes to the assignment structure compared with previous years, timed with the introduction of the new syllabi. These have been designed to provide consistency in approach for a student whether they are completing the assessment for a module by examination, assignment or integrative project. The more significant changes include:

- For the current academic year tutors at CIM centres will mark assignments. These are then moderated by CIM assessors. An integrative project is marked by CIM assessors only.
- No resubmission of assignments as per an examination. In previous years, a range of assignments were being submitted. Where a student does not achieve the 50 per cent

pass mark, they are requested to retake the assessment for the module through examination or assignment/integrative project.

o Whichever assessment route is selected is fixed rather than having the option to change at the last minute. Past history has shown that students sometimes begin on an assignment route, change to an examination at the last minute due to not meeting a deadline and then score badly in the examination. The paths to an assignment or examination are different and therefore it is unadvisable to switch, which is the reason for the change of rule.

o In the 2002–2003 academic year word limits for questions and assignments were introduced. This was introduced due to assignments being submitted which were of a wide variety of lengths. These ranged from under 2000 words to over 25 000 words. Where a student is completing four modules by assignment this would equal over 100 000 words – the equivalent of a medium-sized textbook or novel. As such, it became impossible for two assignments to be considered together. Therefore the words 'limit guidance' were introduced in order to provide equality for all students undertaking assessment by assignment.

o Two sets of assignments per year as with the examination route. With this change students are required to complete the assignment aimed at the nearest examination session. Previously, students had between 3 and 9 months to complete an assignment depending upon whether it was given out in September for a June deadline or March for the June deadline. Therefore a decision was made to follow the examination route with the intention of giving all students equal time to complete an assignment.

These summarize the key changes which have occurred due to the introduction of new syllabi with the assignment/integrative project route in order that there is parity of assessment at all levels and using all formats. Some of these changes have been significant, others minor. However, all the changes have been considered thoughtfully and with the best intentions for the student in mind.

Use of case studies

For anyone who is not working or has difficulty accessing information on their or another organization, there are a number of case studies available which allow the completion of a module using a case-based approach rather than basing it upon an organization identified by the student. These case studies are provided on a request-only basis through your accredited CIM centre and should only be used as a last resort. Using a case study as the basis for your assignment will not mean an easier approach to the assignment. However, they do provide an opportunity to undertake assignments when no other alternative exists. Each case study comes with a certain amount of information which can be used specifically for the completion of a question. Additional information may need to be assumed or researched in order to create a comprehensive assignment.

Submission of assignments/integrative project

The following information will aid both yourself, your tutor who marks your work and also the CIM assessor who will be moderating both your work and the integrative project. In addition, the flow diagram represents the process of an assignment/integrative project from start to final mark.

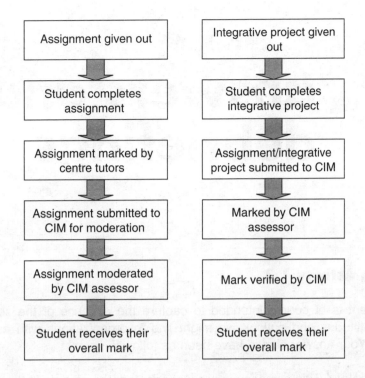

When completing and submitting assignments or the integrative project, refer to the following for guidance:

o Read through each question before starting out. Particularly with the core question there will be a considerable amount work to undertake. Choose your optional questions wisely.

o Answer the question set and use the mark guidance given regarding the marking scheme.

o Reference each question within the assignment and use a bibliography.

o Complete all documentation thoroughly. This is designed to aid both the CIM and yourself.

o Ensure that the assignment is bound as per instructions given. Currently, assignments are requested not to be submitted in plastic wallets or folders as work can become detached or lost. Following the submission, instructions provided aid both the CIM administrators and the CIM assessor who will be marking (integrative project) or moderating (assignments) your work.

o Complete the candidate declaration sheet showing that you have undertaken this work yourself. *Please note that if you wish the information contained in your assignment to remain confidential you must state this on the front of the assignment.* While CIM assessors will not use any information pertaining to your or another organization, CIM may wish to use the answer to a question as an example.

An assignment will be marked by a tutor at your CIM centre followed by moderation by a CIM assessor. The integrative project will be marked by a CIM assessor as per an examination with moderation by the CIM. To ensure objectivity by CIM assessors there exists a mark-in meeting, prior to any marking, in order that standardization can occur. The senior assessor for each subject also undertakes further verification of both examinations and assessments to ensure parity between each type of assessment.

Based on the appendix written by David C. Lane,
Former Senior Moderator (Advanced Certificate),
February 2003

appendix 3
answers and debriefings

Unit 1

Debriefing Activity 1.2

Each statement is of course intended to capture the essence of the sort of differences in managerial attitudes and outlook we might find in organizations with each of the different orientations. Your answer should have been as follows:

Company A = No. 4 This company is product oriented: the attitude is that a good product will sell itself.

Company B = No. 2 This company is sales oriented: the attitude is that aggressive hard selling is required.

Company C = No. 1 This company is marketing oriented: the attitude is that even though it is sometimes difficult, everyone in the company must try to satisfy the customer.

Company D = No. 3 The company is production oriented. The attitude is characterized by an almost exclusive focus on production efficiency and effectiveness.

Debriefing Activity 1.3

Although you may have used different words, your answers should have indicated the following:

Factor	Marketing-oriented era
Demand	Latent demand low
Average disposable income	High
General level of education	High
Mass media/access to information	Well developed/high
Supply/industry capacity	Overcapacity
Competition	Severe/global

318

Debriefing Activity 1.7

Exam hint Use the initial letters APIC to help you remember the key tasks of marketing managers:

A: Analysis – The first stage in marketing management's tasks. Customers, markets, competitors, and company strengths and weaknesses must be analysed. Examples from recruitment advertisements include 'market analysis'/'building of customer database'.

P: Planning – Includes objective setting, choice of target markets, marketing strategies and tactics. Examples from recruitment advertisements include 'develop long-range marketing plans', 'new product/service development', 'corporate identity'.

I: Implementation – Includes staffing, allocating tasks, budgeting and organizing. Examples from recruitment advertisements include 'handling hybrid staff/line role', 'leading change process'.

C: Control – Evaluating progress against objectives and targets. Correcting any deficiencies. Example from recruitment advertisement includes 'strong bottom-line orientation'.

Debriefing Question 1.1

The four consumer rights that President Kennedy referred to in his speech in 1962 were as follows:

1. The right to safety
2. The right to be informed
3. The right to choose
4. The right to be heard.

Since Kennedy's speech outlining these four basic rights, the consumer movement has gathered pace, first in America and then in Western Europe. Consumers have become increasingly critical of what are admittedly sometimes questionable practices of a minority of marketers. They are also increasingly aware of their rights, and demand that these be protected. Many of the worst excesses of marketing in years gone by are now covered by legislation that protects consumers. Above all, consumers have become much better organized and skilled in protecting themselves. In the United Kingdom, for example, in addition to the legal protection afforded to consumers, a number of consumer organizations look after and promote consumers' interests. Some of these are official, such as consumer watchdogs set up to monitor marketing activities and particularly prices in the now privatized utilities of electricity, gas and water. Others are unofficial, such as local pressure groups that will respond to what they see as any infringement of their rights by local companies. There are even specialist consumer magazines, which report on the marketing activities of companies and in particular look at how customers can get the best value. Perhaps the best example of such a magazine in the United Kingdom is *Which?*, produced and published by the Consumers' Association.

Debriefing Activity 1.10

The results of consumerism have included an increase in various acts and legislation designed to protect consumers, and an increased awareness on the part of marketers of the need to ensure that consumers' views and welfare are protected. Enlightened marketers see consumerism not as a threat but an opportunity to respond to changing customer needs and requirements. The most successful companies have been those that have responded positively to the consumer movement and have been proactive in developing marketing programmes to take account of the movement.

There are plenty of examples of how the consumer movement has in one way or another affected how products are produced and marketed, and even if they are marketed at all. For example, in the interests of health, cigarette advertising in many countries is now at least severely constrained and often banned completely. Similarly, many food products are now marketed on the basis of the fact that they are healthier than their predecessors of several years ago. Consumers are demanding and getting healthier and safer products from marketers.

Debriefing Activity 1.11

Here are some examples of products and services whose marketing has been affected by an increased interest on the part of the consumer in health and safety:

- Lower tar tobacco products
- Low fat products
- Low cholesterol products
- Exercise products
- Sun blocks
- Air bag crash protectors in cars.

Debriefing Activity 1.12

Here are just some examples of issues associated with marketing that are frequently raised as causing problems for the environment:

- Products that use/deplete scarce resources, for exmaple hardwood forests.
- Products whose manufacture, use, or disposal of pollutes rivers and so on.
- Products that endanger species.
- Products whose manufacture, use, or disposal of pollutes the atmosphere.

Debriefing Activity 1.13

Examples of products that have specifically been marketed to take account of green issues and concerns include:

- Unleaded petrol
- Fake furs
- Chlorine-free detergents
- CFC-free aerosols and refrigeration
- Biodegradable plastics
- Recyclable packaging
- Wood products made from managed forests.

Unit 2

Debriefing Activity 2.2

The accuracy of any model is only as good as the information upon which the model is based. A BCG matrix type model requires a great deal of accurate market and company information before the model can be used as a meaningful management tool. In addition to presenting strategic alternatives, a well-prepared BCG matrix is valuable because it forces objective consideration of the elements of the portfolio in relation to each other.

However, a number of criticisms can be made of the BCG matrix as a marketing management tool. In particular, that:

o The matrix is oversimplified relying as it does on two variables only – market share and market growth.
o Often it is difficult to identify the 'actual' market in which the rate of growth is measured.
o There is an assumption about profitability and market share which may not be the case for all industries.
o The exact information about the largest competitor may not be accessible.

Debriefing Activity 2.4

Since the GE matrix uses several dimensions to assess SBUs instead of only two and is based on return on investment rather than simply cash flow, it is believed that it offers a substantial improvement over the BCG approach. There are, however, limitations associated with the GE-matrix approach:

o It only offers broad strategy guidelines, with no indications as to precisely what needs to be done to achieve the strategy.
o There is no precise indication as to how to weight the various elements of market attractiveness or how to score business strengths against these.
o Evaluation and scoring are subjective, as are the points of division in the matrix into high, medium and low segments.
o The technique is much more complex than the BCG approach, and requires more extensive data gathering and processing.
o The approach does not explicitly take account of possible relationships between various SBUs or product market areas.
o There is nothing to prove that there is any relation between market attractiveness and business position, and how these are related to return on investment.

Debriefing Activity 2.5

The approach is similar to the conventional concept of the product life cycle, as it identifies the stage, specifies the characteristics of each stage, and suggests appropriate strategies for each stage. Porter has developed the notion of the industry life cycle further by linking it to the strategic position of the individual organization. This strategic position is categorized in terms of whether the individual organization is a leader or a follower.

Debriefing Activity 2.6

Lack of empirical evidence to support the underpinning ideas is the main criticism, coupled with its very simple approach to strategy selection. There is little doubt that industries do pass through different stages and that individual companies in these industries do have different competitive positions. However, this model suggests that analysing just these two factors enables a correct strategy to be identified and selected, which is of course incorrect, as strategic decisions are much more complex than this model would imply.

Debriefing Activity 2.7

Like the BCG approach, it assumes that the same set of factors is universally applicable for assessing the prospects of any product or business. Relevant factors and their relative importance will vary according to both the firm's products and the individual characteristics of each company. In addition, like the GE portfolio, the matrix does not provide any guidelines on how to implement the strategies suggested in each cell of the matrix.

Debriefing Activity 2.9

The following is a brief explanation of Porter's three core strategies and their implications:

1. *Cost leadership* – This is a strategy based on having the lowest costs in the industry. It therefore requires the company to pursue ways of reducing cost, such as economies of scale, efficiencies in design and production and so on. Essentially it is not a marketing strategy as such, more a financial one. The problem with this approach is that it is not market/customer oriented and can leave a company vulnerable to its more marketing-oriented competitors.
2. *Differentiation* – This strategy is based on offering the market something distinct and different from competitors. For example, the differentiation may be based on, say, having the highest quality in the industry, or perhaps the speediest delivery. This is a more marketing-oriented approach than cost leadership but needs to be based on differences that are valuable to customers and can be protected from competitors.
3. *Focus* – As implied by the title of this strategy, it is based on targeting specific segments of the market rather than adopting an industry-wide approach. Companies that focus can become specialists in supplying particular markets but can be vulnerable to market trends and larger competitors.

Debriefing Activity 2.10

Examples of variables used to segment consumer and b2b markets are shown below:

○ **Consumer bases**

  - Demographics, for example age, sex, race, religion
  - Socio-economic, for example income, occupation, social class
  - Geographic, for example country, region, type of housing
  - Personality and lifestyle, for example extrovert, introvert
  - Purchase occasion, for example regular, special, distress
  - User status, for example first-time, non-user, regular user
  - Usage rate, for example heavy, light, medium
  - Benefits sought, for example quality, service, economy.

   o **Business-to-business**

      – Demographic, for example industry type, end use, company size
      – Geographic, for example country, region
      – Purchasing organization, for example centralized, decentralized
      – User status, for example non-user, first-time, regular
      – Usage rate, for example heavy, light, medium
      – Benefits sought, for example delivery, quality, service, economy.

Unit 3

Debriefing Activity 3.2

Some of the advantages and disadvantages of each targeting strategy are as follows:

   o Undifferentiated targeting

      (a) Advantages, for example low cost, economies of scale, simple
      (b) Disadvantages, for example not customer oriented.

   o Differentiated targeting

      (a) Advantages, for example customer oriented, spreads risk
      (b) Disadvantages, for example potentially high cost.

   o Concentrated targeting

      (a) Advantages, for example customer oriented, specialized skills
      (b) Disadvantages, for example high risk/vulnerable to market change.

Unit 4

Debriefing Activity 4.1

Clearly, there are two different views here – customers are seeking to derive some kind of satisfaction whereas those who sell to customers seek to provide that satisfaction and in return for this require some kind of recompense. Although customers pay money for something specific and identifiable, they are in fact paying for something incorporating promotion, availability and perceived value. This has been termed a 'bundle of satisfactions', which can be tangible or intangible and Figure 4.1 explains this more fully.

Debriefing Activity 4.2

There are obvious answers here, for example fitted curtains ordered by the housewife are for privacy at night. However, curtains are also part of the furnishings of a room and in most cases they are purchased to co-ordinate with the decoration of the rest of the room. The décor of the room might then produce a feeling of 'homeliness'. The fitted curtains might come from a good quality yet expensive store, and if this is the case, the housewife might well be able to impress her friends with the purchase. There are many more possible 'bundles of satisfactions' that might be considered, depending upon the motives of the housewife.

A simple satisfaction might be in the case of the 8-year-old child who has just purchased an ice cream, which might be simply the sheer potential delight of what is to come!

The important thing to remember is that satisfactions will differ according to the buyer behaviour of the individual making the purchase. In other words, buyers' motives for purchase will be different, and this indeed is what makes marketing interesting in terms of considering the complexities of human behaviour. You should then be able to work out many and varied need satisfactions for the other examples.

Debriefing Activity 4.13

It is important to note that products can be, and often are, at different stages of their life cycles in different parts of the world. Obviously, the international marketer in particular needs to consider this in using the notion of the life-cycle stages for planning strategy. This applies to every stage of the product life cycle but if we consider, as we do here, the introductory stage, a good example of a product being at different stages in different parts of the world is the home computer or PC. In the United States, these products are well in the growth stage with regard to diffusion in the market place. In the United Kingdom, however, the PC has only just begun to enter this growth stage. In the Eastern Bloc countries and in many developing countries, the home computer has only just entered the introduction stage of the life cycle.

Debriefing Activity 4.14

With reference to our earlier comment regarding products being at different stages of the life cycle in different countries, digital television is now in the growth stage in the United Kingdom but towards its peak of growth and even entering maturity in Japan.

Debriefing Activity 4.15

Again remember that products may be at different stages according to country, but three products that are in the maturity or saturation phases of the product life cycle, at least in the United Kingdom, would be mobile phones, video cassette recorders and microwave ovens.

Debriefing Activity 4.19

Taking the United Kingdom as the market, as mentioned earlier, the home PC is now moving into the growth stage of its diffusion. In the early stages of this process, the innovator categories who were the first to purchase their home computers were a relatively small group of consumers who had a high degree of technical knowledge and interest in computers. Put simply, they were 'computer freaks' who were more interested in the technical aspects of the product. As the product has begun to move through the market place, however, we have begun to see the emergence of the early adopters and now the early majority group. The early adopters were often again technically oriented customers but many of this group were interested in the games aspect of PCs. The early majority, however, although still interested in these entertainment aspects, are beginning to use computers as tools to help them in their family and sometimes business lives. In short, this group are much more interested in everyday uses of their computers. Eventually, the late majority will enter the market as prices continue to drop while uses expand. Finally, the laggards will enter when eventually, and probably still with some reluctance, they begin to see the potential benefits of the home PC.

Debriefing Activity 4.20

Needless to say, and as you probably appreciate, there is indeed a relationship between the two. In fact, essentially they are opposite sides of the same coin 'so as to speak'. The adoption process effectively underpins the diffusion process and hence the product life cycle. The product adoption process, however, relates to the steps and stages which an individual passes through en route to either accepting or rejecting a new product. Diffusion, on the other hand, represents a summary or collective view of the individual adoption processes. Quite simply, the more individuals who adopt a new product or service, and the quicker they do this, the greater and speedier would be the rate of diffusion in the market. The diffusion process represents adoption over time and the product life-cycle model represents this on a cumulative basis.

Debriefing Activity 4.22

Obviously, your answers to this activity will depend upon the examples you have selected, but in the case of your industrial product, the major functions of packaging are likely to be much more closely related to the more functional aspects of the package such as protection and ease of use. In the case of the non-food consumer product such as clothing, the functions of the packaging will again be protection and ease of use but in addition, if it is a clothing product, the packaging will also have to facilitate the handling of the product before purchase, and possibly information in terms of care of the product and so on. Finally, for our processed food item for sale in a typical supermarket, the packaging must again protect and these days prevent tampering, but also must facilitate stacking and display. Perhaps above all, the packaging must serve to differentiate the product and act as the 'silent sales person'.

Debriefing Activity 4.23

There are many examples where marketers have prolonged the life cycles of brands and kept them fresh, exciting and successful. Perhaps one of the best of these examples is the Lucozade brand. Initially positioned as a glucose drink primarily for the sick, eventually as consumers became more informed, the brand waned in this market. Recognizing this, the brand-management team began to position and promote the brand as a 'pick-me-up' drink for the tired housewife midway through her morning chores. As lifestyles changed, and in particular as health and fitness became particularly important in the lifestyles of many consumers in developed economies, the brand was positioned even more strongly as an energy drink. Using well-known sports people in their advertising, the brand managers of Lucozade have managed to establish the brand as one of the leading ones in the energy drink market.

Debriefing Activity 4.24

Your thoughts are probably centring around the product life cycle as a vehicle for longer-term planning, and the product mix for both long- and short-term planning. Perhaps too you have thought about the product adoption process, and where most customers might be in this process, in relation to short-term planning.

After you have gone through this unit, you should be able to cite more product tools that might be appropriate for inclusion when formulating your answer to this particular question.

Unit 5

Debriefing Activity 5.3

Clearly your examples may be specific to your own organization, but here are some typical examples of the different types of cost:

1. Fixed costs, for example rent and rates, leases, cost of capital
2. Variable costs, for example raw materials, labour, power, transportation
3. Neither of the above. If you were puzzled by this category of costs, it is because some costs are neither truly fixed nor truly variable, that is they are semi-fixed/variable. These are costs that vary to some extent with output/sales. For example, in the lease of some equipment there may be both a fixed and variable element to the cost, for example a photocopier.

Debriefing Activity 5.4

1. Using the information provided, contribution = selling price − variable costs = £20 − £10 = £10
2. Breakeven point = fixed costs/contribution = 100 000/10 = 10 000 units.

Debriefing Activity 5.5

The effect on breakeven point is as follows:

1. = 6667 units
2. = 20 000 units.

Shown on the breakeven chart we have the following:

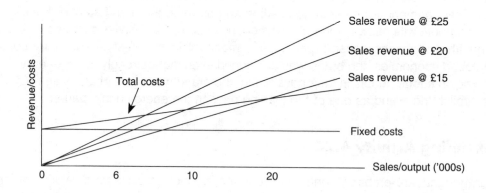

Debriefing Question 5.1

You should have the following answers for the diagrams:

1. Introduction (likely to be highly price inelastic)
2. Growth (more price elastic, due to competition)
3. Maturity (less price elastic, due to brand loyalty)
4. Decline (a return to high price elasticity).

Debriefing Activity 5.6

Examples of markets that fit the range of descriptions in the unit are as follows:

1. Extremely competitive markets, for example food retailing, commodity markets, air travel, holidays
2. Moderate competition, for example alcoholic beverages, coffee, toothpaste, detergents
3. Little or no competition, for example privatized utilities.

Debriefing Activity 5.7

Admittedly, these are very broad generalizations, but on the information given the indication for prices would be:

The ABC company wishes to achieve rapid market growth	Lower
The XYZ company wants quick returns on capital employed	Higher
The LPT company wishes to promote a quality image	Higher
The NYZ company is targeting socio-economic groups D/E	Lower

Debriefing Activity 5.8

Do not worry if your list in the activity differs slightly from the one shown below, but in addition to costs, competition, competitors and company considerations, here are examples of other factors:

o Legal/regulatory considerations
o Dealer and distributor considerations
o Taxation, for example VAT
o Government subsidies
o Tariffs/duties.

Debriefing Activity 5.10

The circumstances that suggest price skimming include:

o Few or no competitors
o High barriers to entry
o A unique/innovatory product
o Price inelastic demand
o No substantial potential scale economies.

Debriefing Activity 5.11

The circumstances that suggest penetration pricing include:

o Extensive competition
o Few barriers to entry
o 'Me too' type products
o High price elasticity
o Potential for substantial scale economies.

Debriefing Activity 5.12

Where you got very good value for money, the marketer probably had set the price too low. You would probably have been prepared to pay more. Where you got very poor value for money, the marketer had probably set the price too high, or at least you paid too much.

Unit 6

Debriefing Activity 6.2

The elements of our channel of distribution are as follows:

- Supplier(s): in this case the manufacturer/marketer
- Customer(s)
- Intermediaries: in this case the retailer
- Outward flows: in this case goods and services
- Inward flows: in this case payments and information.

Debriefing Activity 6.3

As you probably guessed, a 'zero-level channel' is a channel with no intermediaries, that is the producer/marketer uses 'direct marketing'. This idea of channel length/levels is shown in Figure 6.2.

Debriefing Activity 6.4

There are many reasons why the marketer might use intermediaries. For example:

- Custom in the industry
- Intermediaries control customer contact
- Intermediary has superior expertise, skills, resources
- Too many customers for the marketer to reach.

Debriefing Question 6.1

The following represent what we feel are the most appropriate types of market coverage for the products listed:

- Rolex watches = Exclusive
- Cigarettes = Intensive
- Mid-priced hi-fi systems = Selective
- Toilet rolls = Intensive
- Haute couture fashion = Exclusive.

Debriefing Activity 6.6

Examples of types of direct marketing from which you were asked to specify four include:

- Door-to-door selling
- In-home marketing, for example party selling

- o Mail-order catalogues
- o Direct mail
- o Telemarketing
- o Marketer's own outlets.

Debriefing Activity 6.7

There are a number of reasons for the growth of direct marketing, four of the major ones being:

1. Potential for reduced costs/improved profits
2. Speed of delivery
3. Increased control on the part of the marketer
4. Potential for better customer feedback.

Debriefing Activity 6.9

Here are just some of the activities you might have on your list:

- o Inventory (stock) management
- o Order processing
- o Warehousing
- o Transport management
- o Materials handling.

You will readily appreciate the potential for savings in these activities.

Debriefing Activity 6.10

You probably managed to think of lots of examples where customer service is affected by a company's physical distribution system. Here are some of the major ones:

- o Order cycle time
- o Minimum order size
- o Ability to handle special orders/rush orders (flexibility)
- o Consistency of delivery times
- o Degree of damage to delivered products.

Unit 7

Debriefing Activity 7.3

There are a number of ways in which the marketer can obtain feedback from customers regarding the effectiveness of marketing communications. Examples of methods/techniques include:

- o Recognition tests
- o Aided recall tests
- o Unaided recall tests
- o Surveys of customer attitudes.

Methods for collecting this information include:

- ○ Customer questionnaires
- ○ Sales-force feedback
- ○ Focus groups.

Debriefing Activity 7.4

The major advantages of advertising as a promotional tool include:

- ○ Potentially low cost per target audience contact (reach).
- ○ Allows repetition of message.
- ○ Enables dramatization of company and its products (impact).
- ○ Can be used to build up long-term image.

Debriefing Activity 7.5

The major advantages of personal selling as a promotional tool include:

- ○ Two-way communication with target audience.
- ○ Facilitation of immediate feedback.
- ○ Flexibility – can respond to individual customer needs.
- ○ Allows cultivation of customer relationships.

Debriefing Question 7.1

1. *Self-liquidating offer* – A promotional campaign where the cost of the sales promotion is covered by income/payments from the customer, for example where, say, a kitchen knife is offered at a 'special' price of £1.00 plus five labels when the cost to the marketer of the knives is £1.00.
2. *Giveaways* – A free gift, for example a toy, is included with the product.
3. *Coupons* – The customer uses coupons obtained from, say, magazines to obtain products at reduced prices.
4. *Premiums* – Items offered free or at a minimum cost for purchasing a product, for example free soaps with purchase of perfumes.
5. *Dealer loaders* – A trade promotion in which retailers that purchase a certain quantity of merchandise receive gifts.
6. *Buy-back allowances* – Again a trade promotion. A certain amount of money is allowed to, say, a retailer according to quantities bought during a promotional deal. For example, if the retailer has purchased say 100 units on special offer, this will qualify for a further additional premium after the initial deal is over.

Debriefing Activity 7.6

The major advantages of publicity/PR as a promotional tool include the following:

- ○ Can be used to promote a company as a whole and hence all its products.
- ○ Often perceived by target audience as less 'biased' than, say, advertising.
- ○ Potentially low cost.

Debriefing Question 7.2

The initial letters of AIDA stand for:

A – Attention
I – Interest
D – Desire
A – Action.

Debriefing Question 7.3

In the innovation-adoption model, the customer is said to pass through the following stages:
Awareness – Interest – Evaluation – Trial – Adoption – Post-adoption confirmation.

Debriefing Activity 7.10

Here are some examples of promotional messages based on unique selling propositions:

1. 'The chocolate that melts in your mouth and not in your hand'.
2. 'The mint with the hole'.
3. 'The snack you can eat between meals without ruining your appetite'.
4. 'Put a tiger in your tank'.

Debriefing Question 7.4

The four most common methods used for setting promotional budgets are:

1. Affordability
2. Percentage of sales
3. Competitive parity
4. Objective and task.

Debriefing Activity 7.12

Among some of the most important factors affecting the choice of promotional mix are the following:

1. Target market/customer type, for example industrial versus consumer.
2. Characteristics and cost-effectiveness of each promotional tool.
3. Marketing/sales strategies, for example 'push versus pull' strategies.
4. The product life cycle.
5. Availability of promotional tools.
6. Company resources/budgets.

Debriefing Activity 7.13

Examples of innovations in packaging that, at the time of their introduction, were very success-ful and gave the marketers using this packaging a competitive advantage include:

o Ring-pull cans
o Pump action toothpaste tubes

- o Flip-top cartons for cigarettes
- o Cardboard containers for milk and juice
- o CFC-free aerosols.

Unit 8

Debriefing Activity 8.1

The reasons you give in the activity will certainly be very varied: you might feel that there are common faults with a particular product (such as component failure) or with the level of help or support available (buying computers or hi-fi products, for instance). Reasons why these might be difficult to address could relate to other aspects of corporate strategy, for example improving the quality of components, or paying and training more skilful and well-informed staff may involve unacceptable cost penalties in markets where competition is predominantly based on price. The purpose of the exercise is to make you think about the ways in which these issues are interrelated; keeping customers satisfied is not simply a matter of dealing with individual issues, but formulating policies that take the whole range of 'marketing-mix variables' into account.

Debriefing Activity 8.2

Briefly, the main characteristics of the 'customer-care' concept are:

- o Interactions between a firm and its customers
- o The 'image' of the firm, or the 'perceptions' customers have of it
- o Gathering information about customer needs and expectations
- o Taking action to meet those needs and fulfil expectations
- o Giving this aspect of the product/service concept a competitive edge.

Debriefing Activity 8.4

The qualities you select will depend on the product of course. What you should get from this exercise is the message that when we actually compare good products with inferior competitors, on most occasions the differences between them do not lie in gross disparities in the generic features of the products, but in the care and attention to the minutiae involved in the choice, purchase and usage process, for example in the helpfulness of service personnel, the range of products available to cater for individual tastes and the details of actual usage. Can the product, say, survive small accidents, or can it be easily cleaned? How are guarantees organized (a simple 'return' system or 'pay and reclaim', which many people dislike)? The list is, and should be, very long and is likely to be product specific, at least in part. Another by-product will be the realization that quality is an emergent property of attending to these details, rather than simply a 'checklist' of ways of behaving. Quality is a by-product of a particular philosophy of behaviour.

Debriefing Activity 8.6

The purpose of this activity is to force you to think about what avenues, which provide the company with such information, actually exist, and how they are used by the companies in question. Handling complaints, for instance, is traditionally seen as 'firefighting' or deflecting customers who might cause trouble – squashing them, deflating them, placating them or keeping them quiet. This orientation demands that these avenues should be opened up, extended and treated as a very serious means of gathering important business information, which requires action. Rather than 'applying plasters', complaints should be the occasion for 'fault detection', so that recurrence can be avoided by getting it right first time. Equally importantly, there should also be means for customer credit to be transmitted to the staff. Staff should not only be aware of customers as potential sources of trouble for them, but also as the barometer for their achievements.

Debriefing Activity 8.7

This answer to the activity should bring out:

- o The importance of a unified focus on the formulation of strategy and on the design of policies and processes.
- o The importance of fostering the idea of achievement, of positive reinforcement for effective action, rather than founding good practice simply on the avoidance of complaints, failures and negative feedbacks.
- o The idea of building up relationships, rather than relying on formal, contractual obligations. Information is the lifeblood of these processes, and flows freely only under conditions of trust.

Debriefing Activity 8.8

Key aspects of the answer to the question in the activity would be:

- o Loss of status and power
- o Deskilling or disempowerment
- o Fear of the unfamiliar.

Debriefing Activity 8.11

This activity tries to make you think about the implications of:

- o A common focus
- o Role differentiation
- o Power differences
- o The role of information.

Debriefing Activity 8.12

Examples of service encounters that could be measured in our travel agency example include the following:

- o Numbers of customers
- o Numbers of staff
- o Types of enquiry
- o Duration of encounters
- o Waiting time
- o Timing and distribution of customers over the working week
- o Numbers of complaints
- o Types of complaint
- o Outcomes of complaints
- o Customer attitudes.

This list could be greatly extended but each of the elements on our list is relatively easy to measure. Virtually, all the tools of marketing research that we discussed in earlier units could be useful here, including:

- ○ Observation
- ○ Experiment
- ○ Surveys.

However, some important aspects of service encounters are difficult or even impossible to measure. These include, for example, variations in personnel responses to customers of different kinds (socio-economic, ethnic, gender, age differences); aspects of 'body language' or extra-linguistic communication are also critical but difficult to measure.

Debriefing Activity 8.13

The main points of this activity are to recognize the importance, on the one hand, of the specific features of the business in question, so that a good answer would start by making an audit or inventory of the situational/environmental features, and specifying informational needs as well as objectives; and, on the other hand, of making a fundamental change to cover every aspect of the organization, that is to apply a set of core principles from which practice can be derived.

Debriefing Activity 8.15

Examples of issues and problems that might arise in trying to collect information for our wine bar example include:

- ○ Where should the research be carried out? If information is collected only in the wine bar itself, you may not be gathering information about potential customers who are being discouraged by the problems you want to address.
- ○ This, on the other hand, raises the issue of how to identify such potential customers in the first place.
- ○ What research methods should we use and in particular, what should the balance be between qualitative and quantitative information?
- ○ What will be the costs of the research and what resource constraints will affect the information-gathering process?
- ○ How beneficial will any information collected actually be in planning customer relations programmes?

Unit 9

Debriefing Question 9.1

Some of the marketing advantages smaller companies have over their larger counterparts in the area of new-product development and innovation include:

- ○ Speed
- ○ Flexibility
- ○ Better communication between management
- ○ A tendency to be more creative and entrepreneurial.

Debriefing Question 9.2

Examples of ways (bases) the smaller company can use to specialize in niche markets include:

- o Specialization by end use
- o Specialization by customer type
- o Specialization by type of product
- o Specialization by geographic area.

Debriefing Activity 9.4

Examples of possible appropriate marketing objectives for our voluntary and not-for-profit organization are as follows:

- o A national police force, for example 'To improve public cooperation and support.'
- o A local charity, for example 'To increase financial contributions from the local community and secure an increased time commitment from local volunteers.'
- o A church, for example 'To increase the average size of congregations and increase financial contributions.'

Debriefing Activity 9.5

Examples of service products include:

- o Banking
- o Insurance
- o Hotels
- o Restaurants
- o Air travel
- o Hairdressing
- o Medical care, dental care
- o Home services, for example plumbing
- o Management consultancy
- o Industrial cleaning.

Debriefing Activity 9.6

Below is a summary of some of the major marketing implications associated with each of the special characteristics of services:

Characteristic	Marketing implications
Perishability	The matching of demand and supply becomes very important. Examples of ways in which this matching process can be managed in service marketing include the following: price discounts/special offers to even out demand fluctuations, for example off-peak pricing, bargain break holidays and so on; well-managed booking and reservation systems; development of complementary service products and/or diversification into new markets in order to equate demand and supply. Shared use of facilities/equipment, for example hospitals sharing medical scanners and so on.
Intangibility	Increased importance of promotion and branding. Company/brand image crucial.

	Increased need to emphasize the benefits rather than features in selling and promotion.
	Need to look for ways in which to increase the tangibility of the service, for example through demonstrations, promotional literature and so on.
	Difficult to conduct market research for new products.
	Concept testing becomes very important.
Variability	Personnel selection and training very important.
	Wherever possible all systems, procedures, ingredients, and so on should be standardized.
	Where necessary/useful make a marketing feature out of variability, for example stress 'customized' aspect.
Inseparability	Often means that direct sale is the only possible channel of distribution.
	Scale of operation may be limited unless the service provider can reduce the need for him/her to be physically present, for example use of franchises, agents and so on.
Non-ownership	Lack of ownership needs to be turned to advantage by stressing benefits this gives rise to, for example an office-cleaning service company might stress the advantages to the customer of not having to have its own equipment or staff for this purpose.

Debriefing Activity 9.7

In fact, virtually every product/market these days has some level of e-commerce activity.

Initially the major applications of e-commerce, and particularly the Internet in consumer markets, were in markets such as books, travel and event tickets and so on where arguably customers do not need to touch, try on and so on the product. In addition to the product markets shown on the list, other products/markets where e-commerce techniques and activities are being used include:

- o Clothing and footwear
- o Gifts and fancy goods
- o Flowers
- o Garden and outdoor products
- o Furniture.

In short, there is virtually nothing these days that is not being or potentially cannot be marketed using e-commerce and the technologies which underpin it.

Debriefing Activity 9.8

Examples of the sorts of data on customers and an indication of the functions other than the marketing function which might generate this data, include:

- o Prices paid – accounts function
- o Product requirements – design function
- o Delivery and out of stock problems – despatch department
- o Customer complaints – switchboard/reception
- o Quality requirements/issues – production department
- o Licensing/brand protection issues – legal department.

Debriefing Activity 9.9

Satellite television enables more sophisticated targeting with respect to advertising because of the following:

- o More specialized programmes, albeit with smaller audiences, can be linked to special interest groups.
- o Satellite television programmes are often broadcast at times when other, terrestrial-based, programmes are not being shown, again allowing access to audiences which would otherwise be difficult to reach.

Debriefing Activity 9.10

Among some of the most important reasons why many consumers increasingly feel that automated customer-handling operations are annoying and frustrating are:

- o Difficulties in getting through in the first instance
- o Having to respond to questions which are not of interest to the caller
- o The time taken to eventually get connected to the person/department being sought
- o The impersonal nature of many of these systems
- o An intense dislike of 'cheesy' piped music
- o A feeling that the organization does not want to talk to its customers.

appendix 4

past examination papers and examiners' reports

The Chartered
Institute of Marketing

Certificate
in Marketing

Marketing Fundamentals

5.24: **Marketing Fundamentals**

Time: 09.30-12.30

Date: **3rd December, 2003**

3 Hours Duration

This examination is in two sections.

PART A – Is compulsory and worth 40% of total marks.

PART B – Has **SIX** questions; select **THREE**. Each answer will be worth 20% of the total marks.

DO NOT repeat the question in your answer, but show clearly the number of the question attempted on the appropriate pages of the answer book.

Rough workings should be included in the answer book and ruled through after use.

© The Chartered Institute of Marketing

Certificate in Marketing

5.24: Marketing Fundamentals

PART A

Caterpillar Develops its Brand in New Directions

For more than 75 years Caterpillar Inc. (often referred to and abbreviated as CAT) has been building some of the world's infrastructure with its heavy machinery and equipment. Having started as a manufacturer of track-type tractors from its base in East Peoria, Illinois, USA, the company has now become one of the world's largest industrial conglomerate businesses with sales of over $20 billion, profits approaching $1 billion, and around 70,000 employees. Caterpillar is the world's leading manufacturer of construction and mining equipment, diesel and natural gas engines and industrial gas turbines. In addition the company is a technology leader in construction, transportation, mining, forestry, energy, logistics, electronics, financing and electric power generation.

The vision of the company is to be the global leader in customer value and its mission revolves around the fundamental principles of 'providing best value to customers', 'growing profitably', 'developing and rewarding people', and 'encouraging social responsibility'. Caterpillar has a presence throughout the developed and less developed world with more than half the company's sales gained outside the USA, contributing nearly $5 billion to US exports. It also has manufacturing sites in Europe, Latin America, Australia and China, which give it better access to key markets, and has established important strategic alliances in less developed countries through joint ventures or affiliated companies.

The growth of the business has been based on a strategy of diversification into related business areas, and a true belief in being customer oriented. This has resulted in more than 300 individual products now being offered to meet a variety of customer needs. It is also a key part of the strategy to provide industry solutions, particularly in the fields of electric power, general construction and mining, where all the specific needs of customers are met through dedicated packages of products and services. The company's strategy is delivered through its 6 Sigma framework which enables it to use the entire value chain to achieve growth, cost reduction and quality improvement targets, and deliver improved shareholder value as a result.

To support its mission Caterpillar utilises its integral global network of more than 200 dealers worldwide. Most of the dealers have a long history of working with the company, are locally owned, and are independent businesses. This is seen to provide the company with a competitive edge, as customers across the globe are able to deal with people who they know and trust. Dealers provide equipment, service and financing support for customers, whilst rental services are delivered through more than 1,200 outlets around the globe. There is also a well-established international parts distribution network, which features 23 centres in 11 countries throughout the world. In addition, the Caterpillar Equipment Training Division provides dedicated support for buyers and users in order to ensure that they get the maximum from their investment in the company's products. Relationships with suppliers are also very strong and support CAT's commitment to excellence based on good planning, together with conformity to high standards of specification, delivery and price for all the materials and components it uses.

In recent years CAT has developed a name as a clothing and footwear brand with merchandise including a range of industrial, casual and childrens' footwear, as well as jackets, shirts, caps and accessories (all of which display the Caterpillar name and the CAT logo). This move into the consumer market has been further developed through a range of scale models of their famous machines, videos of CAT machines in action, and childrens' caps and T-shirts based on the "I Love CAT Machines" strap line.

Source: The above data has been based on a real life organisation, but details have been changed for assessment purposes and do not reflect the current management practices.

PART A

Question 1.

The company is now considering launching a further extension to its product portfolio by creating a board game for children based on the "I Love CAT Machines" theme. You work as a Brand Assistant in the Merchandise Division of Caterpillar and have been asked by your Manager to write a report that:

a. Explains how branding has been used by Caterpillar to develop its business.

(10 marks)

b. Outlines the components of a marketing plan for the "I Love CAT Machines" game.

(10 marks)

c. Explains in detail how the company would use each element of the marketing mix to support the product in the childrens' games market.

(20 marks)
(40 marks in total)

PART B – Answer THREE Questions Only

Question 2.

a. Using examples from a service organisation of your choice, illustrate how the unique characteristics of services affect its marketing activities.

(12 marks)

b. Explain the part played by people in providing value for the customers of the organisation chosen in Part A of this question.

(8 marks)
(20 marks in total)

Question 3.

Using illustrative examples:

a. Explain the benefits that marketing can provide to business organisations, consumers, and society.

(12 marks)

b. Identify some of the ethical and social responsibility issues that face modern marketers.

(8 marks)
(20 marks in total)

Question 4.

You are employed as a Marketing Assistant with a firm that manufactures household cleaning products.

a. Explain the importance to the firm of introducing new products.

(8 marks)

b. Using an appropriate example from the above business, explain the stages of the new product development process.

(12 marks)
(20 marks in total)

Question 5.

a.   Use examples from a Fast Moving Consumer Goods (FMCG) market to describe the range of different communications tools that can be used to promote a product.

(10 marks)

b.   Explain the factors that influence the selection of the various communications tools adopted.

(10 marks)
(20 marks in total)

Question 6.

a.   Identify the range of environmental factors that influence the marketing of a soft drinks brand (soft drinks, for example, being orange juice) in an international context.

(10 marks)

b.   Explain how each of these factors affects the development of the marketing mix for the brand.

(10 marks)
(20 marks in total)

Question 7.

Relationship marketing is regarded as being a key factor in the success of marketing today. Using an example of a consumer service:

a.   Explain the concept of relationship marketing and why you think it is important to marketing success.

(10 marks)

b.   Examine the role played by Information and Communications Technologies (ICT) in developing and maintaining long-term relationships between buyers and sellers.

(10 marks)
(20 marks in total)

The Chartered
Institute of Marketing

Certificate in Marketing

Examiners Report

24: **Marketing Fundamentals**
Date: **December 2003**

© The Chartered Institute of Marketing

General Strengths and Weaknesses of Candidates

This report has been written after discussion with the Examining Team and most of the comments made are common across many centres. It was generally felt that candidates have not handled this paper very well in comparison with the June 2003 sitting, as the pass rate was significantly lower than the previous session, with only around half of the candidates achieving pass grades. Candidates and tutors should use Examiner's Report and Specimen Answers to help them prepare. It is very good practice to consider the Examiner's Report in particular as it is the intention of the Senior Examiner when writing it to give a clear guide on what is expected by examiners and to indicate the major pitfalls that may be encountered and ways of avoiding them.

Strengths

1. **Using appropriate models, theories, concepts or frameworks.** The best answers tended to display an excellent understanding of the theory, by illustrating models and then applying them to the question set. It is important that when using such approaches, and illustrating them in your answers that they are accurately presented/labelled and correctly cited.

2. **Application of theory to the case or examples.** The best candidates do not just cite the theory; they illustrate understanding by applying the theory to the case or to an example. This assists in explaining what, how and why particular aspects of marketing activity should be undertaken. This is always required in the compulsory case study in Part A and also often in other questions, so it is important that candidates strive to use relevant illustrative material wherever possible. Good candidates clearly demonstrated their understanding by referring to appropriate examples to back up their answers – especially in the case study, where reference to the Caterpillar Brand was required, and the plan outline and mix needed to be developed with the new product in mind.

3. **Good layout and presentation.** The best answers are usually well structured and presented, and utilise the appropriate format where required. This gives the Examiner confidence in the candidate's work as well as assisting in the flow of understanding, and ease of marking. The use of underlining of headings, bullet points with explanation, and clear structures based on the requirements of the various tasks set is advisable. The good candidates do not just reiterate information given in the case study but focus on demonstrating that they are able to explain specifically what the question requires and therefore avoid using up precious time in the exam for little return.

Weaknesses

1. **Lack of understanding of key areas of the syllabus.** As an example this was evident in the compulsory case study - Question 1 (a) where only very limited understanding of branding was displayed by many candidates, together with only very limited knowledge of the benefits of marketing to different

stakeholders, and poor knowledge of service characteristics which were confused with the services marketing mix.

2. **Lack of understanding of question requirements.** Not identifying exactly what the questions is asking for – as in Question 2 (a) which required linking service characteristics to the extended mix. One way of improving this is by using past paper questions to undertake question analysis, which focuses on developing structured answers based on keywords and then developing content around this.

3. **Reluctance to comply with the question requirements.** Many candidates chose to ignore exactly what was required in some questions and generally wrote about the key subject of the question –such as Question 5 (b), which required an explanation of the factors influencing the selection of communications techniques, but often discussed the benefits of some of the more obvious aspects of communications such as advertising media.

4. **Including everything about the subject- even if not related to the question requirements.** This costs the candidates precious time and often happens when they do not know what to include for the actual response. Also, this practice is very tedious for the Examining team, as they have to 'search' for the actual answer. Again, this was very evident in Question 1 (b), which required an outline of the components of a marketing plan for 10 marks, but which tended to elicit massive theory dumps on every aspect of the planning process, far beyond what was necessary.

5. **Lack of practical examples.** As already mentioned, the best marks for questions are awarded to candidates who offer examples, which demonstrate an understanding of the theory to which they are referring. This time, however, not many candidates managed to include relevant examples within their answers, and sometimes included ones out of context – e.g. in Question 4 on NPD, not applying to household cleaning products but something completely different. Candidates should try to demonstrate knowledge and understanding by including examples related to the area in question.

6. **Poor time management and examination technique.** This is still a problem in some centres - especially at certain international centres where many candidates do not answer the required parts of a question or do not answer the required number of questions. Tutors should try to ensure that their students have an opportunity to sit a mock examination prior to the actual examination, which can assist in improving examination technique.

2. Strengths and Weaknesses by Question

PART A Mini Case – Caterpillar

Question 1a

Explain how branding has been used by the company to build its business.

Strengths:

- Some good understanding of and illustrative explanation of the principle of branding.
- Some good application to caterpillar, explaining how the brand was used a basis for growth, particularly through brand extension and stretching (using the case material as evidence).

Weaknesses:

- Poor explanation and definitions of branding.
- Over-emphasis on definitions rather than marketing principle.
- Weak development of issues in case scenario leading to short answers.
- Weak answers regurgitated information from the case study.

Question 1b

Outline the components of a marketing plan for the launch of the new product discussed in the case.

Strengths:

- Generally very competent level of knowledge of the components of a marketing plan.
- Reasonable illustration to the case context and the new product situation presented.

Weaknesses:

- Incomplete plans with many sections omitted and overemphasis on PEST, SWOT, and mix aspects leading to unbalanced answers – omission of objectives, strategy and monitoring and control.
- Proposals lacking in relevant detail in parts.
- Too much written of little relevance for the number of marks allocated – too many irrelevant models and frameworks included.

Question 1c

Explanation of role of marketing mix in supporting launch of product.

Strengths:

- Generally good coverage of key elements of mix and some use of appropriate extended mix elements.
- Some good selective use of mix variables with emphasis given to needs of target market.
- Consistency with answers to parts a and b, in particular building on branding theme.

Weaknesses:

- Too little written by many candidates.
- Use of definitional content rather than specific details of mix variables in context.
- Incoherent and poorly integrated marketing offers developed.
- Did not recognise key significance of branding aspects of the case.

PART B

Question 2

For a chosen organisation, illustrate the link between service characteristics and the marketing mix, and explain the role of people in delivering customer value.

Strengths:

- Some very good instances of detailed knowledge and understanding of the characteristics of services.
- Detail well developed and linked to extended marketing mix activities.
- Particularly strong knowledge of the people element of the extended mix and resultant contribution to customer (dis) satisfaction in service businesses.
- Use of good illustrative material from an appropriate well chosen example organisation.

Weaknesses:

- Lack of knowledge of service characteristics.
- Confusion of the services marketing mix with the characteristics, and omission of some mix variables in discussion.
- Failing to make the link between the characteristics and the mix.
- Poor understanding of how people contribute to customer requirements in services.

Question 3

Using examples explain the benefits of marketing to various stakeholders and identify some ethical and social responsibility issues facing contemporary marketers.

Strengths:

- Very good understanding of benefits to consumers and organisations, and also wider society.
- Detailed explanation using relevant examples.
- Good well-developed list of E&SR facets based with some explanation and theoretical justification integrated across both parts of the question.

Weaknesses:

- Limited coverage of key points – short answers tending to focus on definitions of marketing.
- Emphasis on customer and organisations, and not society.
- Failure to develop sufficient points relating to the E&SR issues.

Question 4

Explain the importance of new products and the NPD process in a given context.

Strengths:

- Understanding of role of new products to business success generally well understood.
- Some very good application to household cleaning products market.
- Stages of NPD process generally well known.
- Good candidates identified significance of new products in terms of how they contribute to future growth and replace old products (PLC analysis).

Weaknesses:

- Some of the weaker candidates had very little insight into why new products are important, thus quite short answers ensued.
- Omissions of detail of illustration and explanation in the NPD process stages and some stages completely overlooked.
- Poor application to the given context.

Question 5

Describe the range of marketing communications available to a FMCG company, and consider factors leading to their selection.

Strengths:

- Wide-ranging coverage of the communications vehicles available, including media options.
- Good description and understanding of the detail of each tool, and explanation of the benefits that each can provide.
- Some candidates provided evidence of a very good knowledge of the criteria for assessing the appropriateness of different promotional methods, particularly in the context of the chosen FMCG market.

Weaknesses:

- Limited knowledge of the range of relevant promotional methods.
- Over-emphasis on advertising media – thus the broad range of options were not considered.
- Limited understanding of the pros and cons of the various methods available.
- Weak candidates had a very poor knowledge of why different tools should be selected.
- Weak candidates discussed general descriptive points relating to each tool rather than understanding significance in terms of achieving specific objectives.

Question 6

In context identify international environmental factors and link to how they influence the marketing of a particular brand.

Strengths:

- Comprehensive coverage of relevant factors using a structured approach.
- Very good identification of factors relevant to the soft drinks market.
- Good explanation of how each factor relates to the identified market and its link to marketing mix variables using a systematic (e.g. 4P) approach.

Weaknesses:

- Limited identification of factors relevant to the given industry.
- Unstructured approach which led to omission of key factors.
- Poor linkage of factors to marketing mix activities.

Question 7

Explain relationship marketing and examine the role played ICT in this form of marketing in context.

Strengths:

- Good candidates explained the principle of RM using examples from a consumer service.
- Key principle of attraction and retention of customers related to marketing success.
- Aspects of relevant theory e.g. ladder of loyalty included by the stronger candidates.
- Significance of ICT e.g. Internet and databases identified in a contemporary consumer marketing context.

Weaknesses:

- Very basic understanding of RM displayed in the weak answers.
- Poor illustrative, applied material included by candidates not fully understanding the key theoretical aspects of RM.
- Limited investigation of how ICT facilitates mutually beneficial long-term relationships between customers and suppliers.

3. Future Themes

It seems clear that there are still a number of candidates who are making the same mistakes session after session, and it also seems clear that they are not aware, (or are not taking any notice), of the guidance offered by Examiner's Reports and the additional helpful sources provided by the CIM. Thus it is strongly recommended that the communication of this Senior Examiner's Report to all tutors and candidates involved with this subject is undertaken as a matter of common practice by those responsible for CIM at Centres.

There is some clear evidence that tutors and candidates are relying heavily on the CIM Workbooks as their main source of reading, although this practice, clearly, does not offer enough reading for candidates to pass this examination. Candidates should consult the CIM reading list and read from the **core texts, quality newspapers and marketing magazines as well as the workbooks.**

Candidates should be taught to practice their time management in terms of the weighting for each part of the question. They should also remember that there will be a small allocation of marks for the presentation of the answer in the format required and students should get used to writing in required formats to ensure that they obtain these marks. Tutors should ensure that students are given an opportunity to sit a mock examination with feedback prior to the actual examination.

There should be some emphasis on encouraging deep learning rather than a surface learning approach where candidates are just learning facts but unable to apply them or offer valid examples. This will allow candidates to analyse the question fully, identify the focus and apply their knowledge to the specific context given.

Tutors and candidates should remember that there are some areas of the syllabus, which often appear on the examination paper and therefore should ensure that they are familiar with the key elements of knowledge in these areas.

In particular the new Senior Examiner would like to emphasise the significance of the need to understand the role of marketing in modern societies, its application in different contexts, and the delivery of satisfaction to customers through a range of tools and techniques (mix variables) as being critical to success in this examination. Additionally it should be noted that future case studies will take a similar form to the one utilised on this occasion, where a well-known organisation forms the basis for examining knowledge and understanding of the fundamentals of marketing theory and practice.

The Chartered
Institute of Marketing

Professional Certificate in Marketing

Marketing Fundamentals

24:	**Marketing Fundamentals**
Time:	**14.00-17.00**
Date:	**9th June, 2004**

3 Hours Duration

This is a generic paper to cover the following qualification: -

- **Certificate in Marketing and IT**

This examination is in two sections.

PART A – Is compulsory and worth 40% of total marks.

PART B – Has **SIX** questions; select **THREE**. Each answer will be worth 20% of the total marks.

All questions relate to both CIM Certificate in Marketing old (pre-July 2002) and new (post-July 2002) Syllabi unless otherwise stated.

DO NOT repeat the question in your answer, but show clearly the number of the question attempted on the appropriate pages of the answer book.

Rough workings should be included in the answer book and ruled through after use.

© The Chartered Institute of Marketing

Professional Certificate in Marketing

24: Marketing Fundamentals

PART A

Robots Set to Join the Dyson Repertoire

James Dyson launched his first product, the Sea Truck, in 1970 when he was an art student in London. Subsequently he invented and marketed the Ballbarrow, the Wheelboat, and the Trolleyball. Many of these innovations have been successful in their own right but it is for the product that revolutionised domestic cleaning that we know him best. Dyson's idea for a bagless vacuum cleaner took 5 years to develop and involved producing over 5,000 prototypes. However in 1991 his idea came to fruition with the launch of the 'G Force' vacuum cleaner which won the International Design Fair prize in Japan. The Japanese were so impressed with the new cleaner's performance that it became a status symbol, which was reflected in a $2,000 price tag.

In 1993, back in Britain with the proceeds of his Japanese venture to invest, the inventor set about conquering the UK market with a 'dual cyclone' machine that collected microscopic particles of dust as well as providing bag-free technology. The DC01 was the first of his range of cleaners to give constant suction and following this the 'Root⁸Cyclone'™ offered even more suction and cleaning power. By 2003 the Dyson range of vacuum cleaners had been extended to include five domestic models which varied in their design to take account of the needs of different customers. It is possible to get both the original upright and the more recently developed cylinder models along with high performing and standard suction specifications, lightweights and compacts. These models come in a range of colours and also offer particular variations for carpets and hard floors, low furniture access, allergy sufferers and a super-powerful 'animal' version for picking up pet hairs. In addition Dyson markets the DC04 constantMax™ to commercial users in buildings such as schools, hospitals and hotels; its main selling propositions being ease of use and maintenance as well as durability and constant suction performance.

Dyson's innovative policy of using its engineers to constantly re-examine existing products of all types also involved them in looking at the washing machine. They identified that standard single-drum machines took a long time to release dirt from the fabrics being washed and that hand washing actually gave better results. So Dyson set about replicating a hand wash action to manipulate and flex the fabric to release dirt more quickly. In 2000 a great deal of research and development finally led to the introduction of their Contrarotator™ washing machine that had two drums, which meant that people would be able to wash larger loads faster and with better results.

In response to a casual remark from a customer asking, "when will you invent a cleaner that you don't have to push around?" James Dyson set about designing the hands-free vacuum cleaner. In the early years of the 21st Century Dyson's DC06 robotic vacuum cleaner is undergoing home trials with a view to it liberating people from the work of floorcare, and also making the whole cleaning process more efficient without even the need to programme the machine. James Dyson's view that the robot should do a better job than a human means that the new machine will not just bounce aimlessly off the furniture and pick up very little dust. The 60,000 hours of research which has been invested in this new product have led to a cleaner being designed which cleans as well as Dyson's other models, but also guides itself more logically than a human would. State of the art technology involving 3 on-board computers and 50 sensory devices has led to the development of the ultimate household-cleaning appliance.

The above data has been based on a real life organisation, but details have been changed for assessment purposes and do not reflect the current management practices.

PART A

Question 1.

You work as an Assistant in the marketing department of Dyson. Write a report that considers each of the following:

a. Explain the concept of market segmentation and identify different ways in which Dyson can segment its markets.

(15 marks)

b. Outline the stages of the new product development process in developing the washing machine.

(15 marks)

c. Explain how Dyson might monitor and control the performance of its products.

(10 marks)
(40 marks in total)

PART B – Answer THREE Questions Only

Question 2.

You are a Marketing Assistant for a producer of a branded range of hair care products:

a.   Explain the factors that should be taken into account when setting the price of one of the products in your range.

(12 marks)

b.   Explain how price could be used to support the brand positioning of your range in the market for hair care products.

(8 marks)
(20 marks in total)

Question 3.

The marketing audit is a key aspect of the marketing planning process. For an organisation of your choice use examples to:

a.   Explain the contents of a marketing audit.

(10 marks)

b.   Explain the sources of marketing information that can be used to undertake a marketing audit.

(10 marks)
(20 marks in total)

Question 4.

You work in the marketing department of a furniture manufacturer:

a.   Explain the range of alternative channels of distribution available to your organisation.

(10 marks)

b.   Explain the factors that should be taken into account when deciding which distribution channels to adopt.

(10 marks)
(20 marks in total)

Question 5.

Firms operating in different business contexts need to take account of the different contexts when organising their marketing activities:

a.   Explain the different characteristics of business to business (b2b) and business to customer (b2c) markets.

(10 marks)

b.   Explain how these differences affect the use of marketing communications techniques in these separate contexts.

(10 marks)
(20 marks in total)

Question 6.

Drawing upon an example of a service product of your choice:

a.   Explain the concept of the product life cycle.

(8 marks)

b.   Outline how the marketing mix will differ at the various stages of the product's life cycle.

(12 marks)
(20 marks in total)

Question 7.

Using examples from marketing practice:

a.   Outline how consumers and wider society might benefit from marketing.

(10 marks)

b.   Explain the benefits of market orientation to business organisations.

(10 marks)
(20 marks in total)

The Chartered
Institute of Marketing

Professional Certificate in Marketing

Marketing Fundamentals

24: **Marketing Fundamentals**

SENIOR EXAMINER'S REPORT FOR JUNE 2004 EXAMINATION PAPER

© The Chartered Institute of Marketing

SENIOR EXAMINER'S REPORT FOR
JUNE 2004 EXAMINATION PAPER

MODULE NAME: Marketing Fundamentals

AWARD NAME: Professional Certificate in Marketing

DATE: 20th July 2004

1. General Strengths and Weaknesses of Candidates

This report has been written after discussion with the Examining Team and most of the comments made are common across many centres. The examination was considered by the Senior Examiner and the examining team as a fair test of the fundamental elements of marketing theory and was designed to elicit standard knowledge and understanding in this area, which should be explained through the use of relevant examples. The case was based on a familiar global brand which many candidates should have been familiar with and the questions covered standard syllabus topics such as segmentation, NPD, pricing, distribution, aspects of marketing planning, services marketing and market orientation.

The performance of candidates was variable and in the main tends to reflect the preparation of those sitting the exam both through individual study and in their study centres. On the basis of the evidence of the marking of scripts it is generally fair to say that some centres do not prepare their candidates well and that students consequently have only a limited chance of passing, whilst candidates from good centres have every opportunity to do well in the examination. In order to ensure the best possible preparation candidates and tutors should use Examiner's Report and Specimen Answers. It is very good practice to consider the Examiner's Report in particular as it is the intention of the Senior Examiner when writing it to give a clear guide on what is expected by Examiners and to indicate the major pitfalls that may be encountered and ways of avoiding them. At the same time evidence of good practice in examinations is highlighted.

<u>Strengths</u>

(1)   **Using appropriate models, theories, concepts or frameworks.** The best answers tended to display an excellent understanding of the theory, by illustrating models and then applying them to the question set. It is important that when using such approaches, and illustrating them in your answers that they are accurately presented/labelled and correctly cited. Good examples of the use of such approaches which were used by the best students in answering Question 2 on pricing by using a 5Cs framework in part (a) and a perceptual map in part (b).

(2)   **Application of theory to the case or examples.** The best candidates do not just cite the theory; they illustrate understanding by applying the theory to

the case or to an example. This assists in explaining what, how and why particular aspects of marketing activity should be undertaken. This is always required in the compulsory case study in Part A and also often in other questions, so it is important that candidates strive to use relevant illustrative material wherever possible. Good candidates clearly demonstrated their understanding by referring to appropriate examples to back up their answers – especially in the case study, where reference to Dyson's position with regard to market segmentation, new product development and the monitoring and control of product performance was required.

(3) **Good layout and presentation.** The best answers are usually well structured and presented, and utilise the appropriate format where required. This gives the Examiner confidence in the candidate's work as well as assisting in the flow of understanding, and ease of marking. The use of underlining of headings, bullet points with explanation, and clear structures based on the requirements of the various tasks set is advisable. The good candidates do not just reiterate information given in the case study but focus on demonstrating that they are able to explain specifically what the question requires and therefore avoid using up precious time in the exam for little return.

Weaknesses
(1) **Lack of understanding of key areas of the syllabus**. As an example this was evident in some answers to the compulsory case study - Question 1 (a) where only a narrow (demographics) knowledge of segmentation was displayed by many candidates, together with only limited understanding of the standard stages of the sequential NPD process together with very sparse knowledge of methods of evaluating and controlling marketing performance. Similarly amongst those attempting Question 7 there was a surprising lack of understanding of the benefits of marketing to various stakeholders.

(2) **Lack of understanding of question requirements**. Not identifying exactly what the questions is asking for – as in Question 3 (a) which required the contents of a marketing audit not a marketing plan or the marketing planning process. One way of improving this is by using past paper questions to undertake question analysis which focuses on developing structured answers based on keywords and then developing content around this.

(3) **Reluctance to comply with the question requirements**. Many candidates chose to ignore exactly what was required in some questions and generally wrote about the key subject of the question –such as Question 5 (b) which required an explanation of how the differences between B2B and B2C affect marketing communications, but tended to elicit answers that simply discussed the differences in the marketing communications mix in these two contexts.

361

(4)   **Including everything about the subject**- even if not related to the question requirements. This costs the candidates precious time and often happens when they do not know what to include for the actual response. Also, this practice is very tedious for the Examining team, as they have to 'search' for the actual answer. This was evident in Question 6 (b) which required an outline of how the marketing mix varies according to the stage of the PLC but which tended to bring forth massive theory dumps on every aspect of the PLC and the marketing mix, far beyond what was necessary. A simple table identifying aspects of the mix (extended to 7Ps for a service) relevant at each of the 4 stages of the PLC would have sufficed.

(5)   **Lack of practical examples**. As already mentioned, the best marks for questions are awarded to candidates who offer examples, which demonstrate an understanding of the theory to which they are referring. Many candidates failed to include relevant examples within their answers, and sometimes included ones out of context – e.g. in Question 4 on distribution, not applying to furniture but something completely different. Candidates should try to demonstrate knowledge and understanding by including examples related to the area in question, particularly when the question specifically request this (i.e. Question 7 on this occasion).

(6)   **Poor time management and examination technique**. This is still a problem in some centres - especially at certain international centres where many candidates do not answer the required parts of a question or do not answer the required number of questions. Tutors should try to ensure that their students have an opportunity to sit a mock examination prior to the actual examination, which can assist in improving examination technique.

2. Strengths and Weaknesses by Question

PART A Mini Case – Dyson

Question 1a

Task: Explain market segmentation and identify possible segmentation approaches for the company.

Strengths:
- Some good definitions of the principle of segmentation (including targeting and positioning)
- Some good application to Dyson involving a comprehensive range of consumer and business segmentation approaches beyond simple demographics to include psychographics, attitudes and behavior and benefits sought.
- Some interesting profiling of customer types

Weaknesses:
- Simplistic explanation of the market segmentation concept
- Over-emphasis on demographic and geographic segmentation bases

- Weak development of possible segmentation variables leading to short answers (i.e. listing rather than explaining in the case context)
- Weak answers regurgitated information from the case study

Question 1b

Task: Outline the stages of the NPD process for the new product in the case.

Strengths:
- Generally very competent level of knowledge of the stages of the sequential NPD process
- Reasonable illustration to the case context and the new product situation presented
- Good students related to the consumer adoption process and linked activities at each stage to this

Weaknesses:
- Some candidates were totally unfamiliar with the standard NPD process
- Omission and/or confusion of sequencing of stages
- Not explained in the context of the case
- Utilisation of the Ansoff Matrix and sometimes the Boston Box or PLC where knowledge of the standard approach was not apparent

Question 1c

Task: Explanation of methods of monitoring and controlling product performance.

Strengths:
- Some good listing of possible methods focusing on research based approaches
- Some good elaboration in the context of the launch of the new Dyson product

Weaknesses:
- Too little written by many candidates indicating a lack of knowledge of this topic
- Over-emphasis on elementary aspects such as customer feedback
- Little detailed understanding of the process of monitoring and control in marketing

PART B

Question 2

Task: In a particular context explain the factors influencing pricing and how price supports brand positioning

Strengths:
- Good range of factors identified often using helpful frameworks
- Detail well developed in context of given product
- Evidence of strategic and operational aspects of pricing decisions
- Use of perceptual maps to link pricing to brand positioning

Weaknesses:
- Difficulty in explaining the key role of price in brand positioning

Question 3

Task: For a chosen organisation explain the contents of a marketing audit and identify sources of audit information

Strengths:
- Some comprehensive audit specifications including micro and internal environments as well as the macro aspects
- Occasional use of a standardised approach (e.g. Kotler)
- Some good coverage of marketing intelligence and research including the use of both external and internal sources of data

Weaknesses:
- Limited coverage of key elements – overemphasis on PEST (macro) elements
- Inclusion of SWOT and other planning models
- Failure to understand the role of the audit in marketing planning
- Focus on external marketing research only

Question 4

Task: In a given context explain the range of distribution channels available and explain the factors influencing channel selection

Strengths:
- Use of distribution maps as an explanatory framework
- Some very good application to the context which made identification of potential channels more selective
- Inclusion of traditional and contemporary channels
- Good candidates identified significance of context in determining the importance of various criteria for channel selection

Weaknesses:
- Some of the weaker candidates had very little knowledge of the wide range of possible channels
- Overemphasis on new (Internet based direct marketing) as opposed to conventional (agent, retail and wholesale) channels
- Poor application to the given context

Question 5

Task: Explain the different characteristics between B2B and B2C markets and outline how these influence differences in marketing communications

Strengths:
- Some good listing of contrasting characteristics using tabular format
- Some clear linkages between marketing communications tools and the identified differences
- Comprehensive coverage of various marketing communication techniques available in the different context by the more capable students

Weaknesses:
- Limited knowledge of the different characteristics
- Focus on difference in the buying unit leading to many other factors being ignored
- Rather narrow understanding of the range of communications methods available
- Failure to link characteristics with promotional tools

Question 6

Task: Using a service product explain the PLC concept and outline how the marketing mix differs at its various stages

Strengths:
- Some good diagrams and separate explanation of PLC stages in context
- Some precise linking of PLC stage to extended (7Ps) mix using a tabular format

Weaknesses:
- Poorly labeled and inaccurate/incomplete PLC diagrams
- Failure to link PLC stage with mix component
- Failure to identify service context and role of extended mix

Question 7

Task: Using practical examples explain the benefits of marketing to consumers, society and businesses

Strengths:
- Good candidates explained the benefits to consumers and society separately in a detailed manner

- Some good identification of the importance of market orientation to business performance
- Good use of definitions of marketing and market orientation to support argument in favour of benefits to individual buyers/organisations and wider society by better candidates

Weaknesses:
- Many short answers giving little more than basic marketing definitions
- Very basic understanding of the role of marketing emphasising the satisfaction of customer requirements only
- Rather theoretical answers that tended to drift around the same point as opposed to providing detailed explanation of specific issues with good examples
- Focus on ethical and social responsibility issues without recognition of wider aspects such as effective used of scarce resources, improved choice, etc.

3. Future Themes

It seems clear that there are still a number of candidates who are making the same mistakes session after session, and it also seems clear that they are not aware, (or are not taking any notice), of the guidance offered by Examiner's Reports and the additional helpful sources provided by the CIM. Thus it is strongly recommended that the communication of this Senior Examiner's Report to all tutors and candidates involved with this subject is undertaken as a matter of common practice by those responsible for CIM at Centres.

There is some clear evidence that tutors and candidates are relying heavily on the CIM Workbooks as their main source of reading, although this practice, clearly, does not offer enough reading for candidates to pass this examination. Candidates should consult the CIM reading list and read from the core texts, quality newspapers and marketing magazines as well as the workbooks.

Candidates should be taught to practice their time management in terms of the weighting for each part of the question. They should also remember that there will be a small allocation of marks for the presentation of the answer in the format required and students should get used to writing in required formats to ensure that they obtain these marks. Tutors should ensure that students are given an opportunity to sit a mock examination with feedback prior to the actual examination.

There should be some emphasis on encouraging deep learning rather than a surface learning approach where candidates are just learning facts but unable to apply them or offer valid examples. This will allow candidates to analyse the question fully, identify the focus and apply their knowledge to the specific context given.

Tutors and candidates should remember that there are some areas of the syllabus, which often appear on the examination paper and therefore should ensure that they are familiar with the key elements of knowledge in these areas.

In particular the Senior Examiner would like to emphasise the significance of the need to understand the role of marketing in modern societies, its application in different contexts, and the delivery of satisfaction to customers through a range of tools and techniques (mix variables) as being critical to success in this examination. Additionally it should be noted that future case studies will take a similar form to the one utilised on this occasion, where a well-known (internationally recognised) organisation forms the basis for examining knowledge and understanding of the fundamentals of marketing theory and practice.

appendix 5
curriculum information and reading list

Aim

The Marketing Fundamentals unit develops a basic knowledge and understanding of marketing, marketing process and the marketing mix. It aims to provide students with a framework on which to build marketing knowledge and skills through the units at this level, through units at later levels and in the workplace.

Related CIM Professional Marketing Standards

Bb.2   Contribute to the production of marketing plans and budgets.
Db.1   Contribute to the development of products and services.
Eb.1   Contribute to the development of pricing policies.
Eb.2   Implement pricing policies.
Fb.1   Develop effective channels to market.
Fb.2   Provide support to channel members.
Hb.1   Contribute to planning and budget preparation.

Learning outcomes

Students will be able to:

5.23.1   Explain the development of marketing and the ways it can benefit business and organizations.

5.23.2   Identify the main steps in, and barriers to, achieving a marketing orientation within the organization.

5.23.3   Explain the context of, and process for, marketing planning and budgeting including related models.

5.23.4   Explain the concept of segmentation and the different bases for effective market segmentation.

5.23.5   Identify and describe the individual elements and tools of the marketing mix.

5.23.6   Identify the basic differences in application of the marketing mix involved in marketing products and services within different marketing contexts.

Knowledge and skill requirements

Element 1: The development of marketing and market orientation (10 per cent)

1.1 Explain the development of marketing as an exchange process, a philosophy of business and a managerial function.

1.2 Recognize the contribution of marketing as a means of creating customer value and as a form of competition.

1.3 Appreciate the importance of a market orientation to organizational performance and identify the factors that promote and impede the adoption of a market orientation.

1.4 Explain the role of marketing in co-ordinating organizational resources both within and outside the marketing function.

1.5 Describe the impacts of marketing actions on society and the need for marketers to act in an ethical and socially responsible manner.

1.6 Examine the significance of buyer–seller relationships in marketing and comprehend the role of relationship marketing in facilitating the retention of customers.

Element 2: Marketing planning and budgeting (20 per cent)

2.1 Explain the importance of the marketing planning process and where it fits into the corporate or organizational planning framework.

2.2 Explain the models that describe the various stages of the marketing planning process.

2.3 Explain the concept of the marketing audit as an appraisal of the external marketing environment and an organization's internal marketing operations.

2.4 Describe the role of various analytical tools in the marketing auditing process.

2.5 Explain the value of marketing research and information in developing marketing plans.

2.6 Explain the importance of objectives and the influences on, and processes for setting, objectives.

2.7 Explain the concept of market segmentation and distinguish effective bases for segmenting consumer and b2b markets.

2.8 Describe the structure of an outline marketing plan and identify its various components.

2.9 Depict the various management structures available for implementing marketing plans, and understand their advantages and disadvantages.

2.10 Examine the factors that affect the setting of marketing budgets.

2.11 Demonstrate an appreciation of the need to monitor and control marketing activities.

Element 3: The marketing mix and related tools (50 per cent)

3.1 Describe the essential elements of targeting and positioning, and the creation of an integrated and coherent marketing mix.

3.2 Describe the wide range of tools and techniques available to marketers to satisfy customer requirements and compete effectively.

3.3 Explain the development of the extended marketing mix concept to include additional components in appropriate contextual settings: product, price, place (distribution), promotion (communications), people, processes, physical evidence and customer service.

3.4 Demonstrate awareness of products as bundles of benefits that deliver customer value and have different characteristics, features and levels.

3.5 Explain and illustrate the product life-cycle concept and recognize its effects on marketing mix decisions.

3.6 Explain and illustrate the principles of product policy: branding, product lines, packaging and service support.

3.7 Explain the importance of introducing new products, and describe the processes involved in their development and launch.

3.8 Explore the range of internal and external factors that influence pricing decisions.

3.9 Identify and illustrate a range of different pricing policies and tactics that are adopted by organizations as effective means of competition.

3.10 Define channels of distribution, intermediaries and logistics, and understand the contribution they make to the marketing effort.

3.11 State and explain the factors that influence channel decisions and the selection of alternative distribution channel options, including the effects of new information and communications technology.

3.12 Describe the extensive range of tools that comprise the marketing communications mix, and examine the factors that contribute to its development and implementation.

3.13 Explain the importance of people in marketing and in particular the contribution of staff to effective service delivery.

3.14 Explain the importance of service in satisfying customer requirements and identify the factors that contribute to the delivery of service quality.

3.15 Examine the effects of information and communication technology on the development and implementation of the marketing mix.

3.16 Explain the importance of measuring the effectiveness of the selected marketing effort and instituting appropriate changes where necessary.

Element 4: Marketing in context (20 per cent)

4.1 Explain the importance of contextual setting in influencing the selection of and emphasis given to marketing mix tools.

4.2 Explain differences in the characteristics of various types of marketing context: FMCG, b2b (supply chain), large or capital project-based, services, voluntary and not-for-profit, sales support (e.g. SMEs), and their impact on marketing mix decisions.

4.3 Compare and contrast the marketing activities of organizations that operate and compete in different contextual settings.

4.4 Explain the global dimension in affecting the nature of marketing undertaken by organizations in an international environmental context.

4.5 Explain the existing and potential impacts of the virtual marketplace on the pattern of marketing activities in given contexts.

Related key skills

Key skill	Relevance to unit knowledge and skills
Communication	Synthesize information from different sources
	Use marketing models to present information
Application of number	Carry out calculations for budgets and measures
Information technology	Use IT tools to support the marketing process
Working with others	
Improving own learning and performance	Apply planning techniques to agree targets and plan how these will be met (methods, timescales, resources)
	Select and use a variety of methods for learning
	Manage time effectively
	Seek feedback to monitor performance and modify approach
	Review progress and provide evidence of meeting targets
Problem-solving	

Assessment

The Chartered Institute of Marketing will normally offer two forms of assessment for this unit from which study centres or students may choose: written examination and an assignment. The Chartered Institute of Marketing may also recognize, or make joint awards for, units at an equivalent level undertaken with other professional marketing bodies and educational institutions.

Recommended support materials

Core texts

Blythe, J. (2004) *Essentials of Marketing*, 3rd edition. Harlow: Prentice Hall.

Masterson, R. and Pickton, D. (2004) *Marketing: An Introduction*, Maidenhead: McGraw-Hill.

Syllabus guides

BPP (2005) *Marketing Fundamentals Study Text*, London: BPP Publishing.

Lancaster, G. and Withey, F. (2005) *Marketing Fundamentals*, Oxford: BH/Elsevier.

Supplementary readings

Adcock, D., Halborg, C. and Ross, C. (2001) *Marketing: Principles and Practice*, 4th edition. Harlow: Prentice Hall.

Blythe, J. (2004) *Essentials of Marketing*, 3rd edition. Harlow: Prentice Hall.

Brassington, F. and Pettitt, S. (2002) *Principles of Marketing*, 3rd edition. Harlow: Pearson Education.

Chaston, I. (2000) *Entrepreneurial Marketing: Successfully Challenging Market Convention*, London: Palgrave.

Drummond, G. (2004) *Introduction to Marketing Concepts*, Butterworth-Heinemann.

Evans, M. and Moutinho, L. (1999) *Contemporary Issues in Marketing*, London: Palgrave.

Hill, E. and O'Sullivan, T. (2004) *Foundation Marketing*, 3rd edition, Prentice Hall.

Kotler, P., Armstrong, G., Saunders, J. and Wong, V. (2004) *Principles of marketing*, 4th European edition. Harlow: Prentice Hall.

Lancaster, G., Massingham, L. and Ashford, R. (2001) *Essentials of Marketing*, 4th edition. Maidenhead: McGraw-Hill.

Palmer, A. (2000) *Principles of Marketing*, Oxford: Oxford University Press.

Smith, P. (2003) *Great Answers to Tough Marketing Questions*, 2nd edition. London: Kogan Page.

BPP (2005) *Marketing Fundamentals: Practice and Revision Kit*, London: BPP Publishing.

Marketing Fundamentals: Success Tape, Learning cassettes by BPP Publishing.

BH (2005) *CIM Revision Cards: Marketing Fundamentals*, Oxford: BH/Elsevier.

Overview and rationale

Approach

This unit has been designed to provide an introduction to the key concepts of marketing to students of the Professional Certificate, many of whom will have little or no previous experience of the discipline. The knowledge and skills that it sets out to impart essential aspects of marketing theory and practice from which both horizontal and vertical integration in the qualifications may take place. Specifically it provides a foundation for Marketing in Practice within the Professional Certificate and an essential platform for the full gamut of the units at Professional Diploma.

The themes it adopts as its cornerstones are the twin facets of marketing as a means of conveying *customer value* and as a form of *competition*. These are seen to define the marketing philosophy and function and thus characterize the types of activities involved in marketing. Moreover these themes are recognized as the core of the marketing planning process, which is introduced in this unit and developed in detail in subsequent units at Professional Diploma and Professional PG Diploma (Marketing Planning and Strategic Marketing Decisions respectively). A comprehensive examination of the range of marketing techniques available to practitioners is included in the knowledge and skills requirements, along with an assessment of their contribution in achieving specific marketing outcomes. In addition, the unit introduces the importance of contextual setting in determining the degree of emphasis given to particular marketing activities, and recognizes that organizational characteristics are a key influence on the composition of the marketing mix adopted.

Horizontally, the content of the unit has been slimmed down to reduce the degree of overlap found between units in the current Certificate syllabus. It now includes societal marketing, social responsibility and relationship marketing (from Marketing Environment) as part of the development of marketing. Customer behaviour and care are now dealt with in Customer Communications. Market research planning has been moved to Marketing Environment. The practical application of basic marketing skills is included in Marketing in Practice, which reinforces marketing in context. ICT is not explicit within this syllabus but should be implicit in marketing mix.

In line with the necessity for the future evolution of the syllabus, the elements of the indicative content together with the associated knowledge and skill requirements offer an essential framework in which any such changes may be integrated.

Syllabus content

The balance of weighting allocated to each of the four elements of the syllabus reflects the importance of the area to the achievement of learning and performance outcomes, and the depth and breadth of material to be covered. Although each area may be regarded as a discrete element, there are clear progressions and overlaps in the knowledge and skills base considered which has important implications for the delivery of the unit.

Element 1: The development of marketing and market orientation
Knowledge and skill requirements here relate to the first two learning outcomes, which focus on the development of marketing and the implementation of a market orientation. This element also includes the new knowledge area of societal marketing the ethical and social responsibility issue. The further new area of relationship marketing is also introduced at this point.

Element 2: Marketing planning and budgeting
The syllabus content in this element relates to the third and fourth learning outcomes that consider the marketing planning and budgeting process, and the market segmentation concept. The material included is intended to provide students with an overview of marketing planning: the process, benefits, models, components and implementation. It will be mainly descriptive and illustrative. However, it is deemed to be fundamental to developing plans that include programmes of mix activities and thus will enhance meaning and understanding in the study of Element 3. Similarly, a grasp of the essentials of segmentation will provide insight into the selection of mix components and overall positioning in accordance with differences in customer requirements and competitive conditions.

Element 3: The marketing mix and related tools
The knowledge and skills areas considered in this element relate directly to the fifth learning outcome which concentrates upon marketing mix activities. The full range of mix components is identified along with some precepts relating to mix formulation and selection. Additionally, some reference is made to the effects of new communications techniques and technologies on the operation of various components of the mix.

Element 4: Marketing in context
The sixth learning outcome is covered in this element which examines how the characteristics of organizational and market contexts influences the configuration and implementation of marketing programmes. Specifically, it considers a range of contrasting, but related, settings and undertakes to provide a comparative assessment of how differences in context affect marketing activities. The virtual marketplace concept and its implications for organizations and their customers is also considered here.

Delivery approach

For many students this unit will provide their first contact with the essentials of marketing theory and the core components of knowledge. Its intention is to provide value to those that participate from both an immediate practical perspective and a longer-term personal/career development standpoint. To this end, studying this unit should enable students to reflect upon the knowledge that they acquire, and enhance their understanding of the role that they play within organizations as well as the activities that they may be involved in. Furthermore it should enable greater understanding of the importance of marketing to a full spectrum of organizations serving markets of differing dimensions.

As a core knowledge and understanding unit, the preferred form of assessment is proposed to be an examination. This should be borne in mind when developing the learning and teaching strategy for the unit.

As the 'spine' of the Professional Certificate and a foundation unit for the Professional Diploma, the indicative content of the syllabus is regarded as being key to future and current understanding in other syllabus areas. It is therefore recommended that the unit be taught in the early stages of a programme of study or ideally as a unit that runs throughout the full period of this stage of study.

The acquisition of the knowledge and skills components covered is regarded as the main outcome of this unit. Specifically, the development of a student's understanding of the essential principles of marketing theory and the ability to illustrate and apply them in context will guide assessment tasks. Particular emphasis should be given to providing students with the opportunity to illustrate key concepts through contemporary examples derived from their own or shared work experiences, and case materials from other sources.

Furthermore, although it is expected that learning outcomes should be achieved as discrete goals of attainment, it is also expected that tutors recognize and impart an understanding of the integrated nature of syllabus content. It is therefore important that tutors make a clear link between the customer value and competition precepts, the integrated mix and its components. The ability to develop, resource and implement marketing activities in a planning framework should also be given due consideration. Tutors should endeavour to ensure that a full range of organizational contexts are studied during the course of the unit.

The critical importance of the core material for continuous and future study may require a mix of learning strategies including some formative assessment. Deeper learning outcomes such as application and understanding may be developed from the acquired knowledge through research exercises, problem-solving activities and case study work.

Additional resources (Syllabus – Professional Certificate in Marketing)

Introduction

Texts to support the individual units are listed in the syllabus for each unit. This appendix shows a list of marketing journals, press and websites that tutors and students may find useful in supporting their studies at Professional Certificate.

Press

Students will be expected to have access to current examples of marketing campaigns and so should be sure to keep up to date with the appropriate marketing and quality daily press, including:

- *Campaign* – Haymarket
- *Internet Business* – Haymarket
- *Marketing* – Haymarket
- *Marketing Business* – CIM
- *Marketing Week* – Centaur
- *Revolution* – Haymarket.

Websites

The Chartered Institute of Marketing

www.cim.co.uk	CIM website containing case studies, reports and news
www.cim.co.uk/learningzone	Website for CIM students and tutors containing study information, past exam papers case 'study examples'. Also access to the marketer articles online
www.cimeducator.com	The CIM site for tutors only

Publications on-line

www.revolution.haynet.com	Revolution magazine
www.brandrepublic.com	Marketing magazine
www.FT.com	A wealth of information for cases (now charging)
www.IPA.co.uk	Need to register – communication resources
www.booksites.net	Financial Times Prentice Hall text websites

Sources of useful information

www.acnielsen.co.uk	AC Nielsen – excellent for research
http://advertising.utexas.edu/world/	Resources for advertising and marketing professionals, students and tutors
www.bized.com	Case studies
www.corporateinformation.com	Worldwide sources listed by country
www.esomar.nl	European body representing research organizations – useful for guidelines on research ethics and approaches
www.dma.org.uk	The direct marketing association
www.eiu.com	The economist intelligence unit
www.euromonitor.com	Euromonitor consumer markets
www.europa.eu.int	The European Commission's extensive range of statistics and reports relating to EU and member countries
www.managementhelp.org/research/research.htm	Part of the 'Free Management Library' – explaining research methods
www.marketresearch.org.uk	The MRS site with information and access to learning support for students – useful links on ethics and code of conduct
www.mmc.gov.uk	Summaries of Competition Commission reports

www.oecd.org	OECD statistics and other information relating to member nations including main economic indicators
www.quirks.com	An American source of information on marketing research issues and projects
www.statistics.gov.uk	UK government statistics
www.un.org	United Nations publish statistics on member nations
www.worldbank.org	World bank economic, social and natural resource indicators for over 200 countries. Includes over 600 indicators covering GNP per capita, growth, economic statistics and so on

Case sites

www.bluelagoon.co.uk	Case – SME website address
www.ebay.com	On-line auction – buyer behaviour
www.glenfiddich.com	Interesting site for case and branding
www.interflora.co.uk	e-Commerce direct ordering
www.moorcroft.co.uk	Good for relationship marketing
www.ribena.co.uk	Excellent targeting and history of communication
www.sothebys.ebay.com	New services offered because of advances in electronic technology

© CIM 2005

Index